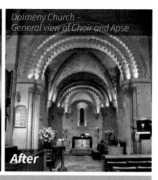

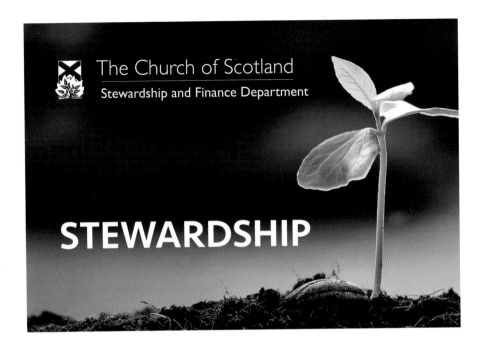

We offer tailored Stewardship programmes for your church.

Inspire and motivate your members with our **money, time and talents** programmes.

Contact us to book your own consultant to work alongside your congregation at **no charge**.

We also assist with:
- Using GRANTfinder to search for potential funders for your project
- Web and text donations, legacies and Gift Aid advice

Email: sfadmin@churchofscotland.org.uk
Tel: 0131 225 5722

Scottish Charity Number: SC011353

www.churchofscotland.org.uk/stewardship

Christian Aid
Scotland

#StandTogether
For dignity.
For equality.
For justice.

Find out more about Christian Aid
prayers, bible readings and
weekly worship at
christianaid.org.uk/Scotland

Augustine United Church
41 George IV Bridge, Edinburgh, EH1 1EL, United Kingdom. Tel: 0131 220 1254.

Sycamore House
290 Bath Street, Glasgow, G2 4JR, United Kingdom. Tel: 0141 221 7475.

Eng and Wales charity no. 1105851 Scot charity no. SC039150 Company no. 5171525 Christian Aid Ireland: NI charity no. NIC101831
Company no. NI059154 and ROI charity no. 20014162 Company no. 426928. The Christian Aid name and logo are trademarks of
Christian Aid. Christian Aid is a key member of ACT Alliance.   Christian Aid July 2018 J72319

The Right Reverend Susan Brown

MODERATOR

The Church of Scotland
YEAR BOOK
2018–2019

133rd year of issue

Editor
David A. Stewart

Published on behalf of
THE CHURCH OF SCOTLAND
by SAINT ANDREW PRESS
121 George Street, Edinburgh EH2 4YN

THE OFFICES OF THE CHURCH

121 George Street
Edinburgh EH2 4YN

0131 225 5722
Fax: 0131 220 3113
www.churchofscotland.org.uk

Office Hours:
Facilities Manager:

Monday–Friday 9:00am–5:00pm
Carole Tait 0131 240 2214

THE COUNCILS OF THE CHURCH

The following five Councils of the Church operate from the Church Offices, 121 George Street, Edinburgh EH2 4YN (0131 225 5722):

- The Council of Assembly
- The Church and Society Council   churchandsociety@churchofscotland.org.uk
- The Ministries Council   ministries@churchofscotland.org.uk
- The Mission and Discipleship Council   mandd@churchofscotland.org.uk
- The World Mission Council   world@churchofscotland.org.uk

The Social Care Council (CrossReach) operates from Charis House, 47 Milton Road East, Edinburgh EH15 2SR

0131 657 2000
Fax: 0131 657 5000
info@crossreach.org.uk
www.crossreach.org.uk

SCOTTISH CHARITY NUMBERS

The Church of Scotland: unincorporated Councils and Committees	SC011353
The Church of Scotland General Trustees	SC014574
The Church of Scotland Investors Trust	SC022884
The Church of Scotland Trust	SC020269

(For the Scottish Charity Numbers of congregations, see Section 7)

First published in 2018 by SAINT ANDREW PRESS, 121 George Street, Edinburgh EH2 4YN on behalf of THE CHURCH of SCOTLAND

Copyright © THE CHURCH of SCOTLAND, 2018

ISBN 978 0 86153 000 7

It is the Publisher's policy only to use papers that are natural and recyclable and that have been manufactured from timber grown in renewable, properly managed forests. All of the manufacturing processes of the papers are expected to conform to the environmental regulations of the country of origin.

Acceptance of advertisements for inclusion in the *Church of Scotland Year Book* does not imply endorsement of the goods or services or of any views expressed within the advertisements.

British Library Cataloguing in Publication Data
A catalogue record for this book is available from the British Library.

Printed and bound by Bell and Bain Ltd, Glasgow

QUICK DIRECTORY

Action of Churches Together in Scotland (ACTS) 01259 216980
Christian Aid London 020 7620 4444
Christian Aid Scotland 0141 221 7475
Church and Society Council 0131 240 2206
Church of Scotland Insurance Co. Ltd 0131 220 4119
Conforti Institute 01236 607120
Council of Assembly 0131 240 2229
CrossReach 0131 657 2000
Eco-Congregation Scotland 0131 240 2274
Ecumenical Officer 0131 240 2208
Gartmore House 01877 382991
Glasgow Lodging House Mission 0141 552 0285
Iona Community 0141 429 7281
IT Department Church of Scotland 0131 240 2245
Legal Questions Committee General Assembly 0131 240 2240
Media Team (Press Office) 0131 240 2268
Media Team (after hours) 07854 783539
Old Churches House, Dunblane (formerly Scottish Churches House) 01786 823663
Pension Trustees (pensions@churchofscotland.org.uk) 0131 240 2255
Place for Hope 07884 580359
Principal Clerk (pcoffice@churchofscotland.org.uk) 0131 240 2240
Priority Areas Office 0141 248 2905
Prison Chaplains 0131 244 8640
Safeguarding Service 0131 240 2256
Scottish Churches Organist Training Scheme (SCOTS) 01592 752403
Scottish Churches Parliamentary Office 0131 240 2276
Scottish Storytelling Centre (The Netherbow) 0131 556 9579
Work Place Chaplaincy Scotland 0131 441 2271
Year Book Editor 0131 441 3362

Pulpit Supply: Fee and Expenses
See www.churchofscotland.org.uk > Resources > Yearbook > Section 3F

Corrections and alterations to the Year Book
Contact the Editor:
yearbookeditor@churchofscotland.org.uk
0131 441 3362

GENERAL ASSEMBLY OF 2019
The General Assembly of 2019 will convene on
Saturday, 18 May 2019

CONTENTS

FROM THE MODERATOR

The Year Book is so much more than a book that marks a calendar year. Its mere presence on the bookshelf marks, for its owner, a sense of belonging to what is beyond the immediate, to every area of Scotland, into England, Europe and even further still. All of us bound together in the net of the Church of Scotland, which itself is part of the far bigger net of the followers of Christ throughout the whole of the world.

But the Year Book does more. As someone who has kept each Year Book since my ordination, the shelf to which I will add this current version now extends to three shelves and although earlier editions are no longer in daily use, I cannot bring myself to throw them out because they contain the names and therefore the memories and stories of so many whose paths I have been fortunate enough to cross.

In its present form, however, it is an incredibly useful and practical tool – and one that perhaps, as ministers, we ought to be more eager to share with our Kirk Sessions as we address the very real challenges we face in 2018–2019. Why not use the figures in a few past books, as well as this Year Book, along with the statistics for mission available on the Church's website, to map the story of faith in your community? It may start conversations about how to realign the work of the congregation to speak to your particular setting.

That apart, the Year Book has the information you need to get in touch with colleagues. Use it to keep in touch. Use it to network. Use it to put others in touch with one another and as you do, give thanks for the family to which we all belong. Enjoy your 2018–2019 Year Book.

Susan M. Brown

BHON MHODARÀTAIR

Chan e dìreach leabhar a tha a' comharrachadh bliadhna tìmeil a tha san Leabhar Bhliadhnail. Tha fiù 's àite air an sgeilp leabhraichean a' comharrachadh dhan neach leis a bheil e faireachdainn de bhuintealas do nì a tha nas fharsainge na gach sgìre de dh'Alba, de Shasainn, dhen Roinn Eòrpa agus eadhon nas fhaide air falbh. Tha gach neach againn air ar ceangal ri chèile ann an lìon Eaglais na h-Alba, a tha fhèin na phàirt de lìon a tha nas motha buileach de luchd-leantainn Chrìosd air feadh an t-saoghail.

Ach tha an Leabhar Bliadhnail a' dèanamh barrachd na sin. Mar neach a tha air gach Leabhar Bliadhnail bho chaidh mi nam mhinistear a chumail, tha an sgeilp ris an cur mi an iris às ùire seo a-nis air leudachadh gu bhith na thrì sgeilpichean agus ged nach eil mi cleachdadh eagrain nas tràithe a-nis gach latha, cha luthaig mi an caith a-mach bhon a tha taisgte annta ainmean, agus mar an ceudna cuimhneachain agus sgeulachdan, uimhir a dhaoine ris an robh mi sealbhach gu leòr coinneachadh.

Sa chruth sa bheil e an-dràsta, ged tha, 's e uidheam air leth feumail agus practaigeach a th' ann – agus fear as dòcha a bu chòir dhuinn mar mhinistearan a bhith nas deònaiche a cho-roinn le ar Seiseanan nuair a tha sinn a' gleac ris na fìor dhùbhlain a tha mu ar coinneimh ann an 2018-2019. Carson nach cleachd sibh na figearan ann an cuid de na seann leabhraichean cuide ris an Leabhar Bhliadhnail seo agus na h-àireamhan airson misein a tha rim faotainn air làrach-lìn na h-Eaglaise gus sgeulachd a' chreideimh nur coimhearsnachd a chlàradh? Dh'fhaodadh gum biodh sin na thoiseach tòiseachaidh air còmhraidhean air mar a b' urrainn obair a' choitheanail ath-dhealbh gus freagairt nas fheàrr air ur suidheachadh sònraichte.

A thuilleadh air sin, tha am fiosrachadh san Leabhar Bhliadhnail a dh' fheumas tu airson ceangal a dhèanamh ri co-obraichean. Cleachd e gus cumail ann an todha. Cleachd e gus lìonradh a thogail. Cleachd e gus feadhainn a chur an aithne feadhainn eile agus, mar a nì thu sin, thoir buidheachas airson an teaghlaich dham buin sinn uile. Gum meal sibh an Leabhar Bliadhnail 2018–2019 agaibh.

An Fhìor Urramach Siùsaidh NicIlleDhuinn
Translation by Professor Boyd Robertson

EDITOR'S PREFACE

I begin by thanking my predecessor (and fellow organist), the Rev. Dr Douglas Galbraith, for his assiduous and painstaking work over the last six editions of the Year Book. I first became acquainted with the 'Red Book' under its longest-serving editor, the Very Rev. Dr Andrew Herron, whilst studying the geography of the Church of Scotland in Edinburgh in the 1970s. Since then it has been a constant companion in visiting churches around Scotland and when serving formerly on the Presbytery of Edinburgh and the Ministries Council. A list of the editorial succession is given overleaf.

There is one major change this year, given that a quarter of all charges are now vacant or in guardianship. For charges which are vacant or in guardianship, and which do not have a named person listed (e.g. Associate Minister, Ordained Local Minster, Auxiliary Minister, Deacon), contact details have been inserted for the Session Clerk (or Session Clerks for linkages) where permission has been given under the General Data Protection Regulation (GDPR).

Lists A to E in Section 6 have been recast in view of the Registration of Ministries Act (Act 2, 2017). As regards those ministers and deacons registered as 'Inactive' under the Act, in the light of the GDPR only those ministers and deacons who have given consent to publication of their details are included in the relevant lists in this edition. The lists of Overseas Resigned and Retired Mission Partners and of Retired Lay Agents, formerly published in the online sections of the Year Book, have been discontinued in view of the GDPR.

Over a hundred people contribute each year to the compilation, production and distribution of the Year Book. My thanks to the Presbytery Clerks and their secretaries, the staff in the Church's offices (in particular those regular correspondents in the Ministries Council and the Communications Department), and to those who compile some of the sections or subsections: Angus Morrison and Boyd Robertson (Gaelic), Roy Pinkerton (list of editors, church grid references, parish and congregational changes, index of parishes and places, and editorial advice), Laurence Wareing (General Assembly report), Stephen Blakey (Forces Chaplains), Jennifer Hamilton (legal names and Scottish charity numbers) and Sandy Gemmill (statistics). Finally, thanks to Claire Ruben of FairCopy (our careful copy editor) and to our contacts at Hymns Ancient and Modern who publish the book via the St Andrew Press.

Corrections, amendments and suggestions are always welcome. As Andrew Herron said in his inimitable style in 1976 'don't write in an aggrieved tone and say that some mistake has "consistently appeared for the last four years". It will go on "consistently appearing" until the Editor learns that it is a mistake'.

David Stewart
yearbookeditor@churchofscotland.org.uk

EDITORS OF THE CHURCH OF SCOTLAND YEAR BOOK

1886–1888	Prepared by **John Anderson Graham** (later Rev Dr J.A. Graham of Kalimpong), Secretary to the Committee on Christian Life and Work (Convener: Rev. A.H. Charteris)
1889–1901	**Rev. J. Aikman Paton**, Inch
1902	In the absence of the editor, most of the work was done by Mr George McAlpine, Secretary to the Committee
1903–1913	**Rev. William Simpson**, Bonhill
1914–1921	**Rev. Arthur Pollok Sim**, Lilliesleaf
1922–1928	**Rev. William S. Buchan**, Liff and Benvie (later Edinburgh: Portobello St James')
1929	**Rev. J. Arnott Hamilton**, Newbattle
1930–1931	**Rev. J. Arnott Hamilton** and **Rev. Louis C. Phillips**, Buckie: South (later Galashiels: Ladhope, Logie and Fala and Soutra) as Joint Editors
1932–1939	**Rev. Louis C. Phillips**
1940–1948	**Rev. Louis C. Phillips** and **Rev. Thomas Caldwell** (Aberlady) as Joint Editors
1949–1950	**Rev. Thomas Caldwell**
1951–1960	**Rev. Joseph S. Easton**, Edinburgh: North Merchiston
1961	No individual editor's name appears on account of changes in the method of compilation
1962–1987	**Rev. Andrew Herron**, Clerk to the Presbytery of Glasgow
1988–1992	**Rev. Andrew Herron** and **Rev. Roy M. Tuton**, Glasgow: Shettleston Old
1993/94–1995/96	**Rev. James G. Black**, East Kilbride: Westwood
1996/97–1999/00	**Rev. A. Gordon McGillivray**, formerly Clerk to the Presbytery of Edinburgh
2000/01–2011/12	**Rev. Ronald S. Blakey**, formerly Secretary to the Assembly Council
2012/13–2017/18	**Rev. D. Douglas Galbraith**, formerly Secretary of the Office for Worship, Doctrine and Artistic Matters

SECTION 1

Assembly Councils, Committees, Departments and Agencies

The symbol > used in website information indicates the headings to be selected as they appear

THE DEPARTMENT OF THE GENERAL ASSEMBLY

The Department of the General Assembly supports the General Assembly and the Moderator, the Council of Assembly and the Ecumenical Relations Committee. In addition, Departmental staff service the following Committees (qv): Assembly Arrangements, Legal Questions, the Committee to Nominate the Moderator, the Nomination Committee, the Committee on Overtures and Cases, and the Committee on Classifying Returns to Overtures. The Clerks of Assembly are available for consultation on matters of Church Law, Practice and Procedure.

Principal Clerk:	Rev. Dr George Whyte
Depute Clerk of the General Assembly:	Ms Christine Paterson LLB DipLP
Executive Assistant to the Principal Clerk:	Ms Susan Taylor
	0131 240 2240
Senior Administration Officer:	Ms Catherine McIntosh MA
(Assembly Arrangements and	0131 225 5722 ext. 2250
Moderatorial Support)	
Secretary to the Council of Assembly:	Rev. Dr Martin Scott
Head of Organisational Programmes:	Ms Catherine Skinner BA MA
Executive Officer (Acting):	Mrs Pauline Wilson MA
Audit and Compliance Officer:	Mrs Debra Livingstone MA FCCA
Senior Administration Officer (Acting):	Ms Carron Lunt
(Council of Assembly,	0131 240 2229
Central Services Committee and	
Nomination Committee)	
Administrator:	Mrs Valerie Jenkins
Interfaith Programme Officer:	Ms Mirella Yandoli MDiv MSt
Worship Development and Mission	Rev. Dr Fiona Tweedie
Statistics Co-ordinator:	0131 240 3007
Ecumenical Officer:	Rev. Dr John L. McPake
Senior Administrator:	Miss Rosalind Milne
(Ecumenical Relations)	0131 240 2208

Personnel in this department are also listed with the Councils and Committees that they serve.

Contact: pcoffice@churchofscotland.org.uk   0131 240 2240   Fax: 0131 240 2239
Further information:
www.churchofscotland.org.uk > About us > Councils, committees > Departments > General Assembly

1. COUNCILS

1.1 THE COUNCIL OF ASSEMBLY

The function of the Council is to co-ordinate, support and evaluate the work of the Councils and Committees of the Church, to assist the General Assembly in determining and implementing policies, and to take necessary administrative decisions in between General Assemblies. The voting members of the Council of Assembly act as the Charity Trustees for the Unincorporated Councils and Committees of the General Assembly: Scottish Charity No. SC011353.

Convener: Dr Sally E. Bonnar MB ChB FRCPsych
Vice-Convener: Mr David Watt BAcc CA CPFA
Secretary: Rev. Dr Martin C. Scott

Contact: Ms Carron Lunt, Senior Administrative Officer
            clunt@churchofscotland.org.uk   0131 240 2229
Further information:
www.churchofscotland.org.uk > About us > Councils, committees > Councils > Council of Assembly

1.2 THE CHURCH AND SOCIETY COUNCIL

The Council seeks to engage on behalf of the Church in national, political and social issues through research, theological reflection, resourcing the local church, and by engaging with leaders in civic society, public bodies, professional associations and other networks. The Council seeks to put the wisdom of local congregations and those with lived experience of poverty and injustice at the heart of its work. Its focus for the next decade, after a consultation involving 10,000 respondents: investing in young people, local communities where people flourish, the health and wellbeing of all, caring for creation, global friendships, an economy driven by equality, doing politics differently.

Convener: Rev. Dr Richard E. Frazer
Vice-Conveners: Wendy Young BSc PGCE MLitt
                          Pauline Edmiston BD
Secretary: Rev. Dr H. Martin J. Johnstone
                          mjohnstone@churchofscotland.org.uk

Contact: churchandsociety@churchofscotland.org.uk   0131 240 2206
Further information:
www.churchofscotland.org.uk > About us > Councils, committees > Councils > Church and Society
www.churchofscotland.org.uk > speak out

1.3   THE MINISTRIES COUNCIL

The Council's remit is to recruit, train and support ministries in every part of Scotland, to monitor their deployment, working in partnership with ecumenical, inter-faith and statutory agencies, and giving priority to the poorest and most marginalised sections of the community.

Convener:	Rev. Neil M Glover
Vice-Conveners:	Dr John Dent MB ChB MMEd
	Rev. Bob Mallinson BD
	Rev. Eleanor J. McMahon BEd BD
	Rev. Sarah Ross BD MTh PGDip

Council Secretary:	Rev. Jayne E. Scott BA MEd MBA
Depute:	Mr Craig Renton
Education and Training:	Mr David Plews MA MTh
Partnership Development:	Mr Daran Golby BA CIPD
Priority Areas:	Ms Shirley Grieve BA PGCE (0141 248 2905)
Recruitment and Support:	Rev. Dr Lezley J Stewart

Contact: ministries@churchofscotland.org.uk 0131 225 5722

Further information:
www.churchofscotland.org.uk > About us > Councils, committees > Councils > Ministries Council
www.churchofscotland.org.uk > Serve > Ministries Council > Ministries in the Church
www.churchofscotland.org.uk/ascend
www.churchofscotland.org.uk > Serve > Go For It
Pulpit Supply Fees: www.churchofscotland.org.uk/yearbook > Section 3F

1.4   THE MISSION AND DISCIPLESHIP COUNCIL

The Council's remit is to stimulate and support the Church by the provision of resources nationally, regionally and locally in worship, witness, mission and discipleship. This includes the development of strategies and materials in the areas of adult education, resourcing elders, work with young adults, young people and children (including those with particular needs and disabilities), as well as in liturgy, and church art and architecture.

Convener:	Rev. Norman A. Smith MA BD
Vice-Conveners:	Rev. W. Martin Fair BA BD DMin
	Rev. Peter M. Gardner MA BD
	Lynne McEwen

Council Secretary:	Rev. Angus R. Mathieson MA BD

Church Without Walls:	Mrs Lesley Hamilton-Messer MA
Congregational Learning:	Mr Ronald H. Clarke BEng MSc PGCE

Resourcing Worship: Mr Graham Fender-Allison BA

Church Art and Architecture:
Convener: Rev. William T. Hogg MA BD
Contact: gentrustees@churchofscotland.org.uk

Contact: Lynn Hall
            mandd@churchofscotland.org.uk
Further information:
www.churchofscotland.org.uk > About us > Councils, committees > Mission and Discipleship
www.resourcingmission.org.uk

Church Art and Architecture www.churchofscotland.org.uk > Resources > Subjects > Art and Architecture resources

For Life and Work see below 2.15
For Saint Andrew Press see below 2.21
For Scottish Storytelling Centre (The Netherbow) see below 2.23

1.5   THE SOCIAL CARE COUNCIL
(CrossReach)
Charis House, 47 Milton Road East, Edinburgh EH15 2SR
0131 657 2000   Fax: 0131 657 5000
info@crossreach.org.uk   www.crossreach.org.uk

The Social Care Council, known as CrossReach, provides social-care services as part of the Christian witness of the Church to the people of Scotland, and engages with other bodies in responding to emerging areas of need. CrossReach operates 72 services across the country.

Convener: Mr Bill Steele
Vice-Conveners: Ms Irene McGugan
                Rev. Thomas S. Riddell

Chief Executive Officer: Viv Dickenson (viv.dickenson@crossreach.org.uk)

Director of Services to Older People: Allan Logan (allan.logan@crossreach.org.uk)
Director of Adult Care Services: Calum Murray (calum.murray@crossreach.org.uk)
Director of Children and Families: Sheila Gordon (sheila.gordon@crossreach.org.uk)
Director of Finance and Resources: Ian Wauchope (ian.wauchope@crossreach.org.uk)
Director of Human Resources and
    Organisational Development: Mari Rennie (mari.rennie@crossreach.org.uk)

Further information: www.crossreach.org.uk

For sharing local experience and initiatives: www.socialcareforum.scot

1.6 THE WORLD MISSION COUNCIL

The aim of the Council is to enable the Church of Scotland – its members, adherents, congregations, and presbyteries - to participate effectively in the Mission of God in the world, following the example and priorities of Jesus Christ, and seeking the guidance of the Holy Spirit. The Gospel story of the walk to Emmaus (Luke 24) provides a paradigm for mission in the 21st Century as a shared journey; through listening to and walking with our partners on our shared journey of faith, the Council seeks to engage in a process of attentive accompaniment with the Church of Scotland's partners worldwide. This involves presence (an incarnational approach to mission in which relationships of mutual respect can be built); practical action (following Jesus' example in reaching out to the poor, the captive, the sick, and the oppressed); and proclamation (both the explicit proclamation of the Good News and being a prophetic voice for the voiceless and exercising advocacy on behalf of the powerless.) The Council is also the principal link with Christian Aid.

Convener:	Very Rev. Dr John P. Chalmers
Vice-Conveners:	Rev. Alan F. Miller BA MA BD
	Mrs Maureen V. Jack MA MEd MSc

Council Secretary:	Rev. Ian W. Alexander BA BD STM
Secretaries:	Mrs Jennie Chinembiri (Africa and Caribbean)
	Ms Carol Finlay (Twinning and Local Development)
	Mr Kenny Roger (Middle East)
	Mr Sandy Sneddon (Asia)

Contact: world@churchofscotland.org.uk   0131 225 5722
Further Information:
www.churchofscotland.org.uk > About us > Councils, committees > Councils > World Mission
www.churchofscotland.org.uk > Serve > World Mission

---

2. DEPARTMENTS, COMMITTEES AND AGENCIES

2.1 ASSEMBLY ARRANGEMENTS COMMITTEE

Convener:	Rev. Fiona E. Smith LLB BD
Vice-Convener:	Rev. Donald G.B. McCorkindale BD DipMin
Secretary:	Principal Clerk
	cmcintosh@churchofscotland.org.uk 0131 240 2240

Further information:
www.churchofscotland.org.uk > About us > General Assembly
www.churchofscotland.org.uk > About us > Councils, committees > Committees > Assembly Arrangements

2.2 CENTRAL PROPERTIES DEPARTMENT

Remit: to provide property, facilities and health and safety services to the Councils and Departments of the central administration of the Church.

Property, Health and Safety Manager: Colin Wallace
Property, Health and Safety Officer: Jacqueline Collins
Property Officer: Eunice Hessell
Support Assistant: Joyce Anderson

Contact: cpd@churchofscotland.org.uk   0131 240 2254

2.3 CHURCH OF SCOTLAND TRUST

Chairman: Mr Thomas C. Watson
Vice-Chairman: Mr W.F. Stuart Lynch
Treasurer: Mrs Anne F. Macintosh BA CA
Secretary and Clerk: Mrs Jennifer M. Hamilton BA NP
jhamilton@churchofscotland.org.uk   0131 240 2222

Further information:
www.churchofscotland.org.uk > About us > Councils, committees > Departments > Church of Scotland Trust

2.4 COMMUNICATIONS DEPARTMENT

Interim Head of Communications: Ruth MacLeod 0131 240 2243
Communications Manager: Helen Silvis 0131 240 2268
Senior Communications Officer: Cameron Brooks 0131 240 2204
Communications Officer: Jane Bristow 0131 240 2204
Communications Officer: Laura Crawford 0131 240 2268
Web Editor: Jill Stevens
Web Developer: Alan Murray
Design Team Leader: Chris Flexen
Senior Designer: Steve Walker

Contact the Media Team after hours: 07854 783539
Contact department: 0131 240 2268
Further information:
www.churchofscotland.org.uk > About us > Councils, committees > Departments > Communications

2.5   ECUMENICAL RELATIONS COMMITTEE

The Committee includes six members appointed by the General Assembly, each attached to one of the five Councils of the Church and the Theological Forum, plus representatives of other denominations in Scotland and Church of Scotland members elected to British and international ecumenical bodies. The Church of Scotland trustee of ACTS and the co-chair of the Joint Commission on Doctrine attend as co-opted members. The General Secretary of ACTS attends as a corresponding member.

Convener:	Rev. Alexander G. Horsburgh MA BD
Vice-Convener:	Rev. Kevin Mackenzie BD DPS
Secretary and Ecumenical Officer:	Rev. Dr John L. McPake
Senior Administrator:	Miss Rosalind Milne

Contact: ecumenical@churchofscotland.org.uk   0131 240 2208

Further information:
www.churchofscotland.org.uk > About us > Councils, committees > Committees > Ecumenical Relations Committee
www.churchofscotland.org.uk > Connect > Ecumenism
www.churchofscotland.org.uk > Resources > Subjects > Ecumenical Resources
World Council of Churches: www.oikumene.org
Churches Together in Britain and Ireland: www.ctbi.org.uk
Action of Churches Together in Scotland: www.acts-scotland.org
For other international ecumenical bodies see Committee's web pages as above
See also 'Other Churches in the United Kingdom' page 20

2.6   FACILITIES MANAGEMENT DEPARTMENT

Facilities Manager:	Carole Tait
	ctait@churchofscotland.org.uk 0131 240 2214

Further information:
www.churchofscotland.org.uk > About us > Councils, committees > Committees > Office management

2.7   FORCES CHAPLAINS COMMITTEE

Convener:	Rev. Dr Marjory A. MacLean
Vice-Convener:	Carolyn Macleod MBE
Secretary:	Mr John K. Thomson, Ministries Council
	jthomson@churchofscotland.org.uk 0131 225 5722

Further information:
www.churchofscotland.org.uk > About us > Councils, committees > Forces Chaplains Committee
A list of Chaplains is found at Section 6 G

2.8 GENERAL TRUSTEES

Chairman:	Mr Raymond K. Young CBE BArch FRIAS
Vice-Chairman:	Mr Roger G.G. Dodd DipBldgCons(RICS) FRICS
Secretary and Clerk:	Mr David D. Robertson LLB NP
Depute Secretary and Clerk:	Mr Keith S. Mason LLB NP
Assistant Secretaries:	Ms Claire L. Cowell LLB (Glebes)
	Mrs Morag J. Menneer BSc MRICS (Glebes)
	Mr Brian D. Waller LLB (Ecclesiastical Buildings)
	Mr. Neil Page BSc MCIOB
Safe Buildings Consultant:	Mr Brian Auld ChEHO MREHIS FRSPH GradIOSH
Energy Conservation:	Mr Robert Lindores FInstPa
Treasurer:	Mrs Anne F. Macintosh BA CA
Finance Manager:	Mr Alex Semple FCCA
Buildings insurance,	Church of Scotland Insurance Services Ltd.
all enquiries to	121 George Street, Edinburgh EH2 4YN
	enquiries@cosic.co.uk 0131 220 4119

Contact: gentrustees@churchofscotland.org.uk   0131 225 5722 ext. 2261
Further information:
www.churchofscotland.org.uk > About us > Councils, committees > Departments > General Trustees

2.9 THE GUILD

The Church of Scotland Guild is a movement within the Church of Scotland whose aim is 'to invite and encourage both women and men to commit their lives to Jesus Christ and to enable them to express their faith in worship, prayer and action'.

Convener:	Patricia Robertson
Vice-Convener:	Marian Macintyre
General Secretary:	Iain W. Whyte BA DCE DMS

Contact: guild@churchofscotland.org.uk   0131 240 2217

Further information:
www.cos-guild.org.uk
www.churchofscotland.org.uk > Serve > The Guild

2.10   HOUSING AND LOAN FUND

Chairman: Rev. Ian Taylor BD ThM
Deputy Chairman: Rev. MaryAnn R. Rennie BD MTh
Secretary: Lin J. Macmillan MA
                        lmacmillan@churchofscotland.org.uk   0131 225 5722 ext. 2310
Property Manager: Hilary J. Hardy
Property Assistant: John Lunn

Further information:
www.churchofscotland.org.uk > About us > Councils, committees > Departments > Housing
and Loan Fund

2.11   HUMAN RESOURCES DEPARTMENT

Head of Human Resources: Elaine McCloghry
Human Resources Managers: Karen Smith
                                   Angela Ocak
Human Resources Advisers: Sarah-Jayne McVeigh
                                   Nicola Bird
                                   Stephanie Thomson

Contact: hr@churchofscotland.org.uk   0131 240 2270

2.12   INFORMATION TECHNOLOGY DEPARTMENT

Information Technology Manager: David Malcolm
                                        0131 240 2247

Contact: itdept@churchofscotland.org.uk   0131 240 2245

Further information:
www.churchofscotland.org.uk > About us > Councils, committees > Committees > IT

2.13   INVESTORS TRUST

Chairman: Ms Catherine Y. Alexander
Vice-Chairman: Mr Brian J. Duffin
Treasurer: Mrs Anne F. Macintosh BA CA
Secretary: Mrs Nicola Robertson
                   investorstrust@churchofscotland.org.uk

Further information:
www.churchofscotland.org.uk > About us > Councils, committees > Departments > Investors Trust

2.14   LAW DEPARTMENT

Solicitor of the Church
and of the General Trustees: Miss Mary Macleod LLB NP
Depute Solicitor: Mrs Jennifer Hamilton BA NP
Senior Solicitor: Mrs Elspeth Annan LLB NP
Solicitors: Miss Susan Killean LLB NP
                              Mrs Anne Steele LLB NP
                              Mrs Jennifer Campbell LLB LLM NP
                              Gregor Buick LLB WS NP
                              Mrs Madelaine Sproule LLB NP
                              Gordon Barclay LLB BSc MSc MPhil PhD
                              David Stihler MA LLB DipLP NP

Contact: lawdept@churchofscotland.org.uk   0131 225 5722 ext. 2230; Fax: 0131 240 2246.

Further information:
www.churchofscotland.org.uk > About us > Councils, committees > Committees > Law

2.15   LEGAL QUESTIONS COMMITTEE

The Committee's remit is to advise the General Assembly on questions of Church and Constitutional Law, assist Agencies of the Assembly in preparing and interpreting legislation, compile statistics and arrange for the care of Church Records.

Convener: Rev. George S. Cowie BSc BD
Vice-Convener: Mrs Barbara Finlayson LLB WS
Secretary: Principal Clerk
Depute Clerk: Ms Christine Paterson LLB DipLP

Contact: staylor@churchofscotland.org.uk   0131 240 2240

Further information:
www.churchofscotland.org.uk > About us > Councils, committees > Committees > Legal
Questions

2.16   LIFE AND WORK
the Church of Scotland's monthly magazine

The magazine's purpose is to keep the Church informed about events in church life at home and abroad and to provide a forum for Christian opinion and debate on a variety of topics. It has an independent editorial policy. Contributions which are relevant to any aspect of the Christian faith are welcome. The website, www.lifeandwork.org, includes up-to-date news, extracts from the magazine and additional features. To subscribe to the magazine through your church, speak to your Life and Work co-ordinator. To receive by post, call the number below or visit the website. A digital download, for reading on PC, tablet and smartphone, is also available.

Editor: Lynne McNeil   magazine@lifeandwork.org   0131 225 5722

Further information:
www.lifeandwork.org
www.churchofscotland.org.uk > News and Events > Life and Work

2.17   NOMINATION COMMITTEE

Convener: Ms Lynsey M. Kimmitt LLB DipLP NP
Vice-Convener: Rev. John K. Collard MA BD
Secretary: Rev. Dr Martin C. Scott

Contact: Mrs Valerie Jenkins, Senior Administration Officer
          vjenkins@churchofscotland.org.uk   0131 240 2229

Further information:
www.churchofscotland.org.uk > About us > Councils, committees > Committees > Nomination
Committee

2.18   PANEL ON REVIEW AND REFORM

The Panel is charged with articulating God's vision of what a Church in need of continual renewal might become and is committed to offering pathways by which congregations, Presbyteries and Agencies of the Church might travel towards that vision.

Convener: Rev. Jennifer M. Adams BEng BD
Vice-Convener: Mrs Christine Cavanagh
Secretary: Ms Amy Bostock

Contact: ABostock@churchofscotland.org.uk   0131 225 5722 ext. 2336

Further information:
www.churchofscotland.org.uk > About us > Councils, committees > Committees > Panel on Review and Reform

2.19   PENSION TRUSTEES

Chairman: Mr Graeme R. Caughey BSc FFIA
Vice-Chairman: Mr Douglas Millar
Secretary and
Pensions Manager: Mr Steven D. Kaney BSc DipPMI Dip IEB
Senior Pensions Administrator: Mrs Fiona McCulloch-Stevenson
Pensions Administrators: Mrs Marshall Rowan
                                Ms Birgit Mosemann
                                Mr Colin Smith

Contact: pensions@churchofscotland.org.uk   0131 240 2255

Further information:
www.churchofscotland.org.uk > About us > Councils, committees > Departments > Pension Trustees

2.20   SAFEGUARDING SERVICE

The service ensures that the Church has robust structures and policies in place for the prevention of harm and abuse of children and adults at risk; and to ensure a timely and appropriate response when harm or abuse is witnessed, suspected or reported.

Convener: Rev. Dr Karen K. Campbell
Vice-Convener: Mrs Caroline Deerin
Service Manager: Ms Julie Main BA DipSW

Contact: safeguarding@churchofscotland.org.uk   0131 240 2256

Further Information:
www.churchofscotland.org.uk > About us > Councils, committees > Departments > Safeguarding Service

2.21   SAINT ANDREW PRESS

Saint Andrew Press is managed on behalf of the Church of Scotland by Hymns Ancient and Modern Ltd and publishes a broad range of titles, ranging from the much-loved William Barclay series of New Testament *Daily Study Bible* commentaries to the resources for the mission and ministry of the contemporary church. The full list of publications can be viewed on the Saint Andrew Press website (see below).

Contact: Christine Smith, Publishing Director christine@hymnsam.co.uk   0207 776 7546

Further information: www.standrewpress.com

2.22   SCOTTISH CHURCHES PARLIAMENTARY OFFICE
121 George Street, Edinburgh EH2 4YN

The Office exists to build fruitful relationships between the Churches and the Scottish and UK Parliaments and Governments, seeking to engage reflectively in the political process, translate their commitment to the welfare of Scotland into parliamentary debate, and contribute their experience and faith-based reflection on it to the decision-making process.

Scottish Churches Parliamentary Officer: Chloe Clemmons MA MA (Human Rights)
                                              chloe.clemmons@scpo.scot
Research and Resource Development Officer: Irene Mackinnon
                                              irene.mackinnon@scpo.scot

Contact: 0131 240 2276

Further information:
www.churchofscotland.org.uk > Speak out > Doing Politics Differently
www.scpo.scot

2.23   SCOTTISH STORYTELLING CENTRE (THE NETHERBOW)
43–45 High Street, Edinburgh EH1 1SR

The integrated facilities of the **Netherbow Theatre** and the **John Knox House**, together with the outstanding conference and reception areas, form an important cultural venue on the Royal Mile in Edinburgh. The Centre captures both the historical roots of storytelling and the forward-looking mission to preserve it: providing advice and assistance nationally in the use of traditional arts in a diversity of settings. Mission and Discipleship Council are pleased to host TRACS (Traditional Arts and Culture Scotland), a grant-funded body who provide an extensive year-round cultural and literary programme.

Contact: reception@scottishstorytellingcentre.com   0131 556 9579

Further information:
www.scottishstorytellingcentre.co.uk

2.24 STEWARDSHIP AND FINANCE DEPARTMENT

General Treasurer: Mrs Anne F. Macintosh BA CA
Deputy Treasurer (Congregational
  Finance): Mr Archie McDowall BA CA
Deputy Treasurer (Unincorporated
  Councils and Committees): Mr Bob Cowan BCom CA
National Stewardship Co-ordinator: Vacant
Finance Managers: Mrs Elaine Macadie BA CA
 Mr Alex Semple FCCA
 Mrs Leanne Thompson BSc CA
Pensions Accountant: Mrs Kay C. Hastie BSc CA

Contact: sfadmin@churchofscotland.org.uk
Further information and details of local consultants:
www.churchofscotland.org.uk > About us > Councils, committees > Departments > Stewardship and Budget
www.churchofscotland.org.uk > Resources > Subjects > National Stewardship Programme

2.25 THEOLOGICAL FORUM

The purpose of the Forum is to continue to develop and bring to expression doctrinal understanding of the Church with reference to Scripture and to the confessional standards of the Church of Scotland, and the implications of this for worship and witness in and beyond contemporary Scotland. It responds to requests to undertake enquiries as they arise, draws the Church's attention to particular matters requiring theological work, and promotes theological reflection throughout the Church.

Convener: Rev. Donald G. MacEwan MA BD PhD
Vice-Convener: Sarah Lane Ritchie BA MDiv MSc PhD
Secretary: Nathalie A. Mareš MA MTh

Contact: NMares@churchofscotland.org.uk
Further Information:
www.churchofscotland.org.uk > About us > Councils, committees > Committees > Theological Forum

SECTION 2

General Information

(1) THE CHURCH OF SCOTLAND AND THE GAELIC LANGUAGE
The Very Revd Dr Angus Morrison and Professor Boyd Robertson

Seirbhis Ghàidhlig an Àrd-sheanaidh
Mar as àbhaist, chumadh seirbhis Ghàidhlig ann an Eaglais nam Manach Liath ann an Dùn Èideann air Didòmhnaich an Àrd-sheanaidh. Air ceann an adhraidh am-bliadhna agus a' searmonachadh bha an t-Urr. Dòmhnall A MacSuain, ministear Chill Tighearna. Mar a tha air tachairt bho chionn grunn bhliadhnachan a-nis, sheinn Còisir Ghàidhlig Lodainn aig toiseach agus deireadh na seirbheis. Rinn Modaràtair an Àrd-sheanaidh, an t-Oll. Urr. Susan Brown, am Beannachadh. An dèidh an adhraidh fhuair an luchd-adhraidh cuireadh gu greim-bìdh agus bha cothrom aca a bhith a' còmhradh agus a' conaltradh.

Tha Eaglais nam Manach Liath air tè de na h-eaglaisean aig Eaglais na h-Alba anns na bailtean mòra far a bheil seirbheis Ghàidhlig air a cumail a h-uile seachdain. Tha seirbheis Ghàidhlig gach Sàbaid cuideachd ann an Eaglais Chaluim Chille ann an Glaschu.

Anns na Meadhanan
Bidh ministearan agus buill eile bho Eaglais na h-Alba a' gabhail pàirt ann am prògraman spioradail air an rèidio agus air an telebhisean.

Bidh mòran ag èisteachd ri Dèanamaid Adhradh air an rèidio madainn agus feasgar na Sàbaid. Air an oidhche bidh seirbhisean à tasglann a' BhBC air an craobh-sgaoileadh, cuid mhath dhiubh bho Eaglais na h-Alba.

Gach latha tron t-seachdain tha Smuain na Maidne ga chraoladh air Rèidio nan Gàidheal. Tha daoine nach eil air chomas seirbheisean eaglais a fhrithealadh a' dèanamh fiughair ris na prògraman spioradail seo. Bidh am BBC a' toirt fiosrachaidh seachad mu sheirbheisean Gàidhlig a tha air an cumail air feadh na dùthcha.

Na Duilleagan Gàidhlig
A h-uile mìos tha Eaglais na h-Alba air a bhith a' foillseachadh dhuilleagan Gàidhlig an lùib na h-iris Mhìosail Life and Work. Bidh cuid mhath de luchd-ionnsachaidh agus feadhainn bho eaglaisean eile a' leughadh nan Duilleag.

Faodar Na Duilleagan a' leughadh cuideachd ann an roinn Gàidhlig den làrach-lìn Life and Work. Aig an àm a tha seo ga sgrìobhadh (An t-Iuchar 2018), thathar a' beachdachadh air dè cho tric sa bhios irisean gam foillseachadh gach bliadhna.

A' Dèanamh Adhartas leis a' Ghàidhlig anns an Eaglais
Ann an 2015 chumadh co-labhairt chudromach anns an robh rannsachadh ga dhèanamh air suidheachadh na Gàidhlig ann an Eaglais na h-Alba. Thugadh An Ciad Ceum air a' cho-labhairt seo.

Mar ath cheum chaidh Buidheann Ghàidhlig Eaglais na h-Alba, a bha air a bhith na tàmh airson beagan bhliadhnaichean, ath-stèidheachadh. Is e amas na Buidhne cleachdadh na Gàidhlig ann am beatha agus obair na h-Eaglaise a bhrosnachadh agus goireasan iomchaidh, a chumas taic ris an amas seo, a leasachadh.

Bho chaidh Àrd Sheanadh 2016 air adhart, chaidh coinneamhan den Bhuidhinn a chumail ann an diofar cheàrnaidhean den dùthaich, nam measg Dùn Èideann, Inbhir Nis, Caol Loch Aillse, Sabhal Mòr Ostaig anns an Eilean Sgitheanach, Glaschu, Steòrnabhagh agus an t-Òban.

Anns a' chiad dhol-a-mach, tha a' Bhuidheann ag amas air Plana Gàidhlig airson Eaglais na h-Alba a dheasachadh. Ged nach robh am Plana buileach deiseil airson fhoillseachadh aig Àrd Sheanadh 2018, chaidh a chrìochnachadh goirid às dèidh sin. Thathar an dòchas gum bi am Plana deireannach an lùib Aithisg Comhairle an Àrd Sheanaidh gu Àrd Sheanadh 2019 gus daoine a bhrosnachadh a dhol an sàs anns an obair a thathar a' toirt air adhart leis a' Bhuidhinn às leth na h-Eaglaise.

Chaidh Òraid Ghàidhlig shoirbheachail, gus crìochnachadh eadar-theangachadh Gàidhlig ùr dhen Tiomnadh Nuadh a chomharrachadh, a cumail air 23 Cèitean 2018 mar thachartas air iomall an Àrd Sheanaidh. B' e am prìomh neach-labhairt an t-Urr. Ruairidh MacIllEathain, ball dhen sgioba eadar-theangachaidh. Bhruidhinn Elaine Duncan bho Chomann Bhìoball na h-Alba cuideachd. Bha mòran an làthair aig an tachartas agus b' e tlachd dha-rìribh a bh' ann fàilte a chur air ministearan agus èildearan bhon Eaglais Shaor.

Thathar an dòchas obair eadar-eaglaiseil air gnothaichean Gàidhlig a thoirt air adhart le eaglaisean eile ann an Alba.

General Assembly Gaelic Service
As always, there was a Gaelic service on the Sunday of the General Assembly in Greyfriars Kirk in Edinburgh. Conducting the service and preaching the sermon was the Rev. Donald A. MacSween, minister of Kiltearn. As has happened for a number of years, the Lothian Gaelic Choir sang at the beginning and conclusion of the service. The Moderator, the Right Rev. Susan Brown, pronounced the benediction.

Following the service, worshippers were invited to a light lunch when they had opportunity for conversation and fellowship.

Greyfriars Kirk is one of the Church of Scotland congregations in the cities which hold weekly Gaelic services. A Gaelic service is also held each Sunday in St Columba's church in Glasgow.

The Media
Ministers and members of the Church of Scotland regularly take part in Gaelic religious programmes on radio and television. The weekly Gaelic service on radio, Dèanamaid Adhradh, broadcast each Sunday morning and repeated in the afternoon, attracts a large audience. Each Sunday evening, services are broadcast from the BBC archives, a good number of them from the Church of Scotland.

The BBC gives information about Gaelic services taking place in different parts of the country.

The Gaelic Supplement
The Church of Scotland publishes a Gaelic supplement, Na Duilleagan Gaidhlig, which is distributed free of charge with *Life and Work.* Learners of Gaelic and members of other churches are regular readers of the Gaelic supplement. The Duilleagan can also be read in the Gaelic supplement section of the *Life and Work* website. At the time of writing (July 2018), discussion is ongoing as to the number of issues planned for each year.

Advancing Gaelic in the Church
In 2015, an important Conference was held to consider the place of Gaelic in the Church of Scotland. The Conference was called An Ciad Ceum (The First Step).

As a subsequent step, the Gaelic Group of the Church of Scotland, which had been dormant for a few years, was reconstituted. The aim of the Group is to encourage the use of Gaelic in the life and work of the Church and to develop suitable resources in support of this aim.

Since the General Assembly of 2016, meetings of the Gaelic Group have been held in different parts of the country, including Edinburgh, Inverness, Kyle of Lochalsh, at Sabhal Mòr Ostaig on Skye, Stornoway, Glasgow and Oban.

As a first priority the Group aim to produce a Gaelic Plan for the Church of Scotland. Although not quite ready for publication by the General Assembly of 2018, it was completed shortly thereafter. It is hoped that the final Plan will be included in the Council of Assembly's Report to the General Assembly of 2019 in order to encourage people to engage with the work being taken forward by the Group on behalf of the Church.

A successful Gaelic Lecture, to mark the completion of the new Gaelic translation of the New Testament, was held on the 23rd of May 2018 as a General Assembly fringe event. The main speaker was Rev Roderick MacLean, a member of the translation team. Elaine Duncan of the Scottish Bible Society also spoke. The event was well attended and it was a particular pleasure to welcome ministers and elders of the Free Church of Scotland.

It is hope to take forward ecumenical working on Gaelic matters with other Churches in Scotland.

(2) OTHER CHURCHES IN THE UNITED KINGDOM

THE UNITED FREE CHURCH OF SCOTLAND
General Secretary: Rev. John Fulton BSc BD, United Free Church Offices, 11 Newton Place, Glasgow G3 7PR (0141 332 3435; freeoffice@ufcos.org.uk; www.uifcos.org.uk).

THE FREE CHURCH OF SCOTLAND
Principal Clerk: Rev. Callum Macleod, 15 North Bank Street, The Mound, Edinburgh EH1 2LS (0131 226 5286; offices@freechurch.org; www.uifcos.org.uk).

FREE CHURCH OF SCOTLAND (CONTINUING)
Principal Clerk: Rev. John MacLeod, Free Church Manse, Portmahomack, Tain IV20 1YL (01862 871467; principalclerk@fccontinuing.org; www.freechurchcontinuing.org).

THE FREE PRESBYTERIAN CHURCH OF SCOTLAND
Clerk of Synod: Rev. Keith M. Watkins, 252 Briercliffe Road, Burnley BB10 2DQ (kmwatkins@fpchurch.org.uk; www.fpchurch.org.uk).

ASSOCIATED PRESBYTERIAN CHURCHES
Clerk of Presbytery: Rev. J.R. Ross Macaskill, Bruach Taibh, 2 Borve, Arnisort, Isle of Skye IV51 9PS (01470 582264; emailjrrm@gmail.com; www.apchurches.org).

THE REFORMED PRESBYTERIAN CHURCH OF SCOTLAND
Clerk of Presbytery: Rev. Peter Loughridge, 3b West Pilton Terrace, Edinburgh EH4 4GY (07791 369626; peterloughridge@hotmail.com; www.rpcscotland.org).

THE PRESBYTERIAN CHURCH IN IRELAND
Clerk of the General Assembly and General Secretary: Rev. Trevor D. Gribben, Assembly Buildings, 2–10 Fisherwick Place, Belfast BT1 6DW (028 9041 7208; clerk@presbyterianireland.org; www.presbyterianireland.org).

THE PRESBYTERIAN CHURCH OF WALES
General Secretary: Rev. Meiron Morris, Tabernacle Chapel, 81 Merthyr Road, Whitchurch, Cardiff CF14 1DD (02920 627465; swyddfa.office@ebcpcw.org.uk; www.ebcpcw.cymru).

THE UNITED REFORMED CHURCH
General Secretary: Rev. John Proctor, Church House, 86 Tavistock Place, London WC1H 9RT
(020 7916 2020; Fax: 020 7916 2021; john.proctor@urc.org.uk; www.urc.org.uk).

UNITED REFORMED CHURCH SYNOD OF SCOTLAND
Synod Clerk: Mr Bill Robson, United Reformed Church, 113 West Regent Street, Glasgow G1
2RU (0141 248 5382; brobson@urcscotland.org.uk; www.urcscotland.org.uk).

BAPTIST UNION OF SCOTLAND
General Director: Rev. Alan Donaldson, 48 Speirs Wharf, Glasgow G4 9TH (0141 423 6169;
admin@scottishbaptist.org.uk; www.scottishbaptist.com).

CONGREGATIONAL FEDERATION IN SCOTLAND
Chair: Rev. May-Kane Logan, 93 Cartside Road, Busby, Glasgow G76 8QD (0141 237 1349;
maycita1@virginmedia.com; www.congregational.org.uk).

RELIGIOUS SOCIETY OF FRIENDS (QUAKERS)
Clerk to the General Meeting for Scotland: Adwoa Bittle (Ms), 4 Burnside Park, Pitcairngreen,
Perth PH1 3BF (01738 583108; adwoabittle@hotmail.co.uk; www.quakerscotland.org).

ROMAN CATHOLIC CHURCH
Mgr Hugh Bradley, General Secretary, Bishops' Conference of Scotland, 64 Aitken Street, Airdrie
ML6 6LT (01236 764061; gensec@bcos.org.uk; www.bcos.org.uk).

THE SALVATION ARMY
Lt-Col. Carol Bailey, Secretary for Scotland and Divisional Commander East Scotland
Division, Scotland Office, 12A Dryden Road, Loanhead EH20 9LZ (0131 440 9101;
carol.bailey@salvationarmy.org.uk; www.salvationarmy.org.uk).

SCOTTISH EPISCOPAL CHURCH
Secretary General: Mr John F. Stuart, 21 Grosvenor Crescent, Edinburgh EH12 5EE (0131 225
6357; secgen@scotland.anglican.org; www.scotland.anglican.org).

THE SYNOD OF THE METHODIST CHURCH IN SCOTLAND
District Administrator: Mrs Fiona Inglis, Methodist Church Office, Old Churches House, Kirk
Street, Dunblane FK15 0AJ (Tel/Fax: 01786 820295; fiona@methodistchurch.plus.com;
methodistchurchinscotland.net).

GENERAL SYNOD OF THE CHURCH OF ENGLAND
Secretary General: Mr William Nye, Church House, Great Smith Street, London SW1P 3NZ
(020 7898 1000; enquiry@churchofengland.org).

---

(3) OVERSEAS CHURCHES

See www.churchofscotland.org.uk > Serve > World Mission > Our partner churches

(4) HER MAJESTY'S HOUSEHOLD IN SCOTLAND
ECCLESIASTICAL

Dean of the Order of the Thistle
and Dean of the Chapel Royal: Very Rev. Prof. Iain R. Torrance Kt DD FRSE

Domestic Chaplains: Rev. Kenneth I. Mackenzie DL BD CPS
Rev. Neil N. Gardner MA BD RNR

Chaplains in Ordinary: Rev. Norman W. Drummond CBE MA BD DUniv FRSE
Very Rev. Angus Morrison MA BD PhD DD
Very Rev. E. Lorna Hood OBE MA BD DD
Rev. Alistair G. Bennett BSc BD
Right Rev. Susan M. Brown BD DipMin
Very Rev. John P. Chalmers BD CPS DD
Rev. Prof. David A.S. Fergusson
OBE MA BD DPhil DD FBA FRSE
Rev. George S. Cowie BSc BD
Rev. Elizabeth M. Henderson MA BD MTh

Extra Chaplains: Rev. John MacLeod MA
Very Rev. James A. Simpson BSc BD STM DD
Very Rev. James Harkness KCVO CB OBE MA DD
Rev. John L. Paterson MA BD STM
Rev. Charles Robertson LVO MA
Very Rev. John B. Cairns KCVO LTh LLB LLD DD
Very Rev. Gilleasbuig I. Macmillan
KCVO MA BD Drhc DD FRSE HRSA FRCSEd
Very Rev. Finlay A.J. Macdonald MA BD PhD DD
Rev. Alastair H. Symington MA BD
Rev. James M. Gibson TD LTh LRAM

(5) RECENT LORD HIGH COMMISSIONERS
TO THE GENERAL ASSEMBLY

* deceased

1969   Her Majesty the Queen attended in person

1980/81   The Earl of Elgin and Kincardine KT DL JP
1982/83   * Colonel Sir John Edward Gilmour Bt DSO TD
1984/85   * Charles Hector Fitzroy Maclean, Baron Maclean of Duart and Morvern
KT GCVO KBE

1986/87	*John Campbell Arbuthnott, Viscount of Arbuthnott KT CBE DSC FRSE FRSA
1988/89	* Sir Iain Mark Tennant KT FRSA
1990/91	The Rt Hon. Donald MacArthur Ross FRSE
1992/93	The Rt Hon. Lord Macfarlane of Bearsden KT FRSE
1994/95	* Lady Marion Fraser KT
1996	Her Royal Highness the Princess Royal LT LG GCVO
1997	The Rt Hon. Lord Macfarlane of Bearsden KT FRSE
1998/99	* The Rt Hon. Lord Hogg of Cumbernauld CBE DL JP
2000	His Royal Highness the Prince Charles, Duke of Rothesay KG KT GCB OM
2001/02	* The Rt Hon. Viscount Younger of Leckie KT KCVO TD PC
	Her Majesty the Queen attended the opening of the General Assembly of 2002
2003/04	The Rt Hon. Lord Steel of Aikwood KT KBE
2005/06	The Rt Hon. Lord Mackay of Clashfern KT
2007	His Royal Highness the Prince Andrew, Duke of York KG KCVO
2008/09	The Rt Hon. George Reid PC MA
2010/11	Lord Wilson of Tillyorn KT GCMG PRSE
2012/13	The Rt Hon. Lord Selkirk of Douglas QC MA LLB
2014	His Royal Highness the Prince Edward, Earl of Wessex KG GCVO
2015/16	The Rt Hon. Lord Hope of Craighead KT PC FRSE
2017	Her Royal Highness the Princess Royal KG KT GCVO QSO
2018	The Duke of Buccleuch and Queensberry KT KBE DL FSA FRSE

(6) RECENT MODERATORS
OF THE GENERAL ASSEMBLY

deceased

1992	Hugh R. Wyllie MA DD FCIBS, Hamilton: Old
1993	*James L. Weatherhead CBE MA LLB DD, Principal Clerk of Assembly
1994	James A. Simpson BSc BD STM DD, Dornoch Cathedral
1995	James Harkness KCVO CB OBE MA DD, Chaplain General (Emeritus)
1996	John H. McIndoe MA BD STM DD, London: St Columba's linked with Newcastle: St Andrew's
1997	*Alexander McDonald BA DUniv CMIWSc, General Secretary, Department of Ministry
1998	Alan Main TD MA BD STM PhD DD, University of Aberdeen
1999	John B. Cairns KCVO LTh LLB LLD DD, Dumbarton: Riverside
2000	Andrew R.C. McLellan CBE MA BD STM DD, Edinburgh: St Andrew's and St George's
2001	John D. Miller BA BD DD, Glasgow: Castlemilk East
2002	Finlay A.J. Macdonald MA BD PhD DD, Principal Clerk of Assembly
2003	Iain R. Torrance Kt DD FRSE, University of Aberdeen
2004	Alison Elliot CBE MA MSc PhD LLD DD FRSE, Associate Director, Centre for Theology and Public Issues
2005	David W. Lacy BA BD DLitt DL, Kilmarnock: Henderson
2006	Alan D. McDonald LLB BD MTh DLitt DD, Cameron linked with St Andrews:

	St Leonard's
2007	Sheilagh M. Kesting BA BD DD DSG, Secretary of Ecumenical Relations Committee
2008	David W. Lunan MA BD DUniv DLitt DD, Clerk to the Presbytery of Glasgow
2009	William C. Hewitt BD DipPS, Greenock: Westburn
2010	John C. Christie BSc BD MSB CBiol, Interim Minister
2011	A. David K. Arnott MA BD, St Andrews: Hope Park linked with Strathkinness
2012	Albert O. Bogle BD MTh, Bo'ness: St Andrew's
2013	E. Lorna Hood OBE MA BD DD, Renfrew: North
2014	John P. Chalmers BD CPS DD, Principal Clerk of Assembly
2015	Angus Morrison MA BD PhD DD, Orwell and Portmoak
2016	G. Russell Barr BA BD MTh DMin, Edinburgh: Cramond
2017	Derek Browning MA BD DMin, Edinburgh: Morningside
2018	Susan M. Brown BD DipMin, Dornoch Cathedral

MATTER OF PRECEDENCE

The Lord High Commissioner to the General Assembly of the Church of Scotland (while the Assembly is sitting) ranks next to the Sovereign and the Duke of Edinburgh and before the rest of the Royal Family.

The Moderator of the General Assembly of the Church of Scotland ranks next to the Lord Chancellor of Great Britain and before the Keeper of the Great Seal of Scotland (the First Minister) and the Dukes.

---

(7) SCOTTISH DIVINITY FACULTIES

[* denotes a Minister of the Church of Scotland]

ABERDEEN

School of Divinity, History and Philosophy
50–52 College Bounds, Old Aberdeen AB24 3DS
Tel 01224 272366; Fax 01224 273750; divinity@abdn.ac.uk

Master of Christ's College: Rev. Professor John Swinton* BD PhD RNM RNMD
christs-college@abdn.ac.uk
Head of School: Paula Sweeney MA PhD
Deputy Head of School: Professor Paul Nimmo MA DipIA, BD ThM PhD
Co-ordinator,
Centre for Ministry Studies Rev. Kenneth S. Jeffrey* BA BD PhD DMin
ksjeffrey@abdn.ac.uk

For teaching staff and further information see www.abdn.ac.uk/sdhp/

ST ANDREWS
University College of St Mary
The School of Divinity, South Street, St Andrews, Fife KY16 9JU
Tel: 01334 462850; Fax: 01334 462852; divinity@st-andrews.ac.uk

Principal and Head of School: Rev. Stephen Holmes BA MA MTh PhD

For teaching staff and further information see www.st-andrews.ac.uk/divinity/rt/staff/

EDINBURGH
School of Divinity and New College
New College, Mound Place, Edinburgh EH1 2LX
0131 650 8959; divinity@ed.ac.uk

Head of School: Professor Helen K. Bond MTheol PhD BD MSt PhD
Principal of New College: Rev. Professor Susan Hardman Moore* MA MAR PhD
Assistant Principal of
New College: Rev. Alison M. Jack* MA BD PhD

For teaching staff and further information see www.ed.ac.uk/schools-departments/divinity/

GLASGOW
School of Critical Studies
Theology and Religious Studies
4 The Square, University of Glasgow, Glasgow G12 8QQ
Tel: 0141 330 6526; Fax: 0141 330 4943

Head of Subject: Dr. Scott Spurlock
Professor of Divinity: Rev. Professor George Pattison
Principal of Trinity College: Rev. Doug Gay* MA BD PhD
Tutor and Clerk: Rev. Sandy C. Forsyth* LLB BD DipLP PhD

For teaching staff and further information see www.gla.ac.uk Subjects A-Z. Theology and
Religious Studies

HIGHLAND THEOLOGICAL COLLEGE UHI
High Street, Dingwall IV15 9HA
Tel: 01349 780000; Fax: 01349 780001;
htc@uhi.ac.uk

Principal of HTC: Rev. Hector Morrison* BSc BD MTh
Vice-Principal of HTC: Jamie Grant PhD MA LLB

For teaching staff and further information see www.htc.uhi.ac.uk

(8) SOCIETIES AND ASSOCIATIONS

1. INTER-CHURCH ASSOCIATIONS

ACTION OF CHURCHES TOGETHER IN SCOTLAND (ACTS) – Eaglaisean Còmhla an Gnìomh an Alba – was formed in 1990 as Scotland's national ecumenical instrument. It brings together nine denominations in Scotland who share a desire for greater oneness between churches, a growth of understanding and common life between churches, and unified action in proclaiming and responding to the gospel in the whole of life. Interim General Secretary: Rev Ian Boa, Jubilee House, Forthside Way, Stirling, FK8 1QZ (01259 216980; ianboa@acts-scotland.org; www.acts-scotland.org).

The FELLOWSHIP OF ST ANDREW: The fellowship promotes dialogue between Churches of the east and the west in Scotland. Further information available from the Secretary, Rev. John G. Pickles, 1 Annerley Road, Annan DG12 6HE (01461 202626; jgpickles@hotmail.com).

The FELLOWSHIP OF ST THOMAS: An ecumenical association formed to promote informed interest in and to learn from the experience of Churches in South Asia (India, Pakistan, Bangladesh, Nepal, Sri Lanka and Burma (Myanmar)). Secretary: Rev. Val Nellist, 28 Glamis Gardens, Dalgety Bay, Dunfermline KY11 9TD (01383 824066; valnellist@btinternet.com; www.fost.org.uk).

FRONTIER YOUTH TRUST: Encourages, resources and supports churches, organisations and individuals working with young people (in particular, disadvantaged young people). Through the StreetSpace initiative, the Trust is able to help churches to explore new ways of engaging young people in the community around mission and fresh expressions of church. All correspondence to: Frontier Youth Trust, 202 Bradford Court, 123/131 Bradford Street, Birmingham B12 0NS (0121-771 2328; frontier@fyt. org.uk; www.fyt.org.uk). For information on StreetSpace, contact Clare McCormack (scotland@streetspace.org.uk).

INTERSERVE GREAT BRITIAN AND IRELAND: An international, evangelical and interdenominational organisation with 160 years of Christian service. The purpose of Interserve is 'to make Jesus Christ known through *wholistic* ministry in partnership with the global church, among the neediest peoples of Asia and the Arab world', and our vision is 'Lives and communities transformed through encounter with Jesus Christ'. Interserve supports over 800 people in cross-cultural ministry in a wide range of work including children and youth, the environment, evangelism, Bible training, engineering, agriculture, business development and health. We rely on supporters in Scotland for the work in Scotland and for sending mission partners from Scotland overseas. Scotland Ministry Facilitator: Grace Penney, 21 Park Avenue, Bishopbriggs, Glasgow G64 2SN (07971 858318; GraceP@isgbi.org; www.interserve.org.uk).

IONA COMMUNITY: We are an ecumenical Christian community with a dispersed worldwide membership of Full Members, Associate Members and Friends. Inspired by our faith and loving concern for the world and its people, we pursue justice and peace in and through community. Our new Glasgow centre hosts a growing programme of events, our work with young people, Wild Goose Publications and the Wild Goose Resource Group. The Iona Community also welcomes guests to share in the common life in the Abbey and MacLeod Centre, Iona and Camas outdoor adventure centre, Mull. Joint Leaders: Ms Christian MacLean and Rev Kathy Galloway, 21 Carlton Court, Glasgow, G5 9JP (0141 429 7281, admin@iona.org.uk; www.iona.org.uk; Facebook: Iona Community; Twitter: @ ionacommunity). Iona Centres Manager: Rev Heinz Toller, Iona Abbey, Isle of Iona, Argyll, PA76 6SN (01681 700404; enquiries@iona.org.uk).

PLACE FOR HOPE: Our churches and faith communities face change, encounter difference and experience conflict at different stages and for a variety of reasons. In times of change or challenge, we know that practical support can help. Place for Hope, a body with its roots in the Church of Scotland and now an independent charity approaching our 10-year anniversary, accompanies and equips people and faith communities where relationships have become strained and helps them move towards living well with difference. Through a skilled and highly trained team of Practitioners, we accompany groups navigating conflict and difficult conversations and resource the church and wider faith communities with peacemakers. Place for Hope can:
– help groups and individuals at a time of crisis
– accompany sensitive or difficult group conversations, such as preparing for change or transition
– provide individual coaching
– host and enable community dialogues on difficult, potentially divisive issues
– offer training, workshops and resources for understanding and working with conflict and change.
Please get in touch for information, or a confidential conversation: 07884 580359; info@ placeforhope.org.uk; www.placeforhope.org.uk.

The ST COLM'S FELLOWSHIP: An association for all from any denomination who have trained, studied or been resident at St Colm's, either when it was a college or later as International House. There is an annual retreat and a meeting for Commemoration; and some local groups meet on a regular basis. Hon. Secretary: Rev. Margaret Nutter, 'Kilmorich', 14 Balloch Road, Balloch G83 8SR (01389 754505; maenutter@gmail.com).

SCOTTISH CHURCHES HOUSING ACTION: Works with Christian denominations across Scotland to tacke homelessness; supports local volunteering to assist homeless people; advice and support on befriending services; and provides consultancy advice on using redundant property for affordable housing. Chief Executive: David Cressey, 44 Hanover

Street, Edinburgh EH2 2DR (0131 477 4500; info@churches-housing.org; www.churches-housing.org).

SCOTTISH CHURCHES ORGANIST TRAINING SCHEME (SCOTS): Established in 1997 as an initiative of the then Panel on Worship, along with the Royal School of Church Music's Scottish Committee and the Scottish Federation of Organists, this is a self-propelled scheme by which a pianist who seeks competence on the organ – and organists who wish to develop their skills – can follow a three-stage syllabus, receiving a certificate at each stage. Participants each have an Adviser whom they meet occasionally for assessment, and also take part in one of the three or four Local Organ Workshops which are held in different parts of Scotland each year. There is a regular e-newsletter, *Scots Wha Play*. Costs are kept low. SCOTS is an ecumenical scheme. Information from Douglas Galbraith (01592 752403; dgalbraith@churchofscotland.org.uk; www.scotsorgan.org.uk > SCOTS).

SCOTTISH JOINT COMMITTEE ON RELIGIOUS AND MORAL EDUCATION: This is an interfaith body that began as a joint partnership between the Educational Institute of Scotland and the Church of Scotland to provide resources, training and support for the work of religious and moral education in schools. Mr Andrew Tomlinson, 121 George Street, Edinburgh EH2 4YN (0131 225 5722; atomlinson@churchofscotland. org.uk), and Mr Lachlan Bradley, 6 Clairmont Gardens, Glasgow G3 7LW (0141 353 3595).

SCRIPTURE UNION SCOTLAND: Scripture Union Scotland's vision is to see the children and young people of Scotland exploring the Bible and responding to the significance of Jesus. SU Scotland works in schools running SU groups and supporting Curriculum for Excellence. Its three activity centres, Lendrick Muir, Alltnacriche and Gowanbank, accommodate school groups and weekends away during term-time. During the school holidays it runs an extensive programme of events for school-age children – including residential holidays (some focused on disadvantaged children and young people), missions and church-based holiday clubs. In addition, it runs discipleship and training programmes for young people and is committed to promoting prayer for, and by, the young people of Scotland through a range of national prayer events and the *Pray for Schools Scotland* initiative. Scripture Union Scotland, 70 Milton Street, Glasgow G4 0HR (Tel: 0141 332 1162; Fax: 0141 352 7600; info@suscotland.org. uk; www.suscotland.org.uk).

STUDENT CHRISTIAN MOVEMENT: SCM is a student-led movement inspired by Jesus to act for justice and show God's love in the world. As a community we come together to pray, worship and explore faith in an open and non-judgemental environment. The movement is made up of a network of groups and individual members across Britain, as well as link churches and chaplaincies. As a national movement we come together at regional and national events to learn more about our faith and spend time as a community, and we take action on issues of social justice chosen by our members. SCM provides resources and training to student groups, churches and chaplaincies on student outreach and engagement, leadership and social action. National Co-ordinator: Hilary Topp, SCM, Grays Court, 3 Nursery Road, Edgbaston, Birmingham B15 3JX (0121 426 4918; scm@movement. org.uk; www.movement.org.uk).

WORLD DAY OF PRAYER: SCOTTISH COMMITTEE: Convener: Mrs Margaret Broster, Bryn a Glyn, 27b Braehead, Beith KA15 1EF (01505 503300; margaretbroster@hotmail.

co.uk). Secretary: Marjorie Paton, Muldoanich, Stirling Street, Blackford, Auchterarder PH4 1QG (01764 682234; marjoriepaton.wdp@btinternet.com; www.wdpscotland.org.uk).

YMCA SCOTLAND: Offers support, training and guidance to churches seeking to reach out to love and serve young people's needs. Chief Executive – National General Secretary: Mrs Kerry Reilly, YMCA Scotland, 1 Chesser Avenue, Edinburgh EH14 1TB (0131 228 1464; kerry@ymcascotland.org; www.ymcascotland.org).

YOUTH FOR CHRIST: Youth for Christ is a national Christian charity committed to taking the Good News of Jesus Christ relevantly to every young person in Great Britain. In Scotland there are 5 locally governed, staffed and financed centres, communicating and demonstrating the Christian faith. Local Ministries Director: Lauren Fox (0121 502 9620; lauren.fox@yfc.co.uk; www.yfc.co.uk/local-centres/scotland).

2. CHURCH OF SCOTLAND SOCIETIES

CHURCH OF SCOTLAND ABSTAINERS' ASSOCIATION: Recognising that alcohol is a major – indeed a growing – problem within Scotland, the aim of the Church of Scotland Abstainers' Association, with its motto 'Abstinence makes sense', is to encourage more people to choose a healthy alcohol-free lifestyle. Further details are available from 'Blochairn', 17A Culduthel Road, Inverness IV24 4AG (jamwall@talktalk.net; www.kirkabstainers.org.uk).

The CHURCH OF SCOTLAND CHAPLAINS' ASSOCIATION: The Association consists of serving and retired chaplains to HM Forces. It holds an annual meeting and lunch on Shrove Tuesday, and organises the annual Service of Remembrance in St Giles' Cathedral on Chaplains' Day of the General Assembly. Hon. Secretary: Rev. Stephen A. Blakey BSc BD, Balduff House, Kilry, Blairgowrie PH11 8HS (01575 560226; SBlakey@churchofscotland.org.uk).

The CHURCH OF SCOTLAND RETIRED MINISTERS' ASSOCIATION: The Association meets in St. Andrew's and St. George's West Church, George St., Edinburgh, normally on the first Monday of the month, from October to April. The group is becoming increasingly ecumenical. Meetings include a talk, which can be on a wide variety of topics, which is followed by afternoon tea. Details of the programme from Hon. Secretary: Rev. David Dutton, 13 Acredales, Haddington EH41 4NT (01620 825999; duttondw@gmail.com).

The CHURCH SERVICE SOCIETY: Founded in 1865 to study the development of Christian worship through the ages and in the Reformed tradition, and to work towards renewal in contemporary worship. It has published since 1928, and continues to publish, a liturgical journal, archived on its website. Secretary: Rev. Dr Douglas Galbraith (01592 752403; dgalbraith@churchofscotland.org.uk; www.churchservicesociety.org).

FORUM OF GENERAL ASSEMBLY AND PRESBYTERY CLERKS: Secretary: Rev. Bryan Kerr, Greyfriars Manse, 3 Bellefield Way, Lanark ML11 7NW (01555 663363; lanark@churchofscotland.org.uk).

COVENANT FELLOWSHIP SCOTLAND (formerly FORWARD TOGETHER): An organisation for evangelicals within the Church of Scotland. Contact the Director, Mr Eric

C. Smith (07715 665728; director@covenantfellowshipscotland.com), or the Chairman, Rev. Prof. Andrew T.B. McGowan (01463 238770; amcgowan@churchofscotland.org.uk; http://covenantfellowshipscotland.com).

The FRIENDS OF TABEETHA SCHOOL, JAFFA: The Friends seek to support the only school run by the Church of Scotland in the world. Based in Jaffa, Israel, it seeks to promote tolerance and understanding amongst pupils and staff alike. President: Irene Anderson. Hon. Secretary: Rev. David J. Smith, 1 Cawdor Drive, Glenrothes KY6 2HN (01592 611963; David.Smith@churchofscotland.org.uk).

The IRISH GATHERING: An informal annual meeting with a guest speaker; all those having a connection with or an interest in the Presbyterian Church in Ireland are very welcome. Secretary: Rev. William McLaren, 23 Shamrock Street, Dundee DD4 7AH (01382 459119; WMcLaren@churchofscotland.org.uk).

SCOTTISH CHURCH SOCIETY: Founded in 1892 to 'defend and advance Catholic doctrine as set forth in the Ancient Creeds and embodied in the Standards of the Church of Scotland', the Society meets for worship and discussion at All Saints' Tide, holds a Lenten Quiet Day, an AGM, and other meetings by arrangement; all are open to non members. Secretary: Rev. W. Gerald Jones MA BD MTh, The Manse, Patna Road, Kirkmichael, Maybole KA19 7PJ (01655 750286; WJones@churchofscotland.org.uk).

SCOTTISH CHURCH THEOLOGY SOCIETY: The Society encourages theological exploration and discussion of the main issues confronting the Church in the twenty-first century. Rev. Alexander Shuttleworth, 62 Toll Road, Kincardine, Alloa FK10 4QZ (01259 731002; AShuttleworth@churchofscotland.org.uk).

SOCIETY OF FRIENDS OF ST ANDREW'S JERUSALEM: In co-operation with the World Mission Council, the Society seeks to provide support for the work of the Congregation of St Andrew's Scots Memorial Church, Jerusalem, and St Andrew's Guesthouse. Hon. Secretary and Membership Secretary: Walter T. Dunlop, c/o World Mission Council, 121 George Street, Edinburgh, EH2 4YN.

3. BIBLE SOCIETIES

The SCOTTISH BIBLE SOCIETY: Chief Executive: Elaine Duncan, 7 Hampton Terrace, Edinburgh EH12 5XU (0131 337 9701; info@scottishbiblesociety.org; https://scottishbiblesociety.org).

WEST OF SCOTLAND BIBLE SOCIETY: Secretary: Rev. Finlay Mackenzie, 6 Shaw Road, Milngavie, Glasgow G62 6LU (07817 680011; f.c.mack51@gmail.com; www.westofscotlandbiblesociety.com).

4. GENERAL

The BOYS' BRIGADE: A volunteer-led Christian youth organisation which was founded in Scotland in 1883 and now operates in many different countries around the world. Our vision is that children and young people experience life to the full (John 10:10). John Sharp, Director for Scotland, Scottish Headquarters, Carronvale House, Carronvale Road,

Larbert FK5 3LH (01324 562008; scottishhq@boys-brigade.org.uk; www.boys-brigade. org.uk/Scotland). Scottish Chaplain for the Brigade: Rev Derek Gunn (scottishchaplain@ boys-brigade.org.uk).

BROKEN RITES: Support group for divorced and separated clergy spouses. (01896 759254; eshirleydouglas@hotmail.co.uk; www.brokenrites.org).

CHRISTIAN AID SCOTLAND: Sally Foster-Fulton, Head of Christian Aid Scotland, Sycamore House, 290 Bath Street, Glasgow G2 4JR (0141 221 7475; glasgow@christian-aid.org). Edinburgh Office: 0131 220 1254.

CHRISTIAN ENDEAVOUR IN SCOTLAND: Challenging and encouraging children and young people in the service of Christ and the Church, especially through the CE Award Scheme: 16 Queen Street, Alloa FK10 2AR (01259 215101; admin@cescotland.org; www. cescotland.org).

DAY ONE CHRISTIAN MINISTRIES: Day One has produced Christian literature for over 35 years. A variety of books are published for both adults and young people, as well as cards, bookmarks and stationery items. Ryelands Road, Leominster, Herefordshire HR6 8NZ. Contact Mark Roberts for further information (01568 613740; mark@dayone.co.uk; www. dayone.org.uk).

ECO-CONGREGATION SCOTLAND: Eco-Congregation Scotland is the largest movement of community-based environment groups in Scotland. We offer a programme to help congregations reduce their impact on climate change and live sustainably in a world of limited resources. 121 George Street, Edinburgh EH2 4YN (0131 240 2274; manager@ ecocongregationscotland.org; www.ecocongregationscotland.org).

GIRLGUIDING SCOTLAND: 16 Coates Crescent, Edinburgh EH3 7AH (Tel: 0131 226 4511; Fax: 0131 220 4828; administrator@girlguiding-scot.org.uk; www.girlguidingscotland.org.uk).

GIRLS' BRIGADE SCOTLAND: 11A Woodside Crescent, Glasgow G3 7UL (0141 332 1765; caroline.goodfellow@girls-brigade-scotland.org.uk; www.girls-brigade-scotland.org.uk).

The LEPROSY MISSION SCOTLAND: Working in over 30 countries, the Leprosy Mission is a global fellowship united by our Christian faith and commitment to seeing leprosy defeated and lives transformed. The Leprosy Mission Scotland, Suite 2, Earlsgate Lodge, Livilands Lane, Stirling FK8 2BG (01786 449266; contactus@leprosymission.scot; www. leprosymission.scot).

RELATIONSHIPS SCOTLAND: Scotland's largest provider of relationship counselling, family mediation and child contact centre services. Chief Executive: Mr Stuart Valentine, 18 York Place, Edinburgh EH1 3EP (Tel: 0345 119 2020; Fax: 0845 119 6089; enquiries@ relationships-scotland.org.uk; www.relationships-scotland.org.uk).

SCOTTISH CHURCH HISTORY SOCIETY: Secretary: Dr Laura Mair, schssec@outlook.com.

SCOTTISH EVANGELICAL THEOLOGY SOCIETY: Secretary: Rev. M.G. Smith, 0/2, 2008 Maryhill Road, Glasgow G20 0AB (0141 570 8680; sets.secretary@gmail.com;

www.s-e-t-s.org.uk).

The SCOTTISH REFORMATION SOCIETY: Chairman: Rev. Kenneth Macdonald. Vice-Chairman: Mr Allan McCulloch. Secretary: Rev. Dr Douglas Somerset. Treasurer: Rev. Andrew W.F. Coghill. The Magdalen Chapel, 41 Cowgate, Edinburgh EH1 1JR (0131 220 1450; info@scottishreformationsociety.org; www.scottishreformationsociety.org).

SCOUTS SCOTLAND: Scottish Headquarters, Fordell Firs, Hillend, Dunfermline KY11 7HQ (01383 419073; hello@scouts.scot; www.scouts.scot).

The SOCIETY IN SCOTLAND FOR PROPAGATING CHRISTIAN KNOWLEDGE: Chairman: Rev. Michael W. Frew; Secretary: Ian Alexander, SSPCK, c/o World Mission, 121 George Street, Edinburgh EH2 4YN (0131 225 5722; SSPCK@churchofscotland.org. uk; www.sspck.co.uk).

TEARFUND: 100 Church Road, Teddington TW11 8QE (0208 977 9144). Director: Lynne Paterson, Tearfund Scotland, Challenge House, 29 Canal Street, Glasgow G4 0AD (0141 332 3621; scotland@tearfund.org; www.tearfund.org/scotland).

The WALDENSIAN MISSIONS AID SOCIETY FOR WORK IN ITALY: David A. Lamb SSC, 36 Liberton Drive, Edinburgh EH16 6NN (0131 664 3059; david@dlamb.co.uk; www. scottishwaldensian.org.uk).

YOUTH SCOTLAND: Balfour House, 19 Bonnington Grove, Edinburgh EH6 4BL (Tel: 0131 554 2561; Fax: 0131 454 3438; office@youthscotland.org.uk; www.youthscotland.org.uk).

THE YOUNG WOMEN'S MOVEMENT: Director: Patrycja Kupiec, Room 1.17 St Margaret's House, 151 London Road, Edinburgh EH7 6AE (0131 652 0248; hello@ywcascotland. org; www.ywcascotland.org).

---

(9) TRUSTS AND FUNDS

ABERNETHY ADVENTURE CENTRES: Full board residential accommodation and adventure activities available for all Church groups, plus a range of Christian summer camps at our four centres across Scotland. 01479 818005; marketing@abernethy.org.uk; www.abernethy.org.uk).

The ARROL TRUST: The Arrol Trust gives small grants to young people between the ages of 16 and 25 for the purposes of travel which will provide education or work experience. Potential recipients would be young people with disabilities or who would for financial reasons be otherwise unable to undertake projects. It is expected that projects would be beneficial not only to applicants but also to the wider community. Application forms are available from Callum S. Kennedy WS, Lindsays WS, Caledonian Exchange, 19A Canning Street, Edinburgh EH3 8HE (0131 229 1212).

The BAIRD TRUST: Assists in the building and repair of churches and halls, and generally assists the work of the Church of Scotland. Apply to Iain A.T. Mowat CA, 182 Bath Street, Glasgow G2 4HG (0141 332 0476; info@bairdtrust.org.uk; www.bairdtrust.org.uk).

The Rev. Alexander BARCLAY BEQUEST: Assists a family member of a deceased minister of the Church of Scotland who at the time of his/her death was acting as his/her housekeeper and who is in needy circumstances, and in certain circumstances assists Ministers, Deacons, Ministries Development Staff and their spouses facing financial hardship. Applications can only be submitted to the trustees by the Ministries Council Pastoral Support Team, 121 George Street, Edinburgh EH2 4YN (0131 225 5722; pastoralsupport@churchofscotland.org.uk).

BELLAHOUSTON BEQUEST FUND: Gives grants to Protestant evangelical denominations in the City of Glasgow and certain areas within five miles of the city boundary for building and repairing churches and halls and the promotion of religion. Apply to Mr Donald B. Reid, Mitchells Roberton, 36 North Hanover Street, Glasgow G1 2AD (0141 552 3422; info@mitchells-roberton.co.uk).

BEQUEST FUND FOR MINISTERS: Provides financial assistance to ministers in outlying districts towards the cost of manse furnishings, pastoral efficiency aids, and personal and family medical or educational (including university) costs. Apply to A. Linda Parkhill CA, 60 Wellington Street, Glasgow G2 6HJ (0141 226 4994; mail@parkhillmackie.co.uk).

CARNEGIE TRUST FOR THE UNIVERSITIES OF SCOTLAND: In cases of hardship, the Carnegie Trust is prepared to consider applications by students of Scottish birth or extraction (at least one parent born in Scotland), or who have had at least two years' education at a secondary school in Scotland, for financial assistance with the payment of their fees for a first degree at a Scottish university. For further details, students should apply to the Secretary, Carnegie Trust for the Universities of Scotland, Andrew Carnegie House, Pittencrieff Street, Dunfermline KY12 8AW (01383 724990; admin@carnegie-trust.org; www.carnegie-trust.org).

CHURCH OF SCOTLAND INSURANCE SERVICES LTD: Arranges Church property and liabilities insurance in its capacity of Insurance Intermediary; also arranges other classes of business including household insurance for members and adherents of the Church of Scotland and insurances for charities. It pays its distributable profits to the Church of Scotland through Gift Aid. It is authorised and regulated by the Financial Conduct Authority. Contact 121 George Street, Edinburgh EH2 4YN (Tel: 0131 220 4119; Fax: 0131 220 3113; b.clarkson@cosic.co.uk; www.cosic.co.uk).

CHURCH OF SCOTLAND MINISTRY BENEVOLENT FUND: Makes grants to retired men and women who have been ordained or commissioned for the ministry of the Church of Scotland and to widows, widowers, orphans, spouses or children of such, who are in need. Apply to Elaine Macadie BA CA, Finance Manager, Ministries Council, 121 George Street, Edinburgh EH2 4YN (0131 225 5722).

The CINTRA BEQUEST: See 'Tod Endowment Trust …' entry below.

CLARK BURSARY: Awarded to accepted candidate(s) for the ministry of the Church of Scotland whose studies for the ministry are pursued at the University of Aberdeen. Applications or recommendations for the Bursary to the Clerk to the Presbytery of Aberdeen, Mastrick Church, Greenfern Road, Aberdeen AB16 6TR.

CRAIGCROOK MORTIFICATION: The Trust has power to award grants or pensions (1) to men and women of 60 years of age or over born in Scotland or who have resided in Scotland for not less than 10 years who appear to be in poor circumstances, and (2) to children of deceased persons who met those conditions at the time of death and who appear to require assistance. The Trust has made single payments but normally awards pensions of £1,000 payable biannually. Ministers are invited to notify the Clerk and Factor, Jennifer Law CA, Exchange Place 3, Semple Street, Edinburgh EH3 8BL (0131 473 3500; charity@scott-moncrieff.com) of deserving persons and should be prepared to act as a referee on the application form.

The DRUMMOND TRUST: Makes grants towards the cost of publication of books of 'sound Christian doctrine and outreach'. The Trustees are also willing to receive grant requests towards the cost of audio-visual programme material, but not equipment, software but not hardware. Requests for application forms should be made to the Secretaries, Hill and Robb Limited, 3 Pitt Terrace, Stirling FK8 2EY (01786 450985; fleurmcintosh@hillandrobb.co.uk). Manuscripts should *not* be sent.

The DUNCAN McCLEMENTS TRUST FOR ECUMENICAL TRAINING: Makes grants towards the cost of attendance at ecumenical assemblies and conferences; gatherings of young people; short courses or conferences promoting ecumenical understanding. Also to enable schools to organise one-off events to promote better understanding among differing communities and cultures with different religious backgrounds. The Trust also helps towards the cost of resources and study materials. Enquiries to: Committee on Ecumenical Relations, Church of Scotland, 121 George Street, Edinburgh EH2 4YN (0131 240 2208; ecumenical@churchofscotland.org.uk).

The David DUNCAN TRUST: Makes grants annually to students for the ministry and students in training to become deacons in the Church of Scotland in the Faculties of Arts and Divinity. Preference is given to those born or educated within the bounds of the former Presbytery of Arbroath. Applications not later than 31 October to Thorntons Law LLP, Brothockbank House, Arbroath DD11 1NE (reference: G.J.M. Dunlop; 01241 872683; gdunlop@thorntons-law. co.uk).

ERSKINE CUNNINGHAM HILL TRUST: Donates 50% of its annual income to the central funds of the Church of Scotland and 50% to other charities. Individual donations are in the region of £1,000. Priority is given to charities administered by voluntary or honorary officials, in particular charities registered and operating in Scotland and relating to the elderly, young people, ex-service personnel or seafarers. Application forms from the Secretary, Alan Ritchie, 121 George Street, Edinburgh EH2 4YN (0131 225 5722; aritchie@cofscotland.org.uk).

ESDAILE TRUST: Assists the education and advancement of daughters of ministers, missionaries and widowed deaconesses of the Church of Scotland between 12 and 25 years of age. Applications are to be lodged by 31 May in each year with the Clerk and Treasurer, Jennifer Law CA, Exchange Place 3, Semple Street, Edinburgh EH3 8BL (0131 473 3500; charity@ scott-moncrieff.com).

FERGUSON BEQUEST FUND: Assists with the building and repair of churches and halls and, more generally, with the work of the Church of Scotland. Priority is given to the Counties of Ayr, Kirkcudbright, Wigtown, Lanark, Dunbarton and Renfrew, and to Greenock, Glasgow, Falkirk and Ardrossan; applications are, however, accepted from across Scotland. Apply to Iain A.T. Mowat CA, 182 Bath Street, Glasgow G2 4HG (0141 332 0476; info@fergusonbequestfund. org.uk; www.fergusonbequestfund.org.uk).

GEIKIE BEQUEST: Makes small grants to students for the ministry, including students studying for entry to the University, preference being given to those not eligible for SAAS awards. Apply to Elaine Macadie BA CA, Finance Manager, Ministries Council, 121 George Street, Edinburgh EH2 4YN by September for distribution in November each year.

James GILLAN'S BURSARY FUND: Bursaries are available for male or female students for the ministry who were born or whose parents or parent have resided and had their home for not less than three years continually in the old counties of Moray or Nairn. Apply to Mr Donald Prentice, St Leonard's, Nelson Road, Forres IV36 1DR (01309 672380).

The GLASGOW SOCIETY OF THE SONS AND DAUGHTERS OF MINISTERS OF THE CHURCH OF SCOTLAND: The Society's primary purpose is to grant financial assistance to children (no matter what age) of deceased ministers of the Church of Scotland. Applications are to be submitted by 1 February in each year. To the extent that funds are available, grants are also given for the children of ministers or retired ministers, although such grants are normally restricted to university and college students. These latter grants are considered in conjunction with the Edinburgh-based Societies. Limited funds are also available for individual application for special needs or projects. Applications are to be submitted by 31 May in each year. Emergency applications can be dealt with at any time when need arises. More information can be found at www.mansebairnsnetwork.org. Application forms may be obtained from the Secretary and Treasurer, Jennifer Law CA, Exchange Place 3, Semple Street, Edinburgh EH3 8BL (0131 473 3500; charity@scott-moncrieff.com).

HAMILTON BURSARY TRUST: Awarded, subject to the intention to serve overseas under the Church of Scotland World Mission Council or to serve with some other Overseas Mission Agency approved by the Council, to a student at the University of Aberdeen (failing which to Accepted Candidate(s) for the Ministry of the Church of Scotland whose studies for the Ministry are pursued at Aberdeen University). Applications or recommendations for the Bursary to the Clerk to the Presbytery of Aberdeen, Mastrick Church, Greenfern Road, Aberdeen AB16 6TR.

Martin HARCUS BEQUEST: Makes annual grants to candidates for the ministry resident within the Presbytery of Edinburgh and currently under the jurisdiction of the Presbytery. Applications to the Principal's Secretary, New College, Mound Place, Edinburgh EH1 2LX (k.mclean@ed.ac.uk) by 15 October.

The HOPE TRUST: Gives some support to organisations involved in combating drink and drugs, and has as its main purpose the promotion of the Reformed tradition throughout the world. There is also a Scholarship programme for Postgraduate Theology Study in Scotland. Apply to Robert P. Miller SSC LLB, Glenorchy House, 20 Union Street, Edinburgh EH1 3LR (Tel: 0131 226 5151; Fax: 0131 225 2608).

KEAY THOM TRUST: The principal purposes of the Keay Thom Trust are:
1. To benefit the widows, daughters or other dependent female relatives of deceased ministers, or wives of ministers who are now divorced or separated, all of whom have supported the minister in the fulfilment of his duties and who, by reason of death, divorce or separation, have been required to leave the manse. The Trust can assist them in the purchase of a house or by providing financial or material assistance whether it be for the provision of accommodation or not.
2. To assist in the education or training of the above female relatives or any other children of deceased ministers.

Further information and application forms are available from Miller Hendry, Solicitors, 10 Blackfriars Street, Perth PH1 5NS (01738 637311; johnthom@millerhendry.co.uk).

LADIES' GAELIC SCHOOLS AND HIGHLAND BURSARY ASSOCIATION: Distributes money to students, preferably with a Highland/Gaelic background, who are training to be ministers in the Church of Scotland. Apply by 15 October in each year to the Secretary, Mrs Marion McGill, 61 Ladysmith Road, Edinburgh EH9 3EY (0131 667 4243; marionmcgill61@ gmail.com).

The LYALL BEQUEST (Scottish Charity Number SC005542): Offers grants to ministers:
1. Grants to individual ministers, couples and families, for a holiday for a minimum of seven nights. No reapplication within a three-year period; and thereafter a 50 per cent grant to those reapplying.
2. Grants towards sickness and convalescence costs so far as not covered by the National Health Service. Applications should be made to the Secretary and Clerk, The Church of Scotland Trust, 121 George Street, Edinburgh EH2 4YN (0131 240 2222; jhamilton@ churchofscotland.org.uk).

REV DR MACINNES AND MRS MACINNES TRUST: Provides grants to (1) retired ministers who have spent part of their ministry in the Counties of Nairn, Ross & Cromarty or Argyll and are solely dependent upon their pensions and preaching fees and (2) widows or widowers of such ministers solely dependent on their pensions. Applications should be made to the Secretary and Clerk, The Church of Scotland Trust, 121 George Street, Edinburgh EH2 4YN (0131 240 2222; jhamilton@churchofscotland.org.uk).

Gillian MACLAINE BURSARY FUND: Open to candidates for the ministry of the Church of Scotland of Scottish or Canadian nationality. Preference is given to Gaelic-speakers. Application forms available from Mr W Stewart Shaw DL BSc, Clerk to the Presbytery of Argyll, 59 Barone Road, Rothesay, Isle of Bute PA20 0DZ (07470 520240; argyll@churchofscotland.org.uk). Closing date for receipt of applications is 31 October.

The E. McLAREN FUND: The persons intended to be benefited are widows and unmarried ladies, preference being given to ladies above 40 years of age in the following order:
(a) Widows and daughters of Officers in the Highland Regiment, and
(b) Widows and daughters of Scotsmen.
Further details from the Secretary, The E. McLaren Fund, Messrs Wright, Johnston & Mackenzie LLP, Solicitors, 302 St Vincent Street, Glasgow G2 5RZ (Tel: 0141 248 3434; Fax: 0141 221 1226; rmd@wjm.co.uk).

THE MEIKLE AND PATON TRUST: Grants are available to Ministers, Missionaries and Christian Workers including staff of the CSC for rest and recuperation at the following hotels: Crieff Hydro; Murraypark Hotel, Crieff; Peebles Hydro; Park Hotel, Peebles; Ballachulish Hotel and Isle of Glencoe Hotel. Grants give a subsidy for overnight residence, such subsidy being decreed by the Trustees at any given time. Booking may be made by telephone or on line and applicants will be required to state their page in the Church of Scotland Year Book or their unique number from the CSC list to obtain Meikle Paton benefit.

MORGAN BURSARY FUND: Makes grants to candidates for the Church of Scotland ministry studying at the University of Glasgow. Apply to the Clerk to the Presbytery of Glasgow, 260

Bath Street, Glasgow G2 4JP (0141 332 6606; glasgow@churchofscotland.org.uk). Closing date October 31.

NEW MINISTERS' FURNISHING LOAN FUND: Makes loans (of £1,000) to ministers in their first charge to assist with furnishing the manse. Apply to Elaine Macadie, Finance Manager, Ministries Council, 121 George Street, Edinburgh EH2 4YN.

NOVUM TRUST: Provides small short-term grants – typically between £200 and £2,500 – to initiate projects in Christian action and research which cannot readily be financed from other sources. Trustees welcome applications from projects that are essentially Scottish, are distinctively new, and are focused on the welfare of young people, on the training of lay people or on new ways of communicating the Christian faith. The Trust cannot support large building projects, staff salaries or individuals applying for maintenance during courses or training. Application forms and guidance notes from novumt@cofscotland.org.uk or Mrs Susan Masterton, Blair Cadell WS, The Bond House, 5 Breadalbane Street, Edinburgh EH6 5JH (0131 555 5800; www.novum.org.uk).

PARK MEMORIAL BURSARY FUND: Provides grants for the benefit of candidates for the ministry of the Church of Scotland from the Presbytery of Glasgow under full-time training. Apply to the Clerk to the Presbytery of Glasgow, 260 Bath Street, Glasgow G2 4JP (0141 332 6606; glasgow@churchofscotland.org.uk). Closing date November 15.

PATON TRUST: Assists ministers in ill health to have a recuperative holiday outwith, and free from the cares of, their parishes. Apply to Alan S. Cunningham CA, Alexander Sloan, Chartered Accountants, 38 Cadogan Street, Glasgow G2 7HF (Tel: 0141 204 8989; Fax: 0141 248 9931; alan.cunningham@alexandersloan.co.uk).

PRESBYTERY OF ARGYLL BURSARY FUND: Open to students who have been accepted as candidates for the ministry and the readership of the Church of Scotland. Preference is given to applicants who are natives of the bounds of the Presbytery, or are resident within the bounds of the Presbytery, or who have a strong connection with the bounds of the Presbytery. Application forms available from Mr W Stewart Shaw DL BSc, Clerk to the Presbytery of Argyll, 59 Barone Road, Rothesay, Isle of Bute PA20 0DZ (07470 520240; argyll@churchofscotland.org.uk). Closing date for receipt of applications is 31 October.

Margaret and John ROSS TRAVELLING FUND: Offers grants to ministers and their spouses for travelling and other expenses for trips to the Holy Land where the purpose is recuperation or relaxation. Applications should be made to the Secretary and Clerk, The Church of Scotland Trust, 121 George Street, Edinburgh EH2 4YN (0131 240 2222; jhamilton@churchofscotland.org.uk).

SCOTLAND'S CHURCHES TRUST: Assists, through grants, with the preservation of the fabric of buildings in use for public worship by any denomination. Also supports the playing of church organs by grants for public concerts, and through tuition bursaries for suitably proficient piano or organ players wishing to improve skills or techniques. SCT promotes visitor interest in churches through the trust's Pilgrim Journeys covering Scotland. Criteria and how to apply at www.scotlandschurchestrust.org.uk. Scotland's Churches Trust, 15 North Bank Street, Edinburgh EH1 2LP (info@scotlandschurchestrust.org.uk).

SCOTTISH CHURCHES HOUSE LEGACY RESERVE: Aim – to enable Scotland's churches and Christian organisations to resource new ways of ecumenical working. Between 1960 and 2011, the former Scottish Churches House in Dunblane was a centre for ecumenical encounter, sharing, challenge and development – the Legacy Reserve aims to continue this ethos. Applications are invited for the funding of projects; completed application forms must be submitted no later than 5th January in any year. Property schemes (such as repairs or purchase) are not eligible. Further details and application forms are available from the Interim General Secretary, Action of Churches Together in Scotland, Jubilee House, Forthside Way, Stirling FK8 1QZ. (01259 216980; ianboa@acts-scotland.org).

SMIETON FUND: To assist ministers who would benefit from a holiday because of a recent pastoral need. Administered at the discretion of the pastoral staff, who will give priority in cases of need. Applications to the Recruitment and Support Secretary, Ministries Council, 121 George Street, Edinburgh EH2 4YN (pastoralsupport@churchofscotland.org.uk).

Mary Davidson SMITH CLERICAL AND EDUCATIONAL FUND FOR ABERDEENSHIRE: Assists ministers who have been ordained for five years or over and are in full charge of a congregation in Aberdeen, Aberdeenshire and the north, to purchase books, or to travel for educational purposes, and assists their children with scholarships for further education or vocational training. Apply to Alan J. Innes MA LLB, 100 Union Street, Aberdeen AB10 1QR (01224 428000).

The SOCIETY FOR THE BENEFIT OF THE SONS AND DAUGHTERS OF THE CLERGY OF THE CHURCH OF SCOTLAND: Annual grants are made to assist in the education of the children (normally between the ages of 12 and 25 years) of ministers of the Church of Scotland. The Society also gives grants to aged and infirm daughters of ministers and ministers' unmarried daughters and sisters who are in need. Applications are to be lodged by 31 May in each year with the Secretary and Treasurer, Jennifer Law CA, Exchange Place 3, Semple Street, Edinburgh EH3 8BL (0131 473 3500; charity@scott-moncrieff.com).

The Nan STEVENSON CHARITABLE TRUST FOR RETIRED MINISTERS: Provides houses, or loans to purchase houses, on similar terms to the Housing and Loan Fund, for any retired paid church worker with a North Ayrshire connection. Secretary and Treasurer: Mrs Christine Thomas, 18 Brisbane Street, Largs KA30 8QN (01475 338564; 07891 838778; cathomas54@gmail.com).

Miss M.E. SWINTON PATERSON'S CHARITABLE TRUST: The Trust can give modest grants to support smaller congregations in urban or rural areas who require to fund essential maintenance or improvement works at their buildings. Apply to Mr Callum S. Kennedy WS, Messrs Lindsays WS, Caledonian Exchange, 19A Canning Street, Edinburgh EH3 8HE (0131 229 1212).

SYNOD OF GRAMPIAN CHILDREN OF THE CLERGY FUND: Makes annual grants to children of deceased ministers. Apply to Rev. Iain U. Thomson, Clerk and Treasurer, 4 Keirhill Gardens, Westhill AB32 6AZ (01224 746743).

SYNOD OF GRAMPIAN WIDOWS' FUND: Makes annual grants (currently £300 p.a.) to widows or widowers of deceased ministers who have served in a charge in the former Synod. Apply to Rev. Iain U. Thomson, Clerk and Treasurer, 4 Keirhill Gardens, Westhill AB32 6AZ (01224 746743).

TOD ENDOWMENT TRUST; CINTRA BEQUEST; TOD ENDOWMENT SCOTLAND HOLIDAY FUND: The Trustees of the Cintra Bequest and of the Tod Endowment Scotland Holiday Fund can consider an application for a grant from the Tod Endowment funds from any ordained or commissioned minister or deacon in Scotland of at least two years' standing before the date of application, to assist with the cost of the beneficiary and his or her spouse or partner and dependants obtaining rest and recuperation in Scotland. The Trustees of the Tod Endowment Scotland Holiday Fund can also consider an application from an ordained or commissioned minister or deacon who has retired. Application forms are available from Mrs Jennifer Hamilton, Deputy Solicitor (for the Cintra Bequest), and from Elaine Macadie BA CA, Finance Manager, Ministries Council (for the Tod Endowment Scotland Holiday Fund). The address in both cases is 121 George Street, Edinburgh EH2 4YN (0131 225 5722). (Attention is drawn to the separate entry above for the Church of Scotland Ministry Benevolent Fund.)

STEPHEN WILLIAMSON & ALEX BALFOUR FUND: Offers grants to Ministers in Scotland, with first priority being given to Ministers in the Presbyteries of Angus and Dundee, followed by the Presbyteries in Fife, to assist with the cost of educational school/ college/university trips for sons and daughters of the Manse who are under 25 years and in full time education. Application for trips in any year will be considered by the Trustees in the January of that year, when the income of the previous financial year will be awarded in grants. The applications for trips in that calendar year must be submitted by 31 December of the preceding year. For applications from outwith the 5 priority Presbyteries the total cost of the trip must be in excess of £500, with the maximum grant which can be awarded being £200. The trustees will always give priority to new applicants. If funds still remain for distribution after the allocation of grants in January further applications for that year will be considered. Applications from the Presbyteries of Angus, Dundee, Dunfermline, Kirkcaldy and St Andrews will be considered at any time of year as the Trustees have retained income for these grants. Applications should be made to the Secretary and Clerk, The Church of Scotland Trust, 121 George Street, Edinburgh EH2 4YN (0131 240 2222; jhamilton@churchofscotland.org.uk).

(10) LONG SERVICE CERTIFICATES

Long Service Certificates, signed by the Moderator, are available for presentation to elders and others in respect of not less than thirty years of service. At the General Assembly of 2015, it was agreed that further certificates could be issued at intervals of ten years thereafter. It should be noted that the period is years of *service*, not (for example) years of ordination in the case of an elder. In the case of Sunday School teachers and Bible Class leaders, the qualifying period is twenty-one years of service. Certificates are not issued posthumously, nor is it possible to make exceptions to the rules, for example by recognising quality of service in order to reduce the qualifying period, or by reducing the qualifying period on compassionate grounds, such as serious illness. Applications for Long Service Certificates should be made in writing to the Principal Clerk at 121 George Street, Edinburgh EH2 4YN by the parish minister, or by the session clerk on behalf of the Kirk Session. Certificates are not issued from this office to the individual recipients, nor should individuals make application themselves. If a note of the award of the Certificate is to be inserted in *Life and Work* contact should be made with that publication direct.

(11) RECORDS OF THE CHURCH OF SCOTLAND

Church records more than fifty years old, unless still in use, should be sent or delivered to the Principal Clerk for onward transmission to the National Records of Scotland. Where ministers or session clerks are approached by a local repository seeking a transfer of their records, they should inform the Principal Clerk, who will take the matter up with the National Records of Scotland.

Where a temporary retransmission of records is sought, it is extremely helpful if notice can be given three months in advance so that appropriate procedures can be carried out satisfactorily.

SECTION 3

Church Procedure

A. THE MINISTER AND BAPTISM

See www.churchofscotland.org.uk > Resources > Yearbook > Section 3A

B. THE MINISTER AND MARRIAGE

See www.churchofscotland.org.uk > Resources > Yearbook > Section 3B

C. CONDUCT OF MARRIAGE SERVICES (CODE OF GOOD PRACTICE)

See www.churchofscotland.org.uk > Resources > Yearbook > Section 3C

D. MARRIAGE AND CIVIL PARTNERSHIP (SCOTLAND) ACT 2014

See www.churchofscotland.org.uk > Resources > Yearbook > Section 3D

E. CONDUCT OF FUNERAL SERVICES: FEES

See www.churchofscotland.org.uk > Resources > Yearbook > Section 3E

F. PULPIT SUPPLY FEES AND EXPENSES

See www.churchofscotland.org.uk > Resources > Yearbook > Section 3F

G. PROCEDURE IN A VACANCY

A full coverage can be found in two handbooks listed under *Interim Moderators and Nominating Committees* on the Ministries Resources pages on the Church of Scotland website, which also includes information on locum appointments:
www.churchofscotland.org.uk > Resources > Subjects > Ministries resources > Interim Moderators and Nominating Committees

SECTION 4

General Assembly 2018

OFFICE-BEARERS OF THE GENERAL ASSEMBLY

The Lord High Commissioner:	The Duke of Buccleuch and Queensberry KT KBE DL FSA FRSE
Moderator:	The Right Rev. Susan M. Brown
Chaplains to the Moderator:	Rev. James C. Stewart Rev. Mary J. Stobo
Principal Clerk:	Rev. Dr George J. Whyte
Depute Clerk:	Ms Christine Paterson
Procurator:	Ms Laura Dunlop QC
Law Agent:	Miss Mary Macleod
Convener of the Business Committee:	Ms Judith J.H. Pearson
Vice-Convener of the Business Committee:	Rev. Fiona E. Smith
Precentor:	Rev. Dr Martin C. Scott
Chief Steward:	Mr Alexander F. Gemmill
Assembly Officer:	Mr William Mearns
Assistant Assembly Officer:	Mrs Karen McKay

THE MODERATOR

The Right Reverend Susan M. Brown BD DipMin

The daughter of a Bilston Glen miner, Susan was in born and brought up in Penicuik. The youngest of three girls (her twin sister was born an hour and a quarter before her), she left Penicuik High School to go to New College to study theology as a first degree. Her call to ministry, which began in her teenage years, was nurtured by the ministers of Penicuik North and her involvement in Sunday School, Youth Group, Scripture Union and Youth with a Mission. Her sense of calling to become a minister of word and sacrament meant she was able to overcome the hesitation of others, not just that women in ministry were unusual at that time (indeed she and most of the rest of us had never come across one) and there was still some resistance to having a woman as a minister, but also that her lack of inches might be an impediment. Fortunately, the church has no height restriction for entrants although the pulpit in Dornoch Cathedral has an extra step-up box so she can be seen over the lectern and Susan often now jokes that she is indeed standing.

Susan and Derek Brown, also a minister who is Lead Chaplain in Raigmore Hospital, met in Sunday School when she was 10 years old. Their friendship developed into romance and they married in their home church in 1981 and have two offspring, Simon and Hannah. Their family has been enhanced over the years with "borrowed" children staying with them for considerable periods of time.

Ordained and appointed to Killearnan in the Black Isle in 1985, Simon was born just over a year after this and often accompanied her on visits. Carried in a sling he, and later his sister, were welcomed in many homes where folk, especially the elderly, delighted in their company. This, and Susan's out-going character and obvious care for the people of her parish encouraged the congregation to grow substantially and develop their outreach in the community which included building a new hall. The call from the congregation was for a six-month terminable tenure but it proved to be so positive that it continued for 13 years until Susan was persuaded to consider a move to Dornoch Cathedral. Inducted to this charge in 1988, she has again encouraged people of the congregation to offer further service to their community and those of their neighbours. The renovated West Church Hall is an ideal base for many community groups.

Thanks to the news headlines in 2000 which brought Susan and the Cathedral into the limelight with the wedding of Madonna to Guy Ritchie and later the baptism of their son Rocco, the Cathedral has continued to be chosen as a venue for tying the knot for people from all over and this forms a fair part of Susan's normal work. She takes seriously her ordination vows to be active in presbytery and the wider church in addition to her parish duties. She was the first woman to be Moderator of both Ross and Sutherland presbyteries. As the World Mission Council convenor of the Europe and Americas committee she travelled widely and was Vice Convenor until becoming Moderator. Previously serving as Vice Convenor of the Ecumenical Relations Committee, she became a Chaplain in Ordinary to the Queen in 2010. Over the years several Readers, trainee ministers and Ordained Local Ministers have benefited from her understanding of people, congregational life and ways of communicating the Gospel, which she is always generously willing to share.

Always keen to see the church at the heart of the community and serving in ways that can fill the gap in people's lives, she has been active in promoting work that has been supported by *Go For It* funding to employ a Community Outreach Worker to help volunteers set up projects that answer identified needs in the community. These include a fortnightly lunch club, a weekly social get-together for adults with learning difficulties, another for teaching them social and cookery skills, a similar one for secondary school children and, under development, a Men's Shed.

Dornoch Beach normally sees Susan out for daily walks with the dog, Finn. While she misses the dog, walking is still an important part of her daily routine. Her theme of "Walking With" throughout the year will encourage others just to be with each other, hearing their stories and telling theirs as we walk with Christ on our journey through life.

It is a great privilege for us to share some of the events of the coming year with Susan. To us she has been a friend and colleague over many years. Her gentle humour and wisdom in her interactions with everyone she meets is a great asset and was evident during the General Assembly as it is in everyday life. We join with the whole church in wishing Susan every blessing. We know that she is an excellent ambassador for Christ and the Church and her insight, energy, and caring nature will be an inspiration and encouragement to others.

Mary Stobo and James Stewart
Moderator's Chaplains

Report from the General Assembly 2018
Theme: Peace be with you!

The 2018 General Assembly began, as always, with formal greetings, well-honed ritual, and the taking on of new responsibilities. Following worship (the unique sound of unaccompanied psalm singing: "All people that on earth do dwell, sing to the Lord with cheerful voice"), the Right Revd Dr Derek Browning presented the name of the Revd Susan Brown, minister of Dornoch Cathedral, to be Moderator for 2018-2019. Mrs Brown, now assuming the 'Right Revd', took up the role exactly 50 years after the General Assembly passed an Act enabling women to be ordained to the Ministry of Word and Sacrament in the Church of Scotland.

The Assembly also greeted the Queen's Lord High Commissioner, His Grace Richard Scott, the Duke of Buccleuch and Queensberry. An Episcopalian with a wife who is Roman Catholic, he spoke movingly of those who have inspired him by expressing their faith in different ways: among them the Church of Scotland minister of his local church, the late Bill Scott, who he described as "the best and kindest of men". He spoke of the faith, founded on the Holy Bible, which helps us overcome difference, allowing diversity to be a cause for celebration rather than division. So, both in his person and in his words, His Grace touched both on a note of outward facing ecumenism and on the potential for deep differences, each of which would surface in different ways throughout the week.

Patterns of peace
The overarching theme chosen for this year's gathering was: "Peace be with you". Commissioners received wrist bands and were invited to pass these on, exchanging bands as many times as they could during the week. The theme was picked up by a number of reporting convenors, most notably perhaps by the convenor of the World Mission Council, which is about making connections worldwide, especially with partner Christian churches. This year's report focussed on conversations across faith boundaries. "There really is no point in saying 'Peace with you!' if we do nothing to help build that peace – interfaith engagement, where we begin to listen to, and start to understand, one another is one component of that process." As if to underline that point, the Assembly's final morning began with an address by Imam Sayed Razawi, Director General of the Scottish Ahlul Bayt Society, a faith-based organisation working to meet the needs of the Scottish Shi'a Muslim community. Addressing the Assembly not just as representative of a diaspora but as a Scotsman, Imam Razawi said that a very Scottish Islam is developing and that our different faith traditions represents different shades of the Creator: an echo perhaps of the World Mission convenor who had showed off a new official, registered Church of Scotland tartan, which he said represents peace well in the interweaving of its colours.

How to be radical?
It was the World Mission Council's special report on Christianity in Africa, however, that really caught the imagination of commissioners. Though its thrust was more about discovering confidence in the living God, and understanding the lessons for Scotland that might be learned from Christians in Africa, the report's examples became linked in commissioners' minds to the idea of being "radical".

Sometimes, the juxtaposition of two Assembly reports has a tangible effect on how one or the other is received. So it was when, following the report on African Christianity, the Council of Assembly presented its draft strategic plan for the Church of Scotland. Its medium-term vision elicited impatience from some quarters, and a frustration that measurable actions had not been identified with sufficient detail. An alternative proposal was put forward: "Instruct the

Council to return to the General Assembly of 2019 with a radical action plan for 2019–2022 to achieve much needed reform within our Church." Examples from the African context were cited in support of such an approach.

One speaker identified the struggle in which commissioners were engaged – to work out how change is effected in a Presbyterian organisation. There is a desire for everyone to have their say, he said, but how would they get the radical change that was being called for? The Assembly is good at pulling things apart, he argued, but not good at crafting something back together again. Against this dilemma was a strongly felt view that time is running out for effective change to be enacted.

A similar argument was made during the Ministries Council report. It was estimated that the number of Church of Scotland ministers is expected to decline by 20 per cent over the next five years, with vacancies increasing faster than Presbytery planning can catch up. Different types of ministry were urged (and again the African context was noted – this time with reference to the training of lay people).

It's sometimes easy to forget that the General Assembly is not a series of annual stand-alone events; rather, each Assembly represents a staging post in an ongoing process. The reports of the Ministries Council are one example – annually taking stock of the current needs and circumstances of the parishes and ministry opportunities for which it takes responsibility, including the Diaconate, which this year presented a new vision statement: *Deacons of Word and Service*. This should not be a surprise for a Christian denomination that speaks of itself as both reformed and always reforming. Indeed this year, the Assembly accepted a request that the Theological Forum take a fresh look at the place of the 1647 Westminster Confession of Faith in the life of the contemporary Church.

Another example of long-term reflection is the decade-long discussion around the subject of same-sex relationships. The issues have appeared under the remit of different committees over the years, always giving rise to debate that is deeply heartfelt and profound. This year the Legal Questions Committee brought not legislation but guidance, outlining the context within which any legislation for the solemnization of same-sex relationships would have to be prepared if that were desired. However, an amendment was brought forward instructing the committee "to prepare legislation enabling those Ministers of Word and Sacrament and deacons who wish to do so to be nominated to solemnize same-sex marriage ceremonies". The amendment was designed to address the present anomaly of a broad Church able to accept ministers in same-sex relationships but unable to bless such relationships. There were attempts to prevent discussion of the amendment but a former moderator argued that peace would not break out by ignoring issues that cause dissent. The amendment was accepted.

Building bridges

At the opening of the Assembly, the outgoing Moderator, the Very Revd Dr Derek Browning, had made a plea to those in local and national government to take seriously the expertise that exists within the Church: "We have been building bridges for generations... It's not simply about 'doing God'; it's about doing humanity."

Nowhere is this more evident than within the report of the Social Care Council – a committee that connects the Church directly with issues faced by other organisations in society. As austerity measures continue to bite, for example, it was noted that the Coalition of Care providers in Scotland, of which the Council is a member, had reported that in 2017 sixty per cent of providers withdrew or decided not to participated in procurement exercises and thirty per cent withdrew from one or more live contracts. It was a sobering statistic as we approach, in 2019, 150 years since the Assembly commissioned the Committee of Life and Work, out of which the Church's current commitment to social care was born. The convenor invited commissioners to consider how they might contribute to the celebration.

Also echoing Dr Browning's words, the convenor of the Church and Society Council highlighted work being taken forward by churches in local situations. He mentioned that politicians in Aberdeen had been "left buzzing" when they heard about the amazing work being done by churches in their communities.

The issue that dominated the Church and Society debate this year was whether or not the Church of Scotland should support disinvestment from the oil and gas industry. Debates like this reveal the breadth of expertise and experience amongst commissioners, in this case from those who have worked in Aberdeen alongside the oil industry to those who have pioneered the use of alternative energy sources locally. In the end, commissioners voted to "eyeball" managers in the industry – engaging with them and challenging them to change – rather than to disinvest.

Personal voices

It is often the personal experiences of commissioners that ground a debate and that raise the level of mutual respect and understanding in a way that certainly impressed one visiting MP this year. To encourage such contributions, most speeches were limited to five minutes this year, but this included the opportunity of five minutes for the seconder of a motion or amendment to speak. This was said to be a small change but with the intention of allowing more voices to be heard.

Two commissioners spoke movingly, for example, about relatives living with dementia and the importance of the Church and church members dealing sensitively with those affected by the disease. Another spoke of the suffering of his compatriots in the Cameroons; another of his ministry to those on the receiving end of homophobic bullying.

The voices of some of the Church's modern saints were also held up in thanksgiving, among them the late Revd Dr Ian Fraser ("a living rebuttal of the heresy that religion and politics don't mix") and, on this 50th anniversary of women in ministry of word and sacrament, Mary Lusk. In a speech marking the occasion, the Revd Dr Margaret Forrester introduced herself as commissioner 007, "licensed to preach". In 1963 she had sat in the gallery of the Assembly Hall and watched Mary Lusk (later Levison) present her petition to become a minister of word and sacrament to the Assembly. Margaret said that the issue of ordaining women had been raised in every decade of the 20th century and was still a live one in the 21st. Her speech was greeted with a rare Assembly standing ovation.

Young at heart

In a week in which the Church of Scotland celebrated its past, claimed its place in the present, and debated intensely the nature of its future, it was left to the Youth Moderator to present the final report of the Assembly. Earlier in the week he had addressed a special event in Princes Street for all those "young at heart"; and the Church of Scotland Guild, too, had demonstrated its commitment to younger generations by selecting four out of its six new three-year projects to reflect the Year of Young People. But here, in the report of the Church of Scotland Youth Assembly, commissioners were reminded that young people as well as old have spent time this past year grappling with the major concerns of the Church.

How, they asked, would the priorities of the Church be agreed? How might we grow through interfaith understanding? And what should Christian discipleship, now and in the future, look like?

Laurence Wareing
(Laurence Wareing produced twice daily podcasts of the
proceedings of the 2018 General Assembly.)

SECTION 5

Presbytery Lists

In each Presbytery list, the congregations ('charges') are listed in alphabetical order. In a linked charge, the names appear under the first named congregation. Under the name of the congregation will be found the name of the minister and, where applicable, that of an associate minister, ordained local minister, auxiliary minister and member of the Diaconate. The years indicated after a name in the congregational section of each Presbytery list are the year of ordination (column 1) and the year of current appointment (column 2). Where only one date is given, it is both the year of ordination and the year of appointment.

In the second part of each Presbytery list, those named, who are either engaged in ministry other than parish or are retired, are listed alphabetically. The first date is the year of ordination, and the following date is the year of appointment or retirement. If the person concerned is retired, then the appointment last held will be shown in brackets.

(GD) Indicates a charge where it is desirable that the minister should have a knowledge of Gaelic.
(GE) Indicates a charge where public worship must be regularly conducted in Gaelic.
(H)   Indicates that a Hearing Aid Loop system has been installed. In Linked charges, the (H) is placed beside the appropriate building as far as possible.
(L)   Indicates that a Chair Lift has been installed.

PRESBYTERY NUMBERS

1	Edinburgh	18	Dumbarton
2	West Lothian	19	Argyll
3	Lothian	20	
4	Melrose and Peebles	21	
5	Duns	22	Falkirk
6	Jedburgh	23	Stirling
7	Annandale and Eskdale	24	Dunfermline
8	Dumfries and Kirkcudbright	25	Kirkcaldy
9	Wigtown and Stranraer	26	St Andrews
10	Ayr	27	Dunkeld and Meigle
11	Irvine and Kilmarnock	28	Perth
12	Ardrossan	29	Dundee
13	Lanark	30	Angus
14	Greenock and Paisley	31	Aberdeen
15		32	Kincardine and Deeside
16	Glasgow	33	Gordon
17	Hamilton	34	Buchan

35	Moray		
36	Abernethy		
37	Inverness		
38	Lochaber		
39	Ross		
40	Sutherland		
41	Caithness		
42	Lochcarron – Skye		
43	Uist		
44	Lewis		
45	Orkney		
46	Shetland		
47	England		
48	International Charges		
49	Jerusalem		

(1) EDINBURGH

The Presbytery meets at Greyfriars Kirk, Edinburgh, on (2018) 6 November, 4 December (in the Moderator's church), and (2019) on 5 February, 2 April, 18 June and 3 September.

Clerk:	REV. MARJORY McPHERSON LLB BD MTh	10/1 Palmerston Place, Edinburgh EH12 5AA edinburgh@churchofscotland.org.uk	0131 225 9137
Depute Clerk:	HAZEL HASTIE MA CQSW PhD AIWS	10/1 Palmerston Place, Edinburgh EH12 5AA HHastie@churchofscotland.org.uk	07827 314374

1 Edinburgh: Albany Deaf Church of Edinburgh (H)

Rosemary A. Addis (Mrs) BD	2014	c/o Ministries Council, 121 George Street, Edinburgh EH2 4YN RAddis@churchofscotland.org.uk	0131 444 2054 07738 983393

Albany Deaf Church is a Mission Initiative of Edinburgh: St Andrew's and St George's West

2 Edinburgh: Balerno (H)

Andre J. Groenewald BA BD MDiv DD	1994	2016	3 Johnsonburn Road, Balerno EH14 7DN AGroenewald@churchofscotland.org.uk	0131 449 7245 0131 449 3830

3 Edinburgh: Barclay Viewforth

Samuel A.R. Torrens BD	1995	2005	**admin@barclaychurch.org.uk** 113 Meadowspot, Edinburgh EH10 5UY STorrens@churchofscotland.org.uk	0131 229 6810 0131 478 2376

4 Edinburgh: Blackhall St Columba's

Benjamin J.A. Abeledo BTh DipTh PTh	1991	2016	**secretary@blackhallstcolumba.org.uk** 5 Blinkbonny Crescent, Edinburgh EH4 3NB BAbeledo@churchofscotland.org.uk	0131 332 4431 0131 343 3708

5 Edinburgh: Bristo Memorial Craigmillar

Drausio P. Goncalves	1993	2013	72 Blackchapel Close, Edinburgh EH15 3SL DGoncalves@churchofscotland.org.uk	0131 657 3266

6 Edinburgh: Broughton St Mary's (H)

Vacant

Session Clerk: Ian Buckingham	ianbucks@hotmail.co.uk	0131 556 4252 0131 557 5051

7 Edinburgh: Canongate (H)

Neil N. Gardner MA BD RNR	1991	2006	The Manse of Canongate, Edinburgh EH8 8BR NGardner@churchofscotland.org.uk	0131 556 3515

8 **Edinburgh: Carrick Knowe (H)**
   Fiona M. Mathieson (Mrs)   1988   2001   ckchurch@talktalk.net   **0131 334 1505**
   BEd BD PGCommEd MTh   21 Traquair Park West, Edinburgh EH12 7AN   0131 334 9774
                                                         FMathieson@churchofscotland.org.uk

9 **Edinburgh: Colinton (H)**
   Rolf H. Billes BD   1996   2009   church.office@colinton-parish.com   **0131 441 2232**
                                                         The Manse, Colinton, Edinburgh EH13 0JR   0131 466 8384
                                                         RBilles@churchofscotland.org.uk

   Gayle J.A. Taylor (Mrs) MA BD   1999   2009   Colinton Parish Church, Dell Road, Edinburgh EH13 0JR   0131 441 2232
   (Associate Minister)   GTaylor@churchofscotland.org.uk

10 **Edinburgh: Corstorphine Craigsbank (H)**   **0131 334 6365**
   Vacant   0131 467 6826
   Session Clerks: Margaret G. Adair   17 Craigs Bank, Edinburgh EH12 8HD   0131 334 5117
                    Elaine Thompson   craigsbanksc@gmail.com   0131 334 0202
                                                         craigsbanksc@gmail.com

11 **Edinburgh: Corstorphine Old (H)**
   Moira McDonald MA BD   1997   2005   corold@aol.com   **0131 334 7864**
                                                         23 Manse Road, Edinburgh EH12 7SW   0131 476 5893
                                                         MMcDonald@churchofscotland.org.uk

12 **Edinburgh: Corstorphine St Anne's (H) (L)**
   James J. Griggs BD MTh ALCM PGCE 2011 2013   office@stannes.corstorphine.org.uk   **0131 316 4740**
                                                         1/5 Morham Gait, Edinburgh EH10 5GH   0131 466 3269
                                                         JGriggs@churchofscotland.org.uk

13 **Edinburgh: Corstorphine St Ninian's (H)**
   James D. Aitken BD   2002   2017   office@st-ninians.co.uk   **0131 539 6204**
                                                         17 Templeland Road, Edinburgh EH12 8RZ   0131 334 2978
                                                         JAitken@churchofscotland.org.uk

14 **Edinburgh: Craiglockhart (H)**
   Gordon Kennedy BSc BD MTh   1993   2012   office@craiglockhartchurch.org   0131 444 1615
                                                         20 Craiglockhart Quadrant, Edinburgh EH14 1HD
                                                         GKennedy@churchofscotland.org.uk

15 **Edinburgh: Craigmillar Park (H)**
   linked with Edinburgh: Reid Memorial (H)   cpkirk@btinternet.com   **0131 667 5862**
   Vacant   reid.memorial@btinternet.com   **0131 662 1203**
   Session Clerk, Craigmillar Park: Pauline   14 Hallhead Road, Edinburgh EH16 5QJ   0131 667 1623
       Weibye   pauline@weibye.net   0131 668 3545
   Session Clerk, Reid Memorial: Elizabeth
       Clark (Mrs)   maretaclark@btinternet.com   0131 667 6705

16	**Edinburgh: Cramond (H)** G. Russell Barr BA BD MTh DMin	1979	1993	**cramond.kirk@blueyonder.co.uk** Manse of Cramond, Edinburgh EH4 6NS GBarr@churchofscotland.org.uk	0131 336 2036
17	**Edinburgh: Currie (H)** V. Easter Smart BA MDiv DMin	1996	2015	**currie_kirk@btconnect.com** 43 Lanark Road West, Currie EH14 5JX ESmart@churchofscotland.org.uk	**0131 451 5141** 0131 449 4719
18	**Edinburgh: Dalmeny linked with Edinburgh: Queensferry (H)** David C. Cameron BD CertMin	1993	2009	1 Station Road, South Queensferry EH30 9HY DavidCCameron@churchofscotland.org.uk	0131 331 1100
19	**Edinburgh: Davidson's Mains (H)** Daniel Robertson BA BD	2009	2016	**life@dmainschurch.plus.com** 1 Hillpark Terrace, Edinburgh EH4 7SX Daniel.Robertson@churchofscotland.org.uk	**0131 312 6282** 0131 336 3078 07909 840654
20	**Edinburgh: Drylaw** Jenny M. Williams BSc CQSW BD (Transition Minister)	1996	2017	15 House o' Hill Gardens, Edinburgh EH4 2AR JWilliams@churchofscotland.org.uk	**0131 343 6643** 0131 531 5786
21	**Edinburgh: Duddingston (H)** James A.P. Jack BSc BArch BD DMin RIBA ARIAS	1989	2001	**dodinskirk@aol.com** Manse of Duddingston, Old Church Lane, Edinburgh EH15 3PX JJack@churchofscotland.org.uk	0131 661 4240
22	**Edinburgh: Fairmilehead (H)** Cheryl McKellar-Young (Mrs) BA BD MSc	2013	2018	**office@fhpc.org.uk** 14 Margaret Rose Drive, Edinburgh EH10 7ER CMcKellarYoung@churchofscotland.org.uk	**0131 445 2374** 07590 230121
23	**Edinburgh: Gorgie Dalry Stenhouse (H)** Peter I. Barber MA BD	1984	1995	90 Myreside Road, Edinburgh EH10 5BZ PBarber@churchofscotland.org.uk	**0131 337 7936** 0131 337 2284
24	**Edinburgh: Gracemount linked with Edinburgh: Liberton (H)** John N. Young MA BD PhD	1996		7 Kirk Park, Edinburgh EH16 6HZ JYoung@churchofscotland.org.uk	0131 664 3067
25	**Edinburgh: Granton (H)** Norman A. Smith MA BD	1997	2005	8 Wardie Crescent, Edinburgh EH5 1AG NSmith@churchofscotland.org.uk	**0131 552 3033** 0131 551 2159

26 Edinburgh: Greenbank (H) (www.greenbankchurch.org)
Martin S. Ritchie MA BD PhD 2018
greenbankchurch@btconnect.com
112 Greenbank Crescent, Edinburgh EH10 5SZ
MRitchie@churchofscotland.org.uk
0131 447 9969
0131 447 4032

27 Edinburgh: Greenside (H)
Guardianship of the Presbytery
80 Pilrig Street, Edinburgh EH6 5AS
0131 556 5588
0131 554 3277   Tel/Fax

28 Edinburgh: Greyfriars Kirk (GE) (H)
Richard E. Frazer BA BD DMin 1986 2003
enquiries@greyfriarskirk.com
12 Tantallon Place, Edinburgh EH9 1NZ
RFrazer@churchofscotland.org.uk
0131 225 1900
0131 667 6610

29 Edinburgh: High (St Giles') (H)
Calum I. MacLeod BA BD 1996 2014
alison.wylie@stgilescathedral.org.uk
St Giles' Cathedral, High Street, Edinburgh EH1 1RE
Calum.MacLeod@churchofscotland.org.uk
0131 225 4363
0131 225 4363

Helen J.R. Alexander BD DipSW 1981 2012
7 Polwarth Place, Edinburgh EH11 1LG
HAlexander@churchofscotland.org.uk
(Assistant Minister)
0131 346 0685

30 Edinburgh: Holy Trinity (H)
Ian A. MacDonald BD MTh 2005 2017
5 Baberton Mains Terrace, Edinburgh EH14 3DG
Ian.Angus.MacDonald@churchofscotland.org.uk
0131 442 3304
0131 281 6153

Rita M. Welsh BA PhD 2017
19 Muir Wood Road, Currie EH14 5JW
RWelsh@churchofscotland.org.uk
(Ordained Local Minister)
0131 451 5943

31 Edinburgh: Inverleith St Serf's (H)
Joanne G. Foster (Mrs) 1996 2012
DipTMus BD AdvDipCouns
78 Pilrig Street, Edinburgh EH6 5AS
JFoster@churchofscotland.org.uk
0131 561 1392

32 Edinburgh: Juniper Green (H)
James S. Dewar MA BD 1983 2000
476 Lanark Road, Juniper Green, Edinburgh EH14 5BQ
JDewar@churchofscotland.org.uk
0131 453 3494

33 Edinburgh: Kirkliston
Margaret R. Lane (Mrs) BA BD MTh 2009
43 Main Street, Kirkliston EH29 9AF
MLane@churchofscotland.org.uk
0131 333 3298
07795 481441

34 Edinburgh: Leith North (H)
Alexander T. McAspurren BD MTh 2002 2011
nlpc-office@btinternet.com
6 Craighall Gardens, Edinburgh EH6 4RJ
AMcAspurren@churchofscotland.org.uk
0131 553 7378
0131 551 5252

35 Edinburgh: Leith St Andrew's (H)
A. Robert A. Mackenzie LLB BD
1993 2013
30 Lochend Road, Edinburgh EH6 8BS
AMacKenzie@churchofscotlandorg.uk
0131 553 2122

36 Edinburgh: Leith South (H)
John S. (Iain) May BSc MBA BD
2012
slpc@dial.pipex.com
37 Claremont Road, Edinburgh EH6 7NN
JMay@churchofscotland.org.uk
0131 554 2578
0131 555 0392

37 Edinburgh: Liberton See Edinburgh: Gracemount

38 Edinburgh: Liberton Northfield (H)
Vacant
9 Claverhouse Drive, Edinburgh EH16 6BR
0131 551 3847
0131 664 5490

39 Edinburgh: Marchmont St Giles' (H)
Karen K. Campbell BD MTh DMin
1997 2002
2 Trotter Haugh, Edinburgh EH9 2GZ
KKCampbell@churchofscotland.org.uk
0131 447 4359
0131 447 2834

40 Edinburgh: Mayfield Salisbury
Scott S. McKenna BA BD MTh MPhil
1994 2000
26 Seton Place, Edinburgh EH9 2JT
SMcKenna@churchofscotland.org.uk
0131 667 1522
0131 667 1286

Kay McIntosh (Mrs) DCS
1990 2018
4 Jacklin Green, Livingston EH54 8PZ
kay@backedge.co.uk
01506 440543

41 Edinburgh: Meadowbank
R. Russell McLarty MA BD
(Transition Minister)
1985 2017
9 Sanderson's Wynd, Tranent EH33 1DA
RussellMcLarty@churchofscotland.org.uk
01875 614496
07751 755986

42 Edinburgh: Morningside (H)
Derek Browning MA BD DMin
1987 2001
office@morningsideparishchurch.org.uk
20 Braidburn Crescent, Edinburgh EH10 6EN
Derek.Browning@churchofscotland.org.uk
0131 447 6745
0131 447 1617

43 Edinburgh: Morningside United (H)
Steven Manders LLB BD STB MTh
2008 2015
1 Midmar Avenue, Edinburgh EH10 6BS
stevenmanders@hotmail.com
0131 447 3152
0131 447 7943
07808 476733

Morningside United is a Local Ecumenical Partnership with the United Reformed Church

44 Edinburgh: Murrayfield (H)
Keith Edwin Graham MA PGDip BD
2008 2014
mpchurch@btconnect.com
45 Murrayfield Gardens, Edinburgh EH12 6DH
KEGraham@churchofscotland.org.uk
0131 337 1091
0131 337 1364

45	**Edinburgh: Newhaven (H)**				
	Peter B. Bluett	2007		158 Granton Road, Edinburgh EH5 3RF PBluett@churchofscotland.org.uk	0131 476 5212
46	**Edinburgh: Old Kirk and Muirhouse (H)**				
	Stephen Ashley-Emery BD DPS	2006	2016	35 Silverknowes Road, Edinburgh EH4 5LL SEmery@churchofscotland.org.uk	0131 476 2580 07484 536297
47	**Edinburgh: Palmerston Place (H)**				
	Colin A.M. Sinclair BA BD	1981	1996	**admin@palmerstonplacechurch.com** 30B Cluny Gardens, Edinburgh EH10 6BJ CSinclair@churchofscotland.org.uk	**0131 220 1690** 0131 447 9598 0131 225 3312 Fax
48	**Edinburgh: Pilrig St Paul's**				
	Mark M. Foster BSc BD	1998	2013	78 Pilrig Street, Edinburgh EH6 5AS MFoster@churchofscotland.org.uk	**0131 553 1876** 0131 332 5736
49	**Edinburgh: Polwarth (H)**				
	Jack Holt BSc BD MTh	1985	2011	**polwarthchurch@tiscali.co.uk)** 88 Craiglockhart Road, Edinburgh EH14 1EP JHolt@churchofscotland.org.uk	**0131 346 2711** 0131 441 6105
50	**Edinburgh: Portobello and Joppa (H)**				
	Stewart G. Weaver BA BD PhD	2003	2014	6 St Mary's Place, Edinburgh EH15 2QF SWeaver@churchofscotland.org.uk	**0131 669 3641** 0131 669 2410
	Lourens de Jager PgDip MDiv BTh	2013	2015	1 Brunstane Road North, Edinburgh EH15 2DL LDeJager@churchofscotland.org.uk	07521 426644
51	**Edinburgh: Priestfield (H)**				
	Donald H. Scott BA BD	1983	2018	13 Lady Road, Edinburgh EH16 5PA Donald.Scott@churchofscotland.org.uk	**0131 667 5644** 0131 468 1254
52	**Edinburgh: Queensferry** See Edinburgh: Dalmeny				
53	**Edinburgh: Ratho**				
	Ian J. Wells BD	1999		2 Freelands Road, Ratho, Newbridge EH28 8NP IWells@churchofscotland.org.uk	0131 333 1346
54	**Edinburgh: Reid Memorial** See Edinburgh: Craigmillar Park				

55	**Edinburgh: Richmond Craigmillar (H)** Elizabeth M. Henderson MA BD MTh	1985 1997	Manse of Duddingston, Old Church Lane, Edinburgh EH15 3PX EHenderson@churchofscotland.org.uk	**0131 661 6561** 0131 661 4240
56	**Edinburgh: St Andrew's and St George's West (H)** Vacant		**info@stagw.org.uk** 25 Comely Bank, Edinburgh EH4 1AJ	**0131 225 3847** 0131 332 5848
57	**Edinburgh: St Andrew's Clermiston** Alistair H. Keil BD DipMin	1989	87 Drum Brae South, Edinburgh EH12 8TD AKeil@churchofscotland.org.uk	0131 339 4149
58	**Edinburgh: St Catherine's Argyle (H)** Stuart D. Irvin BD	2013	5 Palmerston Road, Edinburgh EH9 1TL SIrvin@churchofscotland.org.uk	**0131 667 7220** 0131 667 9344
59	**Edinburgh: St Cuthbert's (H)** Peter Sutton AKC BA BD MThCouns	2017	**office@st-cuthberts.net** St Cuthbert's Church, 5 Lothian Road, Edinburgh EH1 2EP PSutton@churchofscotland.org.uk	**0131 229 1142** 07718 311319
60	**Edinburgh: St David's Broomhouse (H)** Michael J. Mair BD	2014	33 Traquair Park West, Edinburgh EH12 7AN MMair@churchofscotland.org.uk	**0131 443 9851** 0131 334 1730
61	**Edinburgh: St John's Colinton Mains** Peter Nelson BSc BD	2015	2 Caiystane Terrace, Edinburgh EH10 6SR PNelson@churchofscotland.org.uk	07500 057889
62	**Edinburgh: St Margaret's (H)** Carolyn (Carol) H.M. Ford DSD RSAMD BD	2003	**stm.parish@virgin.net** 43 Moira Terrace, Edinburgh EH7 6TD CFord@churchofscotland.org.uk	**0131 554 7400** 0131 669 7329
63	**Edinburgh: St Martin's** William M. Wishart BD	2017	1 Toll House Gardens, Tranent EH33 2QQ BWishart@churchofscotland.org.uk	01875 704071
64	**Edinburgh: St Michael's (H)** Vacant Session Clerk: Douglas Bannatyne		**office@stmichaels-kirk.co.uk** douglasbannatyne@msn.com	0131 444 2935

65	**Edinburgh: St Nicholas' Sighthill**				
	Thomas M. Kisitu MTh PhD	1993	2015	122 Sighthill Loan, Edinburgh EH11 4NT TMKisitu@churchofscotland.org.uk	0131 442 3978
66	**Edinburgh: St Stephen's Comely Bank**				
	George Vidits BD MTh	2000	2015	8 Blinkbonny Crescent, Edinburgh EH4 3NB GVidits@churchofscotland.org.uk	**0131 315 4616** 0131 332 3364
67	**Edinburgh: Slateford Longstone**				
	Vacant				
	Session Clerk: Suzanne Riddoch			50 Kingsknowe Road South, Edinburgh EH14 2JW suzanne@slatefordlongstone.org.uk	0131 466 5308 07866 012971
68	**Edinburgh: Stockbridge (H)**				
	John A. Cowie BSc BD DMin	1983	2013	stockbridgechurch@btconnect.com 19 Eildon Street, Edinburgh EH3 5JU JCowie@churchofscotland.org.uk	**0131 552 8738** 0131 557 6052 07506 104416
69	**Edinburgh: The Tron Kirk (Gilmerton and Moredun)**				
	Cameron Mackenzie BD	1997	2010	467 Gilmerton Road, Edinburgh EH17 7JG Cammy.Mackenzie@churchofscotland.org.uk	0131 664 7538
	Janet R. McKenzie (Mrs) (Ordained Local Minister)	2016		80C Colinton Road, Edinburgh EH14 1DD JMcKenzie@churchofscotland.org.uk	0131 444 2054 07980 884653
	Liz Crocker DipComEd DCS	1985	2015	77c Craigcrook Road, Edinburgh EH4 3PH ECrocker@churchofscotland.org.uk	0131 332 0227
70	**Edinburgh: Wardie (H)**				
	Ute Jaeger-Fleming MTh CPS	2008	2015	churchoffice@wardie.org.uk 35 Lomond Road, Edinburgh EH5 3JN UJaeger-Fleming@churchofscotland.org.uk	**0131 551 3847** 0131 552 0190
	Edinburgh: Wardie was formerly known as Edinburgh: Leith Wardie				
71	**Edinburgh: Willowbrae (H)**				
	A. Malcolm Ramsay BA LLB DipMin (Transition Minister)	1986	2017	19 Abercorn Road, Edinburgh EH8 7DP MRamsay@churchofscotland.org.uk	**0131 661 8259** 0131 652 2938

Abernethy, William LTh	1979 1993	(Glenrothes: St Margaret's)	120/1 Willowbrae Road, Edinburgh EH8 7HW	0131 661 0390
Alexander, Ian W. BA BD STM	1990 2010	Secretary, World Mission Council	121 George Street, Edinburgh EH2 4YN IAlexander@churchofscotland.org.uk	0131 225 5722
Anderson, Robert S. BD MA	1988 2010	(Scottish Churches World Exchange)		

Name	Ord.	Ind.	Charge / Appointment	Address	Tel.
Armitage, William L. BSc BD	1976	2006	(Edinburgh: London Road)	Flat 7, 4 Papermill Wynd, Edinburgh EH7 4GJ; bill@billarm.plus.com	0131 558 8534
Baird, Kenneth S. MSc PhD BD MIMarEST	1998	2009	(Edinburgh: Leith North)	3 Maule Terrace, Gullane EH31 2DB	01620 843447
Barrington, Charles W.H. MA BD	1997	2007	(Associate: Edinburgh: Balerno)	502 Lanark Road, Edinburgh EH14 5DH	0131 453 4826
Beckett, David M. BA BD	1964	2002	(Edinburgh: Greyfriars, Tolbooth and Highland Kirk)	31/1 Sciennes Road, Edinburgh EH9 1NT; davidbeckett3@aol.com	0131 667 2672
Bicket, Matthew S. BD	1989	2017	(Carnoustie: Panbride)	9/2 Connaught Place, Edinburgh EH6 4RQ	0131 552 8781
Blakey, Ronald S. MA BD MTh	1962	2000	(Assembly Council)	24 Kimmerghame Place, Edinburgh EH4 2GE; kathleen.blakey@gmail.com	0131 343 6352; 07851 598101
Booth, Jennifer (Mrs) BD	1996	2004	(Associate: Edinburgh: Leith South)	39 Lilyhill Terrace, Edinburgh EH8 7DR	0131 661 3813
Borthwick, Kenneth S. MA BD	1983	2016	(Edinburgh: Holy Trinity)	34 Rodger Crescent, Armadale EH48 3GR; kennysamuel@aol.com	07735 749594
Boyd, Kenneth M. (Prof.) MA BD PhD FRCPE	1970		(University of Edinburgh: Medical Ethics)	1 Doune Terrace, Edinburgh EH3 6DY; k.boyd@ed.ac.uk	0131 225 6485
Brady, Ian D. BSc ARCST BD	1967	2001	(Edinburgh: Corstorphine Old)	28 Frankfield Crescent, Dalgety Bay, Dunfermline KY11 9LW; bradye500@gmail.com	01383 825104
Brook, Stanley A. BD MTh	1977	2016	(Newport-on-Tay)	4 Scotstoun Green, South Queensferry EH30 9YA; stan_brook@btinternet.com	0131 331 4237
Brown, William D. MA	1963	1989	(Wishaw: Thornlie)	9/3 Craigend Park, Edinburgh EH16 5XY; wdbrown@surefish.co.uk	0131 672 2936
Brown, William D. BD CQSW	1987	2013	(Edinburgh: Murrayfield)	79 Cambee Park, Edinburgh EH16 6GG; wdb@talktalk.net	0131 261 7297
Cameron, John W.M. MA BD	1957	1996	(Edinburgh: Liberton)	10 Plewlands Gardens, Edinburgh EH10 5JP	0131 447 1277
Chalmers, Murray MA	1965	2006	(Hospital Chaplain)	8 Easter Warriston, Edinburgh EH7 4QX	0131 552 4211
Clark, Christine M. (Mrs) BA BD MTh	2006	2017	(Hospital Chaplain, NHS Greater Glasgow and Clyde)	40 Pentland Avenue, Edinburgh EH13 0HY; christine.clark7@aol.co.uk	
Clinkenbeard, William W. BSc BD STM	1966	2000	(Edinburgh: Carrick Knowe)	3/17 Western Harbour Breakwater, Edinburgh EH6 6PA; bjclinks@compuserve.com	
Cook, John MA BD	1967	2005	(Edinburgh: Leith St Andrew's)	26 Silverknowes Court, Edinburgh EH4 5NR	0131 312 8447
Curran, Elizabeth M. (Miss) BD	1995	2008	(Aberlour)	Blackford Grange, 39/2 Blackford Avenue, Edinburgh EH9 3HN; ecurran8@aol.com	0131 664 1358
Cuthell, Tom C. MA BD MTh	1965	2007	(Edinburgh: St Cuthbert's)	Flat 10, 2 Kingsburgh Crescent, Waterfront, Edinburgh EH5 1JS	0131 476 3864
Davidson, D. Hugh MA	1965	2009	(Edinburgh: Inverleith)	Flat 1/2, 22 Summerside Place, Edinburgh EH6 4NZ; hdavidson35@btinternet.com	0131 554 8420
Davidson, Ian M.P. MBE MA BD	1954	1994	(Stirling: Allan Park South with Church of the Holy Rude)	13/8 Craigend Park, Edinburgh EH16 5XX; ian.m.p.davidson@btinternet.com	0131 664 0074
Dawson, Michael S. BTech BD	1979	2005	(Associate: Edinburgh: Holy Trinity)	9 The Broich, Alva FK12 5NR; mixpen.dawson@btinternet.com	01259 769309
Dilbey, Mary D. (Miss) BD	1997	2002	(West Kirk of Calder)	41 Bonaly Rise, Edinburgh EH13 0QU	0131 441 9092
Donald, Alistair P. MA PhD BD	1999	2009	Chaplain: Heriot-Watt University	The Chaplaincy, Heriot-Watt University, Edinburgh EH14 4AS; a.p.donald@hw.ac.uk	0131 451 4508
Douglas, Alexander B. BD	1979	2014	(Edinburgh: Blackhall St Columba's)	15 Inchview Gardens, Dalgety Bay, Dunfermline KY11 9SA; alexandjill@douglas.net	01383 242872

Name			Position	Address	Telephone
Doyle, Ian B. MA BD PhD	1946	1991	(Department of National Mission)	21 Lygon Road, Edinburgh EH16 5QD	0131 667 2697
Drummond, Rhoda (Miss) DCS	1960	1987	(Deacon)	Flat K, 23 Grange Loan, Edinburgh EH9 2ER	0131 668 3631
Dunn, W. Iain C. DA LTh	1983	1998	(Edinburgh: Pilrig and Dalmeny Street)	10 Fox Covert Avenue, Edinburgh EH12 6UQ	0131 334 1665
Embleton, Brian M. BD	1976	2015	(Edinburgh: Reid Memorial)	54 Edinburgh Road, Peebles EH45 8EB bmembleton@gmail.com	01721 602157
Embleton, Sara R. (Mrs) BA BD MTh	1988	2010	(Edinburgh: Leith St Serf's)	54 Edinburgh Road, Peebles EH45 8EB srembleton@gmail.com	01721 602157
Evans, Mark BSc MSc DCS	1988	2006	Head of Spiritual Care NHS Fife	13 Easter Drylaw Drive, Edinburgh EH4 2QA mark.evans59@nhs.net	0131 343 3089 (Home) 01383 674136 (Office)
Farquharson, Gordon MA BD DipEd	1998	2007	(Stonehaven: Dunnottar)	26 Learmonth Court, Edinburgh EH4 1PB gfarqu@talktalk.net	0131 343 1047
Faulds, Norman L. MA BD FSAScot	1968	2000	(Aberlady with Gullane)	10 West Fenton Court, West Fenton, North Berwick EH39 5AE	01620 842331
Fergusson, David A.S. (Prof.) OBE MA BD DPhil DD FBA FRSE	1984	2000	University of Edinburgh: New College	23 Riselaw Crescent, Edinburgh EH10 6HN	0131 447 4022
Forrester, Margaret R. (Mrs) MA BD DD	1974	2003	(Edinburgh: St Michael's)	25 Kingspark Road, Edinburgh EH12 6DZ margaret@rosskeen.org.uk	0131 337 5646
Fraser, Liam J. LLB BD MTh PhD	2017		Campus Minister, University of Edinburgh	Edinburgh University Campus Ministry (EUCAM), 138–140 The Pleasance, Edinburgh EH8 9RR lfraser@churchofscotland.org.uk	07949 468341
Fraser, Shirley A. (Miss) MA BD	1992	2008	(Scottish Field Director: Friends International)	6/50 Roseburn Drive, Edinburgh EH12 5NS	0131 347 1400
Frew, Michael W. BSc BD	1978	2017	(Edinburgh: Slateford Longstone)	37 Swanston Terrace, Edinburgh EH10 7DN	07712 162375
Gardner, John V.	1997	2003	(Glamis, Inverarity and Kinnettles)	75/1 Lockharton Avenue, Edinburgh EH14 1BD jvgardner66@googlemail.com	0131 443 7126
Gilmour, Ian Y. BD	1985	2018	(Edinburgh: St Andrew's and St George's West)	297 South Trinity Road, Edinburgh EH5 3PN ianyg@gmail.com	07794 149852
Gordon, Margaret (Mrs) DCS	1998	2012	(Edinburgh: Currie)	92 Lanark Road West, Currie EH14 5LA	0131 449 2554
Graham, W. Peter MA BD	1967	2008	(Presbytery Clerk: Edinburgh)	23/6 East Comiston, Edinburgh EH10 6RZ	0131 445 5763
Hardman Moore, Susan (Prof.) MA MAR PhD	2013		Ordained Local Minister, New College	c/o New College, Mound Place, Edinburgh EH1 2LX SHardman-Moore@churchofscotland.org.uk	0131 650 8908
Harkness, James CB OBE QHC MA DD	1961	1995	(Chaplain General: Army)	13 Saxe Coburg Place, Edinburgh EH3 5BR	07811 345699
Hay, Jared W. BA MTh DipMin DMin	1987	2017	(Edinburgh: Priestfield)	39 Netherbank, Edinburgh EH16 6YR jaredhay3110@gmail.com	0131 343 1297 07906 662515
Inglis, Ann (Mrs) LLB BD	1986	2015	(Langton and Lammermuir Kirk)	34 Echline View, South Queensferry EH30 9XL revainglis@gmail.com	0131 629 0233
Irving, William D. LTh	1985	2005	(Golspie)	122 Swanston Muir, Edinburgh EH10 7HY	0131 441 3384
Kingston, David V.F. BD DipPTh	1993	2015	(Chaplain: Army)	2 Cleuch Avenue, North Middleton, Gorebridge EH23 4RP	01875 822026
Lamont, Stewart J. BSc BD	1972	2015	(Airbirlot with Carmyllie)	13/1 Grosvenor Crescent, Edinburgh EH12 5EL lamontsj@gmail.com	07557 532012
Lawson, Kenneth C. MA BD	1963	1999	(Adviser in Adult Education)	56 Easter Drylaw View, Edinburgh EH4 2QP	0131 539 3311
Logan, Anne T. (Mrs) MA BD MTh DMin PhD	1981	2012	(Edinburgh: Stockbridge)	Sunnyside Cottage, 18 Upper Broomieknowe, Lasswade EH18 1LP annetlogan@sky.com	0131 663 9550

Name			Role	Address	Phone
McCabe, George	1963	1996	(Airdrie High)	The Elms Care Home, White House Loan, Edinburgh EH9 2EX	01875 819655
Macdonald, Peter J. BD DipMin	1986	2017	(Leader of the Iona Community)	63 Jim Bush Drive, Prestonpans EH32 9GB PMacdonald@churchofscotland.org.uk	07946 715166
Macdonald, William J. BD	1976	2002	(Board of National Mission: New Charge Development)	1/13 North Werber Park, Edinburgh EH4 1SY	0131 332 0254
MacGregor, Margaret S. (Miss) MA BD DipEd	1985	1994	(Calcutta)	16 Learmonth Court, Edinburgh EH4 1PB	0131 332 1089
McGregor, Alistair G.C. QC BD	1987	2002	(Edinburgh: Leith North)	22 Primrose Bank Road, Edinburgh EH5 3JG	0131 551 2802
McGregor, T. Stewart MBE MA BD	1957	1998	(Chaplain: Edinburgh Royal Infirmary)	19 Lonsdale Terrace, Edinburgh EH3 9HL cetsm@uwclub.net	0131 229 5332
Mackenzie, James G. BA BD	1980	2005	(Jersey: St Columba's)	26 Drylaw Crescent, Edinburgh EH4 2AU jgmackenzie@jerseymail.co.uk	0131 332 3720
Maclean, Ailsa G. (Mrs) BD DipCE	1979	2017	(Chaplain: George Heriot's School)	28 Swan Spring Avenue, Edinburgh EH10 6NJ	0131 445 1320
Macmillan, Gilleasbuig I. KCVO MA BD DrHc DD FRSE HRSA FRCSEd	1969	2013	(Edinburgh: High (St Giles'))	207 Dalkeith Road, Edinburgh EH16 5DS gmacmillan1@btinternet.com	0131 667 5732
MacMurchie, F. Lynne LLB BD	1998	2003	Healthcare Chaplain	Edinburgh Community Mental Health Chaplaincy, 41 George IV Bridge, Edinburgh EH1 1EL	0131 220 5150
McNab, John L. MA BD	1997	2013	Ministries Council	121 George Street, Edinburgh EH2 4YN	0131 225 5722
McPake, John M. LTh	2000	2014	(Edinburgh: Liberton Northfield)	9 Claverhouse Drive, Edinburgh EH16 6BR john_mcpake9@yahoo.co.uk	0131 658 1754
McPheat, Elspeth DCS	1985	2001	Deacon: CrossReach	53 Wood Street, Grangemouth FK3 8LS elspeth176@sky.com	01324 282406
McPhee, Duncan C. MA BD	1953	1993	(Department of National Mission)	8 Belvedere Park, Edinburgh EH6 4LR	0131 552 6784
Macpherson, Colin C.R. MA BD	1958	1996	(Dunfermline St Margaret's)	7 Eva Place, Edinburgh EH9 3ET	0131 667 1456
McPherson, Marjory (Mrs) LLB BD MTh	1990	2017	Presbytery Clerk: Edinburgh	10/1 Palmerston Place, Edinburgh EH12 5AA MMcPherson@churchofscotland.org.uk	0131 225 9137
Manners, Stephen MA BD	1989	2017	(South Ronaldsay and Burray)	124 Fernieside Crescent, Edinburgh EH17 7DH sk.manners@me.com	0131 468 0480
Mathieson, Angus R. MA BD	1988	2018	Secretary, Mission and Discipleship Council	21 Traquair Park West, Edinburgh EH12 7AN AMathieson@churchofscotland.org.uk	0131 334 9774
Moir, Ian A. MA BD	1962	2000	(Adviser for Urban Priority Areas)	28/6 Comely Bank Avenue, Edinburgh EH4 1EL	0131 332 2748
Morrison, Mary B. (Mrs) MA BD DipEd	1978	2000	(Edinburgh: Stenhouse St Aidan's)	174 Craigcrook Road, Edinburgh EH4 3PP	0131 336 4706
Moyes, Sheila A. (Miss) DCS	1957		(Deacon)		
Mulligan, Anne MA DCS	1974	2013	(Deacon: Hospital Chaplain)	27A Craigour Avenue, Edinburgh EH17 1NH mulliganne@aol.com	0131 664 3426
Munro, John P.L. MA BD PhD	1977	2007	(Kinross)	5 Marchmont Crescent, Edinburgh EH9 1HN jplmunro@yahoo.co.uk	0131 623 0198
Munro, John R. BD	1976	2017	(Edinburgh: Fairmilehead)	23 Braid Farm Road, Edinburgh EH10 6LE revjohnmunro@hotmail.com	0131 446 9363
Nicol, Douglas A.O. MA BD	1974	2018	(Hobkirk and Southdean with Ruberslaw)	1/2 North Werber Park, Edinburgh EH4 1SY Douglas.Nicol@churchofscotland.org.uk	07811 437075
Orr, Sheena BA MSc MBA BD	2011	2018	Chaplaincy Adviser, Scottish Prison Service	Calton House, 5 Redheughs Rigg, South Gyle, Edinburgh EH12 9DQ sheena.orr@sps.pnn.gov.uk	0131 244 8640
Paterson, Douglas S. MA BD	1976	2010	(Edinburgh: St Colm's)	4 Ards Place, High Street, Aberlady EH32 0DB	01875 870192

Name	Dates	Position	Address	Phone
Plate, Maria A.G. (Miss) BA LTh CQSW DSW	1983 2000	(South Ronaldsay and Burray)	Flat 29, 77 Barnton Park View, Edinburgh EH4 6EL riaplate@gmail.com	0131 339 8539
Rennie, Agnes M. (Miss) DCS	1974 2012	(Deacon)	3/1 Craigmillar Court, Edinburgh EH16 4AD	0131 661 8475
Ridland, Alistair K. MA BD	1982 2000	Chaplain: Western General Hospital	13 Stewart Place, Kirkliston EH29 0BQ	0131 333 2711
Robertson, Charles LVO MA	1965 2005	(Edinburgh: Canongate)	3 Ross Gardens, Edinburgh EH9 3BS canongate1@aol.com	0131 662 9025
Robertson, Norma P. (Miss) BD DMin MTh	1993 2002	(Kincardine O'Neil with Lumphanan)	Flat 5, 2 Burnbrae Drive, Grovewood Hill, Edinburgh EH12 8AS	0131 339 6701
Robertson, Pauline (Mrs) DCS BA CertTheol	2003 2016	Port Chaplain, Sailors' Society	6 Ashville Terrace, Edinburgh EH6 8DD probertson@sailors-society.org	0131 554 6564 07759 436303
Ross, Keith W. MA BD	1984 2015	(Congregational Development Officer)	Easter Bavelaw House, Pentland Hills Regional Park, Balerno EH14 7JS keithwross@outlook.com	07855 163449
Schofield, Melville F. MA	1960 2000	(Chaplain: Western General Hospital)	25 Rowantree Grove, Currie EH14 5AT	0131 466 0952
Scott, Jayne E. BA MEd MBA	1988 2016	Secretary, Ministries Council	121 George Street, Edinburgh EH2 4YN JScott@churchofscotland.org.uk	0131 225 5722
Scott, Martin C. DipMusEd RSAM BD PhD	1986 2016	Secretary, Council of Assembly	121 George Street, Edinburgh EH2 4YN MScott@churchofscotland.org.uk	0131 225 5722
Smith, Angus MA LTh	1965 2006	(Chaplain to the Oil Industry)	3/7 West Powburn, West Savile Gait, Edinburgh EH9 3EW	0131 667 1761
Stark, Suzi BD	2013 2016	Hospice Chaplain	St Columba's Hospice, 15 Boswall Road, Edinburgh EH5 3RW SStark@churchofscotland.org.uk	0131 551 1381
Stephen, Donald M. TD MA BD ThM	1962 2001	(Edinburgh: Marchmont St Giles')	10 Hawkhead Crescent, Edinburgh EH16 6LR donaldmstephen@gmail.com	0131 658 1216
Stevenson, John MA BD PhD	1963 2001	(Department of Education)	12 Swanston Gardens, Edinburgh EH10 7DL	0131 445 3960
Stewart, Lezley J. BD ThM MTh DMin	2000 2017	Ministries Council	121 George Street, Edinburgh EH2 4YN LStewart@churchofscotland.org.uk	0131 225 5722
Stitt, Ronald J. Maxwell LTh BA ThM BREd DMin FSAScot	1977 2012	(Hamilton: Gilmour and Whitehill)	413 Gilmerton Road, Edinburgh EH17 7JJ	
Swan, David BVMS BD	2005 2016	(Aberdeen: Cove)	250/3 Lanark Road, Edinburgh EH14 2LR davidswan97@gmail.com	07944 598988
Tait, John M. BSc BD	1985 2012	(Edinburgh: Pilrig St Paul's)	82 Greenend Gardens, Edinburgh EH17 7QH johnmtait@me.com	0131 258 9105
Taylor, William R. MA BD MTh	1983 2018	(Chaplaincy Adviser, Scottish Prison Service)	33 Kingsknowe Drive EH14 2JY wlretl@outlook.com	0131 443 5590 07447 258525
Teague, Yvonne (Mrs) DCS	1965 2002	(Board of Ministry)	46 Craigcrook Avenue, Edinburgh EH4 3PX y.teague.1@blueyonder.co.uk	0131 336 3113
Telfer, Iain J.M. BD DPS	1978 2001	Chaplain: Royal Infirmary of Edinburgh	Royal Infirmary of Edinburgh, 51 Little France Crescent, Edinburgh EH16 4SA	0131 242 1997
Thomson, Donald M. BD	1975 2013	(Tullibody: St Serf's)	50 Sighthill Road, Edinburgh EH11 4NY donnethomson@tiscali.co.uk	
Torrance, Iain R. (Prof.) Kt DD FRSE	1982 2012	(President: Princeton Theological Seminary)	25 The Causeway, Duddingston Village, Edinburgh EH15 3QA irt@ptsem.edu	0131 661 3092

Tweedie, Fiona J. BSc PhD	2011 2014	Ordained Local Minister: Mission Statistics Co-ordinator	121 George Street, Edinburgh EH2 4YN FTweedie@churchofscotland.org.uk	0131 225 5722
Watson, Nigel G. MA	1998 2012	(Associate: East Kilbride: Old/Stewartfield/West)	7 St Catherine's Place, Edinburgh EH9 1NU nigel.g.watson@gmail.com	0131 662 4191
Webster, Peter BD	1977 2014	(Edinburgh: Portobello St James')	51 Kempock Street, Gourock PA19 1NF peterwebster101@hotmail.com	01475 321916
Whyte, George J. BSc BD DMin	1981 2017	Principal Clerk	Church Offices, 121 George Street, Edinburgh EH2 4YN GWhyte@churchofscotland.org.uk	0131 240 2240
Wigglesworth, J. Christopher MBE BSc PhD BD	1968 1999	(St Andrew's College, Selly Oak)	12 Leven Terrace, Edinburgh EH3 9LW wiggles@talk21.com	0131 228 6335
Wilson, John M. (Ian) MA	1964 1995	(Adviser in Religious Education)	27 Bellfield Street, Edinburgh EH15 2BR ianandshirley@talktalk.net	0131 669 5257
Wynne, Alistair T.E. BA BD	1982 2009	(Nicosia Community Church, Cyprus)	Flat 6, 14 Bumbrae Drive, Edinburgh EH12 8AS awynne2@googlemail.com	0131 339 6462

EDINBURGH ADDRESSES

Albany	at St Andrew's and St George's West
Balerno	Johnsburn Road, Balerno
Barclay Viewforth	Barclay Place
Blackhall St Columba's	Queensferry Road
Bristo Memorial	Peffermill Road, Craigmillar
Broughton St Mary's	Bellevue Crescent
Canongate	Canongate
Carrick Knowe	North Saughton Road
Colinton	Dell Road
Corstorphine	
Craigsbank	Craigs Crescent
Old	Kirk Loan
St Anne's	Kaimes Road
St Ninian's	St John's Road
Craiglockhart	Craiglockhart Avenue
Craigmillar Park	Craigmillar Park
Cramond	Cramond Glebe Road
Currie	Kirkgate, Currie
Dalmeny	Main Street, Dalmeny
Davidson's Mains	Quality Street
Drylaw	Groathill Road North
Duddingston	Old Church Lane, Duddingston
Fairmilehead	Frogston Road West, Fairmilehead
Gorgie Dalry Stenhouse	Gorgie Road
Gracemount	Gracemount Primary School
Granton	Boswall Parkway
Greenbank	Braidburn Terrace
Greenside	Royal Terrace
Greyfriars Kirk	Greyfriars Place
High (St Giles')	High Street
Holy Trinity	Hailesland Place, Wester Hailes
Inverleith St Serf's	Ferry Road
Juniper Green	Lanark Road, Juniper Green
Kirkliston	The Square, Kirkliston
Leith	
North	Madeira Street off Ferry Road
St Andrew's	Easter Road
South	Kirkgate, Leith
Liberton	Kirkgate, Liberton
Northfield	Gilmerton Road, Liberton
Marchmont St Giles'	Kilgraston Road
Mayfield Salisbury	Mayfield Road x West Mayfield
Meadowbank	Dalziel Place x London Road
Morningside	Cluny Gardens
Morningside United	Bruntsfield Place x Chamberlain Rd
Murrayfield	Abinger Gardens
Newhaven	Pennywell Gardens
Old Kirk and Muirhouse	Craighall Road
Palmerston Place	Palmerston Place
Pilrig St Paul's	Pilrig Street
Polwarth	Polwarth Terrace x Harrison Road
Portobello and Joppa	Abercorn Terrace
Priestfield	Dalkeith Road x Marchhall Place
Queensferry	The Loan, South Queensferry
Ratho	Baird Road, Ratho
Reid Memorial	West Savile Terrace
Richmond Craigmillar	Niddrie Mains Road
St Andrew's and St George's West	George Street
St Andrew's Clermiston	Clermiston View
St Catherine's Argyle	Grange Road x Chalmers Crescent
St Cuthbert's	Lothian Road
St David's Broomhouse	Broomhouse Crescent
St John's Colinton Mains	Oxgangs Road North
St Margaret's	Restalrig Road South
St Martin's	Magdalene Drive
St Michael's	Slateford Road
St Nicholas' Sighthill	Calder Road
St Stephen's Comely Bank	Comely Bank
Slateford Longstone	Kingsknowe Road North
Stockbridge	Saxe Coburg Street
The Tron Kirk	Craigour Gardens and
(Gilmerton and Moredun)	Ravenscroft Street
Wardie	Primrosebank Road
Willowbrae	Willowbrae Road

(2) WEST LOTHIAN

Meets in the church of the incoming Moderator on the first Tuesday of September and in St John's Church Hall, Bathgate, on the first Tuesday of every other month, except June and December, when the meeting is on the second Tuesday, and January, July and August, when there is no meeting.

Clerk: REV. DUNCAN SHAW BD MTh   St John's Manse, Mid Street, Bathgate **EH48 1QD**   **01506 653146**
westlothian@churchofscotland.org.uk

Abercorn (H) linked with Pardovan, Kingscavil (H) and Winchburgh (H)
A. Scott Marshall DipComm BD   1984   1998   The Manse, Winchburgh, Broxburn EH52 6TT   01506 890919
SMarshall@churchofscotland.org.uk

Derek R. Henderson MA DipTP DipCS   2017   45 Priory Road, Linlithgow EH49 6BP   01506 844787
(Ordained Local Minister)   DHenderson@churchofscotland.org.uk   07968 491441

Armadale (H)
Julia C. Wiley (Ms) MA(CE) MDiv   1998   2010   70 Mount Pleasant, Armadale, Bathgate EH48 3HB   01501 730358
JWiley@churchofscotland.org.uk

Margaret Corrie (Miss) DCS   1989   2013   44 Sunnyside Street, Camelon, Falkirk FK1 4BH   07955 633969
MCorrie@churchofscotland.org.uk

Avonbridge (H) linked with Torphichen (H)
Ann Lyall DCS   1980   2017   Manse Road, Torphichen, Bathgate EH48 4LT   01506 635957
(Interim Deacon)   ALyall@churchofscotland.org.uk   07467 124474

Bathgate: Boghall (H)
Christopher G. Galbraith BA LLB BD   2012   1 Manse Place, Ash Grove, Bathgate EH48 1NJ   01506 652715
CGalbraith@churchofscotland.org.uk

Bathgate: High (H)
Sandra Black BSc BD   1988   2017   36 Glencairn Drive, Glasgow G41 4PW   07703 822057
(Interim Minister)   SBlack@churchofscotland.org.uk

Bathgate: St John's (H)
Duncan Shaw BD MTh   1975   1978   St John's Manse, Mid Street, Bathgate EH48 1QD   01506 653146
westlothian@churchofscotland.org.uk

Blackburn and Seafield (H)
Vacant
Session Clerk: Elaine Wood (Ms)
The Manse, 5 MacDonald Gardens, Blackburn, Bathgate EH47 7RE
elainewood173@gmail.com
01506 652825
01501 229811
07894 728667

Blackridge (H) linked with Harthill: St Andrew's (H)
Vacant
Session Clerk, Blackridge: Jean Mowitt (Mrs)
East Main Street, Harthill, Shotts ML7 5QW
jean.mowitt@yahoo.com
01501 751239
01501 752378
07590 901933

Session Clerk: Harthill: Alexander Kennedy
alex.kend@gmail.com
01501 752594

Breich Valley (H)
Robert J. Malloch BD   1987   2013
Breich Valley Manse, Stoneyburn, Bathgate EH47 8AU
RMalloch@churchofscotland.org.uk
01501 763142

Broxburn (H)
Jacobus Boonzaaier BA BCom(OR) BD MDiv PhD   1995   2015
2 Church Street, Broxburn EH52 5EL
JBoonzaaier@churchofscotland.org.uk
01506 337560

Fauldhouse: St Andrew's (H)
Scott Raby LTh   1991   2018
7 Glebe Court, Fauldhouse, Bathgate EH47 9DX
SRaby@churchofscotland.org.uk
01501 771190

Harthill: St Andrew's See Blackridge

Kirknewton (H) and East Calder (H)
Alistair J. Cowper BSc BD   2011   2018
8 Manse Court, East Calder, Livingston EH53 0HF
ACowper@churchofscotland.org.uk
01506 884585
07791 524504

Brenda Robson PhD
(Auxiliary Minister)   2005   2014
2 Baird Road, Ratho, Newbridge EH28 8RA
BRobson@churchofscotland.org.uk
0131 333 2746

Kirk of Calder (H)
John M. Povey MA BD   1981
19 Maryfield Park, Mid Calder, Livingston EH53 0SB
JPovey@churchofscotland.org.uk
01506 882495

Linlithgow: St Michael's (H)
Vacant
info@stmichaels-parish.org.uk
St Michael's Manse, Kirkgate, Linlithgow EH49 7AL

Thomas S. Riddell BSc CEng FIChemE
(Auxiliary Minister)   1993   1994
4 The Maltings, Linlithgow EH49 6DS
TRiddell@churchofscotland.org.uk
01506 842195
01506 843251

Linlithgow: St Ninian's Craigmailen (H)
W. Richard Houston BSc BD   1998   29 Philip Avenue, Linlithgow EH49 7BH   01506 202246
                                        WHouston@churchofscotland.org.uk

Livingston: Old (H)
Nelu I. Balaj BD MA ThD   2010   2017   Manse of Livingston, Charlesfield Lane, Livingston EH54 7AJ   01506 411888
                                        NBalaj@churchofscotland.org.uk
Gordon J. Pennykid BD DCS   2015   8 Glenfield, Livingston EH54 7BG   07747 652652
                                        GPennykid@churchofscotland.org.uk

Livingston United
Ronald G. Greig MA BD   1987   2008   2 Eastcroft Court, Livingston EH54 7ET   01506 467426
                                        RGreig@churchofscotland.org.uk
Stephanie Njeru BA   2015   13 Eastcroft Court, Livingston EH54 7ET   01506 461020
                                        stephanie.njeru@methodist.org.uk

Livingston United is a Local Ecumenical Partnership shared with the Scottish Episcopal, Methodist and United Reformed Churches

Pardovan, Kingscavil and Winchburgh See Abercorn

Polbeth Harwood linked with West Kirk of Calder (H)
Jonanda Groenewald BA BD MTh DD   1999   2014   3 Johnsburn Road, Balerno EH14 7DN   0131 261 7977
                                                JGroenewald@churchofscotland.org.uk
Alison Quilter   2018   27 Northfield Meadows, Longridge, Bathgate EH47 8SA   07741 985597
(Ordained Local Minister)   AQuilter@churchofscotland.org.uk

Strathbrock (H)
Vacant
Session Clerk: Lynne McEwen   1 Manse Park, Uphall, Broxburn EH52 6NX   01506 852550
                                                lynnemcewen@hotmail.co.uk   01506 855513

Torphichen See Avonbridge

Uphall: South (H)
Ian D. Maxwell MA BD PhD   1977   2013   8 Fernlea, Uphall, Broxburn EH52 6DF   01506 239840
                                                IMaxwell@churchofscotland.org.uk

West Kirk of Calder (H) See Polbeth Harwood

Whitburn: Brucefield (H)
Alexander M. Roger BD PhD — 1982 2014 — 48 Gleneagles Court, Whitburn, Bathgate EH47 8PG — ARoger@churchofscotland.org.uk — 01501 229354

Whitburn: South (H)
Angus Kerr BD CertMin ThM DMin — 1983 2013 — 5 Mansewood Crescent, Whitburn, Bathgate EH47 8HA — AKerr@churchofscotland.org.uk — 01501 740333

Name			Role	Address	Email	Tel
Black, David W. BSc BD	1968	2008	(Strathbrock)	66 Bridge Street, Newbridge EH28 8SH	dw.black666@yahoo.co.uk	0131 333 2609
Darroch, Richard J.G. BD MTh MA(CMS)	1993	2010	(Whitburn: Brucefield)	23 Barnes Green, Livingston EH54 8PP	richdarr@aol.com	01506 436648
Dunleavy, Suzanne BD DipEd	1990	2016	(Bridge of Weir: St Machar's Ranfurly)	44 Tantallon Gardens, Bellsquarry, Livingston EH54 9AT	suzanne.dunleavy@btinternet.com	
Dunphy, Rhona B. (Mrs) BD DPTheol DrPhil	2005	2016	Ministries Council	92 The Vennel, Linlithgow EH49 7ET	RDunphy@churchofscotland.org.uk	07791 007158
Jamieson, Gordon D. MA BD	1974	2012	(Head of Stewardship)	41 Goldpark Place, Livingston EH54 6LW	gdj1949@talktalk.net	01506 412020
Kenton, Marc B. BTh MTh	1997	2018	(Strathbrock)			
Mackay, Kenneth J. MA BD	1971	2007	(Edinburgh: St Nicholas' Sighthill)	46 Chuckethall Road, Livingston EH54 8FB	knth_mackay@yahoo.co.uk	01506 410884
MacLaine, Marilyn (Mrs) LTh	1995	2009	(Inchinnan)	37 Bankton Brae, Livingston EH54 9LA	marilynmaclaine@btinternet.com	01506 400619
MacRae, Norman I. LTh	1966	2003	(Inverness: Trinity)	144 Hope Park Gardens, Bathgate EH48 2QX	normanmacrae@talktalk.com	01506 635254
Merrilees, Ann (Miss) DCS	1994	2006	(Deacon)	23 Cuthill Brae, West Calder EH55 8QE	mabmerrilees@gmail.com	01501 762909
Nelson, Georgina MA BD PhD DipEd	1990	1995	Hospital Chaplain, NHS Lothian	63 Hawthorn Bank, Seafield, Bathgate EH47 7EB	georgina.nelson@nhslothian.scot.nhs.uk	
Nicol, Robert M.	1984	1996	(Jersey: St Columba's)	59 Kinloch View, Blackness Road, Linlithgow EH49 7HT	revrob.nicol@tiscali.co.uk	01506 670391
Orr, J. McMichael MA BD PhD	1949	1986	(Aberfoyle with Port of Menteith)		mikeandmargorr@googlemail.com	
Smith, Graham W. BA BD FSAScot	1995	2016	(Livingston: Old)	76 Bankton Park East, Livingston EH54 9BN	smithgraham824@gmail.com	01506 442917
Thomson, Phyllis (Miss) DCS	2003	2010	(Deacon)	63 Caroline Park, Mid Calder, Livingston EH53 0SJ		01506 883207
Trimble, Robert DCS	1988	1998	(Deacon)	5 Templar Rise, Dedridge, Livingston EH54 6PJ		01506 412504
Walker, Ian BD MEd DipMS	1973	2007	(Rutherglen: Wardlawhill)	92 Carseknowe, Linlithgow EH49 7LG	walk102822@aol.com	01506 844412

(3) LOTHIAN

Meets at Musselburgh: St Andrew's High Parish Church at 7pm on the last Thursday in February, April, June and November, and in a different church on the last Thursday in September.

Clerk:	**MR JOHN D. McCULLOCH DL**	20 Tipperwell Way, Howgate, Penicuik EH26 8QP lothian@churchofscotland.org.uk	**01968 676300**
Depute Clerk:	**REV MICHAEL D. WATSON**	47 Crichton Terrace, Pathhead EH37 5QZ MWatson@churchofscotland.org.uk	**01875 320043**

Aberlady (H) linked with Gullane (H)

Brian C. Hilsley LLB BD	1990	2015	The Manse, Hummel Road, Gullane EH31 2BG BHilsley@churchofscotland.org.uk	01620 843192

Athelstaneford linked with Whitekirk and Tyninghame

Vacant		The Manse, Athelstaneford, North Berwick EH39 5BE flxra2@gmail.com	01620 880378 01620 880536
Session Clerk, Athelstaneford: Helen M. Napier (Mrs)			
Session Clerk, Whitekirk and Tyninghame: Thomas S. Torrance (Dr)		ttorr@globalnet.co.uk	0131 447 3324 07742 302947

Belhaven (H) linked with Spott

Neil H. Watson BD	2017	The Manse, Belhaven Road, Dunbar EH42 1NH NWatson@churchofscotland.org.uk	01368 860672 07974 074549

Bilston linked with Glencorse (H) linked with Roslin (H)

John R. Wells BD DipMin	1991	2005	31A Manse Road, Roslin EH25 9LG wellsjr3@aol.com	0131 440 2012

Bonnyrigg (H)

John Mitchell LTh CertMin	1991	28 Shiel Hall Crescent, Rosewell EH24 9DD JMitchell@churchofscotland.org.uk	0131 448 2676

Cockenzie and Port Seton: Chalmers Memorial (H)

Robin N. Allison BD DipMin	1994	2 Links Road, Port Seton, Prestonpans EH32 0HA RAllison@churchofscotland.org.uk	01875 812225

Cockenzie and Port Seton: Old (H)
Guardianship of the Presbytery
Session Clerk: Eizabeth W. Malcolm (Miss)   malcolm771@btinternet.com   01875 813659

Cockpen and Carrington (H) linked with Lasswade (H) and Rosewell (H)
Lorna M. Souter MA BD MSc   2016   11 Pendreich Terrace, Bonnyrigg EH19 2DT   0131 663 6392
                                        LSouter@churchofscotland.org.uk   07889 566418
Elisabeth G.B. Spence BD DipEd   1995 2016   18 Castell Maynes Avenue, Bonnyrigg EH19 3RW   07432 528205
(Pioneer Minister, Hopefield Connections)   ESpence@churchofscotland.org.uk

Dalkeith: St John's and King's Park (H)
Keith L. Mack BD MTh DPS   2002   13 Weir Crescent, Dalkeith EH22 3JN   0131 454 0206
                                      KMack@churchofscotland.org.uk

Dalkeith: St Nicholas' Buccleuch (H)
Alexander G. Horsburgh MA BD   1995 2004   16 New Street, Musselburgh EH21 6JP   0131 653 3318
                                                AHorsburgh@churchofscotland.org.uk

Dirleton (H) linked with North Berwick: Abbey (H)
David J. Graham BSc BD PhD   1982 1998   **abbeychurch@btconnect.com**   **01620 892800**
                                              Sydserff, Old Abbey Road, North Berwick EH39 4BP   01620 890800
                                              DGraham@churchofscotland.org.uk

Dunbar (H)
Gordon Stevenson BSc BD   2010   The Manse, 10 Bayswell Road, Dunbar EH42 1AB   01368 865482
                                    revgstev@gmail.com

Dunglass
Suzanne G. Fletcher (Mrs) BA MDiv MA   2001 2011   The Manse, Cockburnspath TD13 5XZ   01368 830713
                                                        SFletcher@churchofscotland.org.uk   07973 960544

Garvald and Morham linked with Haddington: West (H)
John D. Vischer   1993 2011   15 West Road, Haddington EH41 3RD   01620 822213
                                   JVischer@churchofscotland.org.uk

Gladsmuir linked with Longniddry (H)
Robin E. Hill LLB BD PhD   2004   The Manse, Elcho Road, Longniddry EH32 0LB   01875 853195
                                     RHill@churchofscotland.org.uk

Glencorse (H) See Bilston

Gorebridge (H)
Mark S. Nicholas MA BD   1999   100 Hunterfield Road, Gorebridge EH23 4TT   01875 820387
MNicholas@churchofscotland.org.uk   07816 047493

Gullane See Aberlady

Haddington: St Mary's (H)
Vacant   1 Nungate Gardens, Haddington EH41 4EE   01620 823109

Haddington: West See Garvald and Morham

Howgate (H) linked with Penicuik: South (H)
Ian A. Cathcart BSc BD   1994   2007   15 Stevenson Road, Penicuik EH26 0LU   01968 674692
ICathcart@churchofscotland.org.uk   07588 441895

Humbie linked with Yester, Bolton and Saltoun
Anikó Schuetz Bradwell MA BD   2015   The Manse, Tweeddale Avenue, Gifford, Haddington EH41 4QN   01620 811193
ASchuetzBradwell@churchofscotland.org.uk

Lasswade and Rosewell See Cockpen and Carrington

Loanhead
Graham L. Duffin BSc BD DipEd   1989   2001   120 The Loan, Loanhead EH20 9AJ   0131 448 2459
GDuffin@churchofscotland.org.uk

Longniddry See Gladsmuir

Musselburgh: Northesk (H)
Alison P. McDonald MA BD   1991   1998   16 New Street, Musselburgh EH21 6JP   0131 665 2128
Alison.McDonald@churchofscotland.org.uk

Musselburgh: St Andrew's High (H) (0131 665 7239)
Vacant   8 Ferguson Drive, Musselburgh EH21 6XA   0131 665 1124
Michael D. Watson   2013   2018   47 Crichton Terrace, Pathhead EH37 5QZ   01875 320043
(Ordained Local Minister)   MWatson@churchofscotland.org.uk

Musselburgh: St Clement's and St Ninian's
Guardianship of the Presbytery
Session Clerk: Ivor A. Highley

110 Inveresk Road, Musselburgh EH21 7AY

0131 665 5674

Musselburgh: St Michael's Inveresk
Malcolm M. Lyon BD   2007   2017

5 Crookston Ct., Crookston Rd., Inveresk, Musselburgh EH21 7TR
MLyon@churchofscotland.org.uk

0131 653 2411

Newbattle (H) (http://freespace.virgin.net/newbattle.focus)
Vacant
Frederick Harrison   2013   2016
   (Ordained Local Minister)
Malcolm T. Muir LTh   2001   2015
   (Associate Minister)

33 Castle Avenue, Gorebridge EH23 4TH
FHarrison@churchofscotland.org.uk
Mayfield and Easthouses Church, Bogwood Court, Mayfield,
   Dalkeith EH22 5DG
MMuir@churchofscotland.org.uk

01875 820908

0131 663 3245
07920 855467

Newton
Guardianship of the Presbytery
Andrew Don MBA   2006   2013
   (Ordained Local Minister)

5 Eskvale Court, Penicuik EH26 8HT
ADon@churchofscotland.org.uk

0131 663 3845
01968 675766

North Berwick: Abbey See Dirleton

North Berwick: St Andrew Blackadder (H) (www.standrewblackadder.org.uk) admin@standrewblackadder.org.uk
Neil J. Dougall BD DipMin DMin   1991   2003

7 Marine Parade, North Berwick EH39 4LD
NDougall@churchofscotland.org.uk

01620 892132

Ormiston linked with Pencaitland
David J. Torrance BD DipMin   1993   2009

The Manse, Pencaitland, Tranent EH34 5DL
DTorrance@churchofscotland.org.uk

01875 340963

Pencaitland See Ormiston

Penicuik: North (H) (Website: www.penicuiknorthkirk.org.uk)
Vacant
Session Clerk: Fiona C. Charleson (Mrs)

93 John Street, Penicuik EH26 8AG
fionacharleson@sky.com

01968 675761
01968 672754
07810 327098

Penicuik: St Mungo's (H)
John C.C. Urquhart MA MA BD | 2010 2017 | 10 Fletcher Grove, Penicuik EH26 0JT | 01968 382116
JCUrquhart@churchofscotland.org.uk | | | 07392 069957

Penicuik: South See Howgate

Prestonpans: Prestongrange
Kenneth W Donald BA BD | 1982 2014 | The Manse, East Loan, Prestonpans EH32 9ED | 01875 813643
KDonald@churchofscotland.org.uk

Roslin See Bilston
Spott See Belhaven

Tranent
Erica M Wishart (Mrs) MA BD | 2014 | 1 Toll House Gardens, Tranent EH33 2QQ | 01875 704071
EWishart@churchofscotland.org.uk | | | 07503 170173

Traprain
David D. Scott BSc BD | 1981 2010 | The Manse, Preston Road, East Linton EH40 3DS | Tel/Fax 01620 860227
DDScott@churchofscotland.org.uk

Tyne Valley (H)
Dale K. London BTh FSAScot | 2011 2018 | Cranstoun Cottage, Ford, Pathhead EH37 5RE | 01875 320314
DLondon@churchofscotland.org.uk

Whitekirk and Tyninghame See Athelstaneford
Yester, Bolton and Saltoun See Humbie

Allison, Ann BSc PhD BD	2000 2017	(Crail with Kingsbarns)	99 Coalgate Avenue, Tranent EH33 1JW revann@sky.com	01875 571778 07857 525439
Andrews, J. Edward MA BD DipCG FSAScot	1985 2005	(Armadale)	Dunnichen, 1B Cameron Road, Nairn IV12 5NS edward.andrews@btinternet.com	01667 459466 07808 720708
Atkins, Yvonne E.S. (Mrs) BD	1997 2018	(Musselburgh: St Andrew's High)	6 Robert de Quincy Place, Prestonpans EH32 9NS	01875 819858
Berry, Geoff T. BD BSc	2009 2011	Army Chaplain	4 Regiment RA, Alanbrooke Barracks, Topcliffe, Thirsk YO7 3EY	
Brown, Ronald H.	1974 1998	(Musselburgh: Northesk)	6 Monktonhall Farm Cottages, Musselburgh EH21 6RZ	0131 653 2531
Buchanan, John DCS	1988	(Deacon)	19 Gillespie Crescent, Edinburgh EH10 4HU	0131 229 0794

Name	Dates	Charge	Address	Telephone
Burt, Thomas W. BD	1982 2013	(Carlops with Kirkurd and Newlands with West Linton: St Andrew's)	7 Arkwright Court, North Berwick EH39 4RT / tomburt@westlinton.com	01620 895494
Cairns, John B. KCVO LTh LLB LLD DD	1974 2009	(Aberlady with Gullane)	Bell House, Roxburghe Park, Dunbar EH42 1LR / johncairns@mail.com	01368 862501
Cobain, Alan R. BD	2000 2017	Army Chaplain	1 Yorks BHQ, Battlesbury Barracks, Woodcock Lane, Warminster BA12 9DT / 1yorks-ai-bhq-padre@mod.gov.uk	
Coltart, Ian O. CA BD	1988 2010	(Arbirlot with Carmyllie)	25 Bothwell Gardens, Dunbar EH42 1PZ	01368 860064
Dick, Andrew B. BD DipMin	1986 2015	(Musselburgh: St Michael's Inveresk)	4 Kirkhill Court, Gorebridge EH23 4TW / dixbit@aol.com	07540 099480
Duncan, Maureen M. (Mrs) BD	1996 2018	(Lochend and New Abbey)	2 Chalybeate, Haddington EH41 4NX / revmo43@gmail.com	01620 248559 / 07443 501738
Frail, Nicola R. BLE MBA MDiv	2000 2012	Army Chaplain	32 Engineer Regiment, Marne Barracks, Catterick Garrison DL10 7NP / nrfscot@hotmail.com	
Fraser, John W. MA BD	1974 2011	(Penicuik: North)	66 Camus Avenue, Edinburgh EH10 6QX / jiiji2005@hotmail.co.uk	0131 623 0647
Glover, Robert L. BMus BD MTh ARCO	1971 2010	(Cockenzie and Port Seton: Chalmers Memorial)	12 Seton Wynd, Port Seton, Prestonpans EH32 0TY / rtglover@btinternet.com	01875 818759
Gordon, Thomas J. MA BD	1974 2009	(Chaplain, Marie Curie Hospice, Edinburgh)	22 Gosford Road, Port Seton, Prestonpans EH32 0HF / tom.swallowsnest@gmail.com	01875 812262
Johnston, June E. BSc MEd BD	2013	Ordained Local Minister	21 Caberston Road, Walkerburn EH43 6AT / June.Johnston@churchofscotland.org.uk	01896 870754 / 07754 448889
Jones, Anne M. (Mrs) BD	1998 2002	(Hospital Chaplain)	7 North Elphinstone Farm, Tranent EH33 2ND / revamjones@aol.com	01875 614442
Kellock, Chris N. MA BD	1998 2012	Army Chaplain	1 Plantation Road, Tidworth SP9 7SJ / nicandchris@hotmail.co.uk	01980 601070
Macaulay, Glendon D. BD	1999 2012	(Falkirk: Erskine)	43 Gavin's Lee, Tranent EH33 2AP / gd.macaulay@btinternet.com	01875 615851
Manson, James A. LTh	1981 2004	(Glencorse with Roslin)	31 Nursery Gardens, Kilmarnock KA1 3JA / jimamanson@gmail.com	01563 535430
Pirie, Donald LTh	1975 2006	(Bolton and Saltoun with Humbie with Yester)	46 Caiystane Avenue, Edinburgh EH10 6SH	0131 445 2654
Scott, Ian G. BSc BD STM	1965 2006	(Edinburgh: Greenbank)	50 Forthview Walk, Tranent EH33 1FE / igscott50@btinternet.com	01875 612907
Simpson, Robert R. BA BD	1994 2014	(Callander)	10 Bellsmains, Gorebridge EH23 4QD / robert@pansmanse.co.uk	01875 820843
Steele, Marilynn J. (Mrs) BD DCS	1999 2012	(Deacon)	2 Northfield Gardens, Prestonpans EH32 9LQ / marilynnsteele@aol.com	01875 811497
Stein, Jock MA BD	1973 2008	(Tulliallan and Kincardine)	35 Dunbar Road, Haddington EH41 3PJ / jstein@handselpress.org.uk	01620 824896
Stein, Margaret E. (Mrs) DA BD DipRE	1984 2008	(Tulliallan and Kincardine)	35 Dunbar Road, Haddington EH41 3PJ / margaretestein@hotmail.com	01620 824896

| Steven, Gordon R. BD DCS | 1997 | 2012 | (Deacon) | 51 Nantwich Drive, Edinburgh EH7 6RB
grsteven@btinternet.com | 0131 669 2054
07904 385256 |
| Torrance, David W. MA BD | 1955 | 1991 | (Earlston) | 38 Forth Street, North Berwick EH39 4JQ
torrance103@btinternet.com | Tel/Fax 01620 895109 |

(4) MELROSE AND PEEBLES

Meets at Innerleithen on the first Tuesday of February, March, May, October, November and December, and on the fourth Tuesday of June, and in places to be appointed on the first Tuesday of September.

| Clerk: | **REV. VICTORIA LINFORD LLB BD** | 20 Wedale View, Stow, Galashiels TD1 2SJ
melrosepeebles@churchofscotland.org.uk | **01578 730237** |
| Depute Clerk: | **REV. JULIE M. RENNICK BTh** | The Manse, High Street, Earlston TD4 6DE
JRennick@churchofscotland.org.uk | **01896 849236** |

Ashkirk linked with Selkirk (H)

| Margaret D.J. Steele (Miss) BSc BD | 2000 | 2011 | 1 Loanside, Selkirk TD7 4DJ
MSteele@churchofscotland.org.uk | 01750 23308 |

Bowden (H) and Melrose (H)

| Rosemary Frew (Mrs) MA BD | 1988 | 2017 | The Manse, Tweedmount Road, Melrose TD6 9ST
RFrew@churchofscotland.org.uk | 01896 822217 |

Broughton, Glenholm and Kilbucho (H) linked with Skirling linked with Stobo and Drumelzier linked with Tweedsmuir (H)

| Vacant | The Manse, Broughton, Biggar ML12 6HQ | 01899 830331 |

Caddonfoot (H) linked with Galashiels: Trinity (H)

| Elspeth Harley BA MTh | 1991 | 2014 | 8 Mossilee Road, Galashiels TD1 1NF
EHarley@churchofscotland.org.uk | **01896 752967**
01896 758485 |

Carlops linked with Kirkurd and Newlands (H) linked with West Linton: St Andrew's (H)

| Stewart M. McPherson BD CertMin
(Interim Minister) | 1991 | 2018 | The Manse, Main Street, West Linton EH46 7EE
SMcPherson@churchofscotland.org.uk | 01968 660221
07814 901429 |

Channelkirk and Lauder
Marion A. (Rae) Clark MA BD   2014
The Manse, Brownsmuir Park, Lauder TD2 6QD
RClark@churchofscotland.org.uk
01578 718996

Earlston
Julie M. Rennick (Mrs) BTh   2005   2011
The Manse, High Street, Earlston TD4 6DE
JRennick@churchofscotland.org.uk
01896 849236

Eddleston (H) linked with Peebles: Old (H)
Malcolm M. Macdougall BD MTh DipCE   1981   2001
7 Clement Gunn Square, Peebles EH45 8LW
MMacdougall@churchofscotland.org.uk
01721 720568

Pamela D. Strachan (Lady) MA (Cantab)   2015
(Ordained Local Minister)
Glenhighton, Broughton, Biggar ML12 6JF
PStrachan@churchofscotland.org.uk
01899 830423
07837 873688

Ettrick and Yarrow
Vacant

Galashiels: Old Parish and St Paul's (H) linked with Galashiels: St John's (H)
Vacant
Woodlea, Abbotsview Drive, Galashiels TD1 3SL
01896 753029

Galashiels: St John's See Galashiels: Old Parish and St Paul's
Galashiels: Trinity See Caddonfoot

Innerleithen (H), Traquair and Walkerburn
Vacant
The Manse, 1 Millwell Park, Innerleithen, Peebles EH44 6JF
01896 830309

Kirkurd and Newlands See Carlops

Lyne and Manor linked with Peebles: St Andrew's Leckie (H)
Malcolm S. Jefferson   2012
Mansefield, Innerleithen Road, Peebles EH45 8BE
MJefferson@churchofscotland.org.uk
St Andrew's Leckie: **01721 723121**
01721 725148

Maxton and Mertoun linked with Newtown linked with St Boswells
Sheila W. Moir (Ms) MTheol   2008
7 Strae Brigs, St Boswells, Melrose TD6 0DH
SMoir@churchofscotland.org.uk
01835 822255

Newtown See Maxton and Mertoun
Peebles: Old See Eddleston

Peebles: St Andrew's Leckie See Lyne and Manor
St Boswells See Maxton and Mertoun
Selkirk See Ashkirk
Skirling See Broughton, Glenholm and Kilbucho
Stobo and Drumelzier See Broughton, Glenholm and Kilbucho

Stow: St Mary of Wedale and Heriot
Victoria J. Linford (Mrs) LLB BD   2010   20 Wedale View, Stow, Galashiels TD1 2SJ   01578 730237
VLinford@churchofscotland.org.uk

Tweedsmuir See Broughton, Glenholm and Kilbucho
West Linton: St Andrew's See Carlops

Name	Years	Charge / Position	Address	Telephone
Arnott, A. David K. MA BD	1971 2010	(St Andrews: Hope Park with Strathkinness)	53 Whitehaugh Park, Peebles EH45 9DB adka53@btinternet.com	01721 725979 07759 709205
Cashman, P. Hamilton BSc	1985 1998	(Dirleton with North Berwick: Abbey)	38 Abbotsford Road, Galashiels TD1 3HR mcashman@tiscali.co.uk	01896 752711
Devenny, Robert P.	2002 2017	(Head of Spiritual Care, NHS Borders)	Blakeburn Cottage, Wester Housebyres, Melrose TD6 9BW	01896 822350
Dick, J. Ronald BD	1973 2012	(Hospital Chaplain)	1 Viewfield Terrace, Leet Street, Coldstream TD12 4BL ron.dick180@yahoo.co.uk	01890 882206
Dobie, Rachel J.W. (Mrs) LTh	1991 2008	(Broughton, Glenholm and Kilbucho with Skirling with Stobo and Drumelzier with Tweedsmuir)	20 Moss Side Crescent, Biggar ML12 6GE revracheldobie@talktalk.net	01899 229244
Dodd, Marion E. (Miss) MA BD LRAM	1988 2010	(Kelso: Old and Sprouston)	Esdaile, Tweedmount Road, Melrose TD6 9ST mariondodd@btinternet.com	01896 822446
Donaldson, David MA BD DMin	1969 2018	(Manish-Scarista)	13 Rose Park, Peebles EH45 8HP davidandjeandonaldson@gmail.com	07817 479866
Duncan, Charles A. MA	1956 1992	(Heriot with Stow: St Mary of Wedale)	10 Elm Grove, Galashiels TD1 3JA	01896 753261
Faris, Janice M. (Mrs) BSc BD	1991 2018	(Innerleithen, Traquair and Walkerburn)	Overdale Cottage, Grange Park Road, Orton Grange, Carlisle CA5 6LT revjfaris@gmail.com	07427 371239
Hogg, Thomas M. BD	1986 2007	(Tranent)	22 Douglas Place, Galashiels TD1 3BT	01896 759381
Hughes, Barry MA	2011	Ordained Local Minister	Dunslair, Cardrona Way, Cardrona, Peebles EH45 9LD BHughes@churchofscotland.org.uk	01896 831197
Kellet, John M. MA	1962 1995	(Leith: South)	4 High Cottages, Walkerburn EH43 6AZ	01896 870351
Kennon, Stanley BA BD	1992 2000	(Chaplain: Royal Navy)	Trinity Manse, 46 Ayr Road, Cumnock KA18 1DW stankennon@outlook.com	01290 422145
Lawrie, Bruce B. BD	1974 2012	(Duffus, Spynie and Hopeman)	5 Thorncroft, Scotts Place, Selkirk TD7 4LN thorncroft54@gmail.com	01750 725427
Levison, Chris L. MA BD	1972 2010	(Health Care Chaplaincy Training and Development Officer)	Gardenfield, Nine Mile Burn, Penicuik EH26 9LT chrislevison@hotmail.com	01968 674566

Macdonald, Finlay A.J. MA BD PhD DD	1971	2010	(Principal Clerk)	8 St Ronan's Way, Innerleithen EH44 6RG finlay_macdonald@btinternet.com	01896 831631
Milloy, A. Miller DPE LTh DipTrMan	1979	2012	(General Secretary: United Bible Societies)	18 Kirtlegairy Crescent, Peebles EH45 9NJ ammilloy@aol.com	01721 723380
Moore, W. Haisley MA	1966	1996	(Secretary: The Boys' Brigade)	1/2 Dovecot Court, Peebles EH45 8FG jillandhaisley@outlook.com	01721 720837
Munson, Winnie (Ms) BD	1996	2006	(Delting with Northmavine)	6 St Cuthbert's Drive, St Boswells, Melrose TD6 0DF wabsmith@btinternet.com	01835 823375
Norman, Nancy M. (Miss) BA MDiv MTh	1988	2012	(Lyne and Manor)	25 March Street, Peebles EH45 8EP nancy.norman1@googlemail.com	01721 721699
Rae, Andrew W.	1951	1987	(Annan: St Andrew's Greenknowe Erskine)	Roseneuk, Tweedside Road, Newtown St Boswells TD6 0PQ	01835 823783
Rennie, John D. MA	1962	1996	(Broughton, Glenholm and Kilbucho with Skirling with Stobo and Drumelzier with Tweedsmuir)	29/1 Rosetta Road, Peebles EH45 8HJ tworennies@talktalk.net	01721 720963
Riddell, John A. MA BD	1967	2006	(Jedburgh: Trinity)	Orchid Cottage, Gingham Row, Earlston TD4 6ET	01896 848784
Siroky, Samuel BA MTh	2003	2017	(Ettrick and Yarrow)	c/o Hopeview House, Yarrow, Selkirk TD7 5LB	01206 621939 07786 797974
Steele, Leslie M. MA BD	1973	2013	(Galashiels: Old and St Paul's)	25 Bardfield Road, Colchester CO2 8LW lms@hotmail.co.uk	
Taverner, Glyn R. MA BD	1957	1995	(Maxton and Mertoun with St Boswells)	Woodcot Cottage, Waverley Road, Innerleithen EH44 6QW	01896 830156
Wallace, James H. MA BD	1973	2011	(Peebles: St Andrew's Leckie)	52 Waverley Mills, Innerleithen EH44 6RH jimwallace121@btinternet.com	01896 831637

(5) DUNS

Meets at Duns, in the Parish Church hall at 7pm on the first Tuesday of September and of December; and at venues to be announced on the first Saturday of February, the first Tuesday of May and the last Tuesday of June. It also meets throughout the year for developmental activities.

Clerk:	MR DAVID S. PHILP	Sea View, West Winds, Upper Burnmouth TD14 5SL duns@churchofscotland.org.uk	01890 781568

Ayton (H) and District Churches

Norman R. Whyte BD MTh DipMin	1982	2006	The Manse, Beanburn, Ayton, Eyemouth TD14 5QY NWhyte@churchofscotland.org.uk	01890 781333

Berwick-upon-Tweed: St Andrew's Wallace Green (H) and Lowick

Adam J.J. Hood MA BD DPhil	1989	2012	3 Meadow Grange, Berwick-upon-Tweed TD15 1NW AHood@churchofscotland.org.uk	01289 332787

Chirnside linked with Hutton and Fishwick and Paxton
Michael A. Taylor DipTh MPhil   2006   2018   Parish Church Manse, The Glebe, Chirnside, Duns TD11 3XL   01890 819109
                                                  MTaylor@churchofscotland.org.uk   07479 985075

Coldingham and St Abbs linked with Eyemouth
Andrew Haddow BEng BD   2012   The Manse, Victoria Road, Eyemouth TD14 5JD   01890 750327
                                  AHaddow@churchofscotland.org.uk

Coldstream and District Parishes (H) linked with Eccles and Leitholm
David J. Taverner MCIBS ACIS BD   1996   2011   36 Bennecourt Drive, Coldstream TD12 4BY   01890 883887
                                                    DTaverner@churchofscotland.org.uk

Duns and District Parishes
Vacant   The Manse, Castle Street, Duns TD11 3DG   01361 883755

Eccles and Leitholm See Coldstream
Eyemouth See Coldingham and St Abbs

Fogo
Guardianship of the Presbytery

Gordon: St Michael's linked with Greenlaw (H) linked with Legerwood linked with Westruther
Thomas S. Nicholson BD DPS   1982   1995   The Manse, Todholes, Greenlaw, Duns TD10 6XD   01361 810316
                                               TNicholson@churchofscotland.org.uk

Greenlaw See Gordon: St Michael's
Hutton and Fishwick and Paxton See Chirnside
Legerwood See Gordon: St Michael's
Westruther See Gordon: St Michael's

Cartwright, Alan C.D. BSc BD   1976   2016   (Fogo and Swinton with Ladykirk and   Drumgray, Edrom, Duns TD11 3PX   01890 819191
                                                Whitsome with Leitholm)   merse.minister@btinternet.com

Gaddes, Donald R.   1961   1994   (Kelso: North and Ednam)   2 Teindhill Green, Duns TD11 3DX   01361 883172
                                                                drgaddes@btinternet.com

Higham, Robert D. BD   1985   2002   (Tiree)   36 Low Greens, Berwick-upon-Tweed TD15 1LZ   01289 302392
Hope, Geraldine H. (Mrs) MA BD   1986   2007   (Foulden and Mordington   4 Well Court, Chirnside, Duns TD11 3UD   01890 818134
                                                  with Hutton and Fishwick and Paxton)   geraldine.hope@virgin.net

Landale, William S.	2005 2016	(Auxiliary Minister)	Green Hope Guest House, Ellemford, Duns TD11 3SG	01361 890242
			WLandale@churchofscotland.org.uk	
Neill, Bruce F. MA BD	1966 2007	(Maxton and Mertoun with Newtown with St Boswells)	18 Brierydean, St Abbs, Eyemouth TD14 5PQ	01890 771569
			bneill@phonecoop.coop	
Paterson, William BD	1977 2001	(Bonkyl and Preston with Chirnside with Edrom Allanton)	Benachie, Gavinton, Duns TD11 3QT	01361 882727
			billdm.paterson@btinternet.com	
Sherrard, H. Dane BD DMin	1971 2013	(Arrochar with Luss)	Mount Pleasant Granary, Mount Pleasant Farm, Duns TD11 4HU	01361 882254
				07801 939138
			dane@mountpleasantgranary.net	
Shields, John M. MBE LTh	1972 2007	(Channelkirk and Lauder)	12 Eden Park, Ednam, Kelso TD5 7RG	01573 229015
			john.shields118@btinternet.com	
Walker, Kenneth D.F. MA BD PhD	1976 2008	(Athelstaneford with Whitekirk and Tyninghame)	Allanbank Kothi, Allanton, Duns TD11 3PY	01890 817102
			walkerkenneth49@gmail.com	
Walker, Veronica (Mrs) BSc BD		Licentiate	Allanbank Kothi, Allanton, Duns TD11 3PY	01890 817102
			walkerkenneth49@gmail.com	

(6) JEDBURGH

Meets at various venues on the first Wednesday of February, March, May, September, October, November and December and on the last Wednesday of June.

| Clerk | REV. LISA-JANE RANKIN BD CPS | 4 Wilton Hill Terrace, Hawick TD9 8BE | 01450 370744 |
| | | jedburgh@churchofscotland.org.uk | |

Ale and Teviot United (H) (Website: www.aleandteviot.org.uk)
Vacant
Session Clerk: John Rogerson   22 The Glebe, Ancrum, Jedburgh TD8 6UX   01835 830318
B166ESS@yahoo.co.uk   07813 367533

Cavers and Kirkton linked with Hawick: Trinity (H)
Vacant
Session Clerk, Cavers: R. Scott Elliot   Trinity Manse, Howdenburn, Hawick TD9 8PH   01450 378248
Session Clerk, Trinity: Muriel Bowie (Mrs)   scott194elliot@btinternet.com   01450 375046
    01450 372195

Cheviot Churches (H) (www.cheviotchurches.org)
Vacant
Session Clerk: Brian Kelly   bjkelly@uwclub.net   01573 420221

Hawick: Burnfoot (www.burnfootparishchurch.org.uk)
Charles J. Finnie LTh DPS   1991 1997   29 Wilton Hill, Hawick TD9 8BA   01450 373181
CFinnie@churchofscotland.org.uk

Hawick: St Mary's and Old (H) linked with Hawick: Teviot (H) and Roberton
Alistair W. Cook BSc CA BD   2008   2017   4 Heronhill Close, Hawick TD9 9RA   01450 378175
ACook@churchofscotland.org.uk   07802 616352

Hawick: Teviot and Roberton See Hawick: St Mary's and Old
Hawick: Trinity See Cavers and Kirkton

Hawick: Wilton linked with Teviothead
Lisa-Jane Rankin BD CPS   2003   4 Wilton Hill Terrace, Hawick TD9 8BE   01450 370744
LRankin@churchofscotland.org.uk

Hobkirk and Southdean (www.hobkirkruberslaw.org) linked with Ruberslaw (www.hobkirkruberslaw.org)
Vacant   The Manse, Denholm, Hawick TD9 8NB   01450 870268
Session Clerk, Hobkirk and Southdean: 01450 860692
David McFadyen
Session Clerk, Ruberslaw: 01450 870362
Alison Henderson (Mrs)

Jedburgh: Old and Trinity (www.jedburgh-parish.org.uk)
Vacant   The Manse, Honeyfield Drive, Jedburgh TD8 6LQ   01835 863417
Session Clerk: Ken Fotheringham   01835 862570

Kelso Country Churches
Vacant   01573 470250
Session Clerk: James Smith   jamessmith484@btinternet.com

Kelso: North (H) and Ednam (H) (www.kelsonorthandednam.org.uk) office@kelsonorthandednam.org.uk
Anna S. Rodwell BD DipMin   1998   2016   The Manse, 24 Forestfield, Kelso TD5 7BX   **01573 224154**
ARodwell@churchofscotland.org.uk   01573 224248
07765 169826

Kelso: Old and Sprouston
Alexander W. Young BD DipMin   1998   2017   The Manse, Glebe Lane, Kelso TD5 7AU   01573 348749
AYoung@churchofscotland.org.uk

Oxnam
Guardianship of the Presbytery
Session Clerk: Morag McKeand (Mrs)   mh.mckeand@btinternet.com   01835 840284

Ruberslaw See Hobkirk and Southdean
Teviothead See Hawick: Wilton

Combe, Neil R. BSc MSc BD	1984 2015	(Hawick: St Mary's and Old with Hawick: Teviot and Roberton)	2 Abbotsview Gardens, Galashiels TD1 3ER neil.combe@btinternet.com	01896 755869
McNicol, Bruce	1967 2006	(Jedburgh: Old and Edgerston)	42 Dounehill, Jedburgh TD8 6LJ mcnicol942@gmail.com	01835 862991
Stewart, Una B. (Ms) BD DipEd	1995 2014	(Law)	10 Inch Park, Kelso TD5 7BQ rev.ubs@virgin.net	01573 219231

HAWICK ADDRESSES

Burnfoot	Fraser Avenue	
	St Mary's and Old	Kirk Wynd
	Teviot	St George's Lane
	Trinity	Central Square
	Wilton	Princes Street

(7) ANNANDALE AND ESKDALE

Meets on the first Tuesday of February, May, September and December, and the third Tuesday of March, June and October. The September meeting is held in the Moderator's charge. The other meetings are held in Dryfesdale Church Hall, Lockerbie, except for the June meeting, which is separately announced.

Clerk:	**REV. ADAM J. DILLON BD ThM**	**3 Ladyknowe, Moffat DG10 9DY** annandaleeskdale@churchofscotland.org.uk	**01683 221370**

Annan: Old (H) linked with Dornock

Vacant		12 Plumdon Park Avenue, Annan DG12 6EY	01461 201405

Annan: St Andrew's (H) linked with Brydekirk

John G. Pickles BD MTh MSc	2011	1 Annerley Road, Annan DG12 6HE JPickles@churchofscotland.org.uk	01461 202626

Applegarth, Sibbaldbie (H) and Johnstone linked with Lochmaben (H)

Paul R. Read BSc MA(Th)	2000 2013	The Manse, Barrashead, Lochmaben, Lockerbie DG11 1QF PRead@churchofscotland.org.uk	01387 810640

Brydekirk See Annan: St Andrew's

Canonbie United (H) linked with Liddesdale (H)
Vacant
Session Clerk, Liddesdale:
  Glynis Cambridge (Mrs)   23 Langholm Street, Newcastleton TD9 0QX   01387 375242
                                            lpctreasurer1@gmail.com   01387 375488

Canonbie United is a Local Ecumenical Partnership shared with the United Free Church

Dalton and Hightae linked with St Mungo
Vacant   The Manse, Hightae, Lockerbie DG11 1JL   01387 811499
Session Clerk, Dalton: Isobel Tinning (Mrs) isobel.tinning@gmail.com   01387 269133
Session Clerk, St Mungo: Avril Bailey (Mrs) avril57.ab@gmail.com   01576 202458

Dornock See Annan: Old

Gretna: Old (H), Gretna: St Andrew's (H), Half Morton and Kirkpatrick Fleming
C. Bryan Haston LTh   1975   The Manse, Gretna Green, Gretna DG16 5DU   01461 338313
                                            CBHaston@churchofscotland.org.uk

Hoddom, Kirtle-Eaglesfield and Middlebie
Frances M. Henderson BA BD PhD   2006   2013   The Manse, Main Road, Ecclefechan, Lockerbie DG11 3BU   01576 300108
                                            FHenderson@churchofscotland.org.uk

Kirkpatrick Juxta linked with Moffat: St Andrew's (H) linked with Wamphray
Adam J. Dillon BD ThM   2003   2008   The Manse, 1 Meadowbank, Moffat DG10 9LR   01683 220128
                                            ADillon@churchofscotland.org.uk

Langholm Eskdalemuir Ewes and Westerkirk
I. Scott McCarthy BD   2010   The Manse, Langholm DG13 0BL   01387 380252
                                            ISMcCarthy@churchofscotland.org.uk

Liddesdale See Canonbie United
Lochmaben See Applegarth, Sibbaldbie and Johnstone

Lockerbie: Dryfesdale, Hutton and Corrie
Vacant
Eric T. Dempster   2016   2018   Annanside, Wamphray, Moffat DG10 9LZ   01576 470496
(Ordained Local Minister)   EDempster@churchofscotland.org.uk

Moffat: St Andrew's See Kirkpatrick Juxta
St Mungo See Dalton

The Border Kirk (Church office: Chapel Street, Carlisle CA1 1JA
David G. Pitkeathly LLB BD   1996   2007   95 Pinecroft, Carlisle CA3 0DB   **01228 591757**
                                               DPitkeathly@churchofscotland.org.uk   01228 593243

Tundergarth
Guardianship of the Presbytery
Session Clerk: David Paterson   jilljoe@tiscali.co.uk   07982 037029

Wamphray See Kirkpatrick Juxta

Name			Role / Note	Address / Email	Phone
Annand, James M. MA BD	1955	1995	(Lockerbie: Dryfesdale)	Dere Cottage, 48 Main Street, Newstead, Melrose TD6 9DX	
Beveridge, S. Edwin P. BA	1959	2004	(Brydekirk with Hoddom)	19 Rothesay Terrace, Edinburgh EH3 7RY	0131 225 3393
Brydson, Angela (Mrs) DCS	2015	2014	Deacon, Lochmaben, Moffat and Lockerbie Grouping	52 Victoria Park, Lockerbie DG11 2AY ABrydson@churchofscotland.org.uk	07543 796820
Byers, Mairi C. (Mrs) BTh CPS	1992	1998	(Jura)	Meadowbank, Plumdon Road, Annan DG12 6SJ aljbyers@hotmail.com	01461 206512
Dawson, Morag A. BD MTh	1999	2016	(Dalton with Highlae with St Mungo)	34 Kennedy Crescent, Tranent EH33 1DP moragdawson@yahoo.co.uk	
Gibb, J. Daniel M. BA LTh	1994	2006	(Aberfoyle with Port of Menteith)	1 Beechfield, Newton Aycliffe DL5 7AX dannygibb@hotmail.co.uk	
Harvey, P. Ruth (Ms) MA BD	2009	2012	Place for Hope	Croslands, Beacon Street, Penrith CA11 7TZ ruth.harvey@placeforhope.org.uk	01768 840749 07403 638339
MacPherson, Duncan J. BSc BD	1993	2002	Chaplain: Army (Dornock)	MP413, Kentigern House, 65 Brown Street, Glasgow G2 8EX	
Seaman, Ronald S. MA	1967	2007		1 Springfield Farm Court, Springfield, Gretna DG16 5EH	01461 337228
Steenbergen, Pauline (Ms) MA BD	1996	2018	Locum Minister, Presbytery	The Vicarage, Townhead Road, Dalston, Cumbria CA5 7LF locum.ae@gmail.com	07743 927182
Vivers, Katherine A.		2004	Auxiliary Minister	Blacket House, Eaglesfield, Lockerbie DG11 3AA KVivers@churchofscotland.org.uk	01461 500412 07748 233011

(8) DUMFRIES AND KIRKCUDBRIGHT

Meets at Dumfries on the last Wednesday of February, April, June, September and November.

Clerk:	REV. DONALD CAMPBELL BD	St George's Church, 50 George Street, Dumfries DG1 1EJ dumfrieskirkcudbright@churchofscotland.org.uk	01387 252965

Balmaclellan and Kells (H) linked with Carsphairn (H) linked with Dalry (H)
David S. Bartholomew BSc MSc PhD BD	1994	The Manse, Dalry, Castle Douglas DG7 3PJ DBartholomew@churchofscotland.org.uk	01644 430380

Caerlaverock linked with Dumfries: St Mary's-Greyfriars' (H)
David D.J. Logan MStJ BD MA	2009 2016	4 Georgetown Crescent, Dumfries DG1 4EQ DLogan@churchofscotland.org.uk	01387 270128 07793 542411

Carsphairn See Balmaclellan and Kells

Castle Douglas (H) linked with The Bengairn Parishes
Alison H. Burnside (Mrs) MA BD	1991	1 Castle View, Castle Douglas DG7 1BG ABurnside@churchofscotland.org.uk	01556 505983
Oonagh Dee (Ordained Local Minister)	2014	Kendoon, Merse Way, Kippford, Dalbeattie DG5 4LL ODee@churchofscotland.org.uk	01556 620001

Closeburn linked with Kirkmahoe
Vacant		The Manse, Kirkmahoe, Dumfries DG1 1ST	01387 710572
Session Clerk, Closeburn: Jack Tait		jacktait1941@gmail.com	01848 331700
Session Clerk, Kirkmahoe: Alexander Fergusson		alexanderfergusson@btinternet.com	01387 253014

Colvend, Southwick and Kirkbean
James F. Gatherer BD	1984	The Manse, Colvend, Dalbeattie DG5 4QN JGatherer@churchofscotland.org.uk	01556 630255

Corsock and Kirkpatrick Durham linked with Crossmichael, Parton and Balmaghie
Sally M.F. Russell BTh MTh	2006	Knockdrocket, Clarebrand, Castle Douglas DG7 3AH SRussell@churchofscotland.org.uk	01556 503645

Crossmichael, Parton and Balmaghie See Corsock and Kirkpatrick Durham

Cummertrees, Mouswald and Ruthwell (H)
Vacant
The Manse, Ruthwell, Dumfries DG1 4NP
01387 870217

Dalbeattie (H) and Kirkgunzeon linked with Urr (H)
Fiona A. Wilson (Mrs) BD   2008
36 Mill Street, Dalbeattie DG5 4HE
FWilson@churchofscotland.org.uk
01556 610708

Dalry See Balmaclellan and Kells

Dumfries: Maxwelltown West (H)
Vacant
Maxwelltown West Manse, 11 Laurieknowe, Dumfries DG2 7AH
01387 247538
Session Clerk: Drew Crossan
andrew@ahrcrossan.co.uk
01387 255265

Dumfries: Northwest
Vacant
c/o Church Office, Dumfries Northwest Church, Lochside Road, Dumfries DG2 0DZ
01387 249964
Session Clerk: Clara Jackson
sessionclerk.dumfriesnorthwest@gmail.com
01387 249964

Dumfries: St George's (H)
Donald Campbell BD   1997
9 Nunholm Park, Dumfries DG1 1JP
DCampbell@churchofscotland.org.uk
01387 252965

Dumfries: St Mary's-Greyfriars' See Caerlaverock

Dumfries: St Michael's and South
Maurice S. Bond MTh BA DipEd PhD   1981
39 Cardoness Street, Dumfries DG1 3AL
MBond@churchofscotland.org.uk
01387 253849

Dumfries: Troqueer (H)
John R. Notman BSc BD   1990
Troqueer Manse, Troqueer Road, Dumfries DG2 7DF
JNotman@churchofscotland.org.uk
01387 253043

Dunscore linked with Glencairn and Moniaive
Joachim J.H. du Plessis BA BD MTh   1975
Wallaceton, Auldgirth, Dumfries DG2 0TJ
JduPlessis@churchofscotland.org.uk
01387 820245

Durisdeer linked with Penpont, Keir and Tynron linked with Thornhill (H)
J. Stuart Mill MA MBA BD DipEd   1976   2013   The Manse, Manse Park, Thornhill DG3 5ER   01848 331191
                                                         JMill@churchofscotland.org.uk

Gatehouse and Borgue linked with Tarff and Twynholm
Valerie J. Ott (Mrs) BA BD   2002   The Manse, Planetree Park, Gatehouse of Fleet, Castle Douglas   01557 814233
                                                          DG7 2EQ
                                                          VOtt@churchofscotland.org.uk

Glencairn and Moniaive See Dunscore

Irongray, Lochrutton and Terregles
Gary J. Peacock MA BD MTh   2015   The Manse, Shawhead, Dumfries DG2 9SJ   01387 730759
                                                          GPeacock@churchofscotland.org.uk

Kirkconnel (H) linked with Sanquhar: St Bride's (H)
Vacant   St Bride's Manse, Glasgow Road, Sanquhar DG6 6BZ   01659 50247

Kirkcudbright (H)
John K. Collard MA BD   1986   2017   6 Bourtree Avenue, Kirkcudbright DG6 4AU   01557 330489
(Interim Minister)   JCollard@churchofscotland.org.uk

Kirkmahoe See Closeburn

Kirkmichael, Tinwald and Torthorwald
Vacant   Manse of Tinwald, Tinwald, Dumfries DG1 3PL   01387 710246
Mhairi Wallace (Mrs)   2013   2017   5 Dee Road, Kirkcudbright DG 4HQ   07701 375064
(Ordained Local Minister)   MWallace@churchofscotland.org.uk

Lochend and New Abbey
Vacant   New Abbey Manse, 32 Main Street, New Abbey, Dumfries DG2 8BY   01387 850490
                                                          revmo@talktalk.net
Elizabeth A. Mack (Miss) DipEd   1994   2018   24 Roberts Crescent, Dumfries DG2 7RS   01387 264847
(Auxiliary Minister)   mackliz@btinternet.com

Penpont, Keir and Tynron See Durisdeer
Sanquhar: St Bride's See Kirkconnel

Tarff and Twynholm See Gatehouse and Borgue
The Bengairn Parishes See Castle Douglas
Thornhill See Durisdeer
Urr See Dalbeattie and Kirkgunzeon

Name			(Charge)	Address	Telephone
Bennett, David K.P. BA	1974	2000	(Kirkpatrick Irongray with Lochrutton with Terregles)	53 Anne Arundel Court, Heathhall, Dumfries DG1 3SL	01387 257755
Campbell, Neil G. BA BD	1988	2018	Chaplain, HM Prison Dumfries	12 Charles Street, Annan DG12 5AJ	01557 620123
Finch, Graham S. MA BD	1977	2016	(Cadder)	32a St Mary Street, Kirkcudbright DG6 4DN gsf231@gmail.com	
Hammond, Richard J. BA BD	1993	2007	(Kirkmahoe)	3 Marchfield Mount, Marchfield, Dumfries DG1 1SE libby.hammond@virgin.net	07764 465783
Hogg, William T. MA BD	1979	2018	(Kirkconnel with Sanquhar St Bride's)	30 Castle Street, Kirkcudbright DG6 4JD WHogg@churchofscotland.org.uk	
Holland, William MA	1967	2009	(Lochend and New Abbey)	Ardshean, 55 Georgetown Road, Dumfries DG1 4DD billholland55@btinternet.com	01387 256131 / 07766 531732
Irving, Douglas R. LLB BD WS	1984	2016	(Kirkcudbright)	17 Galla Crescent, Dalbeattie DG5 4JY douglas.irving@outlook.com	01556 610156
Kelly, William W. BSc BD	1994	2014	(Dumfries: Troqueer)	6 Vitality Way, Craigie, Perth, WA 6025, Australia ww.kelly@yahoo.com	
McKay, David M. MA BD	1979	2007	(Kirkpatrick Juxta with Moffat: St Andrew's with Wamphray)	20 Auld Brig View, Auldgirth, Dumfries DG2 0XE davidmckay20@tiscali.co.uk	01387 740013
McKenzie, William M. DA	1958	1993	(Dumfries: Troqueer)	41 Kingholm Road, Dumfries DG1 4SR mckenzie.dumfries@btinternet.com	01387 253688
McLauchlan, Mary C. (Mrs) LTh	1997	2013	(Mochrum)	3 Ayr Street, Moniaive, Thornhill DG3 4HP mary@revmother.co.uk	01848 200786
Owen, John J.C. LTh	1967	2001	(Applegarth and Sibbaldbie with Lochmaben)	5 Galla Avenue, Dalbeattie DG5 4JZ jj.owen@onetel.net	01556 612125
Sutherland, Colin A. LTh	1995	2007	(Blantyre: Livingstone Memorial)	71 Caulstran Road, Dumfries DG2 9FJ colin.csutherland@btinternet.com	01387 279954
Williamson, James BA BD	1986	2009	(Cummertrees with Mouswald with Ruthwell)	12 Mulberry Drive, Dunfermline KY11 8BZ jimwill@rcmkirk.fsnet.co.uk	01383 734872
Wotherspoon, Robert C. LTh	1976	1998	(Corsock and Kirkpatrick Durham with Crossmichael and Parton)	5 Goddards Green Cottages, Goddards Green, Beneden, Cranbrook TN17 4AW	01580 243091

DUMFRIES ADDRESSES

Maxwelltown West	Laurieknowe	
Northwest	Lochside Road	
St George's	George Street	
St Mary's-Greyfriars	St Mary's Street	
St Michael's and South	St Michael's Street	
Troqueer	Troqueer Road	

(9) WIGTOWN AND STRANRAER

Meets at Glenluce, in the church hall, on the first Tuesday of March, October and December for ordinary business; on the first Tuesday of September for formal business followed by meetings of committees; on the first Tuesday of November, February and May for worship followed by meetings of committees; and at a church designated by the Moderator on the first Tuesday of June for Holy Communion followed by ordinary business.

| Clerk: | **MR SAM SCOBIE** | 40 Clenoch Parks Road, Stranraer DG9 7QT | 01776 703975 |
| | | wigtownstranraer@churchofscotland.org.uk | |

Ervie Kirkcolm linked with Leswalt
Guardianship of the Presbytery

Session Clerk, Ervie-Kirkcolm:			
Jennifer Comery (Mrs)		Skellies Knowe West, Leswalt, Stranraer DH9 0RY	01776 854277
Session Clerk, Leswalt: Fiona McColm (Mrs)		sessionclerk@leswaltparishchurch.org.uk	01776 870555

Glasserton and Isle of Whithorn linked with Whithorn: St Ninian's Priory

| Alexander I. Currie BD CPS | 1990 | The Manse, Whithorn, Newton Stewart DG8 8PT | 01988 500267 |
| | | ACurrie@churchofscotland.org.uk | |

Inch linked with Portpatrick linked with Stranraer: Trinity (H)

John H. Burns BSc BD	1985	1988	Bayview Road, Stranraer DG9 8BE	01776 702383
			JBurns@churchofscotland.org.uk	
Pamela A. Bellis BA (Ordained Local Minister)	2014	2018	Mayfield, Dunragit, Stranraer DG9 8PG	01581 400378
			PBellis@churchofscotland.org.uk	07751 379249

Kirkcowan (H) linked with Wigtown (H)

| Eric Boyle BA MTh | 2006 | Seaview Manse, Church Lane, Wigtown, Newton Stewart DG8 9HT | 01988 402314 |
| | | EBoyle@churchofscotland.org.uk | |

Kirkinner linked with Mochrum linked with Sorbie (H)

Jeffrey M. Mead BD	1978	1986	The Manse, Kirkinner, Newton Stewart DG8 9AL	01988 840643
			JMead@churchofscotland.org.uk	
Joyce Harvey (Mrs) (Ordained Local Minister)	2013	2017	4a Allanfield Place, Newton Stewart DG8 6BS	01671 403693
			JHarvey@churchofscotland.org.uk	

Kirkmabreck linked with Monigaff (H)

Stuart Farmes	2011	2014	Creebridge, Newton Stewart DG8 6NR SFarmes@churchofscotland.org.uk	01671 403361

Kirkmaiden (H) linked with Stoneykirk

Christopher Wallace BD DipMin	1988	2016	Church Road, Sandhead, Stranraer DG9 9JJ Christopher.Wallace@churchofscotland.org.uk	01776 830757

Leswalt See Ervie Kirkcolm

Luce Valley

Stephen Ogston MPhys MSc BD	2009	2017	Glenluce, Newton Stewart DG8 0PU SOgston@churchofscotland.org.uk	01581 300319

Mochrum See Kirkinner
Monigaff See Kirkmabreck

Penninghame (H)

Edward D. Lyons BD MTh	2007		The Manse, 1A Corvisel Road, Newton Stewart DG8 6LW ELyons@churchofscotland.org.uk	01671 404425

Portpatrick See Inch
Sorbie See Kirkinner
Stoneykirk See Kirkmaiden

Stranraer: High Kirk (H)

Vacant			Stoneleigh, Whitehouse Road, Stranraer DG9 0JB	01776 700616

Stranraer: Trinity See Inch
Whithorn: St Ninian's Priory See Glasserton and Isle of Whithorn
Wigtown See Kirkcowan

Baker, Carolyn M. (Mrs) BD	1997 2008	(Ochiltree with Stair)	Clanary, 1 Maxwell Drive, Newton Stewart DG8 6EL cncbaker@btinternet.com	
Cairns, Alexander B. MA	1957 2009	(Turin)	Beechwood, Main Street, Sandhead, Stranraer DG9 9JG dorothycairns@aol.com	01776 830389
Sheppard, Michael J. BD	1987 2016	(Ervie, Kirkcolm with Leswalt)	4 Mill Street, Drummore, Stranraer DG9 9PS michaelsheppard00@gmail.com	01776 840369

(10) AYR

Meets in the Carrick Centre, Maybole (except as shown), on the first Tuesday of September , the fourth Tuesday of October (in Girvan: North), the first Tuesday of December, (2019) the first Tuesday of March, the first Tuesday of May, and the third Tuesday of June (in the Moderator's church). A conference is held in January.

| Clerk: | REV. KENNETH C. ELLIOTT BD BA CertMin | 68 St Quivox Road, Prestwick KA9 1JF
ayr@churchofscotland.org.uk | 01292 478788 |
| Presbytery Office: | | Prestwick South Parish Church, 50 Main Street, Prestwick KA9 1NX | 01292 678556 |

Alloway (H)
Neil A. McNaught BD MA — 1987 1999 — 1A Parkview, Alloway, Ayr KA7 4QG — 01292 441252
NMcNaught@churchofscotland.org.uk

Annbank (H) linked with Tarbolton
Vacant
Session Clerk, Annbank: Audrey Brown (Mrs) — The Manse, Tarbolton, Mauchline KA5 5QL — 01292 540969
Session Clerk, Tarbolton: Maureen McNae (Mrs) — Thebroonsat53@aol.com
Maureen@mcnae.net

Auchinleck (H) linked with Catrine
Stephen F. Clipston MA BD — 1982 2006 — 28 Mauchline Road, Auchinleck KA18 2BN — 01290 424776
SClipston@churchofscotland.org.uk

Ayr: Auld Kirk of Ayr (St John the Baptist) (H)
David R. Gemmell MA BD — 1991 1999 — 58 Monument Road, Ayr KA7 2UB — Tel/Fax 01292 262580
DGemmell@churchofscotland.org.uk

Ayr: Castlehill (H)
Vacant
Session Clerk: Douglas Owens — 3 Old Hillfoot Road, Ayr KA7 3LW — 01292 263001
jdoayr@aol.com

Ayr: Newton Wallacetown (H)
Abi T. Ngunga GTh LTh MDiv MTh PhD — 2001 2014 — 9 Nursery Grove, Ayr KA7 3PH — 01292 264251
ANgunga@churchofscotland.org.uk

Ayr: St Andrew's (H)
Vacant
Session Clerk: Ian Lamberton   Ian.lamberton@outlook.com

Ayr: St Columba (H)
Fraser R. Aitken MA BD   1978 1991   3 Upper Crofts, Alloway, Ayr KA7 4QX   01292 443747
                                           FAitken@churchofscotland.org.uk

Ayr: St James' (H)
Barbara V. Suchanek-Seitz CertMin DTh   2016   1 Prestwick Road, Ayr KA8 8LD   01292 262420
                                                BSuchanek-Seitz@churchofscotland.org.uk

Ayr: St Leonard's (H) linked with Dalrymple
Brian R. Hendrie BD   1992 2015   35 Roman Road, Ayr KA7 3SZ   01292 283825
                                           BHendrie@churchofscotland.org.uk

Ayr: St Quivox (H)
Vacant
Session Clerk: 11 Springfield Avenue, Prestwick KA9 2HA 01292 478306

Ballantrae (H) linked with St Colmon (Arnsheen Barrhill and Colmonell)
Vacant   The Manse, 1 The Vennel, Ballantrae, Girvan KA26 0NH   01465 831252
                                           clairestrain@live.co.uk
Session Clerk, Ballantrae: Claire Strain (Mrs)
Session Clerk, St Colmon: Claire Pirrie (Mrs)   stcolmon.sessionclerk@gmail.com

Barr linked with Dailly linked with Girvan: South
Ian K. McLachlan MA BD   1999   30 Henrietta Street, Girvan KA26 9AL   01465 713370
                                           IMcLachlan@churchofscotland.org.uk

Catrine See Auchinleck

Coylton linked with Drongan: The Schaw Kirk
Vacant   4 Hamilton Place, Coylton, Ayr KA6 6JQ   01292 571442
Douglas T. Moore   2003 2015   9 Midton Avenue, Prestwick KA9 1PU   01292 671352
(Auxiliary Minister)   DMoore@churchofscotland.org.uk

Craigie Symington linked with Prestwick South (H)
Kenneth C. Elliott BD BA Cert Min   1989   office@pwksouth.plus.com
                                                          68 St Quivox Road, Prestwick KA9 1JF   01292 478788
                                                          KElliott@churchofscotland.org.uk

Tom McLeod   2014 2015   3 Martnaham Drive, Coylton KA6 6JE   01292 570100
(Ordained Local Minister)   TMcleod@churchofscotland.org.uk

Crosshill (H) linked with Maybole
Vacant   The Manse, 16 McAdam Way, Maybole KA19 8FD   01655 883710
Session Clerk, Crosshill: Jackie Dunlop (Mr)   01655 889948
Session Clerk, Maybole: Allan Hutchison   ahutchison185@yahoo.com   01655 882469

Dailly See Barr

Dalmellington linked with Patna Waterside
Vacant   2016   4 Carsphairn Road, Dalmellington, Ayr KA6 7RE   01292 551503
Morag Crossan BA   1A Church Hill, Dalmellington KA26 9AN   07861 736071
(Ordained Local Minister)   MCrossan@churchofscotland.org.uk

Dalrymple See Ayr: St Leonard's
Drongan: The Schaw Kirk See Coylton

Dundonald (H)
Vacant   64 Main Street, Dundonald, Kilmarnock KA2 9HG   01563 850243
Session Clerk: Pam Kavanagh   RKavampsev@aol.com   01563 850976

Fisherton (H) linked with Kirkoswald (H)
Ian R. Stirling BSc BD MTh MSc   1990 2016   The Manse, Kirkoswald, Maybole KA19 8HZ   01655 760532
                                                          IStirling@churchofscotland.org.uk

Girvan: North (Old and St Andrew's) (H)
Richard G. Moffat BD   1994 2013   38 The Avenue, Girvan KA26 9DS   01465 713203
                                                          RMoffat@churchofscotland.org.uk

Girvan: South See Barr

Kirkmichael linked with Straiton: St Cuthbert's
W. Gerald Jones MA BD MTh   1984   1985   The Manse, Patna Road, Kirkmichael, Maybole   KA19 7PJ   01655 750286
                                                                                   WJones@churchofscotland.org.uk

Kirkoswald See Fisherton

Lugar linked with Old Cumnock: Old (H)
John W. Paterson BSc BD DipEd   1994   33 Barrhill Road, Cumnock KA18 1PJ   01290 420769
                                                                                   JPaterson@churchofscotland.org.uk

Mauchline (H) linked with Sorn
David A. Albon BA MCS   1991   2011   4 Westside Gardens, Mauchline   KA5 5DJ   01290 518528
                                                                                   DAlbon@churchofscotland.org.uk

Maybole See Crosshill

Monkton and Prestwick: North (H)
David Clarkson BSc BA MTh   2010   40 Monkton Road, Prestwick KA9 1AR   01292 471379
                                                                                   DClarkson@churchofscotland.org.uk

Muirkirk (H) linked with Old Cumnock: Trinity
Vacant   46 Ayr Road, Cumnock KA18 1DW   01290 422145
Session Clerk, Muirkirk: Sylvia McGlynn (Miss)   hiddendepths@hotmail.com   01290 661203
Session Clerk, Trinity: Kay Mitchell (Mrs)   kaymitch14@sky.com   01290 424919

New Cumnock (H)
Helen E. Cuthbert MA MSc BD   2009   37 Castle, New Cumnock, Cumnock KA18 4AG   01290 338296
                                                                                   HCuthbert@churchofscotland.org.uk

Ochiltree linked with Stair
Morag Garrett (Mrs) BD   2011   2017   10 Mauchline Road, Ochiltree, Cumnock KA18 2PZ   01290 700365
                                                                                   MGarrett@churchofscotland.org.uk

Old Cumnock: Old See Lugar
Old Cumnock: Trinity See Muirkirk
Patna Waterside See Dalmellington

Prestwick: Kingcase (H)
Ian Wiseman BTh DipHSW   1993   2015   office@kingcase.freeserve.co.uk
15 Bellrock Avenue, Prestwick KA9 1SQ
IWiseman@churchofscotland.org.uk   01292 479571

Prestwick: St Nicholas' (H)
George R. Fiddes BD   1979   1985   3 Bellevue Road, Prestwick KA9 1NW
GFiddes@churchofscotland.org.uk   01292 477613

Prestwick: South See Craigie Symington
St Colmon (Arnsheen Barrhill and Colmonell) See Ballantrae
Sorn See Mauchline
Stair See Ochiltree
Straiton: St Cuthbert's See Kirkmichael
Tarbolton See Annbank

Troon: Old (H)
David B. Prentice-Hyers BA MDiv   2003   2013   85 Bentinck Drive, Troon KA10 6HZ
DPrentice-Hyers@churchofscotland.org.uk   01292 313644

Troon: Portland (H)
Vacant
Session Clerk: John Reid   89 South Beach, Troon KA10 6HX
session@troonportlandchurch.org.uk   01292 318929
01292 314475

Troon: St Meddan's (H)
Derek A. Peat BA BD MTh   2013   st.meddan@virgin.net
27 Bentinck Drive, Troon KA10 6HX
DPeat@churchofscotland.org.uk   01292 319163

James Hogg   2018   james.hogg@me.com
(Ordained Local Minister)

Anderson, Robert A. MA BD DPhil	1980	2017	(Blackburn and Seafield)	Aiona, 8 Old Auchans View, Dundonald KA2 9EX robertanderson307@btinternet.com	01563 850554 07484 206190
Birse, G. Stewart CA BD BSc	1980	2013	(Ayr: Newton Wallacetown)	9 Calvinston Road, Prestwick KA9 2EL stewart.birse@gmail.com	01292 474556
Blackshaw, Christopher J. BA(Theol) Chris Blackshaw is a Methodist Minister	2015	2017	Pioneer Minister, Farming Community	Livestock Auction Mart, Whitefordhill, Ayr KA6 5JW CBlackshaw@churchofscotland.org.uk	01292 262241 07989 100818
Blyth, James G.S. BSc BD	1963	1986	(Glenmuick)	40 Robsland Avenue, Ayr KA7 2RW	01292 261276
Bogle, Thomas C. BD	1983	2003	(Fisherton with Maybole: West)	38 McEwan Crescent, Mossblown., Ayr KA6 5DR	01292 521215

Name			Description	Address	Phone
Brown, Jack M. BSc BD	1977	2012	(Applegarth, Sibbaldbie and Johnstone with Lochmaben)	69 Berelands Road, Prestwick KA9 1ER jackm.brown@tiscali.co.uk	01292 477151
Crichton, James MA BD MTh	1969	2010	(Crosshill with Dalrymple)	54 Dalblair Court, Ayr KA7 1UT crichton.james@btinternet.com	07464 675434
Crumlish, Elizabeth A. BD	1995	2015	Path of Renewal Co-ordinator	53 Ayr Road, Prestwick KA9 1SY ECrumlish@churchofscotland.org.uk	
Dickie, Michael M. BSc	1955	1994	(Ayr: Castlehill)	8 Noltmire Road, Ayr KA8 9ES	01292 618512
Geddes, Alexander J. MA BD	1960	1998	(Stewarton: St Columba's)	2 Gregory Street, Mauchline KA5 6BY sandy270736@gmail.com	01290 518597
Gillon, D. Ritchie M. BD DipMin	1994	2017	(Paisley: St Luke's)	12 Fellhill street. Ayr KA7 3JF revgillon@hotmail.com	01292 270018
Glencross, William M. LTh	1968	1999	(Bellshill: Macdonald Memorial)	1 Lochay Place, Troon KA10 7HH	01292 317097
Grant, J. Gordon MA BD PhD	1957	1997	(Edinburgh: Dean)	33 Fullarton Drive, Troon KA10 6LE	01292 311852
Guthrie, James A.	1969	2005	(Corsock and Kirkpatrick Durham with Crossmichael and Parton)	2 Barrhill Road, Pinwherry, Girvan KA26 0QE p.h.m.guthrie@btinternet.com	01465 841236
Hannah, William BD MCAM MIPR	1987	2001	(Muirkirk)	8 Dovecote View, Kirkintilloch, Glasgow G66 3HY carrickhill34@outlook.com	0141 776 1337
Harper, David L. BSc BD	1972	2012	(Troon: St Meddan's)	19 Calder Avenue, Troon KA10 7JT d.l.harper@btinternet.com	01292 312626
Jackson, Nancy		2009	Auxiliary Minister	35 Auchentrae Crescent, Ayr KA7 4BD nancyjaxon@btinternet.com	01292 262034
Johnston, William R. BD	1998	2016	(Ochiltree linked with Stair)	30 Annfield Glen Road, Ayr KA7 3RP	01292 282663
Keating, Glenda K. (Mrs) MTh	1996	2015	(Craigie Symington)	8 Wardlaw Gardens, Irvine KA11 2EW kirkglen@btinternet.com	01294 218820
Laing, Iain A. MA BD	1971	2009	(Bishopbriggs: Kenmuir)	9 Annfield Road, Prestwick KA9 1PP iandrlaing@yahoo.co.uk	01292 471732
Lennox, Lawrie I. MA BD DipEd	1991	2006	(Cromar)	7 Carwinshoch View. Ayr KA7 4AY lennox127@btinternet.com	01292 288658
Lochrie, John S. BSc BD MTh PhD	1967	2008	(St Colmon)	Cosyglen, Kilkerran, Maybole KA19 8LS	01465 811262
McGurk, Andrew F. BD	1983	2011	(Largs: St John's)	15 Fraser Avenue, Troon KA10 6XF afmcg.largs@talk21.com	01292 676008
McIntyre, Allan G. BD	1985	2017	(Greenock: St Ninian's)	9a Templehill, Troon KA10 6BQ agmcintyre@lineone.net	07876 445626
McNidder, Roderick H. BD	1987	1997	Chaplain: NHS Ayrshire and Arran Trust	6 Hollow Park, Alloway, Ayr KA7 4SR roddymcnidder@sky.com	01292 442554
McPhail, Andrew M. BA	1968	2002	(Ayr: Wallacetown)	25 Maybole Road, Ayr KA7 2QA	01292 282108
MacPherson, Gordon C. MA BD MTh	1963	1988	(Associate, Kilmarnock: Henderson)	6 Crosbie Place, Troon KA10 6EY ggmacpherson@btinternet.com	01292 679146
Matthews, John C. MA BD OBE	1992	2010	(Glasgow: Ruchill Kelvinside)	12 Arrol Drive, Ayr KA7 4AF mejohnmatthews@gmail.com	01292 264382
Mayes, Robert BD	1982	2017	(Dundonald)	Garfield Cottage, Som Road, Mauchline KA5 6HQ bobmayes3@gmail.com	01290 519869

Name			Charge	Address	Phone
Milliken, Jamie BD RN	2005	2018	Royal Naval Chaplain	1 Westward Way, Barassie, Troon KA10 6TX	07929 349045
Morrison, Alistair H. BTh DipYCS	1985	2004	(Paisley: St Mark's Oldhall)	92 St Leonard's Road, Ayr KA7 2PU alistairmorrison@gmail.com	01292 266021
Ness, David T. LTh	1972	2008	(Ayr: St Quivox)	17 Winston Avenue, Prestwick KA9 2EZ dtness@gmail.com	01292 471625
Ogston, Edgar J. BSc BD	1976	2017	(North West Lochaber)	14 North Park Avenue, Girvan KA26 9DH edgar.ogston@macfish.com	01465 713081
Rae, Scott M. MBE BD CPS	1976	2016	(Muirkirk with Old Cumnock: Trinity)	2 Primrose Place, Kilmarnock KA1 2RR scottrae1@btopenworld.com	01563 532711
Russell, Paul R. MA BD	1984	2006	Hospital Chaplain, NHS Ayrshire and Arran	23 Nursery Wynd, Ayr KA7 3NZ russellpr@btinternet.com	01292 618020
Sanderson, Alastair M. BA LTh	1971	2007	(Craigie with Symington)	26 Main Street, Monkton, Prestwick KA9 2QL alel@sanderson29.fsnet.co.uk	01292 475819
Simpson, Edward V. BSc BD	1972	2009	(Glasgow: Giffnock South)	8 Paddock View, Thorntoun, Crosshouse, Kilmarnock KA2 0BH eddie.simpson3@talktalk.net	01563 522841
Symington, Alastair H. MA BD	1972	2012	(Troon: Old)	1 Cavendish Place, Troon KA10 6JG revdahs@virginmedia.com	01292 312556
Young, Rona M. (Mrs) BD DipEd	1991	2015	(Ayr: St Quivox)	16 Macintyre Road, Prestwick KA9 1BE revronyoung@hotmail.com	01292 471982
Yorke, Kenneth B.	1982	2009	(Dalmellington with Patna Waterside)	13 Annfield Terrace, Prestwick KA9 1PS kenyorke@yahoo.com	01292 670476

AYR ADDRESSES

Ayr
Auld Kirk	Kirkport (116 High Street)
Castlehill	Castlehill Road x Hillfoot Road
Newton Wallacetown	Main Street
St Andrew's	Park Circus
St Columba	Midton Road x Carrick Park
St James'	Prestwick Road x Falkland Park Road
St Leonard's	St Leonard's Road x Monument Road

Girvan
North	
South	Montgomerie Street Stair Park

Prestwick
Kingcase	Waterloo Road
Monkton and Prestwick North	Monkton Road
St Nicholas	Main Street
South	Main Street

Troon
Old	Ayr Street
Portland	St Meddan's Street
St Meddan's	St Meddan's Street

(11) IRVINE AND KILMARNOCK

The Presbytery meets at 7:00pm in the Howard Centre, Portland Road, Kilmarnock, on the first Tuesday in September, December and March and on the fourth Tuesday in June for ordinary business, and at different locations on the first Tuesday in October, November, February and May for mission. The September meeting commences with the celebration of Holy Communion.

Clerk:	REV. H. TAYLOR BROWN BD CertMin	14 McLelland Drive, Kilmarnock KA1 1SE	01563 529920 (Home)	
		HBrown@churchofscotland.org.uk		
Depute Clerk:	VERY REV. WILLIAM HEWITT BD DipPS	60 Woodlands Grove, Kilmarnock KA3 1TZ	01563 533312 (Home)	
		billhewitt1@btinternet.com		
Presbytery Office:		Howard Centre, 5 Portland Road, Kilmarnock KA1 2BT	01563 526295 (Office)	
		irvinekilmarnock@churchofscotland.org.uk		

The Presbytery office is staffed each Tuesday, Wednesday and Thursday from 9am until 12:30pm.

Ayrshire Mission to the Deaf				
Richard C. Durno DSW CQSW	1989	2013	31 Springfield Road, Bishopbriggs, Glasgow G64 1PJ	(Voice/Text/Fax) 0141 772 1052
			richard.durno@btinternet.com	(Voice/Text/Voicemail) (Mbl) 07748 607721
Caldwell linked with Dunlop				
Alison McBrier MA BD	2011	2017	4 Dampark, Dunlop, Kilmarnock KA3 4BZ	01560 673686
			AMcBrier@churchofscotland.org.uk	
Crosshouse (H)				
T. Edward Marshall BD	1987	2007	27 Kilmarnock Road, Crosshouse, Kilmarnock KA2 0EZ	01563 524089
			TMarshall@churchofscotland.org.uk	
Darvel				
Vacant			46 West Main Street, Darvel KA17 0AQ	
Dreghorn and Springside				
Vacant				
Dunlop See Caldwell				
Fenwick (H) linked with Kilmarnock: Riccarton (H)				
Colin A. Strong BSc BD	1989	2007	2 Jasmine Road, Kilmarnock KA1 2HD	01563 549490
			CStrong@churchofscotland.org.uk	

Galston (H)
Kristina I. Hine BS MDiv   2011   2016
60 Brewland Street, Galston KA4 8DX
KHine@churchofscotland.org.uk
01563 820136
01563 821549

Hurlford (H)
Ada V. MacLeod MA BD PGCE   2013   2018
12 Main Road, Crookedholm, Kilmarnock KA3 6JT
AVMacLeod@churchofscotland.org.uk
01563 539739

Irvine: Fullarton (H) (www.fullartonchurch.co.uk)
Neil Urquhart BD DipMin   1989
48 Waterside, Irvine KA12 8QJ
NUrquhart@churchofscotland.org.uk
01294 279909

Irvine: Girdle Toll (H) (www.girdletoll.fsbusiness.co.uk) linked with Irvine: St Andrew's (H) (01294 276051)
Ian W. Benzie BD   1999   2008
St Andrew's Manse, 206 Bank Street, Irvine KA12 0YD
Ian.Benzie@churchofscotland.org.uk
01294 216139

Irvine: Mure (H)
Vacant
9 West Road, Irvine KA12 8RE
01294 279916

Irvine: Old (H)
Vacant
22 Kirk Vennel, Irvine KA12 0DQ
01294 273503
01294 279265

Irvine: Relief Bourtreehill (H)
Vacant
4 Kames Court, Irvine KA11 1RT
01294 216939

Irvine: St Andrew's (H) See Irvine: Girdle Toll

Kilmarnock: Kay Park (H) (www.kayparkparishchurch.co.uk)
Vacant
52 London Road, Kilmarnock KA3 7AJ
01563 574106
01563 523113 Tel/Fax

Kilmarnock: New Laigh Kirk (H)
David S. Cameron BD   2001   2009
1 Holmes Farm Road, Kilmarnock KA1 1TP
David.Cameron@churchofscotland.org.uk
01563 525416

Kilmarnock: Riccarton See Fenwick

Kilmarnock: St Andrew's and St Marnock's
James McNaughtan BD DipMin — 1983 — 2008 — 35 South Gargieston Drive, Kilmarnock KA1 1TB — JMcNaughtan@churchofscotland.org.uk — 01563 521665

Kilmarnock: St John's Onthank (H)
Allison E. Becker BA MDiv — 2015 — 2017 — 84 Wardneuk Drive, Kilmarnock KA3 2EX — ABecker@churchofscotland.org.uk — 07716 162380

Kilmarnock: St Kentigern's (www.stkentigern.org.uk)
Vacant — 1 Thirdpart Place, Kilmarnock KA1 1UL — 01563 571280

Kilmarnock: South
H. Taylor Brown BD CertMin — 1997 — 2012 — 14 McLelland Drive, Kilmarnock KA1 1SE — HBrown@churchofscotland.org.uk — **01563 524705** / 01563 529920

Kilmaurs: St Maur's Glencairn (H)
John A. Urquhart BD — 1993 — 9 Standalane, Kilmaurs, Kilmarnock KA3 2NB — John.Urquhart@churchofscotland.org.uk — 01563 538289

Newmilns: Loudoun (H)
Vacant — Loudoun Manse, 116A Loudoun Road, Newmilns KA16 9HH — 01560 320174

Stewarton: John Knox
Gavin A. Niven BSc MSc BD — 2010 — 27 Avenue Street, Stewarton, Kilmarnock KA3 5AP — GNiven@churchofscotland.org.uk — 01560 482418

Stewarton: St Columba's (H)
Vacant — 1 Kirk Glebe, Stewarton, Kilmarnock KA3 5BJ — 01560 485113

Name			Charge	Address	Phone
Black, Andrew R. BD	1987	2018	(Irvine Relief Bourtreehill)	4 Nursery Wynd, Kilwinning KA13 6ER	
Brockie, Colin G.F. BSc(Eng) BD SOSc	1967	2007	(Presbytery Clerk, Irvine and Kilmarnock)	36 Braehead Court, Kilmarnock KA3 7AB colin@brockie.org.uk	01563 559960
Campbell, John A. JP FIEM	1984	1998	(Irvine: St Andrew's)	Flowerdale, Balmoral Road, Rattray, Blairgowrie PH10 7AF extrevjack@aol.com	01250 872795
Cant, Thomas M. MA BD	1964	2004	(Paisley: Laigh Kirk)	3 Meikle Cutstraw, Stewarton, Kilmarnock KA3 5HU revtmcant@aol.com	01560 480566
Christie, Robert S. MA BD ThM	1964	2001	(Kilmarnock: West High)	24 Homeroyal House, 2 Chalmers Crescent, Edinburgh EH9 1TP	

Name	Years	Charge	Address / Email	Telephone
Clancy, P. Jill (Mrs) BD DipMin	2000 2017	Prison Chaplain, HMP Barlinnie and HMP Kilmarnock	27 Cross Street, Galston KA4 8AA jgibson@totalise.co.uk	07956 557087
Davidson, James BD DipAFH	1989 2002	(Wishaw: Old)	13 Redburn Place, Irvine KA12 9BQ	01294 312515
Garrity, T. Alan W. BSc BD MTh	1969 2008	(Bermuda)	17 Solomon's View, Dunlop, Kilmarnock KA3 4ES alangarrity@btinternet.com	01560 486879
Gillon, C. Blair BD	1975 2007	(Glasgow: Ibrox)	East Muirshiel Farmhouse, Dunlop, Kilmarnock KA3 4EJ charlesgillon21@gmail.com	01560 483778
Godfrey, Linda BSc BD	2012 2014	(Ayr: St Leonard's with Dalrymple)	9 Taybank Drive, Ayr KA7 4RL godfreykayak@aol.com	07825 663866
Hall, William M. BD	1972 2010	(Kilmarnock: Old High Kirk)	33 Cairns Terrace, Kilmarnock KA1 2JG revwillie@talktalk.net	01563 525080
Hare, Malcolm M.W. BA BD	1956 1994	(Kilmarnock: St Kentigern's)	Flat 5, The Courtyard, Auchlochan, Lesmahagow, Lanark ML11 0GS	
Hewitt, William C. BD DipPS	1977 2012	(Presbytery Clerk: Glasgow)	60 Woodlands Grove, Kilmarnock KA3 1TZ billhewitt1@btinternet.com	01563 533312
Horsburgh, Gary E. BA	1977 2015	(Dreghorn and Springside)	1 Woodlands Grove, Kilmarnock KA3 1TY garyhorsburgh@hotmail.co.uk	01563 624508
Hosain Lamarti, Samuel BD MTh PhD	1979 2006	(Stewarton: John Knox)	7 Dalwhinnie Crescent, Kilmarnock KA3 1QS samlamar@pobroadband.co.uk	01563 529632
Huggett, Judith A. (Miss) BA BD	1990 1998	Lead Chaplain, NHS Ayrshire and Arran	4 Westmoor Crescent, Kilmarnock KA1 1TX judith.huggett@aaaht.scotnhs.uk	
Lacy, David BA BD Dlitt DL	1976 2017	(Kilmarnock: Kay Park)	4 Cairns Terrace, Kilmarnock KA1 2JG DLacy@churchofscotland.org.uk	01563 624034 0797 476 0272
Lind, George K. BD MCIBS	1998 2017	(Stewarton: St. Columba's)	Endrig, 98 Loudoun Road, Newmilns KA16 9HQ gklind@gmail.com	07872 051432
McAllister, Anne C. BSc DipEd CCS	2013 2016	(Ordained Local Minister)	39 Bowes Rigg, Stewarton, Kilmarnock KA3 5EN AMcAllister@churchofscotland.org.uk	01560 483191
McCulloch, James D. BD MIOP MIP3 FSAScot	1996 2016	(Hurlford)	18 Edradour Place, Dunsmuir Park, Kilmarnock KA3 1US mccullochmanse1@btinternet.com	01563 535833
MacLeod, Malcolm (Calum) BA BD	1979 2018	(Rutherglen: Old)	12 Main Road, Crookedholm, Kilmarnock KA3 6JT	01563 539739
Scott, Thomas T.	1968 1989	(Kilmarnock: St Marnock's)	6 North Hamilton Place, Kilmarnock KA1 2QN tomtscott@btinternet.com	01563 531415
Shaw, Catherine A.M. MA	1998 2006	(Auxiliary Minister)	40 Merrygreen Place, Stewarton, Kilmarnock KA3 5EP catherine.shaw@tesco.net	01560 483352
Urquhart, Barbara (Mrs) DCS	1986 2017	(Deacon)	9 Standalane, Kilmaurs, Kilmarnock KA3 2NB barbaraurquhart1@gmail.com	01563 538289
Wark, Alexander C. MA BD STM	1982 2017	(Mid Deeside)	43 Mure Avenue, Kilmarnock KA 3 1TT alecwark@yahoo.co.uk	01563 559581
Watt, Kim	2015	Ordained Local Minister, Presbytery	Reddans Park Gate, The Crescent, Stewarton, Kilmarnock KA3 5AY KWatt@churchofscotland.org.uk	01560 482267
Welsh, Alex M. MA BD	1979 2007	Hospital Chaplain, NHS Ayrshire and Arran	8 Greenside Avenue, Prestwick KA9 2HB alexandevelyn@hotmail.com	01292 475341

IRVINE and KILMARNOCK ADDRESSES

Irvine
Dreghorn and Springside	Townfoot x Station Brae	Relief Bourtreehill	Crofthead, Bourtreehill	Riccarton	Old Street
Fullarton	Marress Road x Church Street	St Andrew's	Caldon Road x Oaklands Ave	St Andrew's and St Marnock's	St Marnock Street
Girdle Toll	Bryce Knox Court	**Kilmarnock**		St John's Onthank	84 Wardneuk Street
Mure	West Road	Ayrshire Mission to the Deaf		St Kentigern's	Dunbar Drive
Old	Kirkgate	Kay Park	10 Clark Street	South	Whatriggs Road
		New Laigh Kirk	London Road John Dickie Street		

(12) ARDROSSAN

Meets at Ardrossan and Saltcoats: Kirkgate, on the first Tuesday of February, March, May, September, October, November and December; and on the second Tuesday of June.

Clerk:	MRS JEAN C. Q. HUNTER BD		The Manse, Shiskine, Isle of Arran KA27 8EP ardrossan@churchofscotland.org.uk	**01770 860380** 07961 299907

Ardrossan: Park

Tanya J. Webster BCom DipAcc BD	2011	35 Ardneil Court, Ardrossan KA22 7NQ TWebster@churchofscotland.org.uk	**01294 463711** 01294 538903

Ardrossan and Saltcoats: Kirkgate (H) (www.kirkgate.org.uk)

Vacant		10 Seafield Drive, Ardrossan KA22 8NU	**01294 472001** 01294 463571

Beith (H)

Roderick I.T. MacDonald BD CertMin	1992 2005	2 Glebe Court, Beith KA15 1ET RMacDonald@churchofscotland.org.uk	**01505 502686** 01505 503858
Fiona Blair DCS	1994 2015	9 West Road, Irvine KA12 8RE FBlair@churchofscotland.org.uk	07495 673428

Brodick linked with Corrie linked with Lochranza and Pirnmill linked with Shiskine (H)

R. Angus Adamson BD	2006	4 Manse Crescent, Brodick, Isle of Arran KA27 8AS RAdamson@churchofscotland.org.uk	01770 302334

Corrie See Brodick

Cumbrae linked with Largs: St John's (H)
Jonathan C. Fleming MA BD   2012   2017   1 Newhaven Grove, Largs KA30 8NS   01475 **674468**
JFleming@churchofscotland.org.uk   01475 329933

Dalry: St Margaret's
Vacant
Marion L.K. Howie (Mrs) MA ARCS   1992   2016   33 Templand Crescent, Dalry KA24 5EZ   01294 **832264**
(Auxiliary Minister)   51 High Road, Stevenston KA20 3DY   01294 832747
MHowie@churchofscotland.org.uk   01294 466571

Dalry: Trinity (H)
Martin Thomson BSc DipEd BD   1988   2004   Trinity Manse, West Kilbride Road, Dalry KA24 5DX   01294 832363
MThomson@churchofscotland.org.uk

Fairlie (H) linked with Largs: St Columba's
Vacant   14 Fairlieburne Gardens, Fairlie, Largs KA29 0ER   01475 **686212**
01475 568515

Kilbirnie: Auld Kirk (H)
Vacant   49 Holmhead, Kilbirnie KA25 6BS   01505 682342

Kilbirnie: St Columba's (H)
Fiona C. Ross (Miss) BD DipMin   1996   2004   Manse of St Columba's, Dipple Road, Kilbirnie KA25 7JU   01505 **685239**
FRoss@churchofscotland.org.uk   01505 683342

Kilmory linked with Lamlash
Lily F. McKinnon (Mrs) MA BD PGCE   1993   2015   The Manse, Lamlash, Isle of Arran KA27 8LE   01770 600074
LMcKinnon@churchofscotland.org.uk

Kilwinning: Mansefield Trinity
Hilary Beresford BD   2000   2018   47 Meadowfoot Road, West Kilbride KA23 9BU   01294 **550746**
HBeresford@churchofscotland.org.uk   01294 822224

Kilwinning: Old
Jeanette Whitecross BD   2002   2011   54 Dalry Road, Kilwinning KA13 7HE   01294 552606
JWhitecross@churchofscotland.org.uk

Isobel Beck BD DCS   2014   2016   16 Patrick Avenue, Stevenston KA20 4AW   07919 193425
IBeck@churchofscotland.org.uk

Lamlash See Kilmory

Largs: Clark Memorial (H)
T. David Watson BSc BD   1988   2014   31 Douglas Street, Largs KA30 8PT   **01475 675186**
                                                            DWatson@churchofscotland.org.uk   01475 672370

Largs: St Columba's See Fairlie
Largs: St John's See Cumbrae
Lochranza and Pirnmill See Brodick

Saltcoats: North
Alexander B. Noble MA BD ThM   1982   2003   25 Longfield Avenue, Saltcoats KA21 6DR   **01294 464679**
                                                            ANoble@churchofscotland.org.uk   01294 604923

Saltcoats: St Cuthbert's (H)
Sarah E.C. Nicol (Mrs) BSc BD MTh   1985   2018   10 Kennedy Road, Saltcoats KA21 5SF   01294 696030
                                                            SNicol@churchofscotland.org.uk

Shiskine See Brodick

Stevenston: Ardeer linked with Stevenston: Livingstone (H)
David A. Sutherland BD   2001   2017   8 Priest Hill View, Stevenston KA20 4AT   01294 608993
                                                            DSutherland@churchofscotland.org.uk

Stevenston: High (H) (www.highkirk.com)
M. Scott Cameron MA BD   2002   Glencairn Street, Stevenston KA20 3DL   01294 463356
                                                            Scott.Cameron@churchofscotland.org.uk

Stevenston: Livingstone See Stevenston: Ardeer

West Kilbride (H) (www.westkilbrideparishchurch.org.uk)
James J. McNay MA BD   2008   The Manse, Goldenberry Avenue, West Kilbride KA23 9LJ   01294 823186
                                                            JMcNay@churchofscotland.org.uk
Mandy R. Hickman RGN   2013   2014   Lagnaleon, 4 Wilson Street, Largs KA30 9AQ   01475 675347
(Ordained Local Minister)   MHickman@churchofscotland.org.uk   07743 760792

Whiting Bay and Kildonan
Elizabeth R.L. Watson (Miss) BA BD — 1981 1982 — The Manse, Whiting Bay, Brodick, Isle of Arran KA27 8RE
EWatson@churchofscotland.org.uk — 01770 700289

Name			(Charge)	Address	Tel
Cruickshank, Norman BA BD	1983	2006	(West Kilbride: Overton)	24D Faulds Wynd, Seamill, West Kilbride KA23 9FA	01294 822239
Davidson, Amelia (Mrs) BD	2004	2011	(Coatbridge: Calder)	11 St Mary's Place, Saltcoats KA21 5NY	
Drysdale, James H. LTh	1987	2006	(Blackbraes and Shieldhill)	10 John Clark Street, Largs KA30 9AH	01475 674870
Falconer, Alan D. MA BD DLitt DD	1972	2011	(Aberdeen: St Machar's Cathedral)	18 North Crescent Road, Ardrossan KA22 8NA alanfalconer@gmx.com	01294 472991
Finlay, William P. MA BD	1968	2000	(Glasgow: Townhead Blochairm)	High Corrie, Brodick, Isle of Arran KA27 8JB	01770 810689
Ford, Alan A. BD	1977	2013	(Glasgow: Springburn)	14 Corsankell Wynd, Saltcoats KA21 6HY alan.andy@btinternet.com	01294 465740
Gordon, David C.	1953	1988	(Gigha and Cara)	South Beach House, South Crescent Road, Ardrossan KA22 8DU	
Hebenton, David J. MA BD	1958	2002	(Ayton and Burnmouth with Grantshouse and Houndwood and Reston)	22B Faulds Wynd, Seamill, West Kilbride KA23 9FA	01294 829228
McCallum, Alexander D. BD	1987	2005	(Saltcoats: New Trinity)	59 Woodcroft Avenue, Largs KA30 9EW sandyandjose@madasafish.com	01475 670133
McCance, Andrew M. BSc	1986	1995	(Coatbridge: Middle)	6A Douglas Place, Largs KA30 8PU	01475 673303
Mackay, Marjory H. (Mrs) BD DipEd CCE	1998	2008	(Cumbrae)	4 Golf Road, Millport, Isle of Cumbrae KA28 0HB marjory.mackay@gmail.com	01475 530388
MacKinnon, Ronald M. DCS	1996	2012	(Deacon)	32 Strathclyde House, Shore Road, Skelmorlie PA17 5AN ronnie@ronniemac.plus.com	01475 521333 07594 427960
MacLeod, Ian LTh BA MTh PhD	1969	2006	(Brodick with Corrie)	Cromla Cottage, Corrie, Isle of Arran KA27 8JB i.macleod829@btinternet.com	01770 810237
Mitchell, D. Ross BA BD	1972	2007	(West Kilbride: St Andrew's)	11 Dunbar Gardens, Saltcoats KA21 6GJ ross.mitchell@virgin.net	
Paterson, John H. BD	1977	2000	(Kirkintilloch: St David's Memorial Park)	Creag Bhan, Golf Course Road, Whiting Bay, Isle of Arran KA27 8QT	01770 700569
Roy, Iain M. MA BD	1960	1997	(Stevenson: Livingstone)	2 The Fieldings, Dunlop, Kilmarnock KA3 4AU	01560 483072
Taylor, Andrew S. BTh FPhS	1959	1992	(Greenock Union)	9 Raillies Avenue, Largs KA30 8QY andrew.taylor_123@btinternet.com	01475 674709
Travers, Robert BA BD	1993	2015	(Irvine Old)	74 Caledonian Road, Stevenston KA20 3LF roberttravers@live.co.uk	01294 279265
Ward, Alan H. MA BD	1978	2013	(Interim Minister)	47 Meadowfoot Road, West Kilbride KA23 9BU	01475 822244 07709 906130

(13) LANARK

Meets on the first Tuesday of February, March, May, September, October, November and December, and on the third Tuesday of June.

Clerk:	REV. BRYAN KERR BA BD	Greyfriars Manse, 3 Bellefield Way, Lanark ML11 7NW lanark@churchofscotland.org.uk www.lanarkpresbytery.org	01555 663363 01555 437050
Depute Clerk:	REV. GEORGE C. SHAND MA BD	16 Abington Road, Symington, Biggar ML12 6JX George.Shand@churchofscotland.org.uk	01899 309400

Biggar (H) linked with Black Mount (www.biggarkirk.btck.co.uk)
Mike Fucella BD MTh   1997   2013   'Candlemas', 6C Leafield Road, Biggar ML12 6AY   01899 229291
MFucella@churchofscotland.org.uk

Black Mount See Biggar

Cairngryffe linked with Libberton and Quothquan (H) linked with Symington (The Tinto Parishes) (www.cairngryffekirk.org.uk; www.libbertonquothquan.org.uk; www.symingtonkirk.com)
George C. Shand MA BD   1981   2014   16 Abington Road, Symington, Biggar ML12 6JX   01899 309400
George.Shand@churchofscotland.org.uk

Carluke: Kirkton (H) www.kirktonchurch.co.uk
Iain D. Cunningham MA BD   1979   1987   9 Station Road, Carluke ML8 5AA   01555 750778
ICunningham@churchofscotland.org.uk   01555 771262

Carluke: St Andrew's (H) (www.carluke-standrewschurch.org)
Helen E. Jamieson (Mrs) BD DipEd   1989   120 Clyde Street, Carluke ML8 5BG   01555 771218
HJamieson@churchofscotland.org.uk

Carluke: St John's (H) (www.carluke-stjohns.org.uk)
Elijah O. Obinna BA MTh PhD   2016   18 Old Bridgend, Carluke ML8 4HN   01555 751730
EObinna@churchofscotland.org.uk   01555 752389

Carnwath (H) linked with Carstairs (carstairschurches.btck.co.uk)
Maudeen I. MacDougall BA BD MTh   1978   2016   11 Range View, Cleghorn, Carstairs, Lanark ML11 8TF   01555 871258
Maudeen.MacDougall@churchofscotland.org.uk

Carstairs See Carnwath

Coalburn and Lesmahagow: Old (H) (www.lopc.org.uk)
Vacant
Session Clerk: Douglas Walsh   9 Elm Bank, Lesmahagow, Lanark ML11 0EA   01555 892425
                                      dougandwilma1@btinternet.com   01555 892848

New charge formed by the union of Coalburn and Lesmahagow: Old

Crossford (H) linked with Kirkfieldbank
Steven Reid BAcc CA BD   1989   1997   74 Lanark Road, Crossford, Carluke ML8 5RE   01555 860415
                                                     SReid@churchofscotland.org.uk

Forth: St Paul's (H) (Website: www.forthstpauls.com)
Elspeth J. MacLean (Mrs) BVMS BD   2011   2015   22 Lea Rig, Forth, Lanark ML11 8EA   01555 728837
                                                          EMacLean@churchofscotland.org.uk

Kirkfieldbank See Crossford

Kirkmuirhill (H) (www.kirkmuirhillchurch.co.uk)
Vacant   The Manse, 2 Lanark Road, Kirkmuirhill, Lanark ML11 9RB   01555 895593
Session Clerk: Catherine Gold (Mrs)   kirkmuirhillchurch@btinternet.com   01555 892409
                                                                                                        01555 893174

Lanark: Greyfriars (www.lanarkgreyfriars.com)
Bryan Kerr BA BD   2002   2007   Greyfriars Manse, 3 Bellefield Way, Lanark ML11 7NW   01555 661510
                                               BKerr@churchofscotland.org.uk   01555 663363

Lanark: St Nicholas' (H) (www.lanark-stnicholas.co.uk)
Louise E. Mackay BSc BD   2017   2 Kaimhill Court, Lanark ML11 9HU   01555 666220
                                                                                       01555 661936

Law (www.lawparishchurch.org.uk)
Paul G.R. Grant BD MTh UKBHC   2003   2018   3 Shawgill Court, Law, Carluke ML8 5SJ   01698 373180
                                                       PGrant@churchofscotland.org.uk

Lesmahagow: Abbeygreen (www.abbeygreen.org.uk)
David S. Carmichael   1982   Abbeygreen Manse, Lesmahagow, Lanark ML11 0DB   01555 893384
                                       David.Carmichael@churchofscotland.org.uk

Libberton and Quothquan See Cairngryffe
Symington See Cairngryffe

The Douglas Valley Church (www.douglasvalleychurch.org)
Vacant
Session Clerk: Andy Robinson

        01555 850000
        01555 851213
        01555 851246

Upper Clyde
Nikki M. Macdonald BD MTh PhD   2014   31 Carlisle Road, Crawford, Biggar ML12 6TP   01864 502139
NMacdonald@churchofscotland.org.uk

Clelland, Elizabeth B. (Mrs) BD	2002	2012	Resident Chaplain, Divine Healing Fellowship (Scotland)	Braehead House Christian Healing and Retreat Centre, Braidwood Road, 01555 860716
				Crossford, Carluke ML8 5NQ
				liz_clelland@yahoo.co.uk
Cowell, Susan G. (Miss) BA BD	1986	1998	(Budapest)	3 Gavel Lane, Regency Gardens, Lanark ML11 9FB 01555 665509
Cutler, James S.H.	1986	2011	(Black Mount with Culter with	12 Kirtlegairy Place, Peebles EH45 9LW 01721 723950
BD CEng MIStructE			Libberton and Quothquan)	revjimc@outlook.com
Findlay, Henry J.W. MA BD	1965	2005	(Wishaw: St Mark's)	2 Alba Gardens, Carluke ML8 5US 01555 759995
				henryfindlay@btinternet.com
Houston, Graham R.	1978	2011	(Cairngryffe with Symington)	3 Alder Lane, Beechtrees, Lanark ML11 9FT 01555 678004
BSc BD MTh PhD				gandih6156@btinternet.com
Seath, Thomas J.G.	1980	1992	(Motherwell: Manse Road)	c/o Orchard Care Home, Crossford, Carluke ML8 5PY
Young, David A.	1972	2003	(Kirkmuirhill)	110 Carlisle Road, Blackwood, Lanark ML11 9RT 01555 893357
				youngdavid@aol.com

(14) GREENOCK AND PAISLEY

Meets on the second Tuesday of September, October, November, December, February, March, April and May, and on the third Tuesday of June.

Clerk: **REV. PETER McENHILL BD PhD**

Presbytery Office: **The Presbytery Office** (see below)
greenockpaisley@churchofscotland.org.uk   **Tel 01505 615033**
'Homelea', Faith Avenue, Quarrier's Village, Bridge of Weir   **Fax 01505 615088**
PA11 3SX

Barrhead: Bourock (H)
Pamela Gordon BD   2006   2014   14 Maxton Avenue, Barrhead, Glasgow G78 1DY   **0141 881 9813**
PGordon@churchofscotland.org.uk   0141 881 8736

Barrhead: St Andrew's (H)
James S.A. Cowan BD DipMin — 1986 1998
10 Arthurlie Avenue, Barrhead, Glasgow G78 2BU
JCowan@churchofscotland.org.uk
0141 881 8442
0141 881 3457

Bishopton (H)
Yvonne Smith BSc BD — 2017
The Manse, Newton Road, Bishopton PA7 5JP
YSmith@churchofscotland.org.uk
01505 862583
01505 862161

Bridge of Weir: Freeland (H)
Kenneth N. Gray BA BD — 1988
15 Lawmarnock Crescent, Bridge of Weir PA11 3AS
aandkgray@btinternet.com
01505 612610
01505 690918

Bridge of Weir: St Machar's Ranfurly
Hanneke Marshall (Mrs) MTh MA PGCE CertMin — 2017
St Andrew's Drive, Bridge of Weir PA11 3SH
Hanneke.Marshall@churchofscotland.org.uk
01505 614364
01505 612975

Elderslie Kirk (H)
Vacant
Interim Moderator: Stephen Smith
282 Main Road, Elderslie, Johnstone PA5 9EF
SSmith@churchofscotland.org.uk
01505 323348
01505 321767
01505 702621

Erskine
Vacant
Interim Moderator: David Stewart
The Manse, 7 Leven Place, Linburn, Erskine PA8 6AS
revdavidst@aol.com
0141 812 4620
0141 570 8103
01475 675159

Gourock: Old Gourock and Ashton (H)
David W.G. Burt BD DipMin — 1989 2014
331 Eldon Street, Gourock PA16 7QN
DBurt@churchofscotland.org.uk
01475 633914

Gourock: St John's (H)
Teri C. Peterson MDiv BMus — 2006 2018
6 Barrhill Road, Gourock PA19 1JX
TPeterson@churchofscotland.org.uk
01475 632143

Greenock: East End linked with Greenock: Mount Kirk
Francis E. Murphy BEng DipDSE BD — 2006
76 Finnart Street, Greenock PA16 8HJ
FMurphy@churchofscotland.org.uk
01475 722338

Greenock: Lyle Kirk

Owen Derrick MDiv MASFL	2007	2016	39 Fox Street, Greenock PA16 8PD ODerrick@churchofscotland.org.uk	01475 717229
Eileen Manson (Mrs) DipCE (Auxiliary Minister)	1994	2014	1 Cambridge Avenue, Gourock PA19 1XT EManson@churchofscotland.org.uk	07840 983657 01475 632401

Greenock: Mount Kirk See Greenock: East End

Greenock: St Margaret's

Morris C. Coull BD	1974	2014	105 Finnart Street, Greenock PA16 8HN MCoull@churchofscotland.org.uk	**01475 781953** 01475 892874

Greenock: St Ninian's

Vacant

Interim Moderator: Karen Harbison — 5 Auchmead Road, Greenock PA16 0PY / KHarbison@churchofscotland.org.uk — 01475 631878 / 01475 721048

Greenock: Wellpark Mid Kirk

Alan K. Sorensen DL BD MTh DipMin FSAScot	1983	2000	101 Brisbane Street, Greenock PA16 8PA ASorensen@churchofscotland.org.uk	01475 721741

Greenock: Westburn

Karen E. Harbison (Mrs) MA BD	1991	2014	50 Ardgowan Street, Greenock PA16 8EP KHarbison@churchofscotland.org.uk	01475 721048

Houston and Killellan (H)

Gary D. Noonan BA	2018		The Manse of Houston, Main Street, Houston, Johnstone PA6 7EL GNoonan@churchofscotland.org.uk	01505 612569

Howwood
Guardianship of the Presbytery

Inchinnan (H)

Ann Knox BD Cert.Healthc.Chap	2017		51 Old Greenock Road, Inchinnan, Renfrew PA4 9PH AKnox@churchofscotland.org.uk	**0141 812 1263** 0141 389 1724 07534 900065

Inverkip (H) linked with Skelmorlie and Wemyss Bay

Archibald Speirs BD	1995	2013	3a Montgomery Terrace, Skelmorlie PA17 5DT ASpeirs@churchofscotland.org.uk	01475 529320

Johnstone: High (H)
Ann C. McCool (Mrs) BD DSD IPA ALCM — 1989 — 2001
76 North Road, Johnstone PA5 8NF
AMcCool@churchofscotland.org.uk
01505 336303
01505 320006

Johnstone: St Andrew's Trinity
Charles M. Cameron BA BD PhD — 1980 — 2013
45 Woodlands Crescent, Johnstone PA5 0AZ
Charles.Cameron@churchofscotland.org.uk
01505 672908

Johnstone: St Paul's (H)
Alistair N. Shaw MA BD MTh PhD — 1982 — 2003
9 Stanley Drive, Brookfield, Johnstone PA5 8UF
Alistair.Shaw@churchofscotland.org.uk
01505 321632
01505 320060

Kilbarchan
Stephen J. Smith BSc BD — 1993 — 2015
The Manse, Church Street, Kilbarchan, Johnstone PA10 2JQ
SSmith@churchofscotland.org.uk
01505 702621

Kilmacolm: Old (H)
Peter McEnhill BD PhD — 1992 — 2007
The Old Kirk Manse, Glencairn Road, Kilmacolm PA13 4NJ
PMcEnhill@churchofscotland.org.uk
01505 873911
01505 873174

Kilmacolm: St Columba (H)
R. Douglas Cranston MA BD — 1986 — 1992
6 Churchill Road, Kilmacolm PA13 4LH
RCranston@churchofscotland.org.uk
01505 873271

Langbank linked with Port Glasgow: St Andrew's (H)
Vacant
Elizabeth Geddes (Mrs) — 2013 — 2017
(Ordained Local Minister)
St Andrew's Manse, Barr's Brae, Port Glasgow PA14 5QA
9 Shillingworth Place, Bridge of Weir PA11 3DY
EGeddes@churchofscotland.org.uk
01475 741486
01505 612639

Linwood (H)
Eileen M. Ross (Mrs) BD MTh — 2005 — 2008
1 John Neilson Avenue, Paisley PA1 2SX
ERoss@churchofscotland.org.uk
01505 328802
0141 887 2801

Lochwinnoch
Guardianship of the Presbytery

Neilston
Fiona E. Maxwell BA BD | 2004 | 2013 | The Manse, Neilston Road, Neilston, Glasgow G78 3NP
FMaxwell@churchofscotland.org.uk | **0141 881 9445**
0141 258 0805

Paisley: Abbey (H)
Alan D. Birss MA BD | 1979 | 1988 | 15 Main Road, Castlehead, Paisley PA2 6AJ
ABirss@churchofscotland.org.uk | **0141 889 7654; Fax 0141 887 3929**
0141 889 3587

Paisley: Glenburn
Vacant
Interim Moderator: Fiona Maxwell | 10 Hawick Avenue, Paisley PA2 9LD
FMaxwell@churchofscotland.org.uk | **0141 884 2602**
0141 884 4903
0141 258 0805

Paisley: Lylesland (H)
Vacant
Interim Moderator: John Murning | 36 Potterhill Avenue, Paisley PA2 8BA
JMurning@churchofscotland.org.uk | **0141 561 7139**
0141 561 9277
0141 316 2678

Paisley: Martyrs' Sandyford
Vacant | 27 Acer Crescent, Paisley PA2 9LR | **0141 889 6603**
0141 884 7400

Paisley: Oakshaw Trinity (H)
Gordon B. Armstrong BD FIAB BRC CertCS | 1998 | 2012 | The Manse, 52 Balgonie Drive, Paisley PA2 9LP
GArmstrong@churchofscotland.org.uk | **0141 887 4647; Fax 0141 848 5139**
0141 587 3124

Oakshaw Trinity is a Local Ecumenical Partnership with the United Reformed Church

Paisley: St Columba Foxbar (H)
Vacant
Interim Moderator: Gordon Armstrong | 13 Corsebar Drive, Paisley PA2 9QD
GArmstrong@churchofscotland.org.uk | **01505 812377**
0141 884 5826
0141 587 3124

Paisley: St Luke's (H)
Vacant
Interim Moderator: William McKaig | 31 Southfield Avenue, Paisley PA2 8BX
bmckaig16@gmail.com | 0141 884 6215
07747 053158

Paisley: St Mark's Oldhall (H)
Vacant | 36 Newtyle Road, Paisley PA1 3JX | **0141 882 2755**
0141 889 4279

Paisley: St Ninian's Ferguslie
Guardianship of the Presbytery
Stuart Stevenson | 2011 | 2017 | 143 Springfield Park, Johnstone PA5 8JT
SStevenson@churchofscotland.org.uk | **0141 887 9436**
0141 886 2131
(Ordained Local Minister)

Paisley: Sherwood Greenlaw (H)
John Murning BD — 1988 — 2014 — 5 Greenlaw Drive, Paisley PA1 3RX — JMurning@churchofscotland.org.uk — **0141 889 7060** / 0141 316 2678

Paisley: Stow Brae Kirk
Robert Craig BA BD DipRS — 2008 — 2012 — 290 Glasgow Road, Paisley PA1 3DP — RCraig@churchofscotland.org.uk — 0141 328 6014

Paisley: Wallneuk North
Peter G. Gill MA BA — 2008 — 5 Glenville Crescent, Paisley PA2 8TW — PGill@churchofscotland.org.uk — **0141 889 9265** / 0141 884 4429

Port Glasgow: Hamilton Bardrainney linked with Port Glasgow: St Martin's
Vacant — 80 Bardrainney Avenue, Port Glasgow PA14 6HD
Interim Moderator: Francis Murphy — FMurphy@churchofscotland.org.uk — 01475 701213 / 01475 722338

Port Glasgow: St Andrew's See Langbank

Port Glasgow: St Martin's See Port Glasgow: Hamilton Bardrainney

Renfrew: North
Philip D. Wallace BSc BTh DTS — 1998 — 2018 — 1 Alexandra Drive, Renfrew PA4 8UB — PWallace@churchofscotland.org.uk — **0141 885 2154** / 0141 886 2074

Renfrew: Trinity (H)
Stuart C. Steell BD CertMin — 1992 — 2015 — 25 Paisley Road, Renfrew PA4 8JH — SSteell@churchofscotland.org.uk — **0141 885 2129** / 0141 387 2464

Skelmorlie and Wemyss Bay See Inverkip

Armstrong, William R. BD	1979 2008	(Skelmorlie and Wemyss Bay)	25A The Lane, Skelmorlie PA17 5AR warmstrong17@tiscali.co.uk	01475 520891
Bell, Ian W. LTh	1990 2011	(Erskine)	40 Brueacre Drive, Wemyss Bay PA18 6HA revianbell@gmail.com	01475 529312
Bell, May (Mrs) LTh	1998 2012	(Johnstone: St Andrew's Trinity)	40 Brueacre Drive, Wemyss Bay PA18 6HA revmaybell22@gmail.com	01475 529312

Name	Years	Note	Address / Email	Phone
Black, Janette M.K. (Mrs) BD	1993 2006	(Assistant: Paisley: Oakshaw Trinity)	5 Craigiehall Avenue, Erskine PA8 7DB	0141 812 0794
Breingan, Mhairi	2011	Ordained Local Minister	6 Park Road, Inchinnan, Renfrew PA4 4QJ MBreingan@churchofscotland.org.uk	0141 812 1425
Campbell, Donald BD	1998 2016	(Houston and Killellan)	1 Herriot Avenue, Kilbirnie KA25 7HZ tofua1951@btinternet.com	01505 684147 07530 394458
Currie, Ian S. MBE BD	1975 2010	(The United Church of Bute)	ianscurrie@tiscali.co.uk	07764 254300
Davidson, Stuart BD	2008 2017	Pioneer Minister: Paisley North End	25H Cross Road, Paisley PA2 9QJ SDavidson@churchofscotland.org.uk	07717 503059
Easton, Lilly C. (Mrs)	1999 2012	(Renfrew: Old)	Flat 0/2, 90 Beith Street, Glasgow G11 6DG revlillyeaston@hotmail.co.uk	0141 586 7628
Fraser, Ian C. BA BD	1983 2008	(Glasgow: St Luke's and St Andrew's)	62 Kingston Avenue, Neilston, Glasgow G78 3JG ianandlindafraser@gmail.com	0141 563 6794
Gray, Greta (Miss) DCS	1992 2014	(Deacon)	67 Crags Avenue, Paisley PA3 6SG greta.gray@ntlworld.com	0141 884 6178
Hood, E. Lorna OBE MA BD DD	1978 2016	(Renfrew: North)	4 Thornly Park Drive, Paisley PA2 7RR revlornahood@gmail.com	0141 384 9516
Kay, David BA BD MTh	1974 2008	(Paisley: Sandyford: Thread Street)	36 Donaldswood Park, Paisley PA2 8RS david.kay500@o2.co.uk	0141 884 2080
Leitch, Maureen (Mrs) BA BD	1995 2011	(Barrhead: Bourock)	Rockfield, 92 Paisley Road, Barrhead G78 1NW maureen.leitch@ntlworld.com	0141 580 2927
MacColl, James C. BSc BD	1966 2002	(Johnstone: St Andrew's Trinity)	20 Dunrobin Avenue, Johnstone PA5 9NW hamishmaccoll@gmail.com	01505 227439
Macdonald, Alexander MA BD	1966 2006	(Neilston)	35 Lochore Avenue, Paisley PA3 4BY alexsmacdonald42@aol.com	0141 889 0066
Mayne, Kenneth A.L. BA MSc CertEd	1976 2018	(Paisley Martyrs' Sandyford)	300 Glasgow Road, Paisley PA1 3DP	
McKaig, William G. BD	1979 2011	(Langbank)	54 Brisbane Street, Greenock PA16 8NT bmckaig16@gmail.com	
Nicol, Joyce M. (Mrs) BA DCS	1974 2006	(Deacon)	93 Brisbane Street, Greenock PA16 8NY joycenicol@hotmail.co.uk	01475 723235 07957 642709
Ross, Duncan DCS	1996 2015	(Deacon)	1 John Neilson Avenue, Paisley PA1 2SX ssomacnud@hotmail.com	0141 887 2801
Simpson, James H. BD LLB	1964 2004	(Greenock: Mount Kirk)	82 Harbourside, Inverkip, Greenock PA16 0BF jameshsimpson@yahoo.co.uk	01475 520582
Smillie, Andrew M. LTh	1990 2005	(Langbank)	7 Turnbull Avenue, West Freeland, Erskine PA8 7DL andrewsmillie@talktalk.net	0141 812 7030
Stewart, David MA DipEd BD MTh	1977 2013	(Howwood)	72 Glen Avenue, Largs KA30 8QQ revdavids@aol.com	01475 675159
Whiteford, Alexander LTh	1996 2013	(Ardersier with Petty)	Cumbrae, 17 Netherburn Gardens, Houston, Johnstone PA6 7NG alex.whiteford@hotmail.co.uk	01505 229611
Whyte, Margaret A. (Mrs) BA BD	1988 2011	(Glasgow: Pollokshaws)	4 Springhill Road, Barrhead G78 2AA mawhyte@hotmail.co.uk	0141 881 4942

GREENOCK AND PAISLEY ADDRESSES

Gourock
Old Gourock
and Ashton   41 Royal Street
St John's   Bath Street x St John's Road

Greenock
East End   Crawfurdsburn Community Centre
Lyle Kirk   Newark Street x Bentinck Street
Mount Kirk   Dempster Street at Murdieston Park
St Margaret's   Finch Road x Kestrel Crescent
St Ninian's   Warwick Road, Larkfield
Wellpark Mid Kirk Cathcart Square

Westburn   9 Nelson Street

Port Glasgow
Hamilton
Bardrainney   Bardrainney Avenue x
                  Auchenbothie Road
St Andrew's   Princes Street
St Martin's   Mansion Avenue

Paisley
Abbey   Town Centre
Glenburn   Nethercraigs Drive off Glenburn Road

Lylesland   Rowan Street off Neilston Road
Martyrs'   King Street
Sandyford   Montgomery Road
Oakshaw Trinity   Churchill
St Columba Foxbar Arnochrie Road, Foxbar
St Luke's   Neilston Road
St Mark's Oldhall Glasgow Road, Ralston
St Ninian's Ferguslie Blackstoun Road
Sherwood Greenlaw Glasgow Road
Stow Brae Kirk   Causeyside Street
Wallneuk North   off Renfrew Road

(16) GLASGOW

Meets at 7pm on the second Tuesday of every month apart from June when it is the third Tuesday. The venue is intimated on the Presbytery website at www.presbyteryofglasgow.org.uk.

Clerk:	REV. GEORGE S. COWIE BSc BD	260 Bath Street, Glasgow G2 4JP	0141 332 6606
		glasgow@churchofscotland.org.uk	Fax 0141 352 6646
		www.presbyteryofglasgow.org.uk	
Treasurer:	MRS ALISON WHITELAW	treasurer@presbyteryofglasgow.org.uk	

1 Banton linked with Twechar
Guardianship of the Presbytery
Session Clerk, Banton: Mary Dixon (Mrs)   magicmaria67@gmail.com   01236 822055
Session Clerk, Twechar: Gena Whyte (Mrs)   whyteg@live.co.uk   0141 777 7704

2 Bishopbriggs: Kenmure
James Gemmell BD MTh   1999   2010   100 Kenmure Avenue, Bishopbriggs, Glasgow G64 2DB   0141 390 3598
                                        JGemmell@churchofscotland.org.uk

3 Bishopbriggs: Springfield Cambridge
Ian Taylor BD ThM   1995   2006   64 Miller Drive, Bishopbriggs, Glasgow G64 1FB   0141 772 1596
                                    ITaylor@churchofscotland.org.uk   0141 772 1540

4 Broom
James A.S. Boag BD CertMin — 1992 — 2007
3 Laigh Road, Newton Mearns, Glasgow G77 5EX
JBoag@churchofscotland.org.uk
Tel 0141 639 3528
0141 639 2916
Fax 0141 639 3528

5 Burnside Blairbeth
William T.S. Wilson BSc BD — 1999 — 2006
59 Blairbeth Road, Burnside, Glasgow G73 4JD
WWilson@churchofscotland.org.uk
0141 634 7383
0141 583 7383

6 Busby
Jeremy C. Eve BSc BD — 1998
17A Carmunnock Road, Busby, Glasgow G76 8SZ
JEve@churchofscotland.org.uk
0141 644 2073
0141 644 3670

7 Cadder
John B. MacGregor BD — 1999 — 2017
231 Kirkintilloch Road, Bishopbriggs, Glasgow G64 2JB
0141 772 7436
0141 576 7127

8 Cambuslang
A. Leslie Milton MA BD PhD — 1996 — 2008
74 Stewarton Drive, Cambuslang, Glasgow G72 8DG
LMilton@churchofscotland.org.uk
0141 641 2028

David Maxwell
(Ordained Local Minister) — 2014 — 2017
248 Old Castle Road, Glasgow G44 5EZ
DMaxwell@churchofscotland.org.uk
0141 569 6379
07779 280074

Karen M. Hamilton (Mrs) DCS — 1995 — 2014
6 Beckfield Gate, Glasgow G33 1SW
KHamilton@churchofscotland.org.uk
0141 558 3195
07514 402612

9 Cambuslang: Flemington Hallside
Vacant
Session Clerk: Anne Clarkson (Mrs)
59 Hay Crescent, Cambuslang, Glasgow G72 6QA
anneclarkson11@gmail.com
0141 641 1049
01698 769207

10 Campsie
Jane M. Denniston MA BD MTh — 2002 — 2016
19 Redhill View, Lennoxtown, Glasgow G66 7BL
Jane.Denniston@churchofscotland.org.uk
01360 310939
01360 310846
07738 123101

11 Chryston (H)
Mark Malcolm MA BD — 1999 — 2008
The Manse, 109 Main Street, Chryston, Glasgow G69 9LA
MMalcolm@churchofscotland.org.uk
0141 779 4188
0141 779 1436
07731 737377

Mark W.J. McKeown
MEng MDiv (Associate Minister) — 2013 — 2014
6 Glenapp Place, Moodiesburn, Glasgow G69 0HS
MMcKeown@churchofscotland.org.uk
01236 263406

12	Eaglesham Andrew J. Robertson BD	2008	2016	The Manse, Cheapside Street, Eaglesham, Glasgow G76 0NS ARobertson@churchofscotland.org.uk	**01355 302087** 01355 303495
13	Fernhill and Cathkin Aquila R. Singh BA PGCE BD	2017		20 Glenlyon Place, Rutherglen, Glasgow G73 5PL ASingh@churchofscotland.org.uk	0141 389 3599
14	Gartcosh (H) (Office 01236 872274) linked with Glenboig David G. Slater BSc BA DipThRS	2011		26 Inchnock Avenue, Gartcosh, Glasgow G69 8EA DSlater@churchofscotland.org.uk	07722 876616
15	Giffnock: Orchardhill S. Grant Barclay LLB DipLP BD MSc PhD	1995	2016	23 Huntly Avenue, Giffnock, Glasgow G46 6LW GBarclay@churchofscotland.org.uk	**0141 638 3604** 0141 387 8254
16	Giffnock: South Catherine J. Beattie (Mrs) BD	2008	2011	164 Ayr Road, Newton Mearns, Glasgow G77 6EE CBeattie@churchofscotland.org.uk	**0141 638 2599** 0141 258 7804
17	Giffnock: The Park Calum D. Macdonald BD	1993	2001	41 Rouken Glen Road, Thornliebank, Glasgow G46 7JD CMacdonald@churchofscotland.org.uk	**0141 620 2204** 0141 638 3023
18	Glenboig See Gartcosh				
19	Greenbank (H) Jeanne N. Roddick BD	2003		Greenbank Manse, 38 Eaglesham Road, Clarkston, Glasgow G76 7DJ JRoddick@churchofscotland.org.uk	**0141 644 1841** 0141 644 1395
20	Kilsyth: Anderson Allan S. Vint BSc BD MTh	1989	2013	Anderson Manse, Kingston Road, Kilsyth, Glasgow G65 0HR AVint@churchofscotland.org.uk	01236 822345 07795 483070

21 Kilsyth: Burns and Old
Robert Johnston BD MSc FSAScot — 2017
The Grange, 17 Glasgow Road, Kilsyth G65 9AE
RJohnston@churchofscotland.org.uk
01236 899901
07810 377582

22 Kirkintilloch: Hillhead
Guardianship of the Presbytery
Bill H Finnie BA PgDipSW CertCRS — 2015
(Ordained Local Minister)
27 Hallside Crescent, Cambuslang, Glasgow G72 7DY
BFinnie@churchofscotland.org.uk
07518 357138

23 Kirkintilloch: St Columba's (H)
Philip Wright BSc MSc PhD BTh — 2017
6 Glenwood Road, Lenzie, Glasgow G66 4DS
PWright@churchofscotland.org.uk
0141 578 0016
07427 623393

24 Kirkintilloch: St David's Memorial Park (H)
Vacant
Session Clerk: Kathleen McKenzie (Mrs)
2 Roman Road, Kirkintilloch, Glasgow G66 1EA
robertmckath@talktalk.net
0141 776 4989
0141 776 1434
0141 775 1737

25 Kirkintilloch: St Mary's
Mark E. Johnstone MA BD — 1993 2001
St Mary's Manse, 60 Union Street, Kirkintilloch, Glasgow G66 1DH
Mark.Johnstone@churchofscotland.org.uk
0141 775 1166
0141 776 1252

26 Lenzie: Old (H)
Louise J.E. McClements BD — 2008 2016
41 Kirkintilloch Road, Lenzie, Glasgow G66 4LB
LMcClements@churchofscotland.org.uk
0141 573 5006

27 Lenzie: Union (H)
Daniel J.M. Carmichael MA BD — 1994 2003
1 Larch Avenue, Lenzie, Glasgow G66 4HX
DCarmichael@churchofscotland.org.uk
0141 776 1046
0141 776 3831

28 Maxwell Mearns Castle
Scott R.McL. Kirkland BD MAR — 1996 2011
122 Broomfield Avenue, Newton Mearns, Glasgow G77 5JR
SKirkland@churchofscotland.org.uk
Tel/Fax **0141 639 5169**
0141 560 5603

29 Mearns (H)
Joseph A. Kavanagh BD DipPTh MTh MTh 1992 — 1998
11 Belford Grove, Newton Mearns, Glasgow G77 5FB
JKavanagh@churchofscotland.org.uk
0141 639 6555
0141 384 2218

No.	Name / Minister	Year(s)	Address	Telephone
30	**Milton of Campsie (H)** Julie H.C. Moody BA BD PGCE	2006	Dunkeld, 33 Birdston Road, Milton of Campsie, Glasgow G66 8BX JMoody@churchofscotland.org.uk	01360 310548 07787 184800
31	**Netherlee (H) (0141 637 2503) linked with Stamperland (H)** Scott C. Blythe MA BD MBA	1997 2017	25 Ormonde Avenue, Netherlee, Glasgow G44 3QY SBlythe@churchofscotland.org.uk	**0141 637 4999** 07706 203786
32	**Newton Mearns (H)** Stuart J. Crawford BD MTh	2017	28 Waterside Avenue, Newton Mearns, Glasgow G77 6TJ SCrawford@churchofscotland.org.uk	**0141 639 7373** 07912 534280
33	**Rutherglen: Old (H)** Vacant Session Clerk: Hugh Miller		31 Highburgh Drive, Rutherglen, Glasgow G73 3RR sessionclerk@rutherglenold.com	0141 534 7477 0141 634 4355
34	**Rutherglen: Stonelaw (H)** Alistair S. May LLB BD PhD	2002	80 Blairbeth Road, Rutherglen, Glasgow G73 4JA AMay@churchofscotland.org.uk	**0141 647 5113** 0141 583 0157
35	**Rutherglen: West and Wardlawhill** Malcolm Cuthbertson BA BD	1984 2017	12 Albert Drive, Rutherglen, Glasgow G73 3RT MCuthbertson@churchofscotland.org.uk	**0844 736 1470** 07864 820612
36	**Stamperland** See Netherlee			
37	**Stepps (H)** Gordon MacRae BD MTh	1985 2014	112 Jackson Drive, Crowwood Grange, Stepps, Glasgow G33 6GF GMacRae@churchofscotland.org.uk	0141 779 5742
38	**Thornliebank (H)** Mike R. Gargrave BD	2008 2014	12 Parkholm Quadrant, Thornliebank, Glasgow G53 7ZH MGargrave@churchofscotland.org.uk	0141 880 5532
39	**Torrance** Nigel L. Barge BSc BD	1991	1 Atholl Avenue, Torrance, Glasgow G64 4JA NBarge@churchofscotland.org.uk	**01360 620970** 01360 622379

40 Twechar See Banton

41 Williamwood
Janet S. Mathieson MA BD — 2003 — 2015
125 Greenwood Road, Clarkston, Glasgow G76 7LL
JMathieson@churchofscotland.org.uk
0141 638 2091
0141 579 9997

42 Glasgow: Anderston Kelvingrove
Guardianship of the Presbytery
Session Clerk: Tom Moffat (Rev)
tom@gallus.org.uk
0141 221 9408
0141 248 1886

43 Glasgow: Baillieston Mure Memorial (0141 773 1216) linked with Glasgow: Baillieston St Andrew's
Vacant
28 Beech Avenue, Baillieston, Glasgow G69 6LF
Alex P. Stuart — 2014
107 Baldorran Crescent, Balloch, Cumbernauld, Glasgow G68 9EX
AStuart@churchofscotland.org.uk
07901 802967
(Ordained Local Minister)

44 Glasgow: Baillieston St Andrew's See Glasgow: Baillieston Mure Memorial

45 Glasgow: Balshagray Victoria Park
Campbell Mackinnon BSc BD — 1982 — 2001
20 St Kilda Drive, Glasgow G14 9JN
CMackinnon@churchofscotland.org.uk
0141 954 9780

46 Glasgow: Barlanark Greyfriars
Willem J. Bezuidenhout BA BD MHEd MEd — 1977 — 2016
4 Rhindmuir Grove, Baillieston, Glasgow G69 6NE
WBezuidenhout@churchofscotland.org.uk
0141 771 6477
0141 771 7103

47 Glasgow: Blawarthill
G. Melvyn Wood MA BD — 1982 — 2009
46 Earlbank Avenue, Glasgow G14 9HL
GMelvynWood@churchofscotland.org.uk
0141 579 6521

48 Glasgow: Bridgeton St Francis in the East (H) (L)
Howard R. Hudson MA BD — 1982 — 1984
10 Albany Drive, Rutherglen, Glasgow G73 3QN
HHudson@churchofscotland.org.uk
0141 556 2830 (Church House: 0141 554 8045)
0141 587 8667

49 Glasgow: Broomhill Hyndland
George C. Mackay
BD CertMin CertEd DipPC — 1994 — 2014
27 St Kilda Drive, Glasgow G14 9LN
GMackay@churchofscotland.org.uk
Ruth Forsythe (Mrs) MCS — 2017
Flat 1/2 41 Bellwood Street, Glasgow G41 3EX
RForsythe@churchofscotland.org.uk
(Ordained Local Minister)
0141 959 8697
07711 569127
0141 649 7755

No.	Name / Qualifications			Address / Email	Telephone
50	**Glasgow: Calton Parkhead** Alison E.S. Davidge MA BD	1990	2008	98 Drumover Drive, Glasgow G31 5RP ADavidge@churchofscotland.org.uk	**0141 554 3866** 07843 625059
51	**Glasgow: Cardonald** Gavin McFadyen BEng BD	2006	2018	133 Newtyle Road, Paisley PA1 3LB GMcFadyen@churchofscotland.org.uk	**0141 882 6264** 0141 887 2726
52	**Glasgow: Carmunnock** G. Gray Fletcher BSc BD	1989	2001	The Manse, 161 Waterside Road, Carmunnock, Glasgow G76 9AJ GFletcher@churchofscotland.org.uk	**0141 644 0655** Tel/Fax 0141 644 1578
53	**Glasgow: Carmyle linked with Glasgow: Kenmuir Mount Vernon** Murdo MacLean BD CertMin	1997	1999	3 Meryon Road, Glasgow G32 9NW Murdo.MacLean@churchofscotland.org.uk	0141 778 2625
	Roland Hunt BSc PhD CertEd (Ordained Local Minister)	2016		4 Flora Gardens, Bishopbriggs, Glasgow G64 1DS RHunt@churchofscotland.org.uk	0141 563 3257
54	**Glasgow: Carntyne** Joan Ross BSc BD PhD	1999	2016	163 Lethamhill Road, Glasgow G33 2SQ JRoss@churchofscotland.org.uk	**0141 778 4186** 0141 770 9247
55	**Glasgow: Carnwadric** Vacant Mary S. Gargrave (Mrs) DCS	1989	2007	62 Loganswell Road, Thornliebank, Glasgow G46 8AX 12 Parkholm Quadrant, Thornliebank, Glasgow G53 7ZH Mary.Gargrave@churchofscotland.org.uk	0141 638 5884 0141 880 5532 07896 866618
56	**Glasgow: Castlemilk (H)** Sarah A. Brown (Ms) MA BD ThM DipYW/Theol PDCCE	2012		156 Old Castle Road, Glasgow G44 5TW Sarah.Brown@churchofscotland.org.uk	**0141 634 1480** 0141 637 5451 07532 457245
	John Paul Cathcart DCS	2000	2017	9 Glen More, East Kilbride, Glasgow G74 2AP Paul.Cathcart@churchofscotland.org.uk	01355 243970 07708 396074
57	**Glasgow: Cathcart Old** Neil W. Galbraith BD CertMin	1987	1996	21 Courthill Avenue, Cathcart, Glasgow G44 5AA NGalbraith@churchofscotland.org.uk	**0141 637 4168** Tel/Fax 0141 633 5248

58	**Glasgow: Cathcart Trinity (H)**			
	Alasdair MacMillan LLB BD	2015	82 Merrylee Road, Glasgow G43 2QZ Alasdair.MacMillan@churchofscotland.org.uk	**0141 637 6658** 0141 633 3744
	Wilma Pearson (Mrs) BD (Associate Minister)	2004	90 Newlands Road, Glasgow G43 2JR WPearson@churchofscotland.org.uk	0141 632 2491
59	**Glasgow: Cathedral (High or St Mungo's)** Vacant Session Clerk: Glen Collie		41 Springfield Road, Bishopbriggs, Glasgow G64 1PL glen.collie@glasgowcathedral.org	**0141 552 6891** 0141 762 2719 01505 329619
60	**Glasgow: Causeway (Tollcross)** Monica Michelin-Salomon BD	1999 2016	228 Hamilton Road, Glasgow G32 9QU MMichelin-Salomon@churchofscotland.org.uk	0141 778 2413
61	**Glasgow: Clincarthill (H)** Stuart Love BA MTh	2016	90 Mount Annan Drive, Glasgow G44 4RZ SLove@churchofscotland.org.uk	**0141 632 4206** 0141 632 2985
62	**Glasgow: Colston Milton** Christopher J. Rowe BA BD	2008	118 Birsay Road, Milton, Glasgow G22 7QP CRowe@churchofscotland.org.uk	**0141 772 1922** 0141 564 1138
63	**Glasgow: Colston Wellpark (H)** Guardianship of the Presbytery Leslie E.T. Grieve (Ordained Local Minister)	2014	23 Hertford Avenue, Kelvindale, Glasgow G12 0LG LGrieve@churchofscotland.org.uk	07813 255052
64	**Glasgow: Cranhill (H)** Muriel B. Pearson (Ms) MA BD PGCE	2004	31 Lethamhill Crescent, Glasgow G33 2SH MPearson@churchofscotland.org.uk	**0141 774 3344** 0141 770 6873 07951 888860
65	**Glasgow: Croftfoot (H)** Robert M. Silver BA BD	1995 2011	4 Inchmurrin Gardens, High Burnside, Rutherglen, Glasgow G73 5RU RSilver@churchofscotland.org.uk	**0141 637 3913** 0141 258 7268
66	**Glasgow: Dennistoun New (H)** Ian M.S. McInnes BD DipMin	1995 2008	31 Pencaitland Drive, Glasgow G32 8RL IMcInnes@churchofscotland.org.uk	**0141 554 1350** 0141 554 1350

67	**Glasgow: Drumchapel St Andrew's** John S. Purves LLB BD	1983	1984	6 Firdon Crescent, Old Drumchapel, Glasgow G15 6QQ john.s.purves@talk21.com	**0141 944 3758** 0141 944 4566
68	**Glasgow: Drumchapel St Mark's** Audrey J. Jamieson BD MTh	2004	2007	146 Garscadden Road, Glasgow G15 6PR AJamieson@churchofscotland.org.uk	0141 944 5440
69	**Glasgow: Easterhouse** Vacant Session Clerk: Graeme Barrie			graeme.barrie@ntlworld.com	**0141 771 8810** 0141 573 3809
70	**Glasgow: Eastwood** James R. Teasdale BA BD	2009	2016	54 Mansewood Road, Eastwood, Glasgow G43 1TL JTeasdale@churchofscotland.org.uk	0141 571 7648
71	**Glasgow: Gairbraid (H)** Donald Michael MacInnes BD	2002	2011	4 Blackhill Gardens, Summerston, Glasgow G23 5NE DMacInnes@churchofscotland.org.uk	0141 946 0604
72	**Glasgow: Gallowgate** Peter L. V. Davidge BD MTh	2003	2009	98 Drumover Drive, Glasgow G31 5RP PDavidge@churchofscotland.org.uk	07765 096599
73	**Glasgow: Garthamlock and Craigend East** Vacant Marion Buchanan (Mrs) MA DCS	1983	2006	16 Almond Drive, East Kilbride, Glasgow G74 2HX MBuchanan@churchofscotland.org.uk	01355 228776 07999 889817
74	**Glasgow: Gorbals** Ian F. Galloway BA BD	1976	1996	6 Stirlingfauld Place, Gorbals, Glasgow G5 9QF IGalloway@churchofscotland.org.uk	07753 686603
75	**Glasgow: Govan and Linthouse** Eleanor J. McMahon BEd BD (Interim Minister) Andrew Thomson BA (Assistant Minister)	1994 1976	2017 2010	81 Moorpark Square, Renfrew PA4 8DB EMcMahon@churchofscotland.org.uk 3 Laurel Wynd, Drumsagard Village, Cambuslang, Glasgow G72 7BH AThomson@churchofscotland.org.uk	07974 116539 0141 641 2936 07772 502774

76	**Glasgow: Hillington Park (H)** Vacant Session Clerk: Tom Smith		61 Ralston Avenue, Glasgow G52 3NB smith.thomas2@sky.com	0141 882 7000 0141 882 0157
77	**Glasgow: Ibrox (H)** Tara P. Granados (Ms) BA MDiv	2018	59 Langhaul Road, Glasgow G53 7SE TGranados@churchofscotland.org.uk	**07380 830030** 07380 830030
78	**Glasgow: John Ross Memorial Church for Deaf People** Richard C. Durno DSW CQSW	1989 1998	**Voice/Text 0141 420 1391; Fax 0141 420 3778** 31 Springfield Road, Bishopbriggs, Glasgow G64 1PJ RDurno@churchofscotland.org.uk	Voice/Text/Fax 0141 772 1052 Voice/Text/Voicemail 07748 607721
79	**Glasgow: Jordanhill** Bruce H Sinclair BA BD	2009 2015	12 Priorwood Gardens, Academy Park, Glasgow G13 1GD BSinclair@churchofscotland.org.uk	**0141 959 2496** 0141 959 1310
80	**Glasgow: Kelvinbridge** Gordon Kirkwood BSc BD MTh MPhil PGCE	1987 2013	Flat 2/2, 94 Hyndland Road, Glasgow G12 9PZ GKirkwood@churchofscotland.org.uk	**0141 339 1750** 0141 334 5352
81	**Glasgow: Kelvinside Hillhead** Vacant Roger D. Sturrock (Prof.) BD MD FCRP (Ordained Local Minister)	2014	36 Thomson Drive, Bearsden, Glasgow G61 3PA RSturrock@churchofscotland.org.uk	**0141 334 2788** 0141 942 7412
82	**Glasgow: Kenmuir Mount Vernon** See Glasgow: Carmyle			
83	**Glasgow: King's Park (H)** Sandra Boyd (Mrs) BEd BD	2007	1101 Aikenhead Road, Glasgow G44 5SL SBoyd@churchofscotland.org.uk	**0141 636 8688** 07919 676242
84	**Glasgow: Kinning Park** Margaret H. Johnston BD	1988 2000	168 Arbroath Avenue, Cardonald, Glasgow G52 3HH MHJohnston@churchofscotland.org.uk	0141 810 3782
85	**Glasgow: Knightswood St Margaret's (H)** Alexander M. Fraser BD DipMin	1985 2009	26 Airthrey Avenue, Glasgow G14 9LJ AFraser@churchofscotland.org.uk	0141 959 7075

86	**Glasgow: Langside** David N. McLachlan BD	1985	2004	36 Madison Avenue, Glasgow G44 5AQ DMcLachlan@churchofscotland.org.uk	**0141 632 7520** 0141 637 0797
87	**Glasgow: Maryhill (H)** Stuart C. Matthews BD MA	2006	2010	251 Milngavie Road, Bearsden, Glasgow G61 3DQ SMatthews@churchofscotland.org.uk	**0141 946 3512** 0141 942 0804
	James Hamilton DCS	1997	2000	6 Beckfield Gate, Glasgow G33 1SW James.Hamilton@churchofscotland.org.uk	0141 558 3195 07584 137314
88	**Glasgow: Merrylea** David P. Hood BD CertMin DipIOB(Scot)	1997	2001	4 Pilmuir Avenue, Glasgow G44 3HX DHood@churchofscotland.org.uk	**0141 637 2009** 0141 637 6700
	Margaret McLellan DCS	1986	2014	18 Broom Road East, Newton Mearns, Glasgow G77 5SD margaretdmclellan@outlook.com	0141 639 6853
89	**Glasgow: Newlands South (H)** R. Stuart M. Fulton BA BD	1991	2017	24 Monreith Road, Glasgow G43 2NY SFulton@churchofscotland.org.uk	**0141 632 3055** 0141 632 2588
90	**Glasgow: Partick South (H)** James Andrew McIntyre BD	2010		3 Branklyn Crescent, Glasgow G13 1GJ Andy.McIntyre@churchofscotland.org.uk	0141 959 3732
91	**Glasgow: Partick Trinity (H)** Timothy D. Sinclair MA MDiv	2018		99 Balshagray Avenue, Glasgow G11 7EQ TSinclair@churchofscotland.org.uk	0141 563 6424
92	**Glasgow: Pollokshaws** Roy J.M. Henderson MA BD DipMin	1987	2013	33 Mannering Road, Glasgow G41 3SW RHenderson@churchofscotland.org.uk	**0141 649 1879** 0141 632 8768
93	**Glasgow: Pollokshields (H)** David R. Black MA BD	1986	1997	36 Glencairn Drive, Glasgow G41 4PW DBlack@churchofscotland.org.uk	0141 423 4000

94 Glasgow: Possilpark
Rosalind (Linda) E. Pollock (Miss) BD ThM ThM — 2001 — 2014 — 108 Erradale Street, Lambhill, Glasgow G22 6PT / RPollock@churchofscotland.org.uk — 0141 336 8028 / 0141 384 5793

95 Glasgow: Queen's Park Govanhill
Elijah W. Smith BA MLitt — 2015 — 32 Queen Mary Avenue, Crosshill, Glasgow G42 8DT / E.Smith@churchofscotland.org.uk — 0141 423 3654 / 07975 998382

Ewan R. Kelly MB CHB BD PhD (Associate Minister) — 1994 — 2018 — Flat 1/2, 17 Overdale Street, Glasgow G42 9PZ / EKelly@churchofscotland.org.uk — 0141 649 2714

96 Glasgow: Renfield St Stephen's
Vacant — Tel: 0141 332 4293; Fax: 0141 332 8482
Session Clerk: Kenneth Rogers — 101 Hill Street, Glasgow G3 6TY / k.rogers@robertson.co.uk — 0141 353 0349 / 0141 954 3854

97 Glasgow: Robroyston
Jonathan A. Keefe BSc BD — 2009 — 7 Beckfield Drive, Glasgow G33 1SR / JKeefe@churchofscotland.org.uk — 0141 558 8414 / 0141 558 2952

98 Glasgow: Ruchazie
Guardianship of the Presbytery
Marion Buchanan (Mrs) MA DCS — 1983 — 2006 — 16 Almond Drive, East Kilbride, Glasgow G74 2HX / MBuchanan@churchofscotland.org.uk — 0141 774 2759 / 01355 228776 / 07999 889817

99 Glasgow: Ruchill Kelvinside
Mark Lowey BD DipTh — 2012 — 2013 — 41 Mitre Road, Glasgow G14 9LE / MLowey@churchofscotland.org.uk — 0141 946 0466 / 0141 959 6718

100 Glasgow: St Andrew and St Nicholas
Lyn M. Peden (Mrs) BD — 2010 — 2015 — 80 Tweedsmuir Road, Glasgow G52 2RX / LPeden@churchofscotland.org.uk — 0141 883 9873

101 Glasgow: St Andrew's East
Barbara D. Quigley (Mrs) MTheol ThM DPS — 1979 — 2011 — 43 Broompark Drive, Glasgow G31 2JB / BQuigley@churchofscotland.org.uk — 0141 554 1485 / 0141 237 7982

102 Glasgow: St Christopher's Priesthill and Nitshill
Douglas M. Nicol BD CA — 1987 — 1996 — 36 Springkell Drive, Glasgow G41 4EZ / DNicol@churchofscotland.org.uk — 0141 881 6541 / 0141 427 7877

103 Glasgow: St Columba (GE)
Guardianship of the Presbytery
Session Clerk: Duncan Mitchell
dpm@addapt.org.uk

0141 221 3305
0141 339 9679

104 Glasgow: St David's Knightswood
Graham M. Thain LLB BD   1988   1999
60 Southbrae Drive, Glasgow G13 1QD
GThain@churchofscotland.org.uk

0141 954 1081
0141 959 2904

105 Glasgow: St Enoch's Hogganfield (H) (www.stenochshogganfield.org.uk) church@st-enoch.org.uk   Tel 0141 770 5694; Fax 08702 840084
Elaine H. MacRae (Mrs) BD   1985   2017
112 Jackson Drive, Crowwood Grange, Stepps, Glasgow G33 6GF
EMacRae@churchofscotland.org.uk

0141 779 5742
07834 269487

106 Glasgow: St George's Tron
Alastair S. Duncan MA BD   1989   2013
(Transition Minister)
29 Hertford Avenue, Glasgow G12 0LG
ADuncan@churchofscotland.org.uk

0141 221 2141
07968 852083

107 Glasgow: St James' (Pollok)
John W. Mann BSc MDiv DMin   2004
30 Ralston Avenue, Glasgow G52 3NA
John.Mann@churchofscotland.org.uk

0141 882 4984
0141 883 7405

108 Glasgow: St John's Renfield www.stjohns-renfield.org.uk
D. Stewart Gillan BSc MDiv PhD   1985   2018
26 Leicester Avenue, Glasgow G12 0LU
SGillan@churchofscotland.org.uk

0141 339 7021
0141 339 4637

109 Glasgow: St Paul's
Daniel Manastireanu BA MTh   2010   2014
38 Lochview Drive, Glasgow G33 1QF
DManastireanu@churchofscotland.org.uk

0141 770 8559
0141 770 1561

110 Glasgow: St Rollox
Jane M. Howitt MA BD   1996   2016
(Transition Minister)
42 Melville Gardens, Bishopbriggs, Glasgow G64 3DE
JHowitt@churchofscotland.org.uk

0141 558 1809
0141 581 0050

111 Glasgow: Sandyford Henderson Memorial (H) (L)
Vacant
Session Clerk: Noel Peacock (Prof.)
66 Woodend Drive, Glasgow G13 1TG
noel.peacock@glasgow.ac.uk

0141 954 9013
0141 334 1611

112 Glasgow: Sandyhills
Vacant
Session Clerk: Maureen Sharp (Mrs)

60 Wester Road, Glasgow G32 9JJ
msharp.sessionclerk@sandyhillschurch.com

0141 778 3415
0141 778 2174
0141 763 2191

113 Glasgow: Scotstoun
Richard Cameron BD DipMin

2000

15 Northland Drive, Glasgow G14 9BE
RCameron@churchofscotland.org.uk

0141 959 4637

114 Glasgow: Shawlands Trinity
Valerie J. Duff (Miss) DMin

1993 2014

29 St Ronan's Drive, Glasgow G41 3SQ
VDuff@churchofscotland.org.uk

0141 258 6782

115 Glasgow: Sherbrooke Mosspark (H)
Thomas L. Pollock
BA BD MTh FSAScot JP

1982 2003

114 Springkell Avenue, Glasgow G41 4EW
TPollock@churchofscotland.org.uk

0141 427 1968
0141 427 2094

New charge formed by the union of Glasgow: Mosspark and Glasgow: Sherbrooke St Gilbert's

116 Glasgow: Shettleston New
W. Louis T. Reddick MA BD

2017

211 Sandyhills Road, Glasgow G32 9NB
LReddick@churchofscotland.org.uk

0141 778 0857
0141 778 1286
07843 083548

117 Glasgow: Springburn (H)
Brian M. Casey MA BD

2014

c/o Springburn Parish Church, 180 Springburn Way,
Glasgow G21 1TU
BCasey@churchofscotland.org.uk

0141 557 2345
07703 166772

118 Glasgow: Temple Anniesland
Fiona M.E. Gardner (Mrs) BD MA MLitt

1997 2011

76 Victoria Park Drive North, Glasgow G14 9PJ
FGardner@churchofscotland.org.uk

0141 530 9745
0141 959 5647

119 Glasgow: Toryglen (H)
Vacant
Session Clerk: Ina Cole (Mrs)

toryglensession@gmail.com

0141 562 4807

120 Glasgow: Trinity Possil and Henry Drummond
Richard G. Buckley BD MTh

1990 1995

50 Highfield Drive, Glasgow G12 0HL
RBuckley@churchofscotland.org.uk

0141 339 2870

121 Glasgow: Tron St Mary's
Rhona E. Graham BA BD   2015
30 Louden Hill Road, Robroyston, Glasgow G33 1GA
RGraham@churchofscotland.org.uk
0141 558 1011
0141 389 8816

122 Glasgow: Wallacewell (New Charge Development)
Daniel L. Frank BA MDiv DMin   1984 2011
8 Streamfield Gate, Glasgow G33 1SJ
DFrank@churchofscotland.org.uk
0141 585 0283

123 Glasgow: Wellington (H)
Vacant
Roger D. Sturrock (Prof.) BD MD FCRP   2014
(Ordained Local Minister)
31 Hughenden Gardens, Glasgow G12 9YH
36 Thomson Drive, Bearsden, Glasgow G61 3PA
RSturrock@churchofscotland.org.uk
0141 339 0454
0141 334 2343
0141 942 7412

124 Glasgow: Whiteinch (Website: www.whiteinchcofs.co.uk)
Alan McWilliam BD MTh   1993 2000
65 Victoria Park Drive South, Glasgow G14 9NX
AMcWilliam@churchofscotland.org.uk
0141 576 9020

125 Glasgow: Yoker
Karen E. Hendry BSc BD   2005
15 Coldingham Avenue, Glasgow G14 0PX
KHendry@churchofscotland.org.uk
0141 952 3620

Name			Note	Address	Phone
Alexander, Eric J. MA BD	1958	1997	(Glasgow: St George's Tron)	77 Norwood Park, Bearsden, Glasgow G61 2RZ	0141 942 4404
Alston, William G.	1961	2009	(Glasgow: North Kelvinside)	Flat 0/2, 5 Knightswood Court, Glasgow G13 2XN williamalston@hotmail.com	0141 959 3113
Beaton, Margaret S. (Miss) DCS	1989	2015	(Deacon)	64 Gardenside Grove, Carmyle, Glasgow G32 8EZ margaretbeaton54@hotmail.com	0141 646 2297 07796 642382
Bell, John L. MA BD FRSCM DUniv	1978	1988	(Iona Community)	148 West Princes Street, Glasgow G4 9DA	0141 387 7628
Birch, James PgDip FRSA FIOC	2001	2007	(Auxiliary Minister)	1 Kirkhill Grove, Cambuslang, Glasgow G72 8EH	0141 583 1722
Black, William B. MA BD	1972	2011	(Stornoway: High)	33 Tankerland Road, Glasgow G44 4EN revwillieblack@gmail.com	0141 637 4717
Blount, A. Sheila (Mrs) BD BA	1978	2010	(Cupar: St John's and Dairsie United)	28 Alcaig Road, Mosspark, Glasgow G52 1NH asheilablount@gmail.com	0141 419 0746
Blount, Graham K. LLB BD PhD	1976	2016	(Presbytery Clerk: Glasgow)	28 Alcaig Road, Mosspark, Glasgow G52 1NH Graham.Blount@churchofscotland.org.uk	0141 419 0746
Brice, Dennis G. BSc BD	1981	1984	(Taiwan)	8 Parkwood Close, Broxbourne, Herts EN10 7PF dbrice1@comcast.net	01702 555333
Campbell, A. Iain MA DipEd	1961	1997	(Busby)	430 Clarkston Road, Glasgow G44 3QF iaingillian@talktalk.net	0141 637 7460

Name			Charge / Role	Address	Telephone
Campbell, John MA BA BSc	1973	2009	(Caldwell)	96 Boghead Road, Lenzie, Glasgow G66 4EN / johncampbell.lenzie@gmail.com	0141 776 0874
Cartledge, Graham R.G. MA BD STM	1977	2015	(Glasgow: Eastwood)	5 Briar Grove, Newlands, Glasgow G43 2TG	0141 637 3228
Carruth, Patricia A. (Mrs) BD	1998	2012	(Coatbridge: Blairhill Dundyvan)	33 Springhill Farm Road, Baillieston, Glasgow G69 6GW	0141 771 3758
Cherry, Alastair J. BA BD FPLD	1982	2009	(Glasgow: Penilee St Andrew's)	8 Coruisk Drive, Clarkston, Glasgow G76 7NG / ajcherry133@gmail.com	0141 571 6052
Clark, Douglas W. LTh	1993	2015	(Lenzie: Old)	2 Poplar Drive, Lenzie, Glasgow G66 4DN / douglaswclark@hotmail.com	0141 776 1298
Cowie, George S. BSc BD	1991	2017	Presbytery Clerk: Glasgow	Renfield St Stephen's Centre, 260 Bath Street, Glasgow G2 4JP / GCowie@churchofscotland.org.uk	0141 332 6066
Cowie, Marian (Mrs) MA BD MTh	1990	2012	(Aberdeen: Midstocket)	120e Southbrae Drive, Glasgow G12 1TZ / mcowieou@aol.com	07740 174969
Cunningham, Alexander MA BD	1961	2002	(Presbytery Clerk: Glasgow)	18 Lady Jane Gate, Bothwell, Glasgow G71 8BW	01698 811051
Cunningham, James S.A. MA BD BLitt PhD	1992	2000	(Glasgow: Barlanark Greyfriars)	'Kirkland', 5 Inveresk Place, Coatbridge ML5 2DA	01236 421541
Drummond, John W. MA BD	1971	2011	(Rutherglen: West and Wardlawhill)	25 Kingsburn Drive, Rutherglen, Glasgow G73 2AN	0141 571 6002
Duff, T. Malcolm F. MA BD	1985	2009	(Glasgow: Queen's Park)	54 Hawkhead Road, Paisley PA1 3NB	0141 570 0614 / 07846 926584
Dutch, Morris M. BD BA Dip BTI	1998	2013	(Costa del Sol)	41 Baronald Drive, Glasgow G12 OHN / mmdutch@yahoo.co.uk	0141 357 2286
Easton, David J.C. MA BD	1965	2005	(Burnside Blairbeth)	6 Peveril Court, Burnside, Glasgow G73 4RE / deaston@btinternet.com	
Farrington, Alexandra LTh	2003	2015	(Campsie)	'Glenburn', High Banton, Kilsyth G65 0RA / revsfarrington@aol.co.uk	01236 824516
Ferguson, James B. LTh	1972	2002	(Lenzie: Union)	3 Bridgeway Place, Kirkintilloch, Glasgow G66 3HW	0141 588 5868
Fleming, Alexander F. MA BD	1966	1995	(Strathblane)	11 Bankwood Drive, Kilsyth, Glasgow G65 0GZ	01236 821461
Forrest, Martin R. BA MA BD	1988	2012	Prison Chaplain	4/1, 7 Blochairn Place, Glasgow G21 2EB / martinrforrest@gmail.com	0141 552 1132
Forsyth, Sandy O. LLB BD DipLP MTh PhD	2009	2017	University of Glasgow: Tutor & Clerk, Trinity College	48 Kerr Street, Kirkintilloch, Glasgow G66 1JZ / AForsyth@churchofscotland.org.uk	0141 777 8194 / 07739 639037
Foster-Fulton, Sally BA BD	1999	2016	Head of Christian Aid Scotland	24 Monreith Road, Glasgow G43 2NY / sallyfulton01@gmail.com	07850 937226
Galloway, Kathy (Mrs) BD MA MLitt	1977	2016	(Head of Christian Aid Scotland)	20 Hamilton Park Avenue, Glasgow G12 8UU / kathygalloway200@btinternet.com	0141 357 4079
Gardner, Peter M. MA BD	1988	2016	Pioneer Minister, Glasgow Arts Community	Flat 3/2, 10 Haggswood Avenue, Glasgow G41 4RE / PGardner@churchofscotland.org.uk	07743 539654
Gay, Douglas C. MA BD PhD	1998	2005	University of Glasgow: Trinity College	39 Athole Gardens, Glasgow G12 9BQ / douggay@mac.com	0141 330 2073 / 07971 321452
Hazlett, W. Ian P. (Prof.-Emer.) BA BD Dr theol DLitt DD		2009	University of Glasgow	Department of Theology & Religious Studies, 4 The Square, University of Glasgow G12 8QQ / i.hazlett@arts.gla.ac.uk	0141 330 2073
Hope, Evelyn P. (Miss) BA BD	1990	1998	(Wishaw: Thornlie)	Flat 0/1, 48 Moss Side Road, Glasgow G41 3UA	0141 649 1522 / 0141 333 9459
Hughes, Helen (Miss) DCS	1977	2008	(Deacon)	2/2, 43 Burnbank Terrace, Glasgow G20 6UQ / helhug35@gmail.com	07752 604817

Name			Position	Address	Tel
Hunter, Alastair G. MSc BD	1976	2010	(University of Glasgow)	487 Shields Road, Glasgow G41 2RG	0141 429 1687
Johnston, Robert W.M. MA BD STM	1964	1999	(Glasgow: Temple Anniesland)	13 Kilmardinny Crescent, Bearsden, Glasgow G61 3NP	0141 931 5862
Johnstone, H. Martin J. MA BD MTh PhD	1989	2015	Secretary: Church and Society Council	3/1, 952 Pollokshaws Road, Glasgow G41 2ET MJohnstone@churchofscotland.org.uk	0141 636 5819
Lang, I. Pat (Miss) BSc	1996	2003	(Dunoon: The High Kirk)	37 Crawford Drive, Glasgow G15 6TW	0141 944 2240
Lloyd, John M. BD CertMin	1984	2009	(Glasgow: Croftfoot)	17 Acacia Way, Cambuslang, Glasgow G72 7ZY	07879 812816
Love, Joanna (Ms) BSc DCS	1992	2009	Iona Community: Wild Goose Resource Group	92 Everard Drive, Glasgow G21 1XQ jo@wildgoose.scot	(Office) 0141 429 7281
Lunan, David W. MA BD DUniv DLitt DD	1970	2002	(Presbytery Clerk: Glasgow)	30 Mill Road, Banton, Glasgow G65 0RD	01236 824110
MacBain, Ian W. BD	1971	1993	(Coatbridge: Coatdyke)	24 Thornyburn Drive, Baillieston, Glasgow G69 7ER	0141 771 7030
McChlery, Lynn M. BA BD	2005	2015	(Eaglesham)	62 Grenville Drive, Cambuslang, Glasgow G72 8DP lmcchlery@btinternet.com	0141 643 9730 07748 118008
MacDonald, Anne (Miss) BA DCS	1980	2002	Healthcare Chaplain	Chaplaincy Office, Glasgow Royal Infirmary G4 0SF	0141 211 4661
MacDonald, Kenneth MA BA	2001	2006	(Auxiliary Minister)	5 Henderland Road, Bearsden, Glasgow G61 1AH	0141 943 1103
McDougall, Hilary N. (Mrs) MA PGCE BD	2002	2013	Congregational Facilitator: Presbytery of Glasgow	16 Central Court, Central Avenue, Cambuslang G72 8DJ hmcdougall@churchofscotland.org.uk	0141 641 8574 07539 321832
MacFadyen, Anne M. (Mrs) BSc BD FSAScot	1995	2003	(Auxiliary Minister)	295 Mearns Road, Glasgow G77 5LT	0141 639 3605
McFarlane, Robert G. BD	2001	2018	(Paisley St Mark's Oldhall)	990 Crookston Road, Glasgow G53 7DY	0141 772 6052
Mackenzie, Gordon R. BScAgr BD	1977	2014	(Chapelhall)	16 Crowhill Road, Bishopbriggs, Glasgow G64 1QY rev.g.mackenzie@btopenworld.com	0141 772 3811
MacKinnon, Charles M. BD	1989	2009	(Kilsyth: Anderson)	36 Hilton Terrace, Bishopbriggs, Glasgow G64 3HB cm.ccmackinnon@gmail.com	0141 810 5789
McLachlan, Eric BD MTh	1978	2005	(Glasgow: Cardonald)	16 Kinpurnie Road, Paisley PA1 3HH eric.janis@btinternet.com	01360 319861
McLachlan, T. Alastair BSc	1972	2009	(Craignish with Kilbrandon and Kilchattan with Kilninver and Kilmelford)	9 Alder Road, Milton of Campsie, Glasgow G66 8HH talastair@btinternet.com	07931 155779
McLaren, D. Muir MA BD MTh PhD	1971	2001	(Glasgow: Mosspark)	House 44, 145 Shawhill Road, Glasgow G43 1SX muir44@yahoo.co.uk	0141 774 2483
McLaughlin, Cathie H. (Mrs)	2014	2018	(Ordained Local Minister)	8 Lamlash Place, Glasgow G33 3XH	0141 776 6235
Macleod, Donald BD LRAM DRSAM	1987	2008	(Blairgowrie)	9 Millersneuk Avenue, Lenzie G66 5HJ donmac2@sky.com	07795 014889
MacLeod, Iain A.	2012	2016	Ordained Local Minister, Presbytery wide	6 Hallydown Drive, Glasgow G13 1UF lMacLeod@churchofscotland.org.uk	0141 423 9600
MacLeod-Mair, Alisdair T. MEd DipTheol	2001	2012	(Glasgow: Baillieston St Andrew's)	2/2, 44 Leven Street, Pollokshields, Glasgow G41 2IE revalisdair@hotmail.com	07811 621671
Macnaughton, J.A. MA BD	1949	1989	(Glasgow: Hyndland)	Lilyburn Care Home, 100 Birdston Road, Milton of Campsie, Glasgow G66 8BY	0131 240 2208
McPake, John L. BA BD PhD	1987	2017	Ecumenical Officer, Church of Scotland	121 George Street, Edinburgh EH2 4YN JMcPake@churchofscotland.org.uk	0141 616 6468
McPherson, James B. DCS	1988	2001	(Deacon)	0/1, 104 Cartside Street, Glasgow G42 9TQ	

Name	Charge	Years	Address	Tel
MacQuarrie, Stuart JP BD BSc MBA	Chaplain: University of Glasgow	1984 2001	The Chaplaincy Centre, University of Glasgow, Glasgow G12 8QQ	0141 330 5419
Martindale, John P.F. BD	(Glasgow: Sandyhills)	1994 2005	Flat 3/2, 25 Albert Avenue, Glasgow G42 8RB	0141 433 4367
Miller, Elsie M. (Miss) DCS	(Deacon)	1974 2001	30 Swinton Avenue, Rowansbank, Baillieston, Glasgow G69 6JR	0141 771 0857
Miller, John D. BA BD DD	(Glasgow: Castlemilk East)	1971 2007	98 Kirkcaldy Road, Glasgow G41 4LD rev.john.miller@btinternet.com	0141 423 0221
Moffat, Thomas BSc BD	(Culross and Torryburn)	1976 2008	Flat 8/1, 8 Cranston Street, Glasgow G3 8GG tom@gallus.org.uk	0141 248 1886
Nelson, Thomas BSc BD	(Netherlee)	1992 2002	11a Crosshill Drive, Rutherglen, Glasgow G73 3QU	0141 534 7834
Ninian, Esther J. (Miss) MA BD	(Newton Mearns)	1993 2015	21 St Ronan's Drive, Burnside, Rutherglen G73 3SR estherninian5914@btinternet.com	0141 647 9720
Owen, Catherine W. MTh	(Wishaw Chalmers)	1984 1987	10 Waverley Park, Kirkintilloch, Glasgow G77 2BP katy.owen@talktalk.net	0141 776 0407
Pacitti, Stephen A. MA	(Black Mount with Culter with Libberton and Quothquan)	1963 2003	157 Nithsdale Road, Glasgow G41 5RD	0141 423 5792
Philip, George M. MA	(Glasgow: Sandyford Henderson Memorial)	1953 1996	Red Cross House, The Erskine Home, Renfrewshire PA7 5PU	
Raeburn, Alan C. MA BD	(Glasgow: Battlefield East)	1971 2010	3 Orchard Gardens, Strathaven ML10 6UN acraeburn@hotmail.com	01357 522924
Ramsay, W.G.	(Glasgow: Springburn)	1967 1999	53 Kelvinvale, Kirkintilloch, Glasgow G66 1RD billram@btopenworld.com	0141 776 2915
Ramsden, Iain R. MStJ BTh	(Killearnan with Knockbain)	1999 2013	Flat 1/1, 15 Cardon Square, Renfrew PA4 8BY s4rev@sky.com	07795 972560
Reid, Iain M.A. BD CQSW	(Paisley Glenburn)	1990 2017	16 Walker Court, Glasgow G16 6QP ireid@churchofscotland.org.uk	0141 577 1200
Ross, Donald M. MA	(Industrial Mission Organiser)	1953 1994	14 Cartsbridge Road, Busby, Glasgow G76 8DH	0141 644 2220
Shackleton, William	(Greenock: Wellpark West)	1960 1996	3 Tynwald Avenue, Burnside, Glasgow G73 4RN	0141 569 9407
Smith, G. Stewart MA BD STM	(Glasgow: King's Park)	1966 2006	33 Brent Road, Stewartfield, East Kilbride, Glasgow G74 4RA stewartandmary@googlemail.com	Tel/Fax 01355 226718
Spencer, John MA BD	(Dumfries: Lincluden with Holywood)	1962 2001	10 Kinkell Gardens, Kirkintilloch, Glasgow G66 2HJ	0141 777 8935
Stewart, Diane E. BD	(Milton of Campsie)	1988 2006	4 Miller Gardens, Bishopbriggs, Glasgow G64 1FG destewart@givemail.co.uk	0141 762 1358
Stewart, Norma D. (Miss) MA MEd BD MTh	(Glasgow: Strathbungo Queen's Park)	1977 2000	127 Nether Auldhouse Road, Glasgow G43 2YS	0141 637 6956
Turner, Angus BD	(Industrial Chaplain)	1976 1998	46 Keir Street, Pollokshields, Glasgow G41 2LA	0141 424 0493
Tuton, Robert M. MA	(Glasgow: Shettleston Old)	1957 1995	6 Holmwood Gardens, Uddingston, Glasgow G71 7BH	01698 321108
Walker, Linda	Auxiliary Minister, Presbytery	2008 2013	18 Valeview Terrace, Glasgow G42 9LA LWalker@churchofscotland.org.uk	0141 649 1340
Walton, Ainslie MA MEd	(University of Aberdeen)	1954 1995	Flat 26, 7 Eastwood Crescent, Thornliebank, Glasgow G46 8NS revainslie@aol.com	0141 638 1548
White, C. Peter BVMS BD MRCVS	(Glasgow: Sandyford Henderson Memorial)	1974 2011	2 Hawthorn Place, Torrance, Glasgow G64 4EA revcpw@gmail.com	01360 622680
White, David M. BA BD DMin	(Kirkintilloch St Columba's)	1988 2016	9 Lapwing Avenue, Lenzie, Glasgow G66 3DJ drdavidmwhite@btinternet.com	0141 578 4357

Name	Dates	Former charge	Address	Email	Phone
Whiteford, John D. MA BD	1989 2016	(Glasgow: Newlands South)	42 Maxwell Drive, East Kilbride, Glasgow G74 4HJ JWhiteford@churchofscotland.org.uk		07809 290806
Whitley, Laurence A.B. MA BD PhD DLitt HonFRCPSG	1975 2017	(Glasgow: Cathedral)	35 Springfield Road, Bishopbriggs, Glasgow G64 1PL labwhitley@btinternet.com		07870 733721
Whyte, James BD	1981 2011	(Fairlie)	32 Torburn Avenue, Giffnock, Glasgow G46 7RB jameswhyte89@btinternet.com		0141 620 3043
Wilson, Phyllis M. (Mrs) DipCom DipRE	1985 2006	(Motherwell: South Dalziel)	Glasgow thomas.wilson38@btinternet.com		
Younger, Adah (Mrs) BD	1978 2004	(Glasgow: Dennistoun Central)	7 Gartocher Terrace, Glasgow G32 0HE		0141 774 6475

GLASGOW ADDRESSES

Banton		Kelvinhead Road, Banton
Bishopbriggs		
Kenmure		Viewfield Road, Bishopbriggs
Springfield		The Leys, off Springfield Road
Broom		Mearns Road, Newton Mearns
Burnside Blairbeth		Church Avenue, Burnside
		Kirkriggs Avenue, Blairbeth
Busby		Church Road, Busby
Cadder		Cadder Road, Bishopbriggs
Cambuslang		
Flemington Hallside		Hutchinson Place
Parish		Arnott Way
Campsie		Main Street, Lennoxtown
Chryston		Main Street, Chryston
		20 Blackwoods Crescent, Moodiesburn
Eaglesham		Montgomery Street, Eaglesham
Fernhill and Cathkin		Neilvaig Drive
Gartcosh		113 Lochend Road, Gartcosh
Giffnock		
Orchardhill		Church Road
South		Eastwood Toll
The Park		Ravenscliffe Drive
Glenboig		Main Street, Glenboig
Greenbank		Eaglesham Road, Clarkston
Kilsyth		
Anderson		Kingston Road, Kilsyth
Burns and Old		Church Street, Kilsyth
Kirkintilloch		
Hillhead		Newdyke Road, Kirkintilloch
St Columba's		Waterside Road nr Auld Aisle Road
St David's Mem Pk		Alexandra Street
St Mary's		Cowgate
Lenzie		
Old		Kirkintilloch Road x Garngaber Ave
Union		65 Kirkintilloch Road
Maxwell		
Mearns Castle		Waterfoot Road
Mearns		Mearns Road, Newton Mearns
Milton of Campsie		Locheil Drive, Milton of Campsie
Netherlee		Ormonde Drive x Ormonde Avenue
Newton Mearns		Ayr Road, Newton Mearns
Rutherglen		
Old		Main Street at Queen Street
Stonelaw		Stonelaw Road x Dryburgh Avenue
West and Wardlawhill		3 Western Avenue
Stamperland		Stamperland Gardens, Clarkston
Stepps		Whitehill Avenue
Thornliebank		61 Spiersbridge Road
Torrance		School Road, Torrance
Twechar		Main Street, Twechar
Williamwood		4 Vardar Avenue, Clarkston

Glasgow

Anderston Kelvingrove		759 Argyle St x Elderslie St
Baillieston		
Mure Memorial		Maxwell Drive, Garrowhill
St Andrew's		Bredisholm Road
Balshagray Victoria Pk		218–230 Broomhill Drive
Barlanark Greyfriars		Edinburgh Rd x Hallhill Rd (365)
Blawarthill		Millbrix Avenue
Bridgeton St Francis		
in the East		26 Queen Mary Street
Broomhill Hyndland		64–66 Randolph Rd (x Marlborough Ave)
Calton Parkhead		122 Helenvale Street
Cardonald		2155 Paisley Road West
Carmunnock		Kirk Road, Carmunnock
Carmyle		155 Carmyle Avenue
Carntyne		358 Carntynehall Road
Carnwadric		556 Boydstone Road, Thornliebank
Castlemilk		1 Dougrie Road
Cathcart		
Old		119 Carmunnock Road
Trinity		90 Clarkston Road
Cathedral		Cathedral Square, 2 Castle Street
Causeway, Tollcross		1134 Tollcross Road
Clincarthill		1216 Cathcart Road
Colston Milton		Egilsay Crescent
Colston Wellpark		1378 Springburn Road
Cranhill		109 Bellrock St (at Bellrock Cr)
Croftfoot		Croftpark Ave x Crofthill Road
Dennistoun New		9 Armadale Street

Drumchapel St Andrew's	153 Garscadden Road
Drumchapel St Mark's	281 Kinfauns Drive
Easterhouse	Boyndie Street
Eastwood	Mansewood Road
Gairbraid	1517 Maryhill Road
Gallowgate	Calton Parkhead halls / 122 Helenvale Street
Garthamlock and Craigend East	46 Porchester Street
Gorbals	1 Errol Gardens
Govan and Linthouse	Govan Cross
Hillington Park	24 Berryknowes Road
Ibrox	Carillon Road x Clifford Street
John Ross Memorial	100 Norfolk Street
Jordanhill	28 Woodend Drive (x Munro Road)
Kelvinbridge	Belmont Street at Belmont Bridge
Kelvinside Hillhead	Observatory Road
Kenmuir Mount Vernon	2405 London Road, Mount Vernon
King's Park	242 Castlemilk Road
Kinning Park	Eaglesham Place
Knightswood St Margaret's	2000 Great Western Road

Langside	167–169 Ledard Road (x Lochleven Road)
Maryhill	1990 Maryhill Road
Merrylea	78 Merrylee Road
Newlands South	Riverside Road x Langside Drive
Partick South	259 Dumbarton Road
Partick Trinity	20 Lawrence Street x Elie Street
Pollokshaws	223 Shawbridge Street
Pollokshields	Albert Drive x Shields Road
Possilpark	124 Saracen Street
Queen's Park Govanhill	170 Queen's Drive
Renfield St Stephen's	260 Bath Street
Robroyston	34 Saughs Road
Ruchazie	4 Elibank Street (x Milncroft Road)
Ruchill Kelvinside	Shakespeare Street nr Maryhill Rd
St Andrew and St Nicholas	224 Hartlaw Crescent
St Andrew's East	681 Alexandra Parade
St Christopher's Priesthill and Nitshill — Priesthill building	100 Priesthill Rd (x Muirshiel Cr)
St Christopher's Priesthill and Nitshill — Nitshill building	36 Dove Street
St Columba	300 St Vincent Street

St David's Knightswood	66 Boreland Drive (nr Lincoln Avenue)
St Enoch's Hogganfield	860 Cumbernauld Road
St George's Tron	163 Buchanan Street
St James' (Pollok)	Lyoncross Road x Byrebush Road
St John's Renfield	22 Beaconsfield Road
St Paul's	30 Langdale St (x Greenrig St)
St Rollox	9 Fountainwell Road
Sandyford Henderson Memorial	Kelvinhaugh Street at Argyle Street
Sandyhills	28 Baillieston Rd nr Sandyhills Rd
Scotstoun	Earlbank Ave x Ormiston Ave
Shawlands Trinity	Shawlands Cross (1114 Pollokshaws Road)
Sherbrooke Mosspark	Nithsdale Rd x Sherbrooke Avenue
Shettleston New	679 Old Shettleston Road
Springburn	180 Springburn Way
Temple Anniesland	869 Crow Road
Toryglen	Glenmore Ave nr Prospecthill Road
Trinity Possil and Henry Drummond	2 Crowhill Street (x Broadholm Street)
Tron St Mary's	128 Red Road
Wallacewell	57 Northgate Rd. Balornock
Wellington	University Ave x Southpark Ave
Whiteinch	1a Northinch Court
Yoker	10 Hawick Street

(17) HAMILTON

Meets at Motherwell: Dalziel St Andrew's Parish Church Halls, on the first Tuesday of February, March, May, September, October, November and December, and on the third Tuesday of June.

Presbytery Office:	Rex House, 103 Bothwell Road, Hamilton ML3 0DW hamilton@churchofscotland.org.uk c/o The Presbytery Office	01698 285672
Clerk:	REV. GORDON A. McCRACKEN BD CertMin DMin	20 Arthur Avenue, Airdrie ML6 9EZ RHamilton@churchofscotland.org.uk
Depute Clerk:	REV. ROBERT A. HAMILTON BA BD	7 Graham Place, Ashgill, Larkhall ML9 3BA 01698 883246
Presbytery Treasurer:	MR ROBERT A. ALLAN	rallan3246@aol.com

1 **Airdrie: Cairnlea (H) (01236 762101) linked with Calderbank**
   Peter H. Donald MA PhD BD   1991   2018   31 Victoria Place, Airdrie ML6 9BU   01236 753159

2 **Airdrie: Clarkston**
   Hanna I. Rankine   2018   66 Wellhall Road, Hamilton ML3 9BY   01236 756862
   HRankine@churchofscotland.org.uk

3 **Airdrie: High linked with Caldercruix and Longriggend**
   Ian R.W. McDonald BSc BD PhD   2007   17 Etive Drive, Airdrie ML6 9QL   01236 760023
   IMcDonald@churchofscotland.org.uk

4 **Airdrie: Jackson**
   Kay Gilchrist (Miss) BD   1996   2008   48 Dunrobin Road, Airdrie ML6 8LR   01236 760154
   KGilchrist@churchofscotland.org.uk

5 **Airdrie: New Monkland (H) linked with Greengairs**
   William Jackson BD CertMin   1994   2015   3 Dykehead Crescent, Airdrie ML6 6PU   01236 761723
   WJackson@churchofscotland.org.uk

6 **Airdrie: St Columba's**
   Margaret F. Currie BEd BD   1980   1987   52 Kennedy Drive, Airdrie ML6 9AW   01236 763173
   MCurrie@churchofscotland.org.uk

7 **Airdrie: The New Wellwynd**
   Robert A. Hamilton BA BD   1995   2001   20 Arthur Avenue, Airdrie ML6 9EZ   01236 763022
   RHamilton@churchofscotland.org.uk

8 **Bargeddie (H)**
   Vacant   The Manse, Manse Road, Bargeddie, Baillieston, Glasgow   G69 6UB 0141 771 1322

9 **Bellshill: Central**
   Kevin M. de Beer BTh   1995   2016   32 Adamson Street, Bellshill ML4 1DT   01698 841176
   KdeBeer@churchofscotland.org.uk   07555 265609

10 **Bellshill: West (H)**
   Calum Stark LLB BD   2011   2015   16 Croftpark Street, Bellshill ML4 1EY   **01698 747581**
   CStark@churchofscotland.org.uk   01698 842877

11 **Blantyre: Livingstone Memorial linked with Blantyre St Andrew's**
Murdo C. Macdonald MA BD 2002 2017 332 Glasgow Road, Blantyre, Glasgow G72 9LQ 01698 769699
Murdo.Macdonald@churchofscotland.org.uk

12 **Blantyre: Old (H)**
Sarah L. Ross (Mrs) BD MTh PGDip 2004 2013 The Manse, Craigmuir Road, High Blantyre, Glasgow G72 9UA 01698 769046
SRoss@churchofscotland.org.uk

13 **Blantyre: St Andrew's** See Blantyre: Livingstone Memorial

14 **Bothwell (H)**
James M. Gibson TD LTh LRAM 1978 1989 Manse Avenue, Bothwell, Glasgow G71 8PQ Tel 01698 853189
JGibson@churchofscotland.org.uk Fax 01698 854903

15 **Calderbank** See Airdrie: Cairnlea

16 **Caldercruix and Longriggend (H)** See Airdrie: High

17 **Chapelhall (H) linked with Kirk o' Shotts (H)**
Vacant The Manse, Russell Street, Chapelhall, Airdrie ML6 8SG 01236 763439
Session Clerk, Chapelhall: Elizabeth Millar (Mrs) millarelizabeth@btinternet.com 01698 870205

18 **Cleland (H) linked with Wishaw: St Mark's**
Graham Austin BD 1997 2008 3 Laburnum Crescent, Wishaw ML2 7EH 01698 384596
GAustin@churchofscotland.org.uk

19 **Coatbridge: Blairhill Dundyvan (H) linked with Coatbridge: Middle**
Vacant 1 Nelson Terrace, East Kilbride, Glasgow G74 2EY 01355 520093
Session Clerk, Blairhill Dundyvan: Myra Fraser myrafraser@hotmail.co.uk 01236 421728

20 **Coatbridge: Calder (H) linked with Coatbridge: Old Monkland**
Vacant 26 Bute Street, Coatbridge ML5 4HF 01236 421516

21 **Coatbridge: Middle** See Coatbridge: Blairhill Dundyvan

22	**Coatbridge: New St Andrew's** Fiona M. Nicolson BA BD	1996	2005	77 Eglinton Street, Coatbridge ML5 3JF FNicolson@churchofscotland.org.uk	01236 437271
23	**Coatbridge: Old Monkland** See Coatbridge: Calder				
24	**Coatbridge: Townhead (H)** Ecilo Selemani LTh MTh	1993	2004	Crinan Crescent, Coatbridge ML5 2LH ESelemani@churchofscotland.org.uk	01236 702914
25	**Dalserf** Vacant Session Clerk: Joan Pollok			Manse Brae, Dalserf, Larkhall ML9 3BN joan.pollok@btinternet.com	01698 882195 07728 337212
26	**East Kilbride: Claremont (H)** Gordon R. Palmer MA BD STM	1986	2003	17 Deveron Road, East Kilbride, Glasgow G74 2HR GPalmer@churchofscotland.org.uk	**01355 238088** 01355 248526
27	**East Kilbride: Greenhills (E)** John Brewster MA BD DipEd	1988		21 Turnberry Place, East Kilbride, Glasgow G75 8TB JBrewster@churchofscotland.org.uk	**01355 221746** 01355 242564
28	**East Kilbride: Moncreiff (H)** Neil Buchanan BD	1991		16 Almond Drive, East Kilbride, Glasgow G74 2HX NBuchanan@churchofscotland.org.uk	**01355 223328** 01355 238639
29	**East Kilbride: Mossneuk** Vacant Jim Murphy (Ordained Local Minister)	2014	2017	30 Eden Grove, Mossneuk, East Kilbride, Glasgow G75 8XU 10 Hillview Crescent, Bellshill ML4 1NX JMurphy@churchofscotland.org.uk	**01355 260954** 01355 234196 01698 740189
30	**East Kilbride: Old (H)** Anne S. Paton BA BD	2001		40 Maxwell Drive, East Kilbride, Glasgow G74 4HJ APaton@churchofscotland.org.uk	**01355 279004** 01355 220732

No.	Name		Address	Telephone
31	**East Kilbride: South (H)**			
	Terry Ann Taylor BA MTh	2005 2017	7 Clamps Wood, St Leonard's, East Kilbride, Glasgow G74 2HB TTaylor@churchofscotland.org.uk	01355 902758
32	**East Kilbride: Stewartfield (New Charge Development)**			
	Douglas W. Wallace MA BD	1981 2001	8 Thistle Place, Stewartfield, East Kilbride, Glasgow G74 4RH DWallace@churchofscotland.org.uk	01355 260879
33	**East Kilbride: West (H)**			
	Mahboob Masih BA MDiv MTh	1999 2008	4 East Milton Grove, East Kilbride, Glasgow G75 8FN MMasih@churchofscotland.org.uk	01355 224469
34	**East Kilbride: Westwood (H)**			
	Kevin Mackenzie BD DPS	1989 1996	16 Inglewood Crescent, East Kilbride, Glasgow G75 8QD Kevin.MacKenzie@churchofscotland.org.uk	**01355 245657** 01355 223992
35	**Greengairs** See Airdrie: New Monkland			
36	**Hamilton: Cadzow (H)**			
	W. John Carswell BS MDiv DPT	1996 2009	3 Carlisle Road, Hamilton ML3 7BZ JCarswell@churchofscotland.org.uk	**01698 428695** 01698 426682
37	**Hamilton: Gilmour and Whitehill (H) linked with Hamilton: West (H) (01698 284670)**			
	Vacant			
	Session Clerk, Gilmour: Ann Paul		annepaul.gandw@gmail.com	01698 284670
	Session Clerk, West: Ian Hindle		ianmarilyn.hindle@googlemail.com	01698 421697 01698 429080
38	**Hamilton: Hillhouse**			
	Christopher A. Rankine MA MTh PgDE	2016	66 Wellhall Road, Hamilton ML3 9BY CRankine@churchofscotland.org.uk	01698 327579
39	**Hamilton: Old (H)**			
	I. Ross Blackman BSc MBA BD	2015	1 Chateau Grove, Hamilton ML3 7DS RBlackman@churchofscotland.org.uk	**01698 281905** 01698 640185
40	**Hamilton: St John's (H)**			
	Joanne C. Hood (Miss) MA BD	2003 2012	9 Shearer Avenue, Ferniegair, Hamilton ML3 7FX JHood@churchofscotland.org.uk	**01698 283492** 01698 425002

41 Hamilton: South (H) (01698 281014) linked with Quarter
Vacant
Session Clerk, South: Joanne Kennedy
Session Clerk, Quarter: Louise Ross
The Manse, Limekilnburn Road, Quarter, Hamilton   ML3 7XA
hamiltonsouthchurch@outlook.com
louise.ross7@btinternet.com
01698 424511
07828 504176
01698 424458

42 Hamilton: Trinity
S. Lindsay A. Turnbull BSc BD   2014
69 Buchan Street, Hamilton   ML3 8JY
Lindsay.Turnbull@churchofscotland.org.uk
01698 284254
01698 284919

43 Hamilton: West See Hamilton: Gilmour and Whitehill

44 Holytown linked with New Stevenston: Wrangholm Kirk
Caryl A.E. Kyle (Mrs) BD DipEd   2008
The Manse, 260 Edinburgh Road, Holytown, Motherwell ML1 5RU
CKyle@churchofscotland.org.uk
01698 832622

45 Kirk o' Shotts (H) See Chapelhall

46 Larkhall: Chalmers (H)
Vacant
Session Clerk: Christine Buck
Quarry Road, Larkhall ML9 1HH
chalmerscos@gmail.com
01698 882238
07518 510664

47 Larkhall: St Machan's (H)
Alastair McKillop BD DipMin   1995   2004
2 Orchard Gate, Larkhall ML9 1HG
AMcKillop@churchofscotland.org.uk
01698 321976

48 Larkhall: Trinity
Vacant
Session Clerk: Wilma Gilmour (Miss)
13 Machan Avenue, Larkhall ML9 2HE
gilmourgilmour@btinternet.com
01698 881401
01698 883002

49 Motherwell: Crosshill (H) linked with Motherwell: St Margaret's
Gavin W.G. Black BD   2006
15 Orchard Street, Motherwell ML1 3JE
GBlack@churchofscotland.org.uk
01698 263410

50 Motherwell: Dalziel St Andrew's (H)
Derek W. Hughes BSc BD DipEd   1990   1996
4 Pollock Street, Motherwell ML1 1LP
DHughes@churchofscotland.org.uk
01698 264097
01698 263414

51 Motherwell: North linked with Wishaw: Craigneuk and Belhaven (H)
Derek H.N. Pope BD   1987   1995
35 Birrens Road, Motherwell ML1 3NS
DPope@churchofscotland.org.uk   01698 266716

52 Motherwell: St Margaret's See Motherwell: Crosshill

53 Motherwell: St Mary's (H)
Bryce Calder MA BD   1995   2017
19 Orchard Street, Motherwell ML1 3JE
BCalder@churchofscotland.org.uk   07986 144834

54 Motherwell: South (H)
Alan W Gibson BA BD   2001   2016
62 Manse Road, Motherwell ML1 2PT
Alan.Gibson@churchofscotland.org.uk   01698 239279

55 Newarthill and Carfin
Elaine W. McKinnon MA BD   1988   2014
Church Street, Newarthill, Motherwell ML1 5HS
EMcKinnon@churchofscotland.org.uk   01698 296850

56 Newmains: Bonkle (H) linked with Newmains: Coltness Memorial (H)
Graham Raeburn MTh   2004
5 Kirkgate, Newmains, Wishaw ML2 9BT
GRaeburn@churchofscotland.org.uk   01698 383858

57 Newmains: Coltness Memorial See Newmains: Bonkle

58 New Stevenston: Wrangholm Kirk See Holytown

59 Overtown
Lorna I. MacDougall MA DipGC BD   2003   2017
The Manse, 146 Main Street, Overtown, Wishaw ML2 0QP
LMacDougall@churchofscotland.org.uk   01698 352090

60 Quarter See Hamilton: South

61 Shotts: Calderhead Erskine
Vacant
Session Clerk: Liam T. Haggart SSC
The Manse, 9 Kirk Road, Shotts ML7 5ET
a2lth@hotmail.com   01501 823204
                                                                          07896 557687

62 Stonehouse: St Ninian's (H)
Stewart J. Cutler BA MSc DipHE 2017
4 Hamilton Way, Stonehouse, Larkhall ML9 3PU
revstewartcutler@gmail.com
01698 791508

Stonehouse: St Ninian's is a Local Ecumenical Partnership with the United Reformed Church

63 Strathaven: Avendale Old and Drumclog (H)
Alan B. Telfer BA BD 1983 2010
4 Fortrose Gardens, Strathaven ML10 6SH
ATelfer@churchofscotland.org.uk
01357 529748
01357 523031

64 Strathaven: Trinity (H)
Shaw J. Paterson BSc BD MSc 1991
15 Lethame Road, Strathaven ML10 6AD
SPaterson@churchofscotland.org.uk
Tel 01357 520019
Fax 01357 529316

65 Uddingston: Burnhead (H)
Les N. Brunger BD 2010
90 Laburnum Road, Uddingston, Glasgow G71 5DB
LBrunger@churchofscotland.org.uk
01698 813716

66 Uddingston: Old (H)
Fiona L.J. McKibbin (Mrs) MA BD 2011
1 Belmont Avenue, Uddingston, Glasgow G71 7AX
FMcKibbin@churchofscotland.org.uk
01698 814015
01698 814757

67 Uddingston: Viewpark (H)
Michael G. Lyall BD 1993 2001
14 Holmbrae Road, Uddingston, Glasgow G71 6AP
MLyall@churchofscotland.org.uk
01698 813113

68 Wishaw: Cambusnethan North (H)
Mhorag Macdonald (Ms) MA BD 1989
350 Kirk Road, Wishaw ML2 8LH
Mhorag.Macdonald@churchofscotland.org.uk
01698 381305

69 Wishaw: Cambusnethan Old and Morningside
Vacant
Session Clerk: Graeme Vincent
22 Coronation Street, Wishaw ML2 8LF
gvincent@theiet.org
01698 384235
01555 752166

70 Wishaw: Craigneuk and Belhaven See Motherwell North

71 Wishaw: Old (H)
Vacant
Session Clerk: Thomas W. Donaldson

130 Glen Road, Wishaw ML2 7NP
tomdonaldson@talktalk.net

01698 **376080**
01698 375134
01698 357605

72 Wishaw: St Mark's See Cleland

73 Wishaw: South Wishaw (H)
Terence C. Moran BD CertMin   1995   2015

3 Walter Street, Wishaw ML2 8LQ
TMoran@churchofscotland.org.uk

01698 **375306**
01698 767459

Name			Charge	Address	Phone
Barrie, Arthur P. LTh	1973	2007	(Hamilton: Cadzow)	30 Airbles Crescent, Motherwell ML1 3AR elizabethbarrie@ymail.com	01698 261147
Baxendale, Georgina M. (Mrs) BD	1981	2014	(Motherwell: South)	32 Meadowhead Road, Plains, Airdrie ML6 7HG georgiebaxendale6@tiscali.co.uk	
Buck, Maxine	2007	2015	Auxiliary Minister, Presbytery	Brownlee House, Mauldslie Road, Carluke ML8 5HW MBuck@churchofscotland.org.uk	01555 759063
Colvin, Sharon E.F. (Mrs) BD LRAM LTCL	1985	2007	(Airdrie: Jackson)	25 Balblair Road, Airdrie ML6 6GQ dibleycol@hotmail.com	01236 590796
Cook, J. Stanley BD Dip PSS	1974	2001	(Hamilton: West)	Mansend, 137A Old Manse Road, Netherton, Wishaw ML2 0EW stancook@blueyonder.co.uk	01698 299600
Donaldson, George M. MA BD	1984	2015	(Caldercruix and Longriggend)	4 Toul Gardens, Motherwell ML1 2FE g.donaldson505@btinternet.com	01698 239477
Doyle, David W. MA BD	1977	2014	(Motherwell: St Mary's)	76 Kethers Street, Motherwell ML1 3HN	01698 263472
Fuller, Agnes A. (Mrs) BD	1987	2014	(Bellshill: West)	10 Carr Quadrant, Mossend, Bellshill ML4 1HZ revamoore2@tiscali.co.uk	01698 841558
Gordon, Alasdair B. BD LLB EdD	1970	1980	(Aberdeen: Summerhill)	Flat 1, 13 Auchingramont Road, Hamilton ML3 6JP alasdairbgordon@hotmail.com	01698 200561 07768 897843
Grier, James BD	1991	2005	(Coatbridge: Middle)	14 Love Drive, Bellshill ML4 1BY	01698 742545
Hunter, James E. LTh	1974	1997	(Blantyre: Livingstone Memorial)	57 Dalwhinnie Avenue, Blantyre, Glasgow G72 9NQ	01698 826177
Jones, Robert BSc BD	1990	2017	(Rosskeen)	3 Grantown Avenue, Airdrie ML6 8HH rob2jones@btinternet.com	07761 782714
Kent, Robert M. MA BD	1973	2011	(Hamilton: St John's)	48 Fyne Crescent, Larkhall ML9 2UX robertmkent@talktalk.net	01698 769244
Lusk, Alastair S. BD	1974	2010	(East Kilbride: Moncreiff)	9 MacFie Place, Stewartfield, East Kilbride, Glasgow G74 4TY	
McAlpine, John BSc	1988	2004	(Auxiliary Minister)	Braeside, 201 Bonkle Road, Newmains, Wishaw ML2 9AA	01698 384610 07918 600720
McCracken, Gordon A. BD CertMin DMin	1988	2015	Presbytery Clerk: Hamilton	1 Kenilworth Road, Lanark ML11 7BL	
McDonald, John A. MA BD	1978	1997	(Cumbernauld: Condorrat)	17 Thomson Drive, Bellshill ML4 3ND	
McKee, Norman B. BD	1987	2010	(Uddingston: Old)	148 Station Road, Blantyre, Glasgow G72 9BW normanmckee946@btinternet.com	01698 827358

Name	Years	Role / Charge	Address / Email	Tel
MacKenzie, Ian C. MA BD	1970 2011	(Interim Minister)	21 Wilson Street, Motherwell ML1 1NP iancmac@blueyonder.co.uk	01698 301230
Melrose, J.H. Loudon MA BD MEd	1955 1996	(Assoc.: Gourock: Old Gourock and Ashton)	1 Laverock Avenue, Hamilton ML3 7DD	01698 427958
Munton, James G. BA	1969 2002	(Coatbridge: Old Monkland)	2 Moorcroft Drive, Airdrie ML6 8ES revjgm1@gmail.com	01236 754848
Murdoch, Iain C. MA LLB DipEd BD	1995 2017	(Wishaw: Cambusnethan Old and Morningside)	2 Pegasus Avenue, Carluke ML8 5TN iaincmurdoch@btopenworld.com	01555 773891
Pandian, Ali R. BA BD PGCertHC	2017	Healthcare Chaplain University Hospital Wishaw	50 Netherton Street, Wishaw ML2 0DP APandian@churchofscotland.org.uk	01698 366779 07966 368344
Price, Peter O. CBE QHC BA FPhS	1960 1996	(Blantyre: Old)	22 Old Bothwell Road, Bothwell, Glasgow G71 8AW peteroprice@sky.com	01698 854032
Salmond, James S. BA BD MTh ThD	1979 2003	(Holytown)	165 Torbothie Road, Shotts ML7 5NE	01698 310370
Spence, Sheila M. (Mrs) MA BD	1979 2010	(Kirk o' Shotts)	12 Machan Avenue, Larkhall ML9 2HE	01698 817582
Stevenson, John LTh	1998 2006	(Cambuslang: St Andrew's)	20 Knowehead Gardens, Uddingston, Glasgow G71 7PY therev20@sky.com	
Stewart, William T. BD	1980 2018	(Glassford with Strathaven East)	68 Townhead Street, Strathaven ML10 6DJ	01357 521138
Thomson, John M.A. TD JP BD ThM	1978 2014	(Hamilton: Old)	8 Skylands Place, Hamilton ML3 8SB jt@john1949.plus.com	01698 422511
Waddell, Elizabeth A. (Mrs) BD	1999 2014	(Hamilton: West)	114 Branchalfield, Wishaw ML2 8QD elizabethwaddell@tiscali.co.uk	01698 382909
Wilson, James H. LTh	1970 1996	(Cleland)	21 Austine Drive, Hamilton ML3 7YE wilsonjh@blueyonder.co.uk	01698 457042
Wyllie, Hugh R. MA DD FCIBS	1962 2000	(Hamilton: Old)	18 Chantinghall Road, Hamilton ML3 8NP	01698 420002
Zambonini, James LIADip	1997 2015	(Auxiliary Minister)	100 Old Manse Road, Netherton, Wishaw ML2 0EP	01698 350889

HAMILTON ADDRESSES

Airdrie
Cairnlea	89 Graham Street
Clarkston	Forrest Street
High	North Bridge Street
Jackson	Glen Road
New Monkland	Glenmavis
St Columba's	Thrashbush Road
The New Wellwynd	Wellwynd

Coatbridge
Blairhill Dundyvan	Blairhill Street
Calder	Calder Street
Middle	Bank Street
New St Andrew's	Church Street
Old Monkland	Woodside Street

Townhead	Crinan Crescent

East Kilbride
Claremont	High Common Road, St Leonard's
Greenhills	Greenhills Centre
Moncreiff	Calderwood Road
Mossneuk	Eden Drive
Old	Montgomery Street
South	Baird Hill, Murray
Stewartfield	Stewartfield Community Centre
West	Kittoch Street
Westwood	Belmont Drive, Westwood

Hamilton
Cadzow	Woodside Walk
Gilmour and Whitehill	Glasgow Road, Burnbank
Hillhouse	Clerkwell Road
Old	Leechlee Road
St John's	Duke Street
South	Strathaven Road
Trinity	Neilsland Square off Neilsland Road
West	Burnbank Road

Motherwell
Crosshill	Windmillhill Street x Airbles Street
Dalziel St Andrew's	Merry Street and Muir Street
North	Chesters Crescent
St Margaret's	Shields Road
St Mary's	Avon Street
South	Gavin Street

Uddingston		
Burnhead	Laburnum Road	
Old	Old Glasgow Road	
Viewpark	Old Edinburgh Road	

Wishaw		
Cambusnethan		
North	Kirk Road	
Old	Kirk Road	

Craigneuk and		
Belhaven		
Old	Craigneuk Street	
St Mark's	Main Street	
South Wishaw	Coltness Road	
	East Academy Street	

(18) DUMBARTON

Meets at Dumbarton, in Riverside Church Halls, on the first Tuesday of February, March, April (if required), May, September, October (if required), November and December; and on the third Tuesday of June at the incoming Moderator's church for the installation of the Moderator.

Clerk:	**VERY REV. JOHN C. CHRISTIE** **BSc BD MSB CBiol**		10 Cumberland Avenue, Helensburgh G84 8QG dumbarton@churchofscotland.org.uk	**01436 674078** **07711 336392**

Alexandria
Elizabeth W. Houston MA BD DipEd	1985	1995	32 Ledrish Avenue, Balloch, Alexandria G83 8JB WHouston@churchofscotland.org.uk	01389 751933

Arrochar linked with Luss
Louis C. Bezuidenhout BA MA BD DD (Transition Minister)	1978	2014	The Manse, Luss, Alexandria G83 8NZ LBezuidenhout@churchofscotland.org.uk	01389 763317

Baldernock (H) linked with Milngavie: St Paul's (H)
Fergus C. Buchanan MA BD MTh	1982	1988	8 Buchanan Street, Milngavie, Glasgow G62 8DD Fergus.Buchanan@churchofscotland.org.uk	**0141 956 4405** 0141 956 1043
David M. White BA BD DMin (Associate Minister)	1988	2018	9 Lapwing Avenue, Lenzie, Glasgow G66 3DJ drdavidmwhite@btinternet.com	0141 578 4357

Bearsden: Baljaffray (H)
Ian K. McEwan BSc PhD BD FRSE	2008		5 Fintry Gardens, Bearsden, Glasgow G61 4RJ IMcEwan@churchofscotland.org.uk	0141 942 0366

Bearsden: Cross (H)
Graeme R. Wilson MCIBS BD ThM DMin	2006	2013	61 Drymen Road, Bearsden, Glasgow G61 2SU GWilson@churchofscotland.org.uk	0141 942 0507

Bearsden: Killermont (H)
Alan J. Hamilton LLB BD PhD   2003   8 Clathic Avenue, Bearsden, Glasgow G61 2HF
AHamilton@churchofscotland.org.uk   0141 942 0021

Bearsden: New Kilpatrick (H)
Roderick G. Hamilton MA BD   1992   2011   **mail@nkchurch.org.uk**
51 Manse Road, Bearsden, Glasgow G61 3PN
Roddy.Hamilton@churchofscotland.org.uk   **0141 942 8827**
0141 942 0035

Bearsden: Westerton Fairlie Memorial (H)
Christine M. Goldie LLB BD MTh DMin   1984   2008   3 Canniesburn Road, Bearsden, Glasgow G61 1PW
CGoldie@churchofscotland.org.uk   **0141 942 6960**
0141 942 2672

Bonhill (H) (01389 756516) linked with Renton: Trinity (H)
Barbara A. O'Donnell BD PGSE   2007   2016   Ashbank, 258 Main Street, Alexandria G83 0NU
BODonnell@churchofscotland.org.uk   01389 752356
07889 251912

Cardross (H)
Margaret McArthur BD DipMin   1995   2015   16 Bainfield Road, Cardross G82 5JQ
MMcArthur@churchofscotland.org.uk   **01389 841322**
01389 849329
07799 556367

Clydebank: Faifley
Gregor McIntyre BSc BD   1991   Kirklea, Cochno Road, Hardgate, Clydebank G81 6PT
Gregor.McIntyre@churchofscotland.org.uk   01389 876836

Clydebank: Kilbowie St Andrew's linked with Clydebank: Radnor Park (H)
Margaret J.B. Yule BD   1992   11 Tiree Gardens, Old Kilpatrick, Glasgow G60 5AT
MYule@churchofscotland.org.uk   01389 875599

Clydebank: Radnor Park See Clydebank: Kilbowie St Andrew's

Clydebank: Waterfront linked with Dalmuir: Barclay
Ruth H.B. Morrison MA BD PhD   2009   2014   16 Parkhall Road, Dalmuir, Clydebank G81 3RJ
RMorrison@churchofscotland.org.uk   **0141 941 3988**
0141 941 3317

Margaret A.E. Nutter   2014   2017   Kilmorich, 14 Balloch Road, Balloch, Alexandria G83 8SR
(Ordained Local Minister)   MNutter@churchofscotland.org.uk   01389 754505

Craigrownie linked with Garelochhead (01436 810589) linked with Rosneath: St Modan's (H)
Christine M. Murdoch BD   1999   The Manse, Argyll Road, Kilcreggan, Helensburgh G84 0JW   01436 842274
                                                                        CMurdoch@churchofscotland.org.uk   07973 331890

Ann J. Cameron (Mrs) CertCS DCE TEFL   2005   2017   Water's Edge, Ferry Road, Rosneath, Helensburgh G84 0RS   01436 831800
(Auxiliary Minister)   ACameron@churchofscotland.org.uk

Dalmuir: Barclay See Clydebank: Waterfront

Dumbarton: Riverside (H) (01389 742551) linked with Dumbarton: St Andrew's (H) linked with Dumbarton: West Kirk (H)
C. Ian W. Johnson MA BD   1997   2014   18 Castle Road, Dumbarton G82 1JF   01389 726685
                                                                        CJohnson@churchofscotland.org.uk

Dumbarton: St Andrew's (H) See Dumbarton: West
Dumbarton: West Kirk See Dumbarton: Riverside

Duntocher: Trinity (H) (L)
Vacant
Session Clerk: Colin G. Dow   The Manse, Roman Road, Duntocher, Clydebank G81 6BT   01389 380038
                                                                        colin.g.dow@ntlworld.com

Garelochhead See Craigrownie

Helensburgh linked with Rhu and Shandon
David T. Young BA BD MTh   2007   35 East Argyle Street, Helensburgh G84 8UP   01436 673365
                                                                        DYoung@churchofscotland.org.uk   07508 628133

Tina Kemp MA   2005   12 Oaktree Gardens, Dumbarton G82 1EU   01389 730477
(Auxiliary Minister)   TKemp@churchofscotland.org.uk

Jamestown (H)
Vacant
Session Clerk: Robert M. Kinloch   26 Kessog's Gardens, Balloch, Alexandria G83 8QJ   01389 756447
                                                                        rkinloch@blueyonder.co.uk   07760 276505

Kilmaronock Gartocharn
Guardianship of the Presbytery
Session Clerk: Angus Kennedy   anguskcn@gmail.com   01389 830301

Luss See Arrochar

Milngavie: Cairns (H)
Andrew Frater BA BD MTh   1987 1994   4 Cairns Drive, Milngavie, Glasgow G62 8AJ
AFrater@churchofscotland.org.uk   **0141 956 4868**
0141 956 1717

Milngavie: St Luke's
Ramsay B. Shields BA BD   1990 1997   70 Hunter Road, Milngavie, Glasgow G62 7BY
RShields@churchofscotland.org.uk   **0141 956 4226**
Tel 0141 577 9171
Fax 0141 577 9181

Milngavie: St Paul's (H) See Baldernock

Old Kilpatrick Bowling
Scott McCrum BD   2015 2018   The Manse, Old Kilpatrick, Glasgow G60 5JQ
SMcCrum@churchofscotland.org.uk   08005 668242

Renton: Trinity See Bonhill
Rhu and Shandon See Helensburgh
Rosneath: St Modan's See Craigrownie

Blackley, Jane M. MA BD	2009	2018	(Brechin: Gardner Memorial with Farnell)	38 Garvel Road, Milngavie, Glasgow G62 7JE	
Booth, Frederick M. LTh	1970	2005	(Helensburgh: St Columba)	Achnashie Coach House, Clynder, Helensburgh G84 0QD boothef@btinternet.com	01436 831858
Christie, John C. BSc BD MSB CBiol	1990	2014	(Interim Minister)	10 Cumberland Avenue, Helensburgh G84 8QG rev.jcc@btinternet.com	01436 674078 07711 336392
Clark, David W. MA BD	1975	2014	(Helensburgh: St Andrew's Kirk with Rhu and Shandon)	3 Ritchie Avenue, Cardross, Dumbarton G82 5LL clarkdw@talktalk.net	01389 849319
Dalton, Mark BD DipMin RN	2002		Chaplain: Royal Navy	HMS Neptune HM Naval Base Clyde, Faslane, Helensburgh G84 8HL mark.dalton242@mod.gov.uk	01436 674321 ext. 6216
Hamilton, David G. MA BD	1971	2004	(Braes of Rannoch with Foss and Rannoch)	79 Finlay Rise, Milngavie, Glasgow G62 6QL davidhamilton40@googlemail.com	0141 956 4202
Harris, John W.F. MA	1967	2012	(Bearsden: Cross)	68 Mitre Road, Glasgow G14 9LL jwfh@sky.com	0141 321 1061
Lees, Andrew P. BD	1984	2017	(Baldernock)	58 Lindores Drive, Stepps G33 6PD andrew.lees@yahoo.co.uk	0141 389 5840
McCutcheon, John	2014		Ordained Local Minister	Flat 2/6 Parkview, Milton Brae, Milton, Dumbarton G82 2TT JMcCutcheon@churchofscotland.org.uk	01389 739034
McIntyre, J. Ainslie MA BD	1963	1984	(University of Glasgow)	60 Bonnaughton Road, Bearsden, Glasgow G61 4DB jamcintyre@hotmail.com	0141 942 5143 07826 013266

Martin, James MA BD DD	1946	1987	(Glasgow: High Carntyne)	Westerton Care Home, 116 Maxwell Avenue, Bearsden, Glasgow G61 1HU — 01389 753039
Miller, Ian H. BA BD	1975	2012	(Bonhill)	Derand, Queen Street, Alexandria G83 0AS / revianmiller@btinternet.com
Moore, Norma MA BD	1995	2017	(Jamestown)	25 Miller Street, Dumbarton G82 2JA / norma-moore@sky.com — 01360 550098
Munro, David P. MA BD STM	1953	1996	(Bearsden: North)	14 Birch Road, Killearn, Glasgow G63 9SQ / david.munro1929@btinternet.com — 0141 956 2897
Ramage, Alastair E. MA BA ADB CertEd	1996	2016	(Auxiliary Minister)	16 Claremont Gardens, Milngavie, Glasgow G62 6PG / sueandalastairramage@btinternet.com
Robertson, Ishbel A. R. MA BD	2013	2018	(Ordained Local Minister)	Oakdene, 81 Bonhill Road, Dumbarton G82 2DU / IRobertson@churchofscotland.org.uk — 01389 763436
Steven, Harold A.M. MStJ LTh FSA Scot	1970	2001	(Baldernock)	9 Cairnhill Road, Bearsden, Glasgow G61 1AT / harold.allison.steven@gmail.com — 0141 942 1598
Taylor, Jane C. BD DipMin	1990	2013	(Insch-Leslie-Premnay-Oyne)	Timbers, Argyll Road, Kilcreggan G84 0JW / jane.c.taylor@btinternet.com — 01436 842336
Wilson, John BD	1985	2010	(Glasgow: Temple Anniesland)	4 Carron Crescent, Bearsden, Glasgow G61 1HJ / reviwilson@btinternet.com — 0141 931 5609
Wright, Malcolm LTh	1970	2003	(Craigrownie with Rosneath: St Modan's)	30 Clairinsh, Drumkinnon Gate, Balloch, Alexandria G83 8SE / malcolmcatherine@msn.com — 01389 720338

DUMBARTON ADDRESSES

Bearsden
Baljaffray — Grampian Way
Cross — Drymen Road
Killermont — Rannoch Drive
New Kilpatrick — Manse Road
Westerton — Crarae Avenue

Clydebank
Fairley — Faifley Road
Kilbowie St Andrew's — Kilbowie Road
Radnor Park — Radnor Street
Waterfront — Town Centre

Dumbarton
Riverside — High Street

St Andrew's — Aitkenbar Circle
West Kirk — West Bridgend

Helensburgh — Colquhoun Square

Milngavie
Cairns — Buchanan Street
St Luke's — Kirk Street
St Paul's — Strathblane Road

(19) ARGYLL

Meets in the Village Hall, Tarbert, Loch Fyne, Argyll on the first Tuesday or Wednesday of March, June, September and December. For details, contact the Presbytery Clerk.

Clerk:	MR W. STEWART SHAW DL BSC	59 Barone Road, Rothesay, Isle of Bute PA20 0DZ / argyll@churchofscotland.org.uk	07470 520240
Treasurer:	REV. DAVID CARRUTHERS BD	The Manse, Park Road, Ardrishaig, Lochgilphead PA30 8HE / DCarruthers@churchofscotland.org.uk	01546 603269

Appin linked with Lismore
Iain C. Barclay MBE TD MA BD MTh   1976   2015
MPhil PhD FRSA
The Manse, Appin PA38 4DD
ICBarclay@churchofscotland.org.uk
Appin 01631 730143
Lismore 01631 760077

Ardchattan (H)
Vacant
Session Clerk: Catherine T. Robb (Miss)
Ardchattan Manse, North Connel, Oban PA37 1RG
catherinerobb02@btinternet.com
01631 710364
01631 720335

Ardrishaig (H) linked with South Knapdale
David Carruthers BD   1998
The Manse, Park Road, Ardrishaig, Lochgilphead PA30 8HE
DCarruthers@churchofscotland.org.uk
01546 603269

Barra (GD) linked with South Uist (GD)
Lindsay Schluter ThE CertMin PhD   1995   2016
The Manse, Cuithir, Isle of Barra HS9 5XU
LSchluter@churchofscotland.org.uk
01871 810230
07835 913963

Campbeltown: Highland (H)
Vacant
Highland Church Manse, Kirk Street, Campbeltown PA28 6BN
01586 551146

Campbeltown: Lorne and Lowland (H)
Vacant
Session Clerk: Jean Durnan (Mrs)
Lorne and Lowland Manse, Castlehill, Campbeltown PA28 6AN
jean.durnan60@btinternet.com
01586 552468
01586 552923

Coll linked with Connel
Vacant
St Oran's Manse, Connel, Oban PA37 1PJ
Coll 01879 230366; Connel 01631 710242

Colonsay and Oronsay (www.islandchurches.org.uk)
Guardianship of the Presbytery

Connel See Coll

Craignish linked with Kilbrandon and Kilchattan linked with Kilninver and Kilmelford (Netherlorn)
Kenneth R. Ross (Prof.) OBE BA BD PhD   1982   2010
The Manse, Kilmelford, Oban PA34 4XA
KRoss@churchofscotland.org.uk
01852 200565

Cumlodden, Lochfyneside and Lochgair linked with Glenaray and Inveraray (West Lochfyneside)
Roderick D.M. Campbell OStJ TD BD   1975   2015   The Manse, Inveraray PA32 8XT   01499 302295
DMin FSAScot   Roderick.Campbell@churchofscotland.org.uk   07469 186495

Dunoon: St John's linked with Kirn and Sandbank (H) (Central Cowal)
Vacant   The Manse, 13 Dhailling Park, Hunter Street, Kirn, Dunoon   01369 702256
                                                                           PA23 8FB
Glenda M. McLaren (Ms) DCS   1990   2006   5 Allan Terrace, Sandbank, Dunoon PA23 8PR   01369 704168
                                                                           Glenda.McLaren@churchofscotland.org.uk

Dunoon: The High Kirk (H) linked with Innellan (H) linked with Toward (H) (South-East Cowal)
Aileen M. McFie (Mrs) BD   2003   2011   7A Mathieson Lane, Innellan, Dunoon PA23 7SH   01369 830276
                                                                           ARobson@churchofscotland.org.uk
Ruth I. Griffiths (Mrs)   2004   Kirkwood, Mathieson Lane, Innellan, Dunoon PA23 7TA   01369 830145
(Auxiliary Minister)   RGriffiths@churchofscotland.org.uk

Gigha and Cara (H) (GD) linked with Kilcalmonell linked with Killean and Kilchenzie (H)
Vacant   The Manse, Muasdale, Tarbert, Argyll PA29 6XD   01583 421432

Glassary, Kilmartin and Ford linked with North Knapdale
Clifford R. Acklam BD MTh   1997   2010   The Manse, Kilmichael Glassary, Lochgilphead PA31 8QA   01546 606926
                                                                           CAcklam@churchofscotland.org.uk

Glenaray and Inveraray See Cumlodden, Lochfyneside and Lochgair

Glenorchy and Innishael linked with Strathfillan
Vacant   The Manse, Dalmally PA33 1AA   01838 200207

Innellan See Dunoon: The High Kirk

Iona linked with Kilfinichen and Kilvickeon and the Ross of Mull
Jenny Earl MA BD   2007   2018   1 The Steadings, Achavaich, Isle of Iona PA76 6SW   07769 994680
                                                                           JEarl@churchofscotland.org.uk

Jura (GD) linked with Kilarrow (H) linked with Kildalton and Oa (GD) (H)
Vacant   The Manse, Bowmore, Isle of Islay PA43 7LH   01496 810271
Session Clerk, Kilarrow: Hugh Smith   uisdean001@gmail.com   01496 810658
Session Clerk, Kildalton and Oa: Dorothy Dennis (Dr)   dorothydennis5792@btinternet.com   01496 302440

Kilarrow See Jura
Kilbrandon and Kilchattan See Craignish
Kilcalmonell See Gigha and Cara

Kilchrenan and Dalavich linked with Muckairn
Thomas W. Telfer BA MDiv   2018   Muckairn Manse, Taynuilt PA35 1HW   01866 822204
TTelfer@churchofscotland.org.uk

Kildalton and Oa See Jura

Kilfinan linked with Kilmodan and Colintraive linked with Kyles (H) (West Cowal)
David Mitchell BD DipPTheol MSc   1988   2006   West Cowal Manse, Kames, Tighnabruaich PA21 2AD   01700 811045
DMitchell@churchofscotland.org.uk

Kilfinichen and Kilvickeon and the Ross of Mull See Iona
Killean and Kilchenzie See Gigha and Cara
Kilmodan and Colintraive See Kilfinan

Kilmore (GD) and Oban (www.obanchurch.com)
Dugald J. Cameron BD DipMin MTh   1990   2007   Kilmore and Oban Manse, Ganavan Road, Oban PA34 5TU   01631 566253
Dugald.Cameron@churchofscotland.org.uk
Christine P. Fulcher BEd   2012   2014   St Blaan's Manse, Southend, Campbeltown PA28 6RQ   01586 830504
(Ordained Local Minister)   CFulcher@churchofscotland.org.uk

Kilmun, Strone and Ardentinny: The Shore Kirk (H)
Vacant   The Manse, Blairmore, Dunoon PA23 8TE   01369 840313
Session Clerk: Elizabeth Paterson (Mrs)   finnartlea@gmail.com   01369 840685

Kilninian and Kilmore linked with Salen (H) and Ulva linked with Tobermory (GD) (H)
linked with Torosay (H) and Kinlochspelvie (North Mull)
John H. Paton BSc BD   1983   2013   The Manse, Gruline Road, Salen, Aros, Isle of Mull PA72 6XF   01680 300001
JPaton@churchofscotland.org.uk

Kilninver and Kilmelford See Craignish
Kirn and Sandbank See Dunoon: St John's
Kyles See Kilfinan
Lismore See Appin

Lochgilphead
Hilda C. Smith (Miss) MA BD MSc   1992   2005   Parish Church Manse, Manse Brae, Lochgilphead PA31 8QZ   01546 602238
HSmith@churchofscotland.org.uk

Lochgoilhead (H) and Kilmorich linked with Strachur and Strathlachlan (Upper Cowal)
Robert K. Mackenzie MA BD PhD   1976   1998   The Manse, Strachur, Cairndow PA27 8DG   01369 860246
RKMackenzie@churchofscotland.org.uk

Muckairn See Kilchrenan and Dalavich

North and West Islay (GD)
Vacant   The Manse, Port Charlotte, Isle of Islay PA48 7TW   01496 850241
New charge formed by the union of Kilchoman, Kilmeny and Portnahaven

North Knapdale See Glassary, Kilmartin and Ford

Rothesay: Trinity (H) (www.rothesaytrinity.org)
Sibyl A. Tchaikovsky BA BD MLitt   2018   12 Crichton Road, Rothesay, Isle of Bute PA20 9JR   01700 503010
STchaikovsky@churchofscotland.org.uk

Saddell and Carradale (H) linked with Southend (H)
Stephen Fulcher BA MA   1993   2012   St Blaan's Manse, Southend, Campbeltown PA28 6RQ   01586 830504
SFulcher@churchofscotland.org.uk

Salen and Ulva See Kilninian and Kilmore

Skipness linked with Tarbert, Loch Fyne and Kilberry (H)
Vacant   The Manse, Cambeltown Road, Tarbert, Argyll PA29 6SX   01880 821012
Session Clerk, Tarbert, Loch Fyne and Kilberry: Janne Leckie (Ms)   Janne.Leckie@argyll-bute.gov.uk   01880 820481

Southend See Saddell and Carradale
South Knapdale See Ardrishaig
South Uist See Barra
Strachur and Strathlachlan See Lochgoilhead and Kilmorich
Strathfillan See Glenorchy and Innishael
Tarbert, Loch Fyne and Kilberry See Skipness

The United Church of Bute
John Owain Jones MA BD FSAScot   1981   2011   10 Bishop Terrace, Rothesay, Isle of Bute PA20 9HF
JJones@churchofscotland.org.uk   01700 504502

Tiree (GD)
Vacant
Session Clerk: vacant
Interim Moderator: Rev. Dr Iain C. Barclay   The Manse, Scarinish, Isle of Tiree PA77 6TN   01879 220377
ICBarclay@churchofscotland.org.uk   01631 730143

Tobermory See Kilninian and Kilmore
Torosay and Kinlochspelvie See Kilninian and Kilmore
Toward See Dunoon: The High Kirk

Name			Position	Address	Phone
Beautyman, Paul H. MA BD	1993	2009	Youth Adviser	130b John Street, Dunoon PA23 7BN PBeautyman@churchofscotland.org.uk	07596 164112
Bell, Douglas W. MA LLB BD	1975	1993	(Alexandria: North)	3 Cairnbaan Lea, Cairnbaan, Lochgilphead PA31 8BA	01546 606815
Cringles, George G. BD	1981	2017	(Coll with Connel)	The Moorings, Ganavan Road, Oban PA34 5TU george.cringles@gmail.com	01631 564215
Crossan, William	2014		Ordained Local Minister	Gowanbank, Kilkerran Road, Campbeltown PA28 6JL	01586 553453
Dunlop, Alistair J. MA	1965	2004	(Saddell and Carradale)	8 Pipers Road, Cairnbaan, Lochgilphead PA31 8UF dunrevn@btinternet.com	01546 600316
Forrest, Alan B. MA	1956	1993	(Uphall: South)	126 Shore Road, Innellan, Dunoon PA23 7SX	01369 830424
Gibson, Elizabeth A. (Mrs) MA MLitt BD	2003	2013	Locum Minister	Mo Dhachaidh, Lochdon, Isle of Mull PA64 6AP egibson@churchofscotland.org.uk	01680 812541
Goss, Alister J. BD DMin	1975	2009	(Industrial Chaplain)	24 Albert Place, Ardnadam, Sandbank, Dunoon PA23 8QF scimwest@hotmail.com	01369 704495
Gray, William LTh	1971	2006	(Kilberry with Tarbert)	Lochnagar, Longsdale Road, Oban PA34 5DZ gray98@hotmail.com	01631 567471
Henderson, Grahame McL. BD	1974	2008	(Kirn)	6 Gerhallow, Bullwood Road, Dunoon PA23 7QB ghende5884@aol.com	01369 702433
Hood, Catriona A.	2006	2018	Auxiliary Minister, South Argyll	Rose Cottage, Whitehouse, Tarbert PA29 6EP CHood@churchofscotland.org.uk	01880 730366
Hood, H. Stanley C. MA BD	1966	2000	(London: Crown Court)	10 Dalriada Place, Kilmichael Glassary, Lochgilphead PA31 8QA	01546 606168
Lamont, Archibald MA	1952	1994	(Kilcalmonell with Skipness)	22 Bonnyton Drive, Eaglesham, Glasgow G76 0LU	
Lind, Michael J. LLB BD	1984	2012	(Campbeltown: Highland)	Maybank, Station Road, Conon Bridge, Dingwall IV7 8BJ mijylind@gmail.com	
Macfarlane, James PhD	1991	2011	(Lochgoilhead and Kilmorich)	'Lindores', 11 Bullwood Road, Dunoon PA23 7QJ mac.farlane@btinternet.com	01369 710626
McIvor, Anne (Miss) SRD BD	1996	2013	(Gigha and Cara)	20 Albyn Avenue, Campbeltown PA28 6LY annemcivor@btinternet.com	07901 964825

Name	Years	(Former charge)	Address	Tel
MacLeod, Roderick MBE MA BD PhD(Edin) PhD(Open)	1966 2011	(Cumlodden, Lochfyneside and Lochgair)	Creag-nam-Barnach, Furnace, Inveraray PA32 8XU / mail@revroddy.co.uk	01499 500629
Marshall, Freda (Mrs) BD FCII	1993 2005	(Colonsay and Oronsay with Kilbrandon and Kilchattan)	Allt Mhaluidh, Glenview, Dalmally PA33 1BE / mail@freda.org.uk	01838 200693
Mill, David KJSI MA BD	1978 2018	(Kilmun, Strone and Ardentinny: The Shore Kirk)	The Hebrides, 107 Bullwood Road, Dunoon PA23 7QN / revandevmill@aol.com	01369 707544
Millar, Margaret R.M. (Miss) BTh	1977 2008	(Kilchrenan and Dalavich with Muckairn)	Fearnoch Cottage, Fearnoch, Taynuilt PA35 1JB / macoje@aol.com	01866 822416
Morrison, Angus W. MA BD	1959 1999	(Kildalton and Oa)	1 Livingstone Way, Port Ellen, Isle of Islay PA42 7EP	01496 300043
Park, Peter B. BD MCIBS	1997 2014	(Fraserburgh: Old)	Hillview, 24 McKelvie Road, Oban PA34 4GB / peterpark9@btinternet.com	01631 565849
Ritchie, Walter M.	1973 1999	(Uphall: South)	Hazel Cottage, Barr Mor View, Kilmartin, Lochgilphead PA31 8UN	01546 510343
Scott, Randolph MA BD	1991 2013	(Jersey: St Columba's)	18 Lochan Avenue, Kirn, Dunoon PA23 8HT / rev.rs@hotmail.com	01369 703175
Stewart, Joseph LTh	1979 2011	(Dunoon: St John's with Sandbank)	7 Glenmorag Avenue, Dunoon PA23 7LG	01369 703438
Taylor, Alan T. BD	1980 2005	(Isle of Mull)	Erray Road, Tobermory, Isle of Mull PA75 6PS	01688 302496
Valerie G.C. Watson MA BD STM	1987 2018	(North and West Islay)	Flat 0/1, 38 Brougham Street, Greenock PA16 8AH	
Wilkinson, W. Brian MA BD	1968 2007	(Glenaray and Inveraray)	3 Achlonan, Taynuilt PA35 1JJ / williambrian35@btinternet.com	01866 822036

ARGYLL Communion Sundays

Parish	Communion Sundays
Ardrishaig	4th Apr, 1st Nov
Barra	2nd Mar, June, Sep, Easter, Advent
Campbeltown	
Highland	1st May, Nov
Lorne and Lowland	1st May, Nov
Craignish	1st Jun, Nov
Cumlodden, Lochfyneside and Lochgair	1st May, 3rd Nov
Dunoon	
St John's	1st Mar, Jun, Nov
The High Kirk	1st Feb, Jun, Oct
Gigha and Cara	1st May, Nov
Glassary, Kilmartin and Ford	1st Apr, Sep
Glenaray and Inveraray	1st Apr, Jul, Oct, Dec
Innellan	1st Mar, Jun, Sep, Dec
Jura	Passion Sun., 2nd Jul, 3rd Nov

Parish	Communion Sundays
Kilarrow	1st Mar, Jun, Sep, Dec
Kilcalmonell	1st Jul, 3rd Nov
Kildalton and Oa	Last Jan, Jun, Oct, Easter
Kilfinan	Last Apr, Oct
Killean and Kilchenzie	1st Mar, Jul, Oct
Kilmodan and Colintraive	1st Apr, Sep
Kilmun, Strone and Ardentinny	Last Jun, Nov
Kilninver and Kilmelford	Last Feb, Jun, Oct
Kirn and Sandbank	2nd Jun, Oct
Kyles	1st May, Nov
Lochgair	Last Apr, Oct
Lochgilphead	2nd Oct (Gaelic)
Lochgilphead and Kilmorich	1st Apr, Nov
North and West Islay	2nd Mar, Jun, Sep, Nov
Kilchoman	1st Aug, Easter
	1st Jul, 2nd Dec, Easter

Parish	Communion Sundays
Kilmeny	2nd May, 3rd Nov
Portnahaven	3rd Jul
North Knapdale	3rd Oct, 2nd May
Rothesay: Trinity	1st Feb, Jun, Nov
Saddell and Carradale	2nd May, 1st Nov
Skipness	2nd May, Nov
Southend	1st Jun, Dec
South Knapdale	4th Apr, 1st Nov
South Uist	
Howmore	1st Jun
Dalburgh	1st Sep
Strachur and Strathlachlan	1st Mar, Jun, Nov
Tarbert and Kilberry	1st May, Oct
The United Church of Bute	1st Mar, Jun, Nov
Toward	Last Feb, May, Aug, Nov

(22) FALKIRK

Meets at Falkirk Trinity Parish Church on the first Tuesday of September, December, March and May, on the fourth Tuesday of October and January and on the third Tuesday of June.

Clerk:	REV. ANDREW SARLE BSc BD	114 High Station Road, Falkirk FK1 5LN falkirk@churchofscotland.org.uk	07565 362074
Depute Clerk and Treasurer:	MR CHRISTOPHER DUNN	3b Afton Road, Cumbernauld G67 2DS depclerk@falkirkpresbytery.org	01236 720874 07799 478880

Airth (H)

James F. Todd BD CPS	1984	2012	The Manse, Airth, Falkirk FK2 8LS JTodd@churchofscotland.org.uk	01324 831120

Blackbraes and Shieldhill linked with Muiravonside

Vacant			81 Stevenson Avenue, Polmont, Falkirk FK2 0GU	01324 717757
Marion Perry (Mrs) (Auxiliary Minister)	2009	2017	17a Tarbolton Road, Cumbernauld, Glasgow G67 2AJ MPerry@churchofscotland.org.uk	01236 898519 07563 180662

Bo'ness: Old (H)

Amanda J. MacQuarrie MA PGCE MTh	2014	2016	10 Dundas Street, Bo'ness EH51 0DG AMacQuarrie@churchofscotland.org.uk	01506 204585

Bo'ness: St Andrew's (Website: www.standonline.org.uk)

Graham D. Astles BD MSc	2007	2016	St Andrew's Manse, 11 Erngath Road, Bo'ness EH51 9DP GAstles@churchofscotland.org.uk	01506 825803 01506 822195

Bonnybridge: St Helen's (H) (www.bbshnc.com)

George MacDonald BTh	2004	2009	The Manse, 32 Reilly Gardens, High Bonnybridge FK4 2BB GMacDonald@churchofscotland.org.uk	01324 874807

Bothkennar and Carronshore

Andrew J. Moore BSc BD		2007	11 Hunter Place, Greenmount Park, Carronshore, Falkirk FK2 8QS AMoore@churchofscotland.org.uk	01324 570525

Brightons (H)
Vacant
Session Clerk: Eric Smith
The Manse, Maddiston Road, Brightons, Falkirk FK2 0JP
sessionclerk@brightonschurch.org.uk
01324 712062
01324 711072

Carriden (H)
Vacant
David C. Wandrum   1993   2017
(Auxiliary Minister)
The Spires, Foredale Terrace, Carriden, Bo'ness EH51 9LW
5 Cawder View, Carrickstone Meadows, Cumbernauld, Glasgow G68 0BN
DWandrum@churchofscotland.org.uk
01506 822141
01236 723288

Cumbernauld: Abronhill (H)
Joyce A. Keyes (Mrs) BD   1996   2003
26 Ash Road, Cumbernauld, Glasgow G67 3ED
JKeyes@churchofscotland.org.uk
01236 723833

Cumbernauld: Condorrat (H)
Grace I.M. Saunders BSc BTh   2007   2011
11 Rosehill Drive, Cumbernauld, Glasgow G67 4EQ
GSaunders@churchofscotland.org.uk
01236 452090

Cumbernauld: Kildrum (H)
Vacant
David Nicholson DCS   1994   1993
64 Southfield Road, Balloch, Cumbernauld, Glasgow G68 9DZ
2D Doonside, Kildrum, Cumbernauld, Glasgow G67 2HX
DNicholson@churchofscotland.org.uk
01236 723304
01236 732260

Cumbernauld: Old (H) (www.cumbernauldold.org.uk)
Elspeth M McKay LLB LLM PGCert BD   2014   2017
Valerie S. Cuthbertson (Miss) DipTMus DCS   2003
The Manse, 23 Baronhill, Cumbernauld, Glasgow G67 2SD
EMcKay@churchofscotland.org.uk
105 Bellshill Road, Motherwell ML1 3SJ
VCuthbertson@churchofscotland.org.uk
01236 728853
01698 259001

Cumbernauld: St Mungo's
Vacant
Contact via Presbytery Clerk
18 Fergusson Road, Cumbernauld, Glasgow G67 1LS
01236 721513

Denny: Old linked with Haggs (H)
Vacant
Contact Denny Old via Presbytery Clerk
Session Clerk, Haggs: R. Murray McCheyne
31 Duke Street, Denny FK6 6NR
mccheyne@blueyonder.co.uk
01324 824508
01324 840137

Denny: Westpark (H) (Website: www.westparkchurch.org.uk)
D. I. Kipchumba Too BTh MTh MSc   2017
13 Baxter Crescent, Denny FK6 5EZ
KToo@churchofscotland.org.uk
01324 882220
07340 868067

Dunipace (H)
Jean W. Gallacher (Miss)
BD CMin CTheol DMin   1989
The Manse, 239 Stirling Street, Dunipace, Denny FK6 6QJ
JGallacher@churchofscotland.org.uk
01324 824540

Falkirk: Bainsford
Vacant
Andrew Sarle BSc BD   2013
(Ordained Local Minister)
1 Valleyview Place, Newcarron Village, Falkirk FK2 7JB
114 High Station Road, Falkirk FK1 5LN
ASarle@churchofscotland.org.uk
01324 621648

Falkirk: Camelon
Stuart W. Sharp MTheol DipPA   2001
30 Cotland Drive, Falkirk FK2 7GE
SSharp@churchofscotland.org.uk
01324 870011
01324 623631

Falkirk: Grahamston United (H)
Ian Wilkie BD PGCE   2001   2007
16 Cromwell Road, Falkirk FK1 1SF
IWilkie@churchofscotland.org.uk
01324 624461
07877 803280 (Mbl)

Anne White BA DipTh   2018
(Ordained Local Minister)
94 Craigleith Road, Grangemouth FK3 0BA
Anne.White@churchofscotland.org.uk
01324 880864

Grahamston United is a Local Ecumenical Partnership with the Methodist and United Reformed Churches

Falkirk: Laurieston linked with Redding and Westquarter
J. Mary Henderson MA BD DipEd PhD   1990   2009
11 Polmont Road, Laurieston, Falkirk FK2 9QQ
JMary.Henderson@churchofscotland.org.uk
01324 621196

Falkirk: St Andrew's West (H)
Alastair M. Horne BSc BD   1989   1997
1 Maggiewood's Loan, Falkirk FK1 5SJ
AHorne@churchofscotland.org.uk
01324 623308

Falkirk: St James'
Vacant – services currently being held jointly at Falkirk: Grahamston United

Falkirk: Trinity (H)
Robert S.T. Allan LLB LLB DipLP BD — 1991   2003
9 Major's Loan, Falkirk FK1 5QF
RAllan@churchofscotland.org.uk
01324 625124

Kathryn I. Brown (Mrs) — 2014
(Ordained Local Minister)
1 Callendar Park Walk, Callendar Grange, Falkirk FK1 1TA
KBrown@churchofscotland.org.uk
01324 617352

Grangemouth: Abbotsgrange
Aftab Gohar MA MDiv PgDip — 1995   2010
8 Naismith Court, Grangemouth FK3 9BQ
AGohar@churchofscotland.org.uk
01324 482109
07528 143784

Grangemouth: Kirk of the Holy Rood
Vacant
Session Clerk: Helen Scott
The Manse, Bowhouse Road, Grangemouth FK3 0EX
sessionclerk.khr@gmail.com
01324 471595
01324 486780

Grangemouth: Zetland (H)
Alison A. Meikle (Mrs) BD — 1999   2015
Ronaldshay Crescent, Grangemouth FK3 9JH
AMeikle@churchofscotland.org.uk
01324 336729

Haggs   See Denny: Old

Larbert: East
Melville D. Crosthwaite BD DipEd DipMin — 1984   1995
1 Cortachy Avenue, Carron, Falkirk FK2 8DH
MCrosthwaite@churchofscotland.org.uk
01324 562402

Larbert: Old (H)
Guardianship of the Presbytery
Session Clerk: Eric Applebe
The Manse, 38 South Broomage Avenue, Larbert FK5 3ED
larbertoldcontact@gmail.com
01324 872760
01324 556551

Larbert: West (H)
Vacant
Session Clerk: Carol Sergeant
11 Carronvale Road, Larbert FK5 3LZ
sessionclerk.larbertwest@gmail.com
01324 562878
01324 554874

Muiravonside   See Blackbraes and Shieldhill

Polmont: Old
Deborah L. van Welie (Ms) MTheol — 2015
3 Orchard Grove, Polmont, Falkirk FK2 0XE
DLVanWelie@churchofscotland.org.uk
01324 713427

Redding and Westquarter See Falkirk: Laurieston

Sanctuary First

Albert O. Bogle BD MTh (Pioneer Minister)	1981	2016	49a Kenilworth Road, Bridge of Allan FK9 4RS AlbertBogle@churchofscotland.org.uk	07715 374557

Sanctuary First is a Presbytery Mission Initiative

Slamannan

Vacant

Monica MacDonald (Mrs) (Ordained Local Minister)		2014	32 Reilly Gardens, High Bonnybridge, Bonnybridge FK4 2BB Monica.MacDonald@churchofscotland.org.uk	01324 874807

Stenhouse and Carron (H)

William Thomson BD	2001	2007	The Manse, 21 Tipperary Place, Stenhousemuir, Larbert FK5 4SX WThomson@churchofscotland.org.uk	01324 416628

Name			(Charge)	Address	Phone
Black, Ian W. MA BD	1976	2013	(Grangemouth: Zetland)	Flat 1R, 2 Carrickvale Court, Carrickstone, Cumbernauld, Glasgow G68 0LA iwblack@hotmail.com	01236 453370
Brown, T. John MA BD	1995	2006	(Tullibody: St Serf's)	1 Callendar Park Walk, Callendar Grange, Falkirk FK1 1TA johnbrown1cpw@talktalk.net	01324 617352
Campbell-Jack, W.C. BD MTh PhD	1979	2011	(Glasgow: Possilpark)	35 Castle Avenue, Airth, Falkirk FK2 8GA c.c-j@homecall.co.uk	01324 832011
Chalmers, George A. MA BD MLitt	1962	2002	(Catrine with Sorn)	3 Cricket Place, Brightons, Falkirk FK2 0HZ	01324 712030
Christie, Helen F. (Mrs) BD	1998	2015	(Haggs)	4B Glencairn Road, Cumbernauld G67 2EN andychristie747@yahoo.com	01236 611583
Goodison, Michael J. BSc BD	2013		Chaplain: Army	40 Comyn Drive, Wallacestone, Falkirk FK2 7FH	07833 028256
Gunn, F. Derek BD	1986	2017	(Airdrie: Clarkston)	6 Yardley Place, Falkirk FK2 7FH	01324 624938
Job, Anne J. BSc BD	1993	2010	(Kirkcaldy: Viewforth with Thornton)	5 Carse View, Airth, Falkirk FK2 8NY aj@ajjob.co.uk	01324 832094
McCallum, John	1962	1998	(Falkirk: Irving Camelon)	11 Burnbrae Gardens, Falkirk FK1 5SB	01324 619766
McDowall, Ronald J. BD	1980	2001	(Falkirk: Laurieston with Redding and Westquarter)	'Kailas', Windsor Road, Falkirk FK1 5EJ	01324 871947
McPherson, William BD DipEd	1993	2003	Chief Executive, The Vine Trust	83 Laburnum Road, Port Seton, Prestonpans EH32 0UD	01875 812252
Mathers, Alexena (Sandra)	2015	2018	(Ordained Local Minister)	10 Ercall Road, Brightons, Falkirk FK2 0RS SMathers@churchofscotland.org.uk	01324 872253
Mathers, Daniel L. BD	1982	2001	(Grangemouth: Charing Cross and West)	10 Ercall Road, Brightons, Falkirk FK2 0RS	01324 872253
Morrison, Iain C. BA BD	1990	2003	(Linlithgow St Ninian's Craigmailen)	Whaligoe, 53 Eastcroft Drive, Polmont, Falkirk FK2 0SU iain@kirkweb.org	01324 713249

Ross, Evan J. LTh   1986 1998   (Cowdenbeath: West with Mossgreen and Crossgates)

Smith, Richard BD   1976 2002   (Denny: Old)

FALKIRK ADDRESSES

Blackbraes and Shieldhill		
Bo'ness: Old	Main St x Anderson Cr	
St Andrew's	Panbrae Road	
	Grahamsdyke Avenue	
Carriden	Carriden Brae	
Cumbernauld: Abronhill	Larch Road	
Condorrat	Main Road	
Kildrum	Clouden Road	
Old	Baronhill	
St Mungo's	St Mungo's Road	

Denny: Old	Denny Cross	
Westpark	Duke Street	
Dunipace	Stirling Street	
Falkirk: Bainsford	Hendry Street, Bainsford	
Camelon	Dorrator Road	
Grahamston United	Bute Street	
Laurieston	Main Falkirk Road	
St Andrew's West	Newmarket Street	
St James'	at Grahamston United	
Trinity	Kirk Wynd	
Grangemouth: Abbotsgrange	Abbot's Road	

Kirk of the Holy Rood	Bowhouse Road	01786 465166
Zetland	Ronaldshay Crescent	
Haggs	Glasgow Road	
Larbert: East	Kirk Avenue	01259 760861
Old	Denny Road x Stirling Road	07525 005028
West	Main Street	01259 762262
Muiravonside	off Vellore Road	
Polmont: Old	Kirk Entry/Bo'ness Road	
Redding and Westquarter	Main Street	
Slamannan	Manse Place	
Stenhouse and Carron	Church Street	01786 447575

5 Arneil Place, Brightons, Falkirk FK2 0NJ

Easter Wayside, 46 Kennedy Way, Airth, Falkirk FK2 8GB   01324 719936   01324 831386

richards@uklinux.net

(23) STIRLING

Meets at the Moderator's church on the first Thursday of September, and at Bridge of Allan Parish Church on the first Thursday of February, March, April, May, June, October, November and December.

Clerk:	**REV. ALAN F. MILLER**	7 Windsor Place, Stirling FK8 2HY	01786 465166
	BA MA BD	AMiller@churchofscotland.org.uk	
Depute Clerk:	**MR EDWARD MORTON**	22 Torry Drive, Alva FK12 5LN	01259 760861
		edmort@aol.com	07525 005028
Treasurer:	**MR MARTIN DUNSMORE**	60 Brookfield Place, Alva FK12 5AT	01259 762262
		m.dunsmore53@btinternet.com	
Presbytery Office:		St Columba's Church, Park Terrace, Stirling FK8 2NA	01786 447575
		stirling@churchofscotland.org.uk	

Aberfoyle (H) linked with Port of Menteith (H) (www.aberfoyleportchurches.org.uk)

Vacant

Session Clerk, Port of Menteith: Sheena Maitland-Makgill-   The Manse, Lochard Road, Aberfoyle, Stirling FK8 3SZ   01877 382391

Crichton (Mrs)   coldon3@btinternet.com   01877 385296

Alloa: Ludgate (www.alloaludgatechurch.org.uk)

Vacant   28 Alloa Park Drive, Alloa FK10 1QY   01259 212709

Alloa: St Mungo's (H) (www.stmungosparish.org.uk)
Sang Y. Cha BD MTh   2011
37A Claremont, Alloa FK10 2DG
SCha@churchofscotland.org.uk
01259 213872

Alva (www.alvaparishchurch.org.uk)
James N.R. McNeil BSc BD   1990   1997
34 Ochil Road, Alva FK12 5JT
JMcNeil@churchofscotland.org.uk
01259 760262

Balfron (www.balfronchurch.org.uk) linked with Fintry (H) (www.fintrykirk.btck.org.uk)
Sigrid Marten   1997   2013
7 Station Road, Balfron, Glasgow G63 0SX
SMarten@churchofscotland.org.uk
01360 440285

Balquhidder linked with Killin and Ardeonaig (H)
Russel Moffat BD MTh PhD   1986   2016
The Manse, Killin FK21 8TN
Russel.Moffat@churchofscotland.org.uk
01567 820247

Bannockburn: Allan (H) (www.allanchurch.org.uk) linked with Cowie and Plean
Vacant
The Manse, Bogend Road, Bannockburn, Stirling   FK7 8NP
janetterussell2000@yahoo.com
Session Clerk, Allan: Janette Russell (Mrs)
01786 814692
01786 833367

Bannockburn: Ladywell (H) (www.ladywellchurch.co.uk)
Elizabeth M.D. Robertson (Miss) BD CertMin   1997
57 The Firs, Bannockburn FK7 0EG
ERobertson@churchofscotland.org.uk
01786 812467

Bridge of Allan (H) (www.bridgeofallanparishchurch.org.uk)
Daniel (Dan) J. Harper BSc BD   2016
29 Keir Street, Bridge of Allan, Stirling   FK9 4QJ
DHarper@churchofscotland.org.uk
01786 834155
01786 832753

Buchanan linked with Drymen (www.drymenchurch.org)
Alexander J. MacPherson BD   1986   1997
Buchanan Manse, Drymen, Glasgow G63 0AQ
AMacPherson@churchofscotland.org.uk
01360 870212

Buchlyvie (H) linked with Gartmore (H)
Vacant
Session Clerk, Buchlyvie: William McLaren
blairgortsniven@aol.com
01360 850285

				Tel/Fax: 01877 331409

Callander (H) (www.callanderkirk.org.uk)
Jeffrey A. McCormick BD   1984   2018   3 Aveland Park Road, Callander FK17 8FD

   JMcCormick@churchofscotland.org.uk

01877 330097

Cambusbarron: The Bruce Memorial (H) (www.cambusbarronchurch.org)
Graham P. Nash MA BD   2006   2012   14 Woodside Court, Cambusbarron, Stirling FK7 9PH

   GPNash@churchofscotland.org.uk

01786 442068

Clackmannan (H) (www.clackmannankirk.org.uk)
Vacant   The Manse, Port Street, Clackmannan FK10 4JH

01259 211255

Cowie (H) and Plean See Bannockburn: Allan

Dollar (H) linked with Glendevon linked with Muckhart (www.dollarparishchurch.org.uk)
Vacant   2 Princes Crescent East, Dollar FK14 7BU

01259 743593

Session Clerk, Dollar: Catherine Gladwin (Mrs)   sessionclerk@dollarparishchurch.org.uk

01259 573476

Session Clerk, Muckhart: Sheena Anderson (Dr)   sheena.c.anderson@btinternet.com

01259 781391

Drymen See Buchanan

Dunblane: Cathedral (H) (www.dunblanecathedral.org.uk)
Colin C. Renwick BMus BD   1989   2014   Cathedral Manse, The Cross, Dunblane FK15 0AQ

   CRenwick@churchofscotland.org.uk

01786 822205

Dorothy U. Anderson (Mrs) LLB DipPL BD   2006   2017   Inverteith, Stirling Road, Doune FK16 6AA

(Associate Minister)   DAnderson@churchofscotland.org.uk

01786 841706

Dunblane: St Blane's (H) linked with Lecropt (H) (www.lecroptkirk.org.uk)
Gary J. Caldwell BSc BD   2007   2015   46 Kellie Wynd, Dunblane FK15 0NR

   GCaldwell@churchofscotland.org.uk

01786 825324

Fallin
Vacant   5 Fincastle Place, Cowie, Stirling FK7 7DS

01786 818413

Fintry See Balfron

Gargunnock linked with Kilmadock linked with Kincardine-in-Menteith (www.blairdrummondchurches.org.uk)
Vacant
Lynne Mack (Mrs)   2013 2014   36 Middleton, Menstrie FK11 7HD   01259 761465
(Ordained Local Minister)   LMack@churchofscotland.org.uk

Gartmore See Buchlyvie
Glendevon See Dollar

Killearn (H) (www.killearnkirk.org.uk)
Vacant
Session Clerk: Carole Young (Mrs)   sessionclerk@killearnkirk.org.uk   01360 550994

Killin and Ardeonaig See Balquhidder
Kilmadock See Gargunnock
Kincardine-in-Menteith See Gargunnock

Kippen (H) linked with Norrieston
Ellen M. Larson Davidson BA MDiv   2007 2015   The Manse, Main Street, Kippen, Stirling FK8 3DN   01786 871249
ELarsonDavidson@churchofscotland.org.uk

Lecropt See Dunblane: St Blane's

Logie (H) (www.logiekirk.co.uk)
Ruth D. Halley BEd BD PGCM   2012   21 Craiglea, Causewayhead, Stirling FK9 5EE   01786 463060
                                            RHalley@churchofscotland.org.uk   07530 307413
Anne F. Shearer BA DipEd   2010   10 Colsnaur, Menstrie FK11 7HG   01259 769176
(Auxilliary Minister)   AShearer@churchofscotland.org.uk

Menstrie (H) (www.menstrieparishchurch.co.uk)
Vacant
Session Clerk: Margaret Perry (Mrs)   mag9per@btinternet.com   01259 761398

Muckhart See Dollar
Norrieston See Kippen
Port of Menteith See Aberfoyle

Sauchie and Coalsnaughton
Margaret Shuttleworth MA BD   2013   62 Toll Road, Kincardine, Alloa FK10 4QZ   01259 731002
                                                                        MShuttleworth@churchofscotland.org.uk

Stirling: Allan Park South (H) (www.apschurch.com)
Guardianship of the Presbytery

Stirling: Church of the Holy Rude (H) (http://holyrude.org) linked with Stirling: Viewfield Erskine (H)
Alan F. Miller BA MA BD   2000   2010   7 Windsor Place, Stirling FK8 2HY   01786 465166
                                                                       AMiller@churchofscotland.org.uk

Stirling: North (H) (www.northparishchurch.com)
Scott McInnes MEng BD   2016   18 Shirras Brae Road, Stirling FK7 0BA   **01786 463376**
                                                                       SMcInnes@churchofscotland.org.uk   01786 357428

Stirling: St Columba's (H) (www.stcolumbasstirling.org.uk)
Alexander M. Millar MA BD MBA   1980   2010   St Columba's Manse, 5 Clifford Road, Stirling FK8 2AQ   **01786 449516**
                                                                     Alexander.Millar@churchofscotland.org.uk   01786 469979

Stirling: St Mark's (www.stmarksstirling.org.uk)
Vacant   10 Laidlaw Street, Stirling FK8 1ZS
Jean T. Porter (Mrs) BD DCS   2006 2008   3 Cochrie Place, Tullibody FK10 2RR   07729 316321
                                                                     JPorter@churchofscotland.org.uk

Stirling: St Ninians Old (H) (www.stniniansold.org.uk)
Gary J. McIntyre BD DipMin   1993   1998   7 Randolph Road, Stirling FK8 2AJ   01786 474421
                                                                     GMcIntyre@churchofscotland.org.uk

Stirling: Viewfield Erskine See Stirling: Church of the Holy Rude

Strathblane (H) (www.strathblanekirk.org.uk)
Murdo M. Campbell BD DipMin   1997 2017   2 Campsie Road, Strathblane, Glasgow G63 9AB   01360 770226
                                                                     MCampbell@churchofscotland.org.uk

Tillicoultry (H) (www.tillicoultryparishchurch.co.uk)
Alison E.P. Britchfield (Mrs) MA BD   1987   2013   The Manse, 17 Dollar Road, Tillicoultry FK13 6PD   01259 750340
                                                                     ABritchfield@churchofscotland.org.uk

Tullibody: St Serf's (H)
Drew Barrie BSc BD | 1984 2016 | 16 Menstrie Road, Tullibody, Alloa FK10 2RG DBarrie@churchofscotland.org.uk | 01259 729804

Name	Appointment	Years	Address / Email	Phone
Allen, Valerie L. (Ms) BMus MDiv DMin	Presbytery Chaplain	1990 2015	16 Pine Court, Doune FK16 6JE VL2allen@btinternet.com	01786 842577
Barr, John BSc PhD BD	(Kilmacolm: Old)	1958 1979	6 Ferry Court, Stirling FK9 5GJ kilbrandon@btinternet.com	07801 291538 01786 472286
Begg, Richard MA BD	Army Chaplain	2008 2016	12 Whiteyetts Drive, Sauchie FK10 3GE rbegg711@aol.com	07766 004292
Boyd, Ronald M.H. BD DipTheol	Chaplain, Queen Victoria School	1995 2010	6 Victoria Green, Queen Victoria School, Dunblane FK15 0JY ron.boyd@qvs.org.uk	01877 339425
Brown, James H. BD	(Helensburgh: Park)	1977 2005	14 Gullipen View, Callander FK17 8HN revjimhbrown@yahoo.co.uk	
Campbell, Andrew B. BD DPS MTh	(Gargunnock with Kilmadock with Kincardine-in-Menteith)	1979 2018	Seahaven, Ganavan, Oban PA34 5TU	
Cloggie, June (Mrs)	(Auxiliary Minister)	1997 2006	11A Tulipan Crescent, Callander FK17 8AR david.cloggie@hotmail.co.uk	01877 331021
Cochrane, James P.N. LTh	(Tillicoultry)	1994 2012	12 Sandpiper Meadow, Alloa Park, Alloa FK10 1QU jamescochrane@pobroadband.co.uk	01259 218883
Cook, Helen (Mrs) BD	Hospital Chaplain	1974 2012	60 Pelstream Avenue, Stirling FK7 0BG revhcook@btinternet.com	01786 464128
Dunnett, Alan L. LLB BD	(Cowie and Plean with Fallin)	1994 2016	9 Tulipan Crescent, Callander FK17 8AR alan.dunnett@sky.com	01877 339640
Dunnett, Linda (Mrs) BA DCS	(Deacon)	1976 2016	9 Tulipan Crescent, Callander FK17 8AR lindadunnett@sky.com	01877 339640 07838 041683
Foggie, Janet P. MA BD PhD	Pioneer Minister, Stirling University	2003 2017	Pioneer Office, Logie Kirk Halls, 15–17 Alloa Road, Stirling FK9 5LH JFoggie@churchofscotland.org.uk	07899 349246
Gaston, A. Ray C. MA BD	(Leuchars: St Athernase)	1969 2002	'Hamewith', 13 Manse Road, Dollar FK14 7AL gaston.arthur@yahoo.co.uk	01259 743202
Gilmour, William M. MA BD	(Lecropt)	1969 2008	14 Pine Court, Doune FK16 6JE	01786 842928
Goodison, Michael J. BSc BD	Chaplain: Army	2013	27 Hunter Crescent, Leuchars KY16 0JP mike.goodison@btinternet.com	
Goring, Iain M. BSc BD	(Interim Minister)	1976 2015	4 Argyle Grove, Dunblane FK15 9DU imgoring@gmail.com	01786 821688
Izett, William A.F.	(Law)	1968 2000	1 Duke Street, Clackmannan FK10 4EF william.izett@talktalk.net	01259 724203
Jack, Alison M. MA BD PhD	Assistant Principal and Lecturer, New College, Edinburgh	1998 2001	5 Murdoch Terrace, Dunblane FK15 9JE alisonjack809@btinternet.com	01786 826953

Name		(Previous charge / role)	Address	Telephone
Landels, James BD CertMin	1990 2015	(Bannockburn: Allan)	11 Ardgay Drive, Bonnybridge, Falkirk FK4 2FH revjimlandels@icloud.com	01324 810685 07860 944266
MacCormick, Moira G. BA LTh	1986 2003	(Buchlyvie with Gartmore)	12 Rankine Wynd, Tullibody, Alloa FK10 2UW mgmaccormick@o2.co.uk	01259 724619
McIntosh, Hamish N.M. MA	1949 1987	(Fintry)	9 Abbeyfield House, 17 Allan Park, Stirling FK8 2QG	01786 479294
McKenzie, Alan BSc BD	1988 2013	(Bellshill: Macdonald Memorial with Bellshill: Orbiston)	89 Drip Road, Stirling FK8 1RN rev.a.mckenzie@btopenworld.com	01786 430450
Malloch, Philip R.M. LLB BD	1970 2009	(Killearn)	8 Michael McParland Drive, Torrance, Glasgow G64 4EE pmalloch@mac.com	01360 620089
Mathew, J. Gordon MA BD	1973 2011	(Buckie: North)	45 Westhaugh Road, Stirling FK9 5GF jg.matthew@btinternet.com	01786 445951
Millar, Jennifer M. (Mrs) BD DipMin	1986 1995	Teacher: Religious and Moral Education	25 Beechwood Gardens, Stirling FK8 2AX ajrmillar@blueyonder.co.uk	01786 469979
Ogilvie, Catriona (Mrs)	1999 2015	(Cumbernauld: Old)	Seberham Flat, 1A Bridge Street, Dollar FK14 7DF catriona.ogilvie1@btinternet.com	01259 742155
Ovens, Samuel B. BD	1982 1993	(Slamannan)	21 Bevan Drive, Alva FK12 5PD	01259 763456
Pryde, W. Kenneth DA BD	1994 2012	(Foveran)	Corrie, 7 Alloa Road, Woodside, Cambus FK10 2NT wkpryde@hotmail.com	01259 721562
Rose, Dennis S. LTh	1996 2016	(Arbuthnott, Bervie and Kinneff)	69 Blackthorn Grove, Menstrie FK11 7DX dennis2327@aol.com	01259 692451
Russell, Kenneth G. BD CCE	1986 2013	Prison Chaplain	Chaplaincy Centre, HM Prison Perth, 3 Edinburgh Road, Perth PH2 7JH kenneth.russell@sps.pnn.gov.uk	01738 458216
Scott, James F.	1957 1997	(Dyce)	5 Gullipen View, Callander FK17 8HN	01877 330565
Sewell, Paul M.N. MA BD	1970 2010	(Berwick-upon-Tweed: St Andrew's Wallace Green and Lowick)	7 Bohun Court, Stirling FK7 7UT paulmsewell@btinternet.com	01786 489969
Sinclair, James H. MA BD DipMin	1966 2004	(Auchencairn and Rerrick with Buittle and Kelton)	16 Delaney Court, Alloa FK10 1RB	01259 729001
Thomson, Raymond BD DipMin	1992 2013	(Slamannan)	8 Rhodders Grove, Alva FK12 5ER	01259 769083
Wilson, Hazel MA BD DMS	1991 2015	(Dundee: Lochee)	2 Boe Court, Springfield Terrace, Dunblane FK15 9LU hmwilson704@gmail.com	01786 825850

STIRLING ADDRESSES

Allan Park South	Dumbarton Road	St Columba's	Park Terrace	Viewfield Erskine	Barnton Street
Holy Rude	St John Street	St Mark's	Drip Road		
North	Springfield Road	St Ninians Old	Kirk Wynd, St Ninians		

(24) DUNFERMLINE

Meets at Dunfermline in St Andrew's Erskine Church, Robertson Road, on the first Thursday of each month, except January, April, July, August and October when there is no meeting, and June when it meets on the last Thursday.

			Office	01383 741495
Clerk:	REV. IAIN M. GREENSHIELDS	38 Garvock Hill, Dunfermline KY12 7UU	Home	07427 477575
	BD DipRS ACMA MSc MTh DD	dunfermline@churchofscotland.org.uk		

Aberdour: St Fillan's (H) (www.stfillans.presbytery.org)

Peter S. Gerbrandy-Baird	2004	St Fillan's Manse, 36 Bellhouse Road, Aberdour, Fife KY3 0TL	01383 861522
MA BD MSc FRSA FRGS		PGerbrandy-Baird@churchofscotland.org.uk	

Beath and Cowdenbeath: North (H) (www.beathandnorth.org.uk)

Vacant		10 Stuart Place, Cowdenbeath KY4 9BN	01383 511033
Session Clerk: Margaret Clark		margaret_clark@hotmail.co.uk	01383 510360

Cairneyhill (H) (01383 882352) (www.cairneyhillchurch.org.uk) linked with Limekilns (H) (01383 873337) (www.limekilnschurch.org)

Norman M. Grant BD	1990	The Manse, 10 Church Street, Limekilns, Dunfermline KY11 3HT	01383 872341
		NGrant@churchofscotland.org.uk	

Carnock and Oakley (H) (www.carnockandoakley.org.uk)

Charles M.D. Lines BA	2010 2017	The Manse, Main Street, Carnock, Dunfermline KY12 9JG	01383 247209
		CLines@churchofscotland.org.uk	07909 762257

Cowdenbeath: Trinity (H) (www.trinitykirk.co.uk)

Vacant		2 Glenfield Road, Cowdenbeath KY4 9EL	01383 510696

Culross and Torryburn (H)

Vacant		The Manse, Culross, Dunfermline KY12 8JD	01383 880231
Interim Moderator: John Belford		john.belford5@tiscali.co.uk	01383 414704

Dalgety (www.dalgety-church.org)

		office@dalgety-church.co.uk	**01383 824092**
Christine M. Sime (Miss) BSc BD	1994 2012	9 St Colme Drive, Dalgety Bay, Dunfermline KY11 9LQ	01383 822316
		CSime@churchofscotland.org.uk	

Dunfermline: Abbey (H) (www.dunfermlineabbey.co.uk)
MaryAnn R. Rennie (Mrs) BD MTh   1998   2012   3 Perdieus Mount, Dunfermline KY12 7XE   01383 727311
MARennie@churchofscotland.org.uk

Dunfermline: East
Andrew A. Morrice MA BD   1999   2010   71 Swift Street, Dunfermline KY11 8SN   01383 223144
AMorrice@churchofscotland.org.uk   07815 719301

Dunfermline: Gillespie Memorial (H) (www.gillespiechurch.org)
Michael A. Weaver BSc BD   2017   **minister@gillespiechurch.org**   **01383 621253**
4 Killin Court, Dunfermline KY12 7XF   01383 724347
MWeaver@churchofscotland.org.uk   07980 492299

Dunfermline: North
Ian G. Thom BSc PhD BD   1990   2007   13 Barbour Grove, Dunfermline KY12 9YB   01383 733471
IThom@churchofscotland.org.uk

Dunfermline: St Andrew's Erskine (www.standrewserskine.org.uk) staechurch@standrewserskine.org.uk)   **01383 841660**
Muriel F. Willoughby (Mrs) MA BD   2006   2013   71A Townhill Road, Dunfermline KY12 0BN   01383 738487
MWilloughby@churchofscotland.org.uk

Dunfermline: St Leonard's (www.stleonardsparishchurch.org.uk)   **01383 620106**
Monika R. W. Redman BA BD   2003   2014   office@stleonardsparishchurch.org.uk   01383 300092
12 Torvean Place, Dunfermline KY11 4YY
MRedman@churchofscotland.org.uk

Dunfermline: St Margaret's (www.stmargscos.org.uk)
Iain M. Greenshields   1984   2007   38 Garvock Hill, Dunfermline KY12 7UU   01383 723955
BD DipRS ACMA MSc MTh DD   IGreenshields@churchofscotland.org.uk   07427 477575

Dunfermline: St Ninian's
Carolann Erskine BD DipPSRP   2009   2018   51 St John's Drive, Dunfermline KY12 7TL   01383 722256
CErskine@churchofscotland.org.uk

Dunfermline: Townhill and Kingseat (H) (www.townhillandkingseatchurchofscotland.org) info@townhillandkingseatchurchofscotland.org
Jean A. Kirkwood BSc PhD BD   2015   7 Lochwood Park, Kingseat, Dunfermline KY12 0UX   01383 723691
JKirkwood@churchofscotland.org.uk

Inverkeithing linked with North Queensferry (www.inverkeithing-parish-church.org.uk)
Colin M. Alston BMus BD BN RN   1975   2012   1 Dover Way, Dunfermline KY11 8HR   01383 621050
CAlston@churchofscotland.org.uk

Kelty (www.keltykirk.org.uk)
Hugh D. Steele LTh DipMin 1994 2013   15 Arlick Road, Kelty KY4 0BH   01383 831362
HSteele@churchofscotland.org.uk

Limekilns See Cairneyhill

Lochgelly and Benarty: St Serf's (www.stserfschurch.co.uk)
Vacant
Pamela Scott (Mrs) DCS   2017   82 Main Street, Lochgelly KY5 9AA   01592 780435
177 Primrose Avenue, Rosyth KY11 2TZ   01383 410530
PScott@churchofscotland.org.uk   07548 819334

North Queensferry See Inverkeithing

Rosyth
Vacant
Morag Crawford (Miss) MSc DCS 1977 1998   42 Woodside Avenue, Rosyth KY11 2LA   01383 412776
118 Wester Drylaw Place, Edinburgh EH4 2TG   0131 332 2253
MCrawford@churchofscotland.org.uk   07970 982563

Saline and Blairingone (www.salineandblairingonechurch.org.uk) linked with Tulliallan and Kincardine (www.tulliallanandkincardine.org.uk)
Alexander J. Shuttleworth MA BD 2004 2013   62 Toll Road, Kincardine, Alloa FK10 4QZ   01259 731002
AShuttleworth@churchofscotland.org.uk

Tulliallan and Kincardine See Saline and Blairingone

Bjarnason, Sven S. CandTheol	1974	2011	(Tomintoul, Glenlivet and Inveraven)	14 Edward Street, Dunfermline KY12 0JW sven@bjarnason.org.uk	01383 724625
Boyle, Robert P. LTh	1990	2010	(Saline and Blairingone)	43 Dunipace Crescent, Dunfermline KY12 7JE boab.boyle@btinternet.com	01383 740980
Brown, Peter MA BD FRAScot	1953	1987	(Holm)	24 Inchmickery Avenue, Dalgety Bay, Dunfermline KY11 5NF	01383 822456
Chalmers, John P. BD CPS DD	1979	2017	(Principal Clerk)	10 Liggars Place, Dunfermline KY12 7XZ	01383 739130
Christie, Arthur A. BD	1997	2018	(Anstruther and Cellardyke: St Ayle with Kilrenny)	194 Foulford Road, Cowdenbeath KY4 9AX revacc@btinternet.com	01383 511326
Farquhar, William E. BA BD	1987	2006	(Dunfermline: Townhill and Kingseat)	29 Queens Drive, Middlewich, Cheshire CW10 0DG	01606 835097
Fisk, Elizabeth A. BD	1996	2016	(Dunfermline St Ninian's)	30 Masterton Road, Dunfermline KY11 8RB elizabethfisk10@hotmail.com	01383 730039
Jenkins, Gordon F.C. MA BD PhD	1968	2006	(Dunfermline: North)	2 Balrymonth Court, St Andrews KY16 8XT jenkinsgordon1@sky.com	01335 477194
Johnston, Thomas N. LTh	1972	2008	(Edinburgh: Priestfield)	71 Main Street, Newmills, Dunfermline KY12 8ST tomjohnston@blueyonder.co.uk	01383 889240

Name		Ordained	Appointed	Address	Phone
Kenny, Elizabeth S.S. BD RGN SCM	(Carnock and Oakley)	1989	2010	5 Cobden Court, Crossgates, Cowdenbeath KY4 8AU esskenny@btinternet.com	07831 763494
Laidlaw, Victor W.N. BD	(Edinburgh: St Catherine's Argyle)	1975	2008	9 Tern Road, Dunfermline KY11 8GA	01383 620134
Leitch, D. Graham MA BD	(Tyne Valley)	1974	2012	9 St Margaret Wynd, Dunfermline KY12 0UT dgrahamleitch@gmail.com	01383 249245
McCulloch, William B BD	(Rome: St Andrew's)	1997	2016	81 Meldrum Court, Dunfermline KY11 4XR revwbmcculloch@hotmail.com	01383 730305
McDonald, Tom BD	(Kelso: North and Ednam)	1994	2015	12 Woodmill Grove, Dunfermline KY11 4JR revtomparadise12@gmail.com	01383 695365
McKay, Violet C.C. BD	(Rosyth)	1988	2017	87 McDonald Street, Dunfermline KY11 8NG vcmckay@btinternet.com	01383 731410
McLellan, Andrew R.C. CBE MA BD STM DD	(HM Chief Inspector of Prisons for Scotland)	1970	2009	4 Liggars Place, Dunfermline KY12 7XZ	01383 725959
Paterson, Andrew E. JP	Auxiliary Minister, Presbytery	1994	2016	6 The Willows, Kelty KY4 0FQ APaterson@churchofscotland.org.uk	01383 830998
Redmayne, David W. BSc BD	(Beath and Cowdenbeath: North)	2001	2017	10 Hawthorn Park, Dunfermline KY12 0DY	01383 738137
Reid, A. Gordon BSc BD	(Dunfermline: Gillespie Memorial)	1982	2008	7 Arkleston Crescent, Paisley PA3 4TG reid501@fsmail.net	0141 842 1542 07773 300989
Reid, David MSc LTh FSAScot	(St Monans with Largoward)	1961	1992	North Lethans, Saline, Dunfermline KY12 9TE	01383 733144
Watt, Robert J. BD	(Dumbarton: Riverside)	1994	2009	101 Birrell Drive, Dunfermline KY11 8FA robertwatt101@gmail.com	01383 735417 07753 683717
Whyte, Iain A. BA BD STM PhD	(Community Mental Health Chaplain)	1968	2005	14 Carlingnose Point, North Queensferry, Inverkeithing KY11 1ER iainisabelwhyte@gmail.com	01383 410732
Whyte, Isabel H. (Mrs) BD	(Chaplain: Queen Margaret Hospital, Dunfermline)	1993	2006	14 Carlingnose Point, North Queensferry, Inverkeithing KY11 1ER iainisabelwhyte@gmail.com	01383 410732

(25) KIRKCALDY

Meets at Kirkcaldy, in the St Bryce Kirk Centre, on the first Tuesday of March, September and June. It meets also on the first Tuesday of November for Holy Communion at the church of the Moderator.

Clerk:	REV. ALAN W.D. KIMMITT BSc BD	40 Liberton Drive, Glenrothes KY6 3PB kirkcaldy@churchofscotland.org.uk	01592 742233
Depute Clerk:	REV. ROBIN J. McALPINE BDS BD MTh	25 Bennochy Avenue, Kirkcaldy KY2 5QE RMcAlpine@churchofscotland.org.uk	01592 643558

Auchterderran Kinglassie
Donald R. Lawrie MA BD DipCouns   1991   2018   7 Woodend Road, Cardenden, Lochgelly KY5 0NE   01592 720508
DLawrie@churchofscotland.org.uk

Auchtertool linked with Kirkcaldy: Linktown (H)
Catriona M. Morrison MA BD   1995   2000   16 Raith Crescent, Kirkcaldy KY2 5NN   **01592 641080**
CMorrison@churchofscotland.org.uk   01592 265536

Marc A. Prowe   2000   2008   16 Raith Crescent, Kirkcaldy KY2 5NN   01592 265536
MProwe@churchofscotland.org.uk

Buckhaven (01592 715577) and Wemyss
Vacant
Jacqueline Thomson (Mrs) MTh DCS   2004   2008   16 Aitken Place, Coaltown of Wemyss, Kirkcaldy KY1 4PA   07806 776560
Jacqueline.Thomson@churchofscotland.org.uk

Burntisland (H)
Alan Sharp BSc BD   1980   2001   21 Ramsay Crescent, Burntisland KY3 9JL   01592 874303
ASharp@churchofscotland.org.uk

Dysart: St Clair (H)
Lynn Brady BD DipMin   1996   2017   42 Craigfoot Walk, Kirkcaldy KY1 1GA   01592 561967
(Interim Minister)   LBrady@churchofscotland.org.uk

Glenrothes: Christ's Kirk (H)
David W Denniston BD DipMin   1981   2018   12 The Limekilns, Glenrothes KY6 3QJ   0800 566 8242
(Interim Minister)   DDenniston@churchofscotland.org.uk   07903 926727

Glenrothes: St Columba's (Rothes Trinity Parish Grouping) (www.st-columbas.com)
Alan W.D. Kimmitt BSc BD   2013   40 Liberton Drive, Glenrothes KY6 3PB   **01592 752539**
Alan.Kimmitt@churchofscotland.org.uk   01592 742233

Glenrothes: St Margaret's (H)
Eileen Miller BD MBACP (Snr. Accred.)   2014   8 Alburne Park, Glenrothes KY7 5RB   **01592 328162**
DipCouns DipComEd   EMiller@churchofscotland.org.uk   01592 752241

Glenrothes: St Ninian's (H) (Rothes Trinity Parish Grouping)
David J. Smith BD DipMin   1992   2017   office@stninians.co.uk   **01592 610560**
1 Cawdor Drive, Glenrothes KY6 2HN   01592 611963
David.Smith@churchofscotland.org.uk

Kennoway, Windygates and Balgonie: St Kenneth's
Allan Morton MA BD PGDip   2018   stkennethsparish@gmail.com   **01333 351372**
                                            2 Fernhill Gardens, Windygates, Leven KY8 5DZ   01333 352329
                                            AMorton@churchofscotland.org.uk

Kinghorn
James Reid BD   1985   1997   17 Myre Crescent, Kinghorn, Burntisland KY3 9UB   01592 890269
                                          JReid@churchofscotland.org.uk

Kirkcaldy: Abbotshall (H) (www.abbotshallchurch.org.uk)
Justin W. Taylor BTh MTh MTh   2018   83 Milton Road, Kirkcaldy KY1 1TP   01592 267915
                                                JTaylor@churchofscotland.org.uk

Kirkcaldy: Bennochy
Robin J. McAlpine BDS BD MTh   1988   2011   25 Bennochy Avenue, Kirkcaldy KY2 5QE   01592 643518
                                                         RMcAlpine@churchofscotland.org.uk

Kirkcaldy: Linktown See Auchtertool

Kirkcaldy: Pathhead (H) (www.pathheadparishchurch.co.uk)
Andrew C. Donald BD DPS   1992   2005   **pathheadchurch@btinternet.com**   **01592 204635**
                                                    73 Loughborough Road, Kirkcaldy KY1 3DB   01592 652215
                                                    ADonald@churchofscotland.org.uk

Kirkcaldy: St Bryce Kirk (H)
J. Kenneth (Ken) Froude MA BD   1979   **office@stbrycekirk.org.uk**   **01592 640016**
                                                 6 East Fergus Place, Kirkcaldy KY1 1XT   01592 264480
                                                 JFroude@churchofscotland.org.uk

Kirkcaldy: Templehall (H)
Vacant   35 Appin Crescent, Kirkcaldy KY2 6EJ   01592 260156

Kirkcaldy: Torbain
Ian J. Elston BD MTh   1999   91 Sauchenbush Road, Kirkcaldy KY2 5RN   01592 263015
                                        IElston@churchofscotland.org.uk

Brian Porteous BSc DipCS   2018   Kirkdene, Westfield Road, Cupar KY15 5DS   01334 653561
(Ordained Local Minister)   BPorteous@churchofscotland.org.uk

Leslie: Trinity (Rothes Trinity Parish Grouping)
Guardianship of the Presbytery
Session Clerk: Alec Redpath   sessionclerk@leslietrinitychurch.co.uk   01592 742636

Leven
Gilbert C. Nisbet CA BD   1993   2007
5 Forman Road, Leven KY8 4HH
GNisbet@churchofscotland.org.uk
01333 303339

Markinch and Thornton
Vacant
Session Clerk: John Wood
7 Guthrie Crescent, Markinch, Glenrothes KY7 6AY
sessionclerk@markinchandthorntonchurch.org.uk
01592 758264
07789 000740

Methil: Wellesley (H)
Gillian Paterson (Mrs) BD   2010
10 Vettriano Vale, Leven KY8 4GD
GPaterson@churchofscotland.org.uk
01333 423147

Methilhill and Denbeath
Elisabeth F. Cranfield (Ms) MA BD   1988
9 Chemiss Road, Methilhill, Leven KY8 2BS
ECranfield@churchofscotland.org.uk
01592 713142

Name			(Charge)	Address	Phone
Adams, David G. BD	1991	2011	(Cowdenbeath: Trinity)	13 Fernhill Gardens, Windygates, Leven KY8 5DZ adams.69@btinternet.com	01333 351214
Cairns, Wilma R.C. (Miss) BD	1999	2018	(Buckhaven and Wemyss)	42 Approach Row, East Wemyss, Kirkcaldy KY1 4LB wilcairns@blueyonder.co.uk	01592 572416
Campbell, Reginald F. BSc BD DipChEd	1979	2015	(Daviot and Dunlichity with Moy, Dalarossie and Tomation)	12 Alloway Drive, Kirkcaldy KY2 6DX campbell1578@talktalk.net	
Collins, Mitchell BD CPS	1996	2005	(Creich, Flisk and Kilmany with Monimail)	6 Netherby Park, Glenrothes KY6 3PL collinsmit@aol.com	01592 742915
Deans, Graham D.S. MA BD MTh MLitt DMin	1978	2017	(Aberdeen: Queen Street)	38 Sir Thomas Elder Way, Kirkcaldy KY2 6ZS graham.deans@btopenworld.com	01592 641429
Dick, James S. MA BTh	1988	1997	(Glasgow Ruchazie)	20 Church Street, Kirkcaldy KY1 2AD jdick63@yahoo.com	01592 369239
Elston, Peter K.	1963	2000	(Dalgety)	6 Cairngorm Crescent, Kirkcaldy KY2 5RF peterkelston@btinternet.com	01592 205622
Ferguson, David J.	1966	2001	(Bellie with Speymouth)	4 Russell Gardens, Ladybank, Cupar KY15 7LT	01337 831406
Forrester, Ian L. MA	1964	1996	(Friockheim Kinnell with Inverkeilor and Lunan)		
Forsyth, Alexander R. TD BA MTh	1973	2013	(Markinch)	8 Bennochy Avenue, Kirkcaldy KY2 5QE 49 Scaraben Crescent, Formonthills, Glenrothes KY6 3HL alex@arforsyth.com	01592 260251 01592 749049 07756 239021
Fowler, Anthony J.R. BSc BD	1982	2018	(Kirkcaldy Templehall)	1 Ratho Place, Kirkcaldy KY2 6XL	01592 752403
Galbraith, D. Douglas MA BD BMus MPhil ARSCM PhD	1965	2005	(Office for Worship, Doctrine and Artistic Matters)	34 Balbirnie Street, Markinch, Glenrothes KY7 6DA dgalbraith@churchofscotland.org.uk	
Gisbey, John E. MA BD MSc DipEd	1964	2002	(Thornhill)	Whitemyre House, 28 St Andrews Road, Largoward, Leven KY9 1HZ	01334 840540

Name			Parish	Address	Phone
Gordon, Ian D. LTh	1972	2001	(Markinch)		
Houghton, Christine (Mrs) BD	1997	2010	(Whitburn: South)	2 Somerville Way, Glenrothes KY7 5GE	01592 742487
				39 Cedar Crescent, Thornton, Kirkcaldy KY1 4BE	01592 772823
				c.houghton1@btinternet.com	
McLeod, Alistair G.	1988	2005	(Glenrothes: St Columba's)	13 Greenmantle Way, Glenrothes KY6 3QG	01592 744558
				alistairmcleod1936@gmail.com	
McNaught, Samuel M. MA BD MTh	1968	2002	(Kirkcaldy: St John's)	6 Munro Court, Glenrothes KY7 5GD	01592 742352
				sjmcnaught@btinternet.com	
Munro, Andrew MA BD PhD	1972	2000	(Glencaple with Lowther)	7 Dunvegan Avenue, Kirkcaldy KY2 5SG	01592 566129
				am.smm@blueyonder.co.uk	
Nicol, George G. BD DPhil	1982	2013	(Falkland with Freuchie)	48 Fidra Avenue, Burntisland KY3 0AZ	01592 873258
				ggnicol@totalise.co.uk	
Paterson, Maureen (Mrs) BSc	1992	2010	(Auxiliary Minister)	91 Dalmahoy Crescent, Kirkcaldy KY2 6TA	01592 262300
				m.e.paterson@blueyonder.co.uk	
Roy, Allistair BD DipSW PgDip	2007	2016	(Glenrothes: St Ninian's)	39 Ravenswood Drive, Glenrothes KY6 2PA	
				minister@revroy.co.uk	
Templeton, James L. BSc BD	1975	2012	(Innerleven: East)	29 Coldstream Avenue, Leven KY8 5TN	01333 427102
				jamietempleton@btinternet.com	
Thomson, John D. BD	1985	2005	(Kirkcaldy: Pathhead)	3 Tottenham Court, Hill Street, Dysart, Kirkcaldy KY1 2XY	01592 655313
					07885 414979
				j.thomson10@sky.com	
Tomlinson, Bryan L. TD	1969	2003	(Kirkcaldy: Abbotshall)	2 Duddingston Drive, Kirkcaldy KY2 6JP	01592 564843
				abbkirk@blueyonder.co.uk	
Wilson, Tilly (Miss) MTh	1990	2012	(Dysart)	6 Citron Glebe, Kirkcaldy KY1 2NF	01592 263134
				tillywilson1@sky.com	
Wright Lynda BEd DCS	1979	2016	Community Chaplaincy Listening Coordinator, NHS Fife	71a Broomhill Avenue, Burntisland KY3 0BP	07835 303395

KIRKCALDY ADDRESSES

Abbotshall	Abbotshall Road	
Bennochy	Elgin Street	
Linktown	Nicol Street x High Street	
Pathhead	Harriet Street x Church Street	
St Bryce Kirk	St Brycedale Avenue x Kirk Wynd	
Templehall	Beauly Place	
Torbain	Lindores Drive	
Viewforth	Viewforth Street x Viewforth Terrace	

(26) ST ANDREWS

Meets on the first Wednesday of the specified months, except in June when it meets on the last Wednesday. Locations: February – St Andrews, March – Cupar St John's, May – Freuchie, June – Crail, September, November and December – locations to be announced.

Clerk: REV. NIGEL J. ROBB FCP MA BD ThM MTh   Presbytery Office, The Basement, 1 Howard Place, St Andrews KY16 9HL   01334 461300
standrews@churchofscotland.org.uk

Depute Clerk: MRS CATHERINE WILSON MBE BSc CPhys HonFInstP FRSA
5 Taeping Close, Cellardyke, Anstruther KY10 3YL   01333 310936
catherine.wilson15@btinternet.com

Anstruther and Cellardyke (H): St Ayle linked with Kilrenny
Vacant
Session Clerk, St Ayle: Eleanor Blair — 16 Taeping Close, Cellardyke, Anstruther KY10 3YL — eleanor_blair@btinternet.com — 01333 313917 / 01333 310438
Session Clerk, Kilrenny: Corinne Peddie (Mrs) — corinne@peddies.com — 07939 252012

Balmerino (H) linked with Wormit (H)
James Connolly   1982 2004 — 5 Westwater Place, Newport-on-Tay DD6 8NS — JConnolly@churchofscotland.org.uk — 01382 542626
   DipTh CertMin MA(Theol) DMin

Boarhills and Dunino linked with St Andrews: Holy Trinity
Guardianship of the Presbytery
Session Clerk, Boarhills and Dunino: Michael Foote — michaelfoote54@gmail.com — 01334 880787
Session Clerk, Holy Trinity: Michael Stewart (Dr) — htsessionclerk@gmail.com — 01334 461270

Cameron linked with St Andrews: St Leonard's (H)
Graeme W. Beebee BD   1993 2017 — **stlencam@btconnect.com** — **01334 478702**
1 Cairnhill Gardens, St Andrews KY16 8QY — GBeebee@churchofscotland.org.uk — 01334 472793

Carnbee linked with Pittenweem
Margaret E.S. Rose BD   2007 — 29 Milton Road, Pittenweem, Anstruther KY10 2LN — MRose@churchofscotland.org.uk — 01333 312838

Ceres, Kemback and Springfield
James W. Campbell BD   1995 2010 — Almbank, Gladney, Ceres, Cupar KY15 5LT — James.Campbell@churchofscotland.org.uk — 01334 829350

Crail linked with Kingsbarns (H)
Vacant
Session Clerk, Crail: Helen Armitage (Mrs) — helenarmitage@btinternet.com — 01333 450516
Session Clerk, Kingsbarns: John (Ian) Ramsay — johnvramsay@btinternet.com — 01333 451480

Creich, Flisk and Kilmany
Guardianship of the Presbytery
Session Clerk: Sheena Fowler (Mrs) — sheena.fowler@btinternet.com — 01337 870216

Cupar: Old (H) and St Michael of Tarvit linked with Monimail
Jeffrey A. Martin BA MDiv   1991 2016 — 76 Hogarth Drive, Cupar KY15 5YU — JMartin@churchofscotland.org.uk — 01334 656181

Cupar: St John's and Dairsie United
Vacant
Session Clerk: Muriel Dymock (Miss)
The Manse, 23 Hogarth Drive, Cupar KY15 5YH
m.dymock164@btinternet.com
01334 650751
01334 653164

East Neuk Trinity (H) linked with St Monans (H)
Vacant
Session Clerk, East Neuk Trinity: Olive Weir (Mrs)
jamandlor1@gmail.com
01333 340642

Edenshead
Vacant
Session Clerk: Rodney McCall
The Manse, Kirk Wynd, Strathmiglo, Cupar KY14 7QS
rodmccall@yahoo.co.uk
01337 860256
01337 827001
New charge formed by the union of Auchtermuchty and Edenshead and Strathmiglo

Falkland linked with Freuchie (H)
Guardianship of the Presbytery
Susan Thorburn MTh   2014   2017
(Ordained Local Minister)
1 Newton Road, Falkland, Cupar KY15 7AQ
3 Daleally Farm Cottages, St Madoes Road, Errol, Perth PH2 7TJ
SThorburn@churchofscotland.org.uk
01337 858557
01821 642681

Freuchie See Falkland

Howe of Fife
William F. Hunter MA BD   1986   2011
The Manse, 83 Church Street, Ladybank, Cupar KY15 7ND
WHunter@churchofscotland.org.uk
01337 832717

Kilrenny See Anstruther and Cellardyke: St Ayle
Kingsbarns See Crail

Largo
Gavin R. Boswell BTheol   1993   2018
GBoswell@churchofscotland.org

Largoward (H)
Guardianship of the Presbytery
Interim Moderator: Catherine Wilson (Mrs)
catherine.wilson15@btinternet.com
01333 310936

Leuchars: St Athernase
John C. Duncan MBE BD MPhil   1987   2016
7 David Wilson Park, Balmullo, St Andrews KY16 0NP
JDuncan@churchofscotland.org.uk
01334 870038

Lindores (H)
Guardianship of Presbytery
Session Clerk: Rosslynn Scott (Ms)

2 Guthrie Court, Cupar Road, Newburgh, Cupar KY14 6HA   01337 842228
rosslyn6@btinternet.com

New charge formed by the union of Abdie and Dunbog and Newburgh

Monimail See Cupar: Old and St Michael of Tarvit

Newport-on-Tay (H)
Amos B. Chewachong BTh MTh PhD   2017

17 East Station Place, Newport-on-Tay DD6 8EG   01382 542893
AChewachong@churchofscotland.org.uk

Pittenweem See Carnbee

St Andrews: Holy Trinity See Boarhills and Dunino

St Andrews: Hope Park and Martyrs (H) linked with Strathkinness
Allan McCafferty BSc BD   1993   2011

20 Priory Gardens, St Andrews KY16 8XX   Tel/Fax 01334 478287
AMcCafferty@churchofscotland.org.uk

St Andrews: St Leonard's See Cameron
St Monans See East Neuk Trinity
Strathkinness See St Andrews: Hope Park and Martyrs

Tayport
Brian H. Oxburgh BSc BD   1980   2011

27 Bell Street, Tayport DD6 9AP   01382 553879
BOxburgh@churchofscotland.org.uk

Wormit See Balmerino

Allardice, Michael MA MPhil   2014   Ordained Local Minister   2 Station Road, Kingskettle, Cupar KY15 7PR   01337 597073
PGCertTHE FHEA   MAllardice@churchofscotland.org.uk   07936 203465

Barron, Jane L. (Mrs) BA DipEd BD   1999 2013   (Aberdeen: St Machar's Cathedral)   In USA: contact via the Presbytery Office
livialouise888@gmail.com

Bradley, Ian C. (Prof.) MA BD DPhil   1990 1999   University of St Andrews   4 Donaldson Gardens, St Andrews KY16 9DN   01334 475389
icb@st-andrews.ac.uk

Cameron, John U.   1974 2008   (Dundee: Broughty Ferry St Stephen's   10 Howard Place, St Andrews KY16 9HL   01334 474474
BA BSc PhD BD ThD   and West)   jucameron@yahoo.co.uk

Name			(Position)	Address	Telephone
Clark, David M. MA BD	1989	2013	(Dundee: The Steeple)	2b Rose Street, St Monans, Anstruther KY10 2BQ / dmclark72@gmail.com	01333 738034
Connolly, Daniel BD DipTheol Dip Min	1983	2015	(Army Chaplain)	2 Cairngreen, Cupar KY15 2SY / dannyconnolly@hotmail.co.uk	07951 078478
Douglas, Peter C. JP	1966	1993	(Boarhills with Dunino)	12 Greyfriars Gardens, St Andrews KY16 8DR	01334 475868
Fairlie, George BD BVMS MRCVS	1971	2002	(Crail with Kingsbarns)	41 Warrack Street, St Andrews KY16 8DR	01334 475868
Fraser, Ann G. BD CertMin	1990	2007	(Auchtermuchty)	24 Irvine Crescent, St Andrews KY16 8LG / anngilfraser@btinternet.com	01334 461329
Gordon, Peter M. MA BD	1958	1995	(Airdrie: West)	3 Cupar Road, Cuparmuir, Cupar KY15 5RH / machrie@madasafish.com	01334 652341
Hamilton, Ian W.F. BD LTh ALCM AVCM	1978	2012	(Nairn: Old)	Mossneuk, 5 Windsor Gardens, St Andrews KY16 8XL / reviwfh@btinternet.com	01334 477745
Harrison, Cameron	2006	2011	(Auxiliary Minister)	Woodfield House, Priormuir, St Andrews KY16 8LP / cameron@harrisonleimon.co.uk	01334 478067
Jeffrey, Kenneth S. BA BD PhD DMin	2002	2014	University of Aberdeen	The North Steading, Dalgairn, Cupar KY15 4PH / ksjeffrey@btopenworld.com	01334 653196
Kesting, Sheilagh M. BA BD DD DSG	1980	2016	(Ecumenical Officer, Church of Scotland)	Restalrig, Chance Inn, Cupar KY15 5QJ / smkesting@btinternet.com	01334 829485
McDonald, William G. MA BD	1959	1975	(Falkirk: Grahamston United)	3 Kinkell Terrace, St Andrews KY16 8DL	01334 479770
MacEwan, Donald G. MA BD PhD	2001	2012	Chaplain: University of St Andrews	Chaplaincy Centre, 3A St Mary's Place, St Andrews KY16 9UY / dgm21@st-andrews.ac.uk	01334 462865 / 07713 322036
McGregor, Duncan J. MIFM	1982	1996	(Channelkirk with Lauder: Old)	14 Mount Melville, St Andrews KY16 8NG	01334 478314
McKimmon, Eric BA BD MTh PhD	1983	2014	(Cargill Burrelton with Collace)	14 Marionfield Place, Cupar KY15 5JN / ericmckimmon@gmail.com	01334 659650
McLean, John P. BSc BPhil BD	1994	2013	(Glenrothes: St Margaret's)	72 Lawmill Gardens, St Andrews KY16 8QS / john@mcleanmail.me.uk	01334 470803
Meager, Peter MA BD CertMgmt(Open)	1971	1998	(Elie with Kilconquhar and Colinsburgh)	7 Lorraine Drive, Cupar KY15 5DY / meager52@btinternet.com	01334 656991
Neilson, Peter MA BD MTh	1975	2016	(Mission Consultant)	Linne Bheag, 2 School Green, Anstruther KY10 3HF / neilson.peter@btinternet.com	01333 310477 / 07818 418608
Paton, Marion J. (Miss) MA BMus BD	1991	2017	(Dundee: St David's High Kirk)	18 Winram Place, St Andrews KY16 8XH / mjpdht@gmail.com	01334 208743
Robb, Nigel J. FCP MA BD ThM MTh	1981	2014	Presbytery Clerk: St Andrews	Presbytery Office, Hope Park and Martyrs' Church, 1 Howard Place, St Andrews KY16 9UY	07966 286958
Strong, Clifford LTh	1983	1995	(Creich, Flisk and Kilmany with Monimail)	60 Maryknowe, Gauldry, Newport-on-Tay DD6 8SL / cliffstrongman@btinternet.com	01382 330445
Torrance, Alan J. (Prof.) MA BD DrTheol	1984	1999	University of St Andrews	Kincaple House, Kincaple, St Andrews KY16 9SH	Home 01334 850755 / Office 01334 462843
Unsworth, Ruth BA BD CertMHS PgDipCBP BABCP	1984	1987	(Glasgow Pollokshaws)	5 Lindsay Gardens, St Andrews KY16 8XB / RUnsworth@churchofscotland.org.uk	07894 802119
Walker, James B. MA BD DPhil	1975	2011	(Chaplain: University of St Andrews)	5 Priestden Park, St Andrews KY16 8DL	01334 472839
Wotherspoon, Ian G. BA LTh	1967	2004	(Coatbridge: St Andrew's)	12 Cherry Lane, Cupar KY15 5DA / wotherspoonrig@aol.com	01334 650710

(27) DUNKELD AND MEIGLE

Meets at Pitlochry on the first Tuesday of February, September and December, on the third Tuesday of April and the fourth Tuesday of October, and at the Moderator's church on the third Tuesday of June.

Clerk:	REV. JOHN RUSSELL MA	Kilblaan, Gladstone Terrace, Birnam, Dunkeld PH8 0DP	01350 728896
		dunkeldmeigle@churchofscotland.org.uk	
Depute Clerk:	REV. R. FRASER PENNY BA BD	Cathedral Manse, Dunkeld PH8 0AW	01350 727249
		RPenny@churchofscotland.org.uk	

Aberfeldy (H) linked with Dull and Weem (H) linked with Grantully, Logierait and Strathtay
Neil M. Glover   2005   2017   The Manse, Taybridge Terrace, Aberfeldy PH15 2BS   01887 820819
NGlover@churchofscotland.org.uk   07779 280074

Alyth (H)
Michael J. Erskine MA BD   1985   2012   The Manse, Cambridge Street, Alyth, Blairgowrie PH11 8AW   01828 632238
erskinemike@gmail.com

Ardler, Kettins and Meigle
Alison Notman BD   2014   The Manse, Dundee Road, Meigle, Blairgowrie PH12 8SB   01828 640074
ANotman@churchofscotland.org.uk

Bendochy linked with Coupar Angus: Abbey
Andrew F. Graham BTh DPS   2001   2016   Caddam Road, Coupar Angus, Blairgowrie PH13 9EF   01828 627864
Andrew.Graham@churchofscotland.org.uk

Blair Atholl and Struan linked with Braes of Rannoch linked with Foss and Rannoch (H)
Vacant   The Manse, Blair Atholl, Pitlochry PH18 5SX   01796 481213
Session Clerk, Blair Atholl and Struan: H.J. Ingram (Mr)   ingramsparky@btinternet.com   01796 481275
Session Clerk, Braes of Rannoch: A.M. Phillips (Miss)   alisonrannoch@outlook.com   01882 633228
Session Clerk, Foss and Rannoch: R. Anderson (Mr)   lizandrab@live.co.uk   01892 632272

Blairgowrie
Vacant   The Manse, Upper David Street, Blairgowrie PH10 6HB   01250 872146
Session Clerk: A. Drummond (Mr)   ajdrummond@btinternet.com   01250 873207

Braes of Rannoch See Blair Atholl and Struan

Caputh and Clunie (H) linked with Kinclaven (H)
Peggy Ewart-Roberts BA BD 2003 2011 Cara Beag, Essendy Road, Blairgowrie PH10 6QU 01250 876897
PEwart-Roberts@churchofscotland.org.uk

Coupar Angus: Abbey See Bendochy
Dull and Weem See Aberfeldy

Dunkeld (H)
R. Fraser Penny BA BD 1984 2001 Cathedral Manse, Dunkeld PH8 0AW 01350 727249
RPenny@churchofscotland.org.uk

Fortingall and Glenlyon linked with Kenmore and Lawers (H)
Anne J. Brennan BSc BD MTh 1999 The Manse, Balnaskeag, Kenmore, Aberfeldy PH15 2HB 01887 830218
ABrennan@churchofscotland.org.uk

Foss and Rannoch See Blair Atholl and Struan
Grantully, Logierait and Strathtay See Aberfeldy
Kenmore and Lawers See Fortingall and Glenlyon
Kinclaven See Caputh and Clunie

Kirkmichael, Straloch and Glenshee linked with Rattray (H)
Linda Stewart (Mrs) BD 1996 2012 The Manse, Alyth Road, Rattray, Blairgowrie PH10 7HF 01250 872462
Linda.Stewart@churchofscotland.org.uk

Pitlochry (H)
Mary M. Haddow (Mrs) BD 2001 2012 Manse Road, Moulin, Pitlochry PH16 5EP **01796 472160**
MHaddow@churchofscotland.org.uk 01796 472774

Rattray See Kirkmichael, Straloch and Glenshee

Tenandry
Guardianship of the Presbytery
Session Clerk: J. Thorpe (Mrs) johnethorpe@btinternet.com 01796 473252

Campbell, Richard S. LTh 1993 2010 (Gargunnock with Kilmadock with 3 David Farquharson Road, Blairgowrie PH10 6FD 01250 876386
Kincardine-in-Menteith) revrichards@yahoo.co.uk
Cassells, Alexander K. MA BD 1961 1997 (Leuchars: St Athernase and Guardbridge) Alt-Na-Feidh, Bridge of Cally, Blairgowrie PH10 7JL 07816 043968

Name			Charge	Address	Telephone
Ewart, William BSc BD	1972	2010	(Caputh and Clunie with Kinclaven)	Cara Beag, Essendy Road, Blairgowrie PH10 6QU ewel@btinternet.com	01250 876897
Knox, John W. MTheol	1992	1997	(Lochgelly: Macainsh)	Heatherlea, Main Street, Ardler, Blairgowrie PH12 8SR	01828 640731
McAlister, D.J.B. MA BD PhD	1951	1989	(North Berwick: Blackadder)	2 Duff Avenue, Moulin, Pitlochry PH16 5EN	01796 473591
MacRae, Malcolm H. MA PhD	1971	2010	(Kirkmichael, Straloch and Glenshee with Rattray)	10B Victoria Place, Stirling FK8 2QU malcolm.macrae1@btopenworld.com	01786 465547
Mowbray, Harry BD CA	2003	2018	(Blairgowrie)	12 Isla Road, Blairgowrie PH10 6RR	
Nelson, Robert C. BA BD	1980	2010	(Isle of Mull, Kilninian and Kilmore with Salen and Ulva with Tobermory with Torosay and Kinlochspelvie)	St Colme's, Perth Road, Birnam, Dunkeld PH8 0BH rcnelson49@btinternet.com	01350 727455
Nicol, Robert D.		2013	Ordained Local Minister	Rappla Lodge, Camserney, Aberfeldy PH15 2JF RNicol@churchofscotland.org.uk	01887 820242
Ormiston, Hugh C. BSc BD MPhil PhD	1969	2004	(Kirkmichael, Straloch and Glenshee with Rattray)	Cedar Lea, Main Road, Woodside, Blairgowrie PH13 9NP	01828 670539
Robertson, Matthew LTh	1968	2002	(Cawdor with Croy and Dalcross)	Inver, Strathtay, Pitlochry PH9 0PG	01887 840780
Rooney, Malcolm I.G. DPE BEd BD	1993	2017	(The Glens and Kirriemuir: Old)	23 Mart Lane, Northmuir, Kirriemuir DD8 4TL malc.rooney@gmail.com	01575 575334 07909 993233
Russell, John MA	1959	2000	Presbytery Clerk: Dunkeld and Meigle	Kilblaan, Gladstone Terrace, Birnam, Dunkeld PH8 0DP	01350 728896
Shannon, W.G. MA BD	1955	1998	(Pitlochry)	19 Knockard Road, Pitlochry PH16 5HJ	01796 473533
Sloan, Robert BD	1997	2014	(Fauldhouse St Andrew's)	3 Gean Grove, Blairgowrie PH10 6TL	01250 875286
Steele, Grace M.F. MA BTh		2014	Ordained Local Minister	12a Farragon Drive, Aberfeldy PH15 2BQ GSteele@churchofscotland.org.uk	01887 820025
Tait, Thomas W. BD MBE	1972	1997	(Rattray)	3 Rosemount Park, Blairgowrie PH10 6TZ	01250 874833
Wallace, Sheila D. (Mrs) DCS BA BD	2009	2017	(Deacon)	Little Orchard, Blair Atholl, Pitlochry PH18 5SH sheilad.wallace53@gmail.com	01796 481647 07733 243046
Whyte, William B. BD	1973	2003	(Nairn: St Ninian's)	The Old Inn, Park Hill Road, Rattray, Blairgowrie PH10 7DS	01250 874401
Wilson, John M. MA BD	1967	2004	(Altnaharra and Farr)	Berbice, The Terrace, Blair Atholl, Pitlochry PH18 5SZ	01796 481619
Wilson, Mary D. (Mrs) RGN SCM DTM	1990	2004	(Auxiliary Minister)	Berbice, The Terrace, Blair Atholl, Pitlochry PH18 5SZ	01796 481619

(28) PERTH

Meets at 10am on the second Saturday of September, March, and June and at 7pm on the second Tuesday of November in venues throughout the Presbytery.

Clerk:	REV. J. COLIN CASKIE BA BD	209 High Street, Perth PH1 5PB perth@churchofscotland.org.uk	01738 451177
Presbytery Office:			

Aberdalgie (H) and Forteviot (H) linked with Aberuthven and Dunning (H)
James W. Aitchison BD   1993   2015   The Manse, Aberdalgie, Perth PH2 0QD   01738 446771
JAitchison@churchofscotland.org.uk

Abernethy and Dron and Arngask
Vacant   3 Manse Road, Abernethy, Perth PH2 9JP   01738 850938
Session Clerk: Bill Macpherson   session.clerk@ada-church.org.uk   01577 830430

Aberuthven and Dunning See Aberdalgie and Forteviot

Almondbank Tibbermore linked with Methven and Logiealmond
Vacant   The Manse, Pitcairngreen, Perth PH1 3EA   01738 583217
Session Clerk, Almondbank Tibbermore: Wilma Lumsden (Mrs)   lummies@talktalk.net   01738 583376

Ardoch (H) linked with Blackford (H)
Mairi Perkins BA BTh   2012   2016   Manse of Ardoch, Feddoch Road, Braco, Dunblane FK15 5RE   01786 880948
MPerkins@churchofscotland.org.uk

Auchterarder (H)
Vacant   22 Kirkfield Place, Auchterarder PH3 1FP   01764 662399
Session Clerk: Anne Robertson (Mrs)   anne@friendlylion.net   01764 664528

Auchtergaven and Moneydie linked with Redgorton and Stanley
Adrian J. Lough BD   2012   22 King Street, Stanley, Perth PH1 4ND   01738 827952
ALough@churchofscotland.org.uk

Blackford See Ardoch

Cargill Burrelton linked with Collace
Steven Thomson BSc BD   2001   2016   The Manse, Manse Road, Woodside, Blairgowrie PH13 9NQ   01828 670384
SThomson@churchofscotland.org.uk

Cleish (H) linked with Fossoway: St Serf's and Devonside
Elisabeth M. Stenhouse BD   2006   2014   Station House, Station Road, Crook of Devon, Kinross KY13 0PG   01577 842128
EStenhouse@churchofscotland.org.uk

Collace See Cargill Burrelton

Comrie (H) linked with Dundurn (H)
Graham McWilliams BSc BD DMin   2005   The Manse, Strowan Road, Comrie, Comrie, Crieff PH6 2ES   01764 670076
GMcWilliams@churchofscotland.org.uk

Crieff (H)
Andrew J. Philip BSc BD   1996   2013   8 Strathearn Terrace, Crieff PH7 3AQ   01764 218976
APhilip@churchofscotland.org.uk

Dunbarney (H) and Forgandenny
Allan J. Wilson BSc MEd BD   2007   Dunbarney Manse, Manse Road, Bridge of Earn, Perth PH2 9DY   01738 812211
AWilson@churchofscotland.org.uk

Dundurn See Comrie

Errol (H) linked with Kilspindie and Rait
John Macgregor BD   2001   2016   South Bank, Errol, Perth PH2 7PZ   01821 642279
John.Macgregor@churchofscotland.org.uk

Fossoway: St Serf's and Devonside See Cleish

Fowlis Wester, Madderty and Monzie linked with Gask (H)
Vacant   Beechview, Abercairney, Crieff PH7 3NF   01764 652116
Session Clerk: Fowlis Wester, Madderty and   sheenacrawford@gmail.com   01764 654270
Monzie: Sheena Crawford (Mrs)

Gask See Fowlis Wester, Madderty and Monzie
Kilspindie and Rait See Errol

Kinross (H)
Alan D. Reid MA BD   1989   2009   15 Green Wood, Kinross KY13 8FG   **01577 862570**
AReid@churchofscotland.org.uk   01577 862952

Methven and Logiealmond See Almondbank Tibbermore

Muthill (H) linked with Trinity Gask and Kinkell
Klaus O.F. Buwert LLB BD DMin   1984   2013   The Manse, Station Road, Muthill, Crieff PH5 2AR   01764 681205
KBuwert@churchofscotland.org.uk

Orwell (H) and Portmoak (H)
Angus Morrison MA BD PhD DD — 1979 — 41 Auld Mart Road, Milnathort, Kinross KY13 9FR / AMorrison@churchofscotland.org.uk — 01577 **862100** / 01577 863461

Perth: Craigie and Moncreiffe
Vacant
Robert F. Wilkie — 2011 2012 — The Manse, 46 Abbot Street, Perth PH2 0EE / 24 Huntingtower Road, Perth PH1 2JS / RWilkie@churchofscotland.org.uk — 01738 623748 / 01738 628301
(Auxiliary Minister)

Perth: Kinnoull (H)
Graham W. Crawford BSc BD STM — 1991 2016 — 1 Mount Tabor Avenue, Perth PH2 7BT / GCrawford@churchofscotland.org.uk — 01738 626046 / 07817 504042
Timothy E.G. Fletcher BA FCMA — 1998 2014 — 3 Ardchoille Park, Perth PH2 7TL / TFletcher@churchofscotland.org.uk — 01738 638189 / 07747 013985
(Auxiliary Minister)

Perth: Letham St Mark's (H)
James C. Stewart BD DipMin — 1997 — 35 Rose Crescent, Perth PH1 1NT / JStewart@churchofscotland.org.uk — 01738 **446377** / 01738 624167
Kenneth D. Mackay DCS — 1996 1998 — 11F Balgowan Road, Perth PH1 2JG / Kenneth.Mackay@churchofscotland.org.uk — 01738 621169 / 07843 883042

Perth: North
Kenneth D. Stott MA BD — 1989 2017 — 2 Cragganmore Place, Perth PH1 3GJ / KStott@churchofscotland.org.uk — 01738 **622298** / 01738 625728

Perth: Riverside
David R. Rankin MA BD — 2009 2014 — 44 Hay Street, Perth PH1 5HS / DRankin@churchofscotland.org.uk — 01738 **622341** / 07810 008754

Perth: St John's Kirk of Perth (H) (01738 633192) linked with Perth: St Leonard's-in-the-Fields (H) (01738 632238)
John A.H. Murdoch BA BD DPSS — 1979 2016 — Ferntower Kinfauns Holdings, Perth PH2 7JY / JMurdoch@churchofscotland.org.uk — 01738 628378 / 07578 558978
Alexander T. Stewart MA BD FSAScot — 1975 2017 — 36 Viewlands Terrace, Perth PH1 1BZ / alex.t.stewart@blueyonder.co.uk — 01738 566675
(Associate Minister)

Perth: St Leonard's-in-the-Fields See Perth: St John's Kirk of Perth

Perth: St Matthew's   Office: 01738 636757; Vestry: 01738 630725
Scott Burton BD DipMin   1999   2007   23 Kincarrathie Crescent, Perth PH2 7HH   01738 626828
SBurton@churchofscotland.org.uk

Redgorton and Stanley See Auchtergaven and Moneydie

St Madoes and Kinfauns
Marc F. Bircham BD MTh   2000   Glencarse, Perth PH2 7NF   01738 860837
MBircham@churchofscotland.org.uk

Scone and St Martins
Vacant
Alan Livingstone   2013   Meadowside, Lawmuir, Methven, Perth PH1 3SZ   01738 840682
(Ordained Local Minister)   ALivingstone@churchofscotland.org.uk

Trinity Gask and Kinkell See Muthill

Ballentine, Ann M. MA BD	1981	2007	(Kirknewton and East Calder)	17 Nellfield Road, Crieff PH7 3DU · annmballentine@gmail.com	01764 652567
Barr, T. Leslie LTh	1969	1997	(Kinross)	8 Fairfield Road, Kelty KY4 0BY · leslie_barr@yahoo.co.uk	
Bertram, Thomas A.	1972	1995	(Patna Waterside)	3 Scrimgeour's Corner, 29 West High Street, Crieff PH7 4AP	07727 718076
Brown, Elizabeth JP RGN	1996	2007	(Auxiliary Minister)	8 Viewlands Place, Perth PH1 1BS · liz.brown@blueyonder.co.uk	01764 652066 / 01738 552391
Brown, Marina D. MA BD MTh	2000	2012	(Hawick: St Mary's and Old)	Moneydie School Cottage, Luncarty, Perth PH1 3HZ · revndb1711@btinternet.com	01738 582163
Cairns, Evelyn BD	2004	2012	(Chaplain: Rachel House)	15 Talla Park, Kinross KY13 8AB · revelyn@btinternet.com	01577 863990
Caskie, J. Colin BA BD	1977	2012	Presbytery Clerk: Perth	13 Anderson Drive, Perth PH1 1JZ · jcolincaskie@gmail.com	01738 445543
Coleman, Sidney H. BA BD MTh	1961	2001	(Glasgow: Merrylea)	'Blaven', 11 Clyde Place, Perth PH2 0EZ · sidney.coleman@blueyonder.co.uk	01738 565072
Craig, Joan H. MTheol	1986	2005	(Orkney: East Mainland)	7 Jedburgh Place, Perth PH1 1SJ · joanhcraig@btinternet.com	01738 580180
Donaldson, Robert B. BSocSc	1953	1997	(Kilchoman with Portnahaven)	11 Strathearn Court, Crieff PH7 3DS	01764 654976
Dunn, W. Stuart LTh	1970	2006	(Motherwell: Crosshill)	10 Macrostie Gardens, Crieff PH7 4LP	01764 655178
Fleming, Hamish K. MA	1966	2001	(Banchory Ternan: East)	36 Earnmuir Road, Comrie, Crieff PH6 2EY · hamishnan@gmail.com	01764 679178

Name			Charge	Address / Email	Tel
Gilchrist, Ewen J. BD DipMin DipComm	1982	2017	(Cults)	9 David Douglas Avenue, Scone PH2 6QQ ewengilchrist@btconnect.com	07747 746418
Graham, Sydney S. DipYL MPhil BD	1987	2009	(Iona with Kilfinichen and Kilvickeon and the Ross of Mull)	'Aspen', Milton Road, Luncarty, Perth PH1 3ES syd@sydgraham-plus.com	01738 829350
Gregory, J.C. LTh	1968	1992	(Blantyre: St Andrew's)	2 Southlands Road, Auchterarder PH3 1BA	01764 664594
Gunn, Alexander M. MA BD	1967	2006	(Aberfeldy with Amulree and Strathbraan with Dull and Weem)	'Navarone', 12 Cornhill Road, Perth PH1 1LR sandygunn@btinternet.com	01738 443216
Halliday, Archibald R. BD MTh	1964	1999	(Duffus, Spynie and Hopeman)	8 Turretbank Drive, Crieff PH7 4LW roberthalliday343@btinternet.com	01764 656464
Kelly, T. Clifford	1973	1995	(Ferintosh)	20 Whinfield Drive, Kinross KY13 8UB	01577 864946
Lawson, James B. MA BD	1961	2002	(South Uist)	4 Cowden Way, Comrie, Crieff PH6 2NW james.lawson7@btopenworld.com	01764 679180
Lawson, Ronald G. MA BD	1964	1999	(Greenock: Wellpark Mid Kirk)	6 East Brougham Street, Stanley, Perth PH1 4NJ	01738 828871
McCarthy, David J. BSc BD	1985	2014	Mission and Discipleship Council	121 George Street, Edinburgh EH2 4YN DMcCarthy@churchofscotland.org.uk	0131 225 5722
McCormick, Alastair F.	1962	1998	(Creich with Rosehall)	14 Balmanno Park, Bridge of Earn, Perth PH2 9RJ	01738 813588
McCrum, Robert BSc BD	1982	2014	(Ayr: St James')	28 Rose Crescent, Perth PH1 1NT robert.mccrum@virgin.net	01738 447906
MacDonald, James W. BD	1976	2012	(Crieff)	'Mingulay', 29 Hebridean Gardens, Crieff PH7 3BP rev_up@btinternet.com	01764 654500
McFadzean, Iain MA BD	1989	2010	Chief Executive: Work Place Chaplaincy Scotland	2 Lowfield Crescent, Luncarty, Perth PH13FG iain.mcfadzean@wpcscotland.co.uk	01738 827338 07969 227696
McGregor, William LTh	1987	2003	(Auchtergaven and Moneydie)	'Ard Choille', 7 Taypark Road, Luncarty, Perth PH1 3FE bill.mcgregor7@btinternet.com	01738 827866
McIntosh, Colin G. MA BD	1976	2013	(Dunblane: Cathedral)	Drumhead Cottage, Drum, Kinross KY13 0PR colinmcintosh4@btinternet.com	01577 840012
MacLaughlan, Grant BA BD	1998	2015	Community Worker, Perth Tulloch Net	Unit 2, Tulloch Square, Perth PH1 2PW grantmac.tullochnet@gmail.com	01738 562731 07790 518041
MacMillan, Riada M. BD	1991	1998	(Perth: Craigend Moncreiffe with Rhynd)	11 Muirend Gardens, Perth PH1 1JR	01738 628867
McNaughton, David J.H. BA CA	1976	1995	(Killin and Ardeonaig)	14 Rankine Court, Wormit, Newport-on-Tay DD6 8TA	
Main, Douglas M. BD	1986	2014	(Errol with Kilspindie and Rait)	14 Madoch Road, St Madoes, Perth PH2 7TT revdmain@sky.com	01738 860867
Malcolm, Alistair BD DPS	1976	2012	(Inverness: Inshes)	11 Kinclaven Gardens, Murthly, Perth PH1 4EX amalcolm067@btinternet.com	01738 710979
Michie, Margaret		2013	Ordained Local Minister: Loch Leven Parish Grouping	3 Loch Leven Court, Wester Balgedie, Kinross KY13 9NE margaretmichie@btinternet.com	01592 840602
Milne, Robert B. BTh	1999	2017	(Broughton, Glenholm and Kilbucho with Skirling with Stobo and Drumelzier with Tweedsmuir)	3 Mid Square, Comrie PH6 2EG rbmilne@aol.com	
Mitchell, Alexander B. BD	1981	2014	(Dunblane: St Blane's)	24 Hebridean Gardens, Crieff PH7 3BP alex.mitchell6@btopenworld.com	01764 652241
Munro, Gillian BSc BD	1989	2018	(Head of Spiritual Care, NHS Tayside)	The Old Town House, 53 Main Street, Abernethy, Perth PH2 9JH munrooth@aol.com	01738 850066

Name			Charge / Role	Address	Tel
Munro, Patricia BSc DCS	1986	2016	(Deacon)	4 Hewat Place, Perth PH1 2UD patmunrodcs@gmail.com	01738 443088 07814 836314
Paton, Iain F. BD FCIS	1980	2006	(Elie with Kilconquhar and Colinsburgh)	Muldoanich, Stirling Street, Blackford, Auchterarder PH4 1QG iain.f.paton@btinternet.com	01764 682234
Pattison, Kenneth J. MA BD STM	1967	2004	(Kilmuir and Logie Easter)	2 Castle Way, St Madoes, Glencarse, Perth PH2 7NY k_pattison@btinternet.com	01738 860340
Philip, Elizabeth MA BA PGCSE DCS	2007		Deacon	8 Strathearn Terrace, Crieff PH7 3AQ ephilipstitch@gmail.com	01764 218976 07970 767851
Redpath, James G. BD DipPTh	1988	2016	(Auchtermuchty with Edenshead and Strathmiglo)	9 Beveridge Place, Kinross KY13 8QY JRedpath@churchofscotland.org.uk	07713 919442
Searle, David C. MA DipTh	1965	2003	(Warden: Rutherford House)	Stonefall Lodge, 30 Abbey Lane, Grange, Errol PH2 7GB dcs@davidsearle.plus.com	01821 641004
Simpson, James A. BSc BD STM DD	1960	2000	(Dornoch Cathedral)	'Dornoch', Perth Road, Bankfoot, Perth PH1 4ED ja@simpsondornoch.co.uk	01738 787710
Sloan, Robert P. MA BD	1968	2007	(Braemar and Crathie)	1 Broomhill Avenue, Perth PH1 1EN sloan12@virginmedia.com	01738 443904
Stenhouse, W. Duncan MA BD	1989	2006	(Dunbarney and Forgandenny)	32 Smeaton Gait, Kinross KY13 8FB	01577 866992
Stewart, Anne E. BD CertMin	1998		Prison Chaplain: HM Prison Castle Huntly	35 Rose Crescent, Perth PH1 1NT anne.stewart2@sps.pnn.gov.uk	01738 624167
Stewart, Robin J. MA BD STM	1959	1995	(Orwell with Portmoak)	'Oakbrae', Perth Road, Murthly, Perth PH1 4HF	01738 710220
Thomson, J. Bruce MA BD	1972	2009	(Scone: Old)	47 Elm Street, Errol, Perth PH2 7SQ RevBruceThomson@aol.com	01821 641039 07850 846404
Thomson, Peter D. MA BD	1968	2004	(Comrie with Dundurn)	34 Queen Street, Perth PH2 0EJ peterthomson208@btinternet.com	01738 622418
Wallace, Catherine PGDipC DCS	1987	2017	Deacon: Honorary Secretary, Diaconate Council	21 Durley Dene Crescent, Bridge of Earn PH2 9RD secretary@churchofscotland.org.uk	01738 621709
Wallace, James K. MA BD STM	1988	2015	Scotus Tours	21 Durley Dene Crescent, Bridge of Earn PH2 9RD jkwministry@hotmail.com	01738 621709
Wylie, Jonathan BSc BD MTh	2000	2015	Chaplain: Strathallan School	Strathallan School, Forgandenny, Perth PH2 9EG chaplain@strathallan.co.uk	01738 815098

PERTH ADDRESSES

Craigie	Abbot Street	
Kinnoull	Dundee Rd near Queen's Bridge	
Letham St Mark's	Rannoch Road	
Moncreiffe	Glenbruar Crescent	
North	Mill Street near Kinnoull Street	
Riverside	Bute Drive	
St John's	St John's Street	
St Leonard's-in-the-Fields	Marshall Place	
St Matthew's	Tay Street	

(29) DUNDEE

Meets at Dundee: The Steeple, Nethergate, on the second Wednesday of February, March, May, September, November and December; and on the fourth Wednesday of June.

Clerk:	REV. JAMES L. WILSON BD CPS	dundee@churchofscotland.org.uk	
Depute Clerk:	MR COLIN D. WILSON	cd.wilson663@iscali.co.uk	07885 618659 / 01382 774059
Presbytery Office:		Whitfield Parish Church, Haddington Crescent, Dundee DD4 0NA	01382 503012

Abernyte linked with Inchture and Kinnaird linked with Longforgan (H)
Marjory A. MacLean LLB BD PhD 1991 2011 The Manse, Longforgan, Dundee DD2 5HB 01382 360238
MMaclean@churchofscotland.org.uk

Auchterhouse (H) linked with Monikie and Newbigging and Murroes and Tealing (H)
Jean de Villiers BATheol BTh HonP'psych 2003 2017 29 Oak Lane, Ballumbie Castle Estate, Dundee DD5 3UQ 01382 351680
JdeVilliers@churchofscotland.org.uk

Dundee: Balgay (H)
Vacant 150 City Road, Dundee DD2 2PW 01382 669600
Session Clerk: Gary Dysart gary.dysart@blueyonder.co.uk 01382 524420

Dundee: Barnhill St Margaret's (H)
Alisa L. McDonald BA MDiv 2008 2018 church.office@btconnect.com 01382 737294
2 St Margaret's Lane, Barnhill, Dundee DD5 2PQ 01382 779278
Alisa.McDonald@churchofscotland.org.uk

Dundee: Broughty Ferry New Kirk (H)
Catherine E.E. Collins (Mrs) MA BD 1993 2006 New Kirk Manse, 25 Ballinard Gardens, Broughty Ferry, Dundee DD5 1BZ 01382 778874
CCollins@churchofscotland.org.uk

Dundee: Broughty Ferry St James' (H)
Guardianship of the Presbytery 2 Ferry Road, Monifieth, Dundee DD5 4NT 01382 534468
Session Clerks: Lyn Edwards (Mrs) lynlocks@hotmail.co.uk 01382 730552
David J.B. Murie d.j.b.murie@gmail.com 01382 320493

Dundee: Broughty Ferry St Luke's and Queen Street
C. Graham D. Taylor BSc BD FIAB   2001
22 Albert Road, Broughty Ferry, Dundee DD5 1AZ
CTaylor@churchofscotland.org.uk
01382 **732094**
01382 779212

Dundee: Broughty Ferry St Stephen's and West (H) linked with Dundee: Dundee (St Mary's) (H)
Keith F. Hall MA BD   1980   1994
33 Strathern Road, West Ferry, Dundee DD5 1PP
KHall@churchofscotland.org.uk
01382 **226271**
01382 778808

Dundee: Camperdown (H)
Guardianship of the Presbytery
Camperdown Manse, Myrekirk Road, Dundee DD2 4SF
01382 **623958**

Dundee: Chalmers-Ardler (H)
Vacant
The Manse, Turnberry Avenue, Dundee DD2 3TP
01382 827439

Dundee: Coldside
Anthony P. Thornthwaite MTh   1995   2011
9 Abercorn Street, Dundee DD4 7HY
AThornthwaite@churchofscotland.org.uk
01382 458314

Dundee: Craigiebank (H) (01382 731173) linked with Dundee: Douglas and Mid Craigie
Edith F. McMillan (Mrs) MA BD   1981   1999
19 Americanmuir Road, Dundee DD3 9AA
EMcMillan@churchofscotland.org.uk
01382 812423

Dundee: Douglas and Mid Craigie See Dundee: Craigiebank

Dundee: Downfield Mains (H)
Nathan S. McConnell BS MA ThM   2005   2016
9 Elgin Street, Dundee DD3 8NL
NMcConnell@churchofscotland.org.uk
01382 **810624/812166**
01382 690196

Dundee: Dundee (St Mary's) See Dundee: Broughty Ferry St Stephen's and West

Dundee: Fintry
Colin M. Brough BSc BD   1998   2002
4 Clive Street, Dundee DD4 7AW
CBrough@churchofscotland.org.uk
01382 458629

Catherine J. Brodie MA BA MPhil PGCE   2017
(Ordained Local Minister)
48h Cleghorn Street, Dundee DD2 2NJ
CBrodie@churchofscotland.org.uk
07432 513375

Dundee: Lochee (H)

Minister	Ordained	Inducted	Address	Phone
Roderick J. Grahame BD CPS DMin	1991	2018	32 Clayhills Drive, Dundee DD2 1SX RGrahame@churchofscotland.org.uk	01382 561872
Willie Strachan MBA DipY&C (Ordained Local Minister)		2013	Ladywell House, Lucky Slap, Monikie, Dundee DD5 3QG WStrachan@churchofscotland.org.uk	01382 370286

Dundee: Logie and St John's Cross (H)

Minister	Ordained	Inducted	Address	Phone
David T. Gray BArch BD	2010	2014	7 Hyndford Street, Dundee DD2 1HQ DGray@churchofscotland.org.uk	**01382 668514** 01382 668653 07789 718622

Dundee: Meadowside St Paul's (H) (01382 225420) linked with Dundee: St Andrew's (H) (01382 224860)

Vacant

Session Clerk, Meadowside St Paul's: Margaret Adamson (Ms)	mspdundee@outlook.com	01382 668624
Session Clerk, St Andrew's: Helen Holden (Mrs)	hholdenuk@yahoo.com	01241 853242

Dundee: Menzieshill

Minister	Inducted	Address	Phone
Robert Mallinson BD	2010	The Manse, Charleston Drive, Dundee DD2 4ED RMallinson@churchofscotland.org.uk	01382 667446 07595 249089

Dundee: St Andrew's See Dundee: Meadowside St Paul's

Dundee: St David's High Kirk (H)

Minister	Ordained	Inducted	Address	Phone
Emma McDonald BD	2013	2018	St David's High Kirk, 119A Kinghorne Road, Dundee DD3 6PW EMcDonald@churchofscotland.org.uk	01382 322955

Dundee: The Steeple (H)

Minister	Ordained	Inducted	Address	Phone
Robert A. Calvert BSc BD DMin	1983	2014	128 Arbroath Road, Dundee DD4 7HR RCalvert@churchofscotland.org.uk	**01382 200031** 01382 522837 07532 029343

Dundee: Stobswell (H)

Minister	Ordained	Inducted	Address	Phone
William McLaren MA BD	1990	2007	23 Shamrock Street, Dundee DD4 7AH WMcLaren@churchofscotland.org.uk	**01382 461397** 01382 459119

Dundee: Strathmartine (H)

Minister	Ordained	Inducted	Address	Phone
Stewart McMillan BD	1983	1990	19 Americanmuir Road, Dundee DD3 9AA SMcMillan@churchofscotland.org.uk	**01382 825817** 01382 812423

Dundee: Trinity (H)
Vacant
Session Clerk: Ian Main   65 Clepington Road, Dundee DD4 7BQ   01382 458764
ian-main@sky.com   01382 783783

Dundee: West
Vacant

Dundee: Whitfield (H)
James L. Wilson BD CPS   1986   2001   53 Old Craigie Road, Dundee DD4 7JD   01382 **503012**
James.Wilson@churchofscotland.org.uk   01382 459249
07885 618659

Fowlis and Liff linked with Lundie and Muirhead (H)
Donna M. Hays (Mrs) MTheol   2004   149 Coupar Angus Road, Muirhead of Liff, Dundee DD2 5QN   01382 580210
DipEd DipTMHA   DHays@churchofscotland.org.uk

Inchture and Kinnaird See Abernyte

Invergowrie (H)
Robert J. Ramsay LLB NP BD   1986   1997   2 Boniface Place, Invergowrie, Dundee DD2 5DW   01382 561118
RRamsay@churchofscotland.org.uk

Longforgan See Abernyte
Lundie and Muirhead See Fowlis and Liff

Monifieth (H)
Fiona J. Reynolds LLB BD   2018   8 Church Street, Monifieth, Dundee DD5 4JP   01382 699183

Monikie and Newbigging and Murroes and Tealing See Auchterhouse

Allan, Jean (Mrs) DCS   1989 2011   (Deacon)   12C Hindmarsh Avenue, Dundee DD3 7LW   01382 827299
jeannieallan45@googlemail.com   07709 959474

Barrett, Leslie M. BD FRICS   1991 2014   (Chaplain: University of Abertay, Dundee)   Dunelm Cottage, Logie, Cupar KY15 4SJ   01334 870396
lesliembarrett@btinternet.com

Campbell, Gordon MA BD CDipAF   2001 2004   Auxiliary Minister: an Honorary Chaplain: 2 Falkland Place, Kingoodie, Invergowrie, Dundee DD2 5DY   01382 561383
DipHSM CMgr MCMI MIHM   University of Dundee   g.a.campbell@dundee.ac.uk
AssocCIPD AFRIN ARSGS FRGS
FSAScot

Name	Ord.	Appt.	Charge / Role	Address	Tel.
Collins, David A. BSc BD	1993	2016	(Auchterhouse with Monikie and Newbigging and Murroes and Tealing)	New Kirk Manse, 25 Ballinard Gardens, Broughty Ferry, Dundee DD5 1BZ revdacollins@btinternet.com	01382 778874
Craik, Sheila (Mrs) BD	1989	2001	(Dundee: Camperdown)	35 Haldane Terrace, Dundee DD3 0HT	01382 802078
Cramb, Erik M. LTh	1973	2004	(Industrial Mission Organiser)	Flat 35, Braehead, Methven Walk, Dundee DD2 3FJ erikcramb@aol.com	01382 526196
Dempster, Colin J. BD CertMin	1990	2016	(Mearns Coastal)	35 Margaret Lindsay Place, Monifieth DD6 4RD Coldcoast@btinternet.com	01382 532368
Donald, Robert M. LTh BA	1969	2004	(Kilmodan and Colintraive)	2 Blacklaw Drive, Birkhill, Dundee DD2 5RJ robandmoiradonald@yahoo.co.uk	01382 581337
Douglas, Fiona C. MBE MA BD PhD	1989	1997	Chaplain: University of Dundee	10 Springfield, Dundee DD1 4JE f.c.douglas@dundee.ac.uk	01382 384157
Fraser, Donald W. MA	1958	2010	(Monifieth)	1 Blake Avenue, Broughty Ferry, Dundee DD5 3LH fraserdonald37@yahoo.co.uk	01382 477491 07531 863316
Galbraith, W. James L. BSc BD MICE	1973	1996	(Kilchrenan and Dalavich with Muckairn)	586 Brook Street, Broughty Ferry, Dundee DD5 2EA Wards of Keithock, Brechin DD9 7PZ	01382 732110 01356 624479
Greaves, Andrew T. BD	1985	2016	(Dundee: West)	48 Marlee Road, Broughty Ferry, Dundee DD5 3EX	01382 736400
Ingram, J.R.	1954	1978	(Chaplain: RAF)	8A Albert Street, Monifieth, Dundee DD5 4JS	01382 532772
Jamieson, David B. MA BD STM	1974	2011	(Monifieth)	1 Kintail Walk, Inchture, Perth PH14 9RY	01828 686029
Kay, Elizabeth (Miss) DipYCS	1993	2007	(Auxiliary Minister)	ekay007@btinternet.com	
Laidlaw, John J. MA	1964	1996	(Adviser in Religious Education)	14 Dalhousie Road, Barnhill, Dundee DD5 2SQ	01382 477458
Laing, David J.H. BD DPS	1976	2014	(Dundee: Trinity)	18 Kerrington Crescent, Barnhill, Dundee DD5 2TN david.laing@live.com	01382 739586
Lillie, Fiona L. (Mrs) BA BD MLitt	1995	2017	(Glasgow: St John's Renfield)	4 McVicars Lane, Dundee DD1 4LH fionalillie@btinternet.com	01382 229082
McLeod, David C. BSc MEng BD	1969	2001	(Dundee: Fairmuir)	6 Carseview Gardens, Dundee DD2 1NE	01382 641371
McMillan, Charles D. LTh	1979	2004	(Elgin: High)	11 Troon Terrace, The Orchard, Ardler, Dundee DD2 3FX	01382 831358
Mair, Michael V.A. MA BD	1967	2007	(Chaplain: Dundee Acute Hospitals)	48 Panmure Street, Monifieth DD5 4EH mvamair@gmail.com	01382 530538
Martin, Janie (Miss) DCS	1979	2008	(Deacon)	16 Wentworth Road, Ardler, Dundee DD2 8SD janimar@aol.com	01382 813786
Mitchell, Jack MA BD CTh	1987	1996	(Dundee: Menzieshill)	29 Carrick Gardens, Ayr KA7 2RT	01575 572503
Pownie, James E. LTh	1969	1995	(Dundee: Chalmers-Ardler)	3 Kirktonhill Road, Kirriemuir DD8 4HU	01382 581790
Rae, Robert LTh	1968	1983	(Carriden)	14 Neddertoun View, Liff, Dundee DD3 5RU	01382 520519
Reid, R. Gordon BSc BD MIET	1993	2010		6 Bayview Place, Monifieth, Dundee DD5 4TN GordonReid@aol.com	07952 349884
Robertson, James H. BSc BD	1975	2014	(Culloden: The Barn)	'Far End', 35 Mains Terrace, Dundee DD4 7BZ jimrob838@gmail.com	01382 522773 07595 465838
Robson, George K. LTh DPS BA	1983	2011	(Dundee: Balgay)	11 Ceres Crescent, Broughty Ferry, Dundee DD5 3JN gkrobson@virginmedia.com	01382 901212
Rose, Lewis (Mr) DCS	1993	2010	(Deacon)	6 Gauldie Crescent, Dundee DD3 0RR lewis_rose48@yahoo.co.uk	01382 816580 07899 790466
Scott, James MA BD	1973	2010	(Drumoak-Durris)	3 Blake Place, Broughty Ferry, Dundee DD5 3LQ jimscott73@yahoo.co.uk	01382 739595

Scoular, Stanley	1963	2000	31 Duns Crescent, Dundee DD4 0RY	01382 501653
Strickland, Alexander LTh	1971	2005	12 Ballumbie Braes, Dundee DD4 0UN	01382 685539
			(Dairsie with Kemback with Strathkinness)	
Taylor, Caroline (Mrs)	1995	2014	(Rosyth)	
			(Leuchars: St Athernase)	
			The Old Dairy, 15 Forthill Road, Broughty Ferry, Dundee DD5 3DH	01382 770198
			caro234@btinternet.com	

DUNDEE ADDRESSES

Balgay	200 Lochee Road
Barnhill St Margaret's	10 Invermark Terrace
Broughty Ferry	
New Kirk	370 Queen Street
St James'	5 Fort Street
St Luke's and Queen Street	5 West Queen Street
St Stephen's and West	96 Dundee Road
Camperdown	22 Brownhill Road
Chalmers-Ardler	Turnberry Avenue

Coldside	
Craigiebank	Isla Street x Main Street
Douglas and Mid Craigie	Craigie Avenue at Greendykes Road
Downfield Mains	Balbeggie Place
Dundee (St Mary's)	Haldane Street off Strathmartine Road
Fintry	Nethergate
Lochee	Fintry Road x Fintry Drive
Logie and St John's Cross	191 High Street, Lochee
	Shaftesbury Rd x Blackness Ave

Meadowside St Paul's	114 Nethergate
Menzieshill	Charleston Drive, Menzieshill
St Andrew's	2 King Street
St David's High Kirk	119A Kinghorne Road
Steeple	Nethergate
Stobswell	170 Albert Street
Strathmartine	507 Strathmartine Road
Trinity	73 Crescent Street
West	130 Perth Road
Whitfield	Haddington Crescent

(30) ANGUS

Meets at Forfar in St Margaret's Church Hall on the first Tuesday of February, March, May, September, November and December; and on the fourth Tuesday of June.

| Clerk: | REV IAN A. McLEAN BSc BD DMin | angus@churchofscotland.org.uk | |
| Presbytery Office: | | St Margaret's Church, West High Street, Forfar DD8 1BJ | 01307 464224 |

Aberlemno (H) linked with Guthrie and Rescobie

Brian Ramsay BD DPS MLitt	1980	1984	The Manse, Guthrie, Forfar DD8 2TP	01241 828243
			BRamsay@churchofscotland.org.uk	

Arbirlot linked with Carmyllie

Brian Dingwall BTh CQSW	1999	2016	The Manse, Arbirlot, Arbroath DD11 2NX	01241 879800
			brian.d12@btinternet.com	07906 656847

Arbroath: Knox's (H) linked with Arbroath: St Vigeans (H)

Vacant	The Manse, St Vigeans, Arbroath DD11 4RF	01241 873206
Session Clerk, St Vigeans: Margaret Pullar (Mrs)	margaret.pullar@btinternet.com	01241 876667

Arbroath: Old and Abbey (H)
Dolly Purnell BD — 2003 2014 — 51 Cliffburn Road, Arbroath DD11 5BA
DPurnell@churchofscotland.org.uk — Tel/Fax **01241 877068**
01241 872196

Arbroath: St Andrew's (H)
W. Martin Fair BA BD DMin — 1992 — **office@arbroathstandrews.org.uk**
92 Grampian Gardens, Arbroath DD11 4AQ
MFair@churchofscotland.org.uk — Tel/Fax 01241 873238

Arbroath: St Vigeans See Arbroath: Knox's

Arbroath: West Kirk (H)
Alasdair G. Graham BD DipMin — 1981 1986 — 1 Charles Avenue, Arbroath DD11 2EY
AGraham@churchofscotland.org.uk — 01241 872244

Barry linked with Carnoustie
Michael S. Goss BD DPS — 1991 2003 — 44 Terrace Road, Carnoustie DD7 7AR
MGoss@churchofscotland.org.uk — 01241 410194
07787 141567

Brechin: Cathedral (H) (www.brechincathedral.org.uk)
Vacant — Chanonry Wynd, Brechin DD9 6JS — **01356 629360**
01356 624980

Brechin: Gardner Memorial (H) linked with Farnell
Vacant
Session Clerk, Gardner Memorial:
  Dorothy Black (Miss) — 15 Caldhame Gardens, Brechin DD9 7JJ
dorothy.black6@btinternet.com — 01356 622034
01356 622614

Carmyllie See Arbirlot
Carnoustie See Barry

Carnoustie: Panbride (H)
Annette Gordon BD — 2017 — 8 Arbroath Road, Carnoustie DD7 6BL
AGordon@churchofscotland.org.uk — 01241 854478

Colliston linked with Friockheim Kinnell linked with Inverkeilor and Lunan (H)
Peter A. Phillips BA — 1995 2004 — The Manse, Inverkeilor, Arbroath DD11 5SA
PPhillips@churchofscotland.org.uk — 01241 830464

Dun and Hillside
Fiona C. Bullock (Mrs) MA LLB BD   2014   4 Manse Road, Hillside, Montrose DD10 9FB   01674 830288
                                                                FBullock@churchofscotland.org.uk

Dunnichen, Letham and Kirkden
Vacant   7 Braehead Road, Letham, Forfar DD8 2PG   01307 818025
Session Clerk: Muriel Gorringe   m.gorringe156@btinternet.com   01307 818748

Eassie, Nevay and Newtyle
Carleen J. Robertson (Miss) BD   1992   2 Kirkton Road, Newtyle, Blairgowrie PH12 8TS   01828 650461
                                                                CRobertson@churchofscotland.org.uk

Edzell Lethnot Glenesk (H) linked with Fern Careston Menmuir
A.S. Wayne Pearce MA PhD   2002   2017   19 Lethnot Road, Edzell, Brechin DD9 7TG   01356 648117
                                                                ASWaynePearce@churchofscotland.org.uk

Farnell See Brechin: Gardner Memorial
Fern Careston Menmuir See Edzell Lethnot Glenesk

Forfar: East and Old (H)
Barbara Ann Sweetin BD   2011   The Manse, Lour Road, Forfar DD8 2BB   01307 248228
                                                                BSweetin@churchofscotland.org.uk

Forfar: Lowson Memorial (H)
Karen Fenwick BSc BD MPhil PhD   2006   1 Jamieson Street, Forfar DD8 2HY   01307 468585
                                                                KFenwick@churchofscotland.org.uk

Forfar: St Margaret's (H)
Margaret J. Hunt (Mrs) MA BD   2014   St Margaret's Manse, 15 Potters Park Crescent, Forfar DD8 1HH   **01307 464224**
                                                                MHunt@churchofscotland.org.uk   01307 462044

Friockheim Kinnell See Colliston

Glamis (H), Inverarity and Kinnettles
Guardianship of the Presbytery

Guthrie and Rescobie See Aberlemno
Inverkeilor and Lunan See Colliston

Kirriemuir: St Andrew's (H) linked with Oathlaw Tannadice
John K. Orr BD MTh   2012   26 Quarry Park, Kirriemuir DD8 4DR   01575 572610
JOrr@churchofscotland.org.uk

Montrose: Old and St Andrew's
Ian A. McLean BSc BD DMin   1981   2008   2 Rosehill Road, Montrose DD10 8ST   01674 672447
IMcLean@churchofscotland.org.uk
Ian Gray   2013   2017   The Mallards, 15 Rossie Island Road, Montrose DD10 9NH   01674 677126
(Ordained Local Minister)   IGray@churchofscotland.org.uk

Montrose: South and Ferryden
Geoffrey Redmayne BSc BD MPhil   2000   2016   Inchbrayock Manse, Usan, Montrose DD10 9SD   01674 675634
GRedmayne@churchofscotland.org.uk

Oathlaw Tannadice See Kirriemuir: St Andrew's

The Glens and Kirriemuir: (www.gkopc.co.uk)   **01575 572819**
Guardianship of the Presbytery
Linda Stevens (Mrs) BSc BD PgDip   2006   17 North Latch Road, Brechin DD9 6LE   01356 623415
(Team Minister)   LStevens@churchofscotland.org.uk   07801 192730

The Isla Parishes
Stephen A. Blakey BSc BD   1977   2018   Balduff House, Kilry, Blairgowrie PH11 8HS   01575 560226
SBlakey@churchofscotland.org.uk

Butters, David	1964	1998	(Turriff: St Ninian's and Forglen)	68A Millgate, Friockheim, Arbroath DD11 4TN eleanorbutters68@btinternet.com	01241 828030
Duncan, Robert F. MTheol	1986	2001	(Lochgelly: St Andrew's)	25 Rowan Avenue, Kirriemuir DD8 4TB	01575 573973
Edwards, Dougal BTh	2013	2017	(Ordained Local Minister)	25 Mackenzie Street, Carnoustie DD7 6HD	01241 852666
Gough, Ian G. MA BD MTh DMin	1974	2009	(Arbroath: Knox's with Arbroath: St Vigeans)	23 Keptie Road, Arbroath DD11 3ED ianggough@btinternet.com	07891 838379
Hastie, George I. MA BD	1971	2009	(Mearns Coastal)	23 Borrowfield Crescent, Montrose DD10 9BR	01674 672290
Morrice, Alastair M. MA BD	1968	2002	(Rutherglen: Stonelaw)	5 Brechin Road, Kirriemuir DD8 4BX ambishkek@swissmail.org	01575 574102
Norrie, Graham MA BD	1967	2007	(Forfar: East and Old)	'Novar', 14A Wyllie Street, Forfar DD8 3DN grahamnorrie@hotmail.com	01307 468152

Reid, Albert B. BD BSc	1966 2001	(Ardler, Kettins and Meigle)	1 Mary Countess Way, Glamis, Forfar DD8 1RF abreid@btinternet.com	01307 840213
Robertson, George R. LTh	1985 2004	(Udny and Pitmedden)	3 Slateford Gardens, Edzell, Brechin DD9 7SX geomag.robertson@btinternet.com	01356 647322
Smith, Hamish G.	1965 1993	(Auchterless with Rothienorman)	11A Guthrie Street, Letham, Forfar DD8 2PS	01307 818973
Thomas, Martyn R.H. CEng MIStructE	1987 2002	(Fowlis and Liff with Lundie and Muirhead of Liff)	14 Kirkgait, Letham, Forfar DD8 2XQ martyn317thomas@btinternet.com	01307 818084
Thomas, Shirley A. (Mrs) DipSocSci AMIA (Aux)	2000 2006	(Auxiliary Minister)	14 Kirkgait, Letham, Forfar DD8 2XQ martyn317thomas@btinternet.com	01307 818084
Watt, Alan G.N. MTh CQSW DipCommEd	1996 2009	(Edzell Lethnot Glenesk with Fern Careston Menmuir)	6 Pine Way, Friockheim, Arbroath DD11 4WF watt455@btinternet.com	01241 826018
Webster, Allan F. MA BD	1978 2013	(Workplace Chaplain)	42 McCulloch Drive, Forfar DD8 2EB allanfwebster@aol.com	01307 464252 07546 276725

ANGUS ADDRESSES

Arbroath: Knox's	Howard Street	Gardner Memorial	South Esk Street	St Margaret's	West High Street
Old and Abbey	West Abbey Street	Carnoustie:	Dundee Street	Kirriemuir: Old	High Street
St Andrew's	Hamilton Green	Panbride	Arbroath Road	St Andrew's	Glamis Road
West Kirk	Keptie Street	Forfar: East and Old	East High Street	Montrose: South and Ferryden	Church Road, Ferryden
Brechin: Cathedral	Bishops Close	Lowson Memorial	Jamieson Street	Old and St Andrew's	High Street

(31) ABERDEEN

Meets on the first Tuesday of February, March, May, September, October, November and December; and on the fourth Tuesday of June. The venue varies.

Clerk:	**REV. JOHN A. FERGUSON BD DipMin DMin**	
Depute Clerk:	**MRS CHERYL BRANKIN BA**	
Treasurer:	**MR ALAN MORRISON**	
Presbytery Office:	**Mastrick Church, Greenfern Road, Aberdeen AB16 6TR** aberdeen@churchofscotland.org.uk	**01224 698119**

Aberdeen: Bridge of Don Oldmachar (www.oldmacharchurch.org) secretary@oldmacharchurch.org			**01224 709299**
David J. Stewart BD MTh DipMin	2000 2012	60 Newburgh Circle, Aberdeen AB22 8QZ DStewart@churchofscotland.org.uk	01224 823283

Joseph K. Somevi BSc MSc PhD MRICS 2015   2018
MRTPI MIEMA CertCRS   (Ordained Local
Minister)
97 Ashwood Road, Aberdeen AB22 8QX
JSomevi@churchofscotland.org.uk
01224 826362
07886 533259

Aberdeen: Craigiebuckler (H) (www.craigiebuckler.org)
Kenneth L. Petrie MA BD   1984   1999
office@craigiebuckler.org.uk
185 Springfield Road, Aberdeen AB15 8AA
KPetrie@churchofscotland.org.uk
01224 315649
01224 315125

Aberdeen: Ferryhill (H) (www.ferryhillparishchurch.org)
J. Peter N. Johnston BSc BD   2001   2013
office@ferryhillparishchurch.org
54 Polmuir Road, Aberdeen AB11 7RT
PJohnston@churchofscotland.org.uk
01224 213093
01224 949192

Aberdeen: Garthdee (H) (www.garthdeechurch.co.uk)
Vacant
Session Clerk: Hilda Smith (Mrs)
admin@garthdeechurch.co.uk
smithh09@hotmail.com
01244 311309

Aberdeen: High Hilton (H) (www.highhilton.zyberweb.com)
G. Hutton B. Steel MA BD   1982   2013
24 Rosehill Drive, Aberdeen AB24 4JJ
Hutton.Steel@churchofscotland.org.uk
01224 494717
01224 493552

Aberdeen: Holburn West (H) (www.holburnwestchurch.org.uk)
Duncan C. Eddie MA BD   1992   1999
31 Cranford Road, Aberdeen AB10 7NJ
DEddie@churchofscotland.org.uk
01224 571120
01224 325873

Aberdeen: Mannofield (H) (www.mannofieldchurch.org.uk)
Keith T. Blackwood BD DipMin   1997   2007
office@mannofieldchurch.org.uk
21 Forest Avenue, Aberdeen AB15 4TU
KBlackwood@churchofscotland.org.uk
01224 310087
01224 315748

Aberdeen: Mastrick (H) (www.mastrickchurch.org.uk)
Susan J. Sutherland (Mrs) BD   2009   2017
8 Corse Wynd, Kingswells, Aberdeen AB15 8TP
SSutherland@churchofscotland.org.uk
01224 694121
01224 279562

Aberdeen: Middlefield (H)
Guardianship of the Presbytery
Session Clerk: Linda A. Forbes (Mrs)
linda56forbes@yahoo.co.uk
01224 691165

Aberdeen: Midstocket (www.midstocketchurch.org.uk)
Vacant
Session Clerk: Alison McLeod (Mrs)
secretary@midstocketchurch.org.uk
182 Midstocket Road, Aberdeen AB15 5HS
alisonmcleod99@sky.com
01224 319519
01224 561358
01224 732227

Aberdeen: Northfield
Scott C. Guy BD   1989   1998   28 Byron Crescent, Aberdeen AB16 7EX   **01224 692332**
SGuy@churchofscotland.org.uk   01224 692332

Aberdeen: Queen's Cross (H) (www.queenscrosschurch.org.uk)   office@queenscrosschurch.org.uk   **01224 644742**
Scott M. Rennie MA BD STM   1999   2009   1 St Swithin Street, Aberdeen AB10 6XH   01224 322549
SRennie@churchofscotland.org.uk

Aberdeen: Rubislaw (H) (www.rubislawparishchurchofscotland.org.uk) rubislawchurch@btconnect.com   **01224 645477**
Robert L. Smith BS MTh PhD   2000   2013   13 Oakhill Road, Aberdeen AB15 5ERR   01224 314773
RSmith@churchofscotland.org.uk

Aberdeen: Ruthrieston West (www.ruthriestonwestchurch.org.uk)
Benjamin D.W. Byun BS MDiv MTh PhD   1992   2008   53 Springfield Avenue, Aberdeen AB15 8JJ   01224 312706
BByun@churchofscotland.org.uk

Aberdeen: St Columba's Bridge of Don (H) (http://stcolumbaschurch.org.uk) administrator@stcolumbaschurch.org.uk   **01224 825653**
Louis Kinsey BD DipMin TD   1991   151 Jesmond Avenue, Aberdeen AB22 8UG   01224 705337
LKinsey@churchofscotland.org.uk

Aberdeen: St George's Tillydrone (H) (https://tillydrone.church)   info@Tillydrone.church   **01224 482204**
Vacant
Session Clerk: Kenneth Williamson   kdwllmsn@yahoo.co.uk   01224 487302

Aberdeen: St John's Church for Deaf People
Mary Whittaker   2011   11 Templand Road, Lhanbryde, Elgin IV30 8BR   Text only 07810 420106
(Auxiliary Minister)
Interim Moderator: Rev Nigel Parker (see Bucksburn Stoneywood); or contact Aberdeen: St Mark's

Aberdeen: St Machar's Cathedral (H) (www.stmachar.com)   office@stmachar.com   **01224 485988**
Barry W. Dunsmore MA BD   1982   2015   39 Woodstock Road, Aberdeen AB15 5EX   01224 314596
BDunsmore@churchofscotland.org.uk

Aberdeen: St Mark's (H) (www.stmarksaberdeen.org.uk)   office@stmarksaberdeen.org.uk   **01224 640672**
Vacant   51 Osborne Place AB25 2BX   01224 646429
Session Clerks: Helen Burr (Mrs)   helen.burr@hotmail.co.uk
           Dianne Morrison (Miss)   diannemorrison@talktalk.net   01224 630161
New charge formed by the union of Aberdeen: Queen Street and Aberdeen: St Mark's

Aberdeen: St Mary's (H)
Elsie J. Fortune (Mrs) BSc BD   2003
stmaryschurch924@btinternet.com
456 King Street, Aberdeen AB24 3DE
EFortune@churchofscotland.org.uk
01224 **487227**
01224 633778

Aberdeen: St Nicholas Kincorth, South of (www.southstnicholas.org.uk)
Edward C. McKenna BD DPS   1989   2002
The Manse, Kincorth Circle, Aberdeen AB12 5NX
EMcKenna@churchofscotland.org.uk
01224 872820

Aberdeen: St Nicholas Uniting, Kirk of (H) (www.kirk-of-st-nicholas.org.uk) mither.kirk@btconnect.com
B. Stephen C. Taylor BA BBS MA MDiv   1984   2005
12 Louisville Avenue, Aberdeen AB15 4TX
BSCTaylor@churchofscotland.org.uk
St Nicholas Uniting is a Local Ecumenical Partnership with the United Reformed Church
01224 **643494** (ext 21)
01224 314318
01224 649242 (Fax)

Aberdeen: St Stephen's (H) (www.st-stephens.co.uk)
Maggie Whyte BD   2010
6 Belvidere Street, Aberdeen AB25 2QS
Maggie.Whyte@churchofscotland.org.uk
01224 **624443**
01224 635694

Aberdeen: South Holburn (H) (www.southholburn.org)
Vacant
Session Clerks: Joyce Lettis (Mrs)
Shelagh Johnstone (Mrs)
54 Woodstock Road, Aberdeen AB15 5JF
joyce@joycelettis.plus.com
shelaghjohnstone@hotmail.com
07498 **781457**
01224 315042
01224 584040
01651 862559

Aberdeen: Stockethill (www.stockethillchurch.org.uk)
Ian M. Aitken MA BD   1999
52 Ashgrove Road West, Aberdeen AB16 5EE
IAitken@churchofscotland.org.uk
01224 686929

Aberdeen: Summerhill (H) (www.summerhillchurch.org.uk)
Michael R.R. Shewan MA BD CPS   1985   2010
36 Stronsay Drive, Aberdeen AB15 6JL
MShewan@churchofscotland.org.uk
01224 324669

Aberdeen: Torry St Fittick's (H) (www.torrychurch.org.uk)
Edmond Gatima BEng BD MSc MPhil PhD   2013
11 Devanha Gardens East, Aberdeen AB11 7UN
EGatima@churchofscotland.org.uk
01224 **899183**
01224 588245

Aberdeen: Woodside (H) (www.woodsidechurch.co.uk)
Markus Auffermann DipTheol   1999   2006
office@talktalk.net
322 Clifton Road, Aberdeen AB24 4HQ
MAuffermann@churchofscotland.org.uk
01224 **277249**
01224 484562

Bucksburn Stoneywood (H) (www.bucksburnstoneywoodchurch.com) 1994
Nigel Parker BD MTh DMin
23 Polo Park, Stoneywood, Aberdeen AB21 9JW
NParker@churchofscotland.org.uk
01224 712411
01224 712635

Cults (H) (www.cultsparishchurch.co.uk)
Shuna M. Dicks BSc BD 2010 2018
cultsparishchurch@btinternet.com
1 Cairnlee Terrace, Bieldside, Aberdeen AB15 9AE
01224 869028
01224 861692

Dyce (H) (www.dyceparishchurch.org.uk)
Manson C. Merchant BD CPS 1992 2008
dyceparishchurch@outlook.com
100 Burnside Road, Dyce, Aberdeen AB21 7HA
MMerchant@churchofscotland.org.uk
01224 771295
01224 722380

Kingswells (www.kingswellschurch.com)
Vacant
Session Clerk: Lorna Graham (Mrs)
Kingswells Manse, Lang Stracht, Aberdeen AB15 8PN
lorna.graham15@btinternet.com
01224 740229
01224 313048

Newhills (H) (www.newhillschurch.org.uk)
Vacant
Session Clerk: Myra Kinnaird (Mrs)
office@newhillschurch.org.uk
myra@no24.co.uk
01224 716161
01358 742164

Peterculter (H) (http://culterkirk.co.uk) 1988 1999
John A. Ferguson BD DipMin DMin
secretary@culterkirk.co.uk
7 Howie Lane, Peterculter AB14 0LJ
JFerguson@churchofscotland.org.uk
01224 735845
01224 735041

Name			Position / Charge	Address	Telephone
Craig, Gordon T. BD DipMin	1988	2012	Chaplain to UK Oil and Gas Industry	The UK Oil and Gas Company, Total House, Tarland Road, Westhill AB32 6JZ gordon.craig@ukoilandgaschaplaincy.com	01224 297532
Falconer, James B. BD	1982	1991	Hospital Chaplain	3 Brimmond Walk, Westhill AB32 6XH	01224 744621
Gardner, Bruce K. MA BD PhD	1988	2011	(Aberdeen: Bridge of Don Oldmachar)	21 Hopetown Crescent, Bucksburn, Aberdeen AB21 9QY drbrucegardner@aol.com	07891 186724
Haddow, Angus H. BSc	1963	1999	(Methlick)	25 Lerwick Road, Aberdeen AB16 6RF DHobson@churchofscotland.org.uk	01224 696362
Hutchison, David S. BSc BD ThM	1991	2015	Chaplain: University of Aberdeen	The Den of Keithfield, Tarves, Ellon AB41 7NU	01651 851501
Lundie, Ann V. (Miss) DCS	1972	2007	(Deacon)	20 Langdykes Drive, Cove, Aberdeen AB12 3HW ann.lundie@btopenworld.com	01224 898416
Maciver, Norman MA BD DMin	1976	2006	(Newhills)	4 Mundi Crescent, Newmachar, Aberdeen AB21 0LY norirene@aol.com	01651 869434
Main, Alan (Prof.) TD MA BD STM PhD DD	1963	2001	(University of Aberdeen)	Kirkfield, Barthol Chapel, Inverurie AB51 8TD amain@talktalk.net	01651 806773

Name			Charge / Role	Address	Telephone
Montgomerie, Jean B. (Miss) MA BD	1973	2006	(Forfar: St Margaret's)	12 St Ronan's Place, Peterculter, Aberdeen AB14 0QX revjeanb@tiscali.co.uk	01224 732350
Phillippo, Michael MTh BSc BVetMed MRCVS	2003	2011	(Auxiliary Minister)	126 St Michael's Road, Newtonhill AB39 3XW	01569 739475
Richardson, Thomas C. LTh ThB	1971	2004	(Cults: West)	19 Kinkell Road, Aberdeen AB15 8HR tomandpatrich@gmail.com	01224 315328
Rodgers, D. Mark BA BD MTh	1987	2003	Head of Spiritual Care, NHS Grampian	63 Cordiner Place, Hilton, Aberdeen AB24 4SB mrodgers@nhs.net	01224 379135
Sefton, Henry R. MA BD STM PhD	1957	1992	(University of Aberdeen)	25 Albury Place, Aberdeen AB11 6TQ	01224 572305
Sheret, Brian S. MA BD DPhil	1982	2009	(Glasgow: Drumchapel Drumry St Mary's)	59 Airyhall Crescent, Aberdeen AB15 7QS	01224 323032
Stewart, James C. MA BD STM FSAScot	1960	2000	(Aberdeen: Kirk of St Nicholas)	54 Murray Terrace, Aberdeen AB11 7SB study@jascstewart.co.uk	01224 587071
Swinton, John (Prof.) BD PhD	1999		University of Aberdeen	51 Newburgh Circle, Bridge of Don, Aberdeen AB22 8XA j.swinton@abdn.ac.uk	01224 825637
Wallace, Hugh M. MA BD	1980	2018	(Newhills)		
Weir, James J.C.M. BD	1991	2018	(Aberdeen: St George's Tillydrone)	114 Hilton Heights, Woodside, Aberdeen AB24 4QF JWeir@churchofscotland.org.uk	01224 901430
Youngson, Elizabeth J.B. BD	1996	2015	(Aberdeen: Mastrick)	47 Corse Drive, The Links, Dubford, Aberdeen AB23 8LN elizabeth.youngson@btinternet.com	07788 294745

ABERDEEN ADDRESSES

Bridge of Don Oldmachar	Ashwood Park	Middlefield	Manor Avenue	St Mark's	Rosemount Viaduct
Craigiebuckler	Springfield Road	Midstocket	Mid Stocket Road	St Mary's	King Street
Cults	Quarry Road, Cults	Northfield	Byron Crescent	St Nicholas Kincorth, South of	Kincorth Circle
Dyce	Victoria Street, Dyce	Peterculter	Craigton Crescent	St Nicholas Uniting, Kirk of	Union Street
Ferryhill	Fonthill Road x Polmuir Road	Queen's Cross	Albyn Place	St Stephen's	Powis Place
Garthdee	Ramsay Gardens	Rubislaw	Queen's Gardens	South Holburn	Holburn Street
High Hilton	Hilton Drive	Ruthrieston West	Broomhill Road	Stockethill	Cairncry Community Centre
Holburn West	Great Western Road	St Columba's Bridge of Don	Braehead Way, Bridge of Don	Summerhill	Stronsay Drive
Kingswells	Old Skene Road, Kingswells	St George's Tillydrone	Hayton Road, Tillydrone	Torry St Fittick's	Walker Road
Mannofield	Great Western Road x Craigton Road	St John's for the Deaf	at St Mark's	Woodside	Church Street, Woodside
Mastrick	Greenfern Road	St Machar's Cathedral	The Chanonry		

(32) KINCARDINE AND DEESIDE

Meets in various locations as arranged on the first Tuesday of September, October, November, December, March and May; and on the last Tuesday of June at 7pm.

Clerk: REV. HUGH CONKEY BSc BD   39 St Ternans Road, Newtonhill, Stonehaven   AB39 3PF   01569 739297
kincardinedeeside@churchofscotland.org.uk

Aberluthnott linked with Laurencekirk (H)
Vacant
Session Clerk, Aberluthnott: Marian Finlayson (Mrs)   Aberdeen Road, Laurencekirk   AB30 1AJ   01561 378838
Session Clerk, Laurencekirk: Vera McBain (Mrs)   marfin_33@btinternet.com   01674 840730
    01561 376181

Aboyne-Dinnet (H) linked with Cromar
Frank Ribbons MA BD DipEd   1985   2011   49 Charlton Crescent, Aboyne   AB34 5GN   01339 887267
FRibbons@churchofscotland.org.uk

Arbuthnott, Bervie and Kinneff
Vacant

Banchory-Ternan: East (H)
Alan J.S. Murray BSc BD PhD   2003   2013   info@banchoryeastchurch.com   01330 **820380**
East Manse, Station Road, Banchory   AB31 5YP   01330 822481
AJSMurray@churchofscotland.org.uk
Amy Pierce BA BDiv   2017   7 Hollybank Crescent, Banchory   AB31 5TX   07814 194997
(Associate Minister, Youth)   amy.pierce@gmail.com

Banchory-Ternan: West (H)
Antony A. Stephen MA BD   2001   2011   The Manse, 2 Wilson Road, Banchory   AB31 5UY   01330 822811
TStephen@churchofscotland.org.uk
Amy Pierce BA BDiv   2017   7 Hollybank Crescent, Banchory   AB31 5TX   07814 194997
(Associate Minister, Youth)   amy.pierce@gmail.com

Birse and Feughside
Vacant   The Manse, Finzean, Banchory   AB31 6PB   01330 850776

Braemar and Crathie
Kenneth I. Mackenzie DL BD CPS   1990   2005   The Manse, Crathie, Ballater   AB35 5UL   01339 742208
KMacKenzie@churchofscotland.org.uk

Cromar See Aboyne-Dinnet

Drumoak (H)-Durris (H)
Jean A. Boyd MSc BSc BA
2016
26 Sunnyside Drive, Drumoak, Banchory   AB31 3EW
JBoyd@churchofscotland.org.uk
01330 811031

Glenmuick (Ballater) (H)
David L.C. Barr
2014
The Manse, Craigendarroch Walk, Ballater   AB35 5ZB
DBarr@churchofscotland.org.uk
01339 756111

Laurencekirk See Aberluthnott

Maryculter Trinity
Melvyn J. Griffiths BTh DipTheol DMin
1978   2014
thechurchoffice@tiscali.co.uk
The Manse, Kirkton of Maryculter, Aberdeen   AB12 5FS
MGriffiths@churchofscotland.org.uk
01224 735983
01224 730150

Mearns Coastal
Guardianship of the Presbytery
Norman D. Lennox-Trewren
(Ordained Local Minister)
2018
The Manse, Kirkton, St Cyrus, Montrose   DD10 0BW
NLennoxTrewren@churchofscotland.org.uk
01674 850880

Mid Deeside
Vacant
Session Clerk: Pam Auckland (Mrs)
The Manse, Torphins, Banchory   AB31 4GQ
aucklandab@aol.com
01339 882276
01339 882722

Newtonhill
Hugh Conkey BSc BD
1987   2001
39 St Ternans Road, Newtonhill, Stonehaven   AB39 3PF
HConkey@churchofscotland.org.uk
01569 730143

Portlethen (H)
Rodolphe Blanchard-Kowal
(Exchange Minister)
2011   2017
18 Rowanbank Road, Portlethen, Aberdeen   AB12 4NX
RKowal@churchofscotland.org.uk
01224 782883
01224 780211

Stonehaven: Dunnottar (H) linked with Stonehaven: South (H)
Vacant
Session Clerk, Dunnottar: Brian Sim
Session Clerk, South: Gordon Edgar
Dunnottar Manse, Stonehaven   AB39 3XL
bsim84@gmail.com
gdaresaybear@tiscali.co.uk
01569 762166
01569 762038
01569 766169

Stonehaven: Fetteresso (H)

| Fyfe Blair BA BD DMin | 1989 | 2009 | office@fetteresso.org
11 South Lodge Drive, Stonehaven AB39 2PN
Fyfe.Blair@churchofscotland.org.uk | 01569 **767689**
01569 762876 |

Stonehaven: South See Stonehaven: Dunnottar

West Mearns

| Brian D. Smith BD | 1990 | 2016 | The Manse, Fettercairn, Laurencekirk AB30 1UE
BSmith@churchofscotland.org.uk | 01561 340203 |

Broadley, Linda J. (Mrs) LTh DipEd	1996	2013	(Dun and Hillside)	Snaefell, Lochside Road, St Cyrus, Montrose DD10 0DB lindabroadley@btinternet.com	01674 850141
Brown, J.W.S. BTh	1960	1995	(Cromar)	10 Forestside Road, Banchory AB31 5ZH iainisobel@aol.com	01330 824353
Duncan, Rosslyn P. BD MTh	2007	2018	(Stonehaven: Dunnottar with Stonehaven: South)		
Hamilton, Helen (Miss) BD	1991	2003	(Glasgow: St James' Pollok)	The Cottage, West Tilbouries, Maryculter, Aberdeen AB12 5GD helenhamilton125@gmail.com	01224 739632
Lamb, A. Douglas MA	1964	2002	(Dalry: St Margaret's)	9 Luther Drive, Laurencekirk AB30 1FE lamb.edzell@talk21.com	01561 376816
Purves, John P. S. MBE BSc BD	1978	2013	(Colombo, Sri Lanka: St Andrew's Scots Kirk)	Lonville Cottage, 20 Viewfield Road, Ballater AB35 5RD john@thepurves.com	01339 754081
Smith, Albert E. BD	1983	2006	(Methlick)	25 Alloway Drive, Paisley PA2 7DS aesmith42@googlemail.com	0141 533 5879
Wallace, William F. BDS BD	1968	2008	(Wick: Pulteneytown and Thrumster)	Lachan Cottage, 2 Station Road, Banchory AB31 5XX williamwallace39@talktalk.net	01330 822259
Watson, John M. LTh	1989	2009	(Aberdeen: St Mark's)	20 Greystone Place, Newtonhill, Stonehaven AB39 3UL johnmutchwatson2065@btinternet.com	01569 730604 07733 334380

(33) GORDON

Meets at various locations on the first Tuesday of February, March, April, May, September, October, November and December, and on the last Tuesday of June.

| Clerk: | REV. G. EUAN D. GLEN BSc BD | The Manse, 26 St Ninians, Monymusk, Inverurie AB51 7HF
gordon@churchofscotland.org.uk | 01467 651470 |

Barthol Chapel linked with Tarves
Alison I. Swindells (Mrs) LLB BD DMin — 1998 — 2017
8 Murray Avenue, Tarves, Ellon AB41 7LZ
ASwindells@churchofscotland.org.uk
01651 851295

Belhelvie (H)
Paul McKeown BSc PhD BD — 2000 — 2005
Belhelvie Manse, Balmedie, Aberdeen AB23 8YR
PMcKeown@churchofscotland.org.uk
01358 742227

Blairdaff and Chapel of Garioch
Martyn S. Sanders BA CertEd — 2013 — 2015
The Manse, Chapel of Garioch, Inverurie AB51 5HE
MSanders@churchofscotland.org.uk
01467 681619
07814 164373

Cluny (H) linked with Monymusk (H)
G. Euan D. Glen BSc BD — 1992
The Manse, 26 St Ninians, Monymusk, Inverurie AB51 7HF
GGlen@churchofscotland.org.uk
01467 651470

Culsalmond and Rayne linked with Daviot (H)
Mary M. Cranfield MA BD DMin — 1989
The Manse, Daviot, Inverurie AB51 0HY
MCranfield@churchofscotland.org.uk
01467 671241

Cushnie and Tough (R) (H)
Vacant
The Manse, Muir of Fowlis, Alford AB33 8JU
01975 581239

Daviot See Culsalmond and Rayne

Echt and Midmar (H)
Sheila M. Mitchell BD MTh — 1995 — 2018
The Manse, Echt, Westhill AB32 7AB
SMitchell@churchofscotland.org.uk
01330 860004

Ellon
Alastair J. Bruce BD MTh PGCE — 2015
The Manse, 12 Union Street, Ellon AB41 9BA
ABruce@churchofscotland.org.uk
01358 723787

Fintray Kinellar Keithhall
Sean Swindells BD DipMin MTh — 1996 — 2016
8 Murray Avenue, Tarves, Ellon AB41 7LZ
SSwindells@churchofscotland.org.uk
01651 851295

Foveran
Richard M.C. Reid BSc BD MTh | 1991 | 2013 | The Manse, Foveran, Ellon AB41 6AP / RReid@churchofscotland.org.uk | 01358 789288

Howe Trinity
John A. Cook MA BD DMin | 1986 | 2000 | The Manse, 110 Main Street, Alford AB33 8AD / John.Cook@churchofscotland.org.uk | 01975 562282

Huntly Cairnie Glass
Thomas R. Calder LLB BD WS | 1994 | The Manse, Queen Street, Huntly AB54 8EB / TCalder@churchofscotland.org.uk | 01466 792630

Insch-Leslie-Premnay-Oyne (H)
Kay Gauld BD STM PhD | 1999 | 2015 | 66 Denwell Road, Insch AB52 6LH / KGauld@churchofscotland.org.uk | 01464 820404

Inverurie: St Andrew's (standrewschurchinverurie.org.uk)
Vacant | standrews@btinternet.com / 27 Buchan Drive, Newmachar, Aberdeen AB21 0NR | **01467 628740** / 01651 862281

Inverurie: West
Rhona P. Cathcart BA BSc BD | 2017 | West Manse, 1 Westburn Place, Inverurie AB51 5QS / RCathcart@churchofscotland.org.uk | 01467 620285

Kemnay
Joshua M. Mikelson BA MDiv | 2008 | 2015 | 15 Kirkland, Kemnay, Inverurie AB51 5QD / JMikelson@churchofscotland.org.uk | Tel/Fax 01467 642219

Kintore (H)
Neil W. Meyer BD MTh | 2000 | 2014 | 28 Oakhill Road, Kintore, Inverurie AB51 0FH / NMeyer@churchofscotland.org.uk | 01467 632219

Meldrum and Bourtie
Alison Jaffrey (Mrs) MA BD FSAScot | 1990 | 2010 | The Manse, Urquhart Road, Oldmeldrum, Inverurie AB51 0EX / AJaffrey@churchofscotland.org.uk | 01651 872250

Methlick
William A. Stalder BA MDiv MLitt PhD | 2014 | The Manse, Manse Road, Methlick, Ellon AB41 7DG
WStalder@churchofscotland.org.uk | 01651 806264

Monymusk See Cluny

New Machar
Douglas G. McNab BA BD | 1999 2010 | The New Manse, Newmachar, Aberdeen AB21 0RD
DMcNab@churchofscotland.org.uk | 01651 862278

Noth
Regine U. Cheyne (Mrs) MA BSc BD | 1988 2010 | Manse of Noth, Kennethmont, Huntly AB54 4NP
RCheyne@churchofscotland.org.uk | 01464 831690

Skene (H)
Stella Campbell MA (Oxon) BD | 2012 | The Manse, Manse Road, Kirkton of Skene, Westhill AB32 6LX
SCampbell@churchofscotland.org.uk | 01224 745955
Marion G. Stewart (Miss) DCS | 1991 1994 | Kirk Cottage, Kirkton of Skene. Westhill AB32 6XE
MStewart@churchofscotland.org.uk | 01224 743407

Strathbogie Drumblade
Neil I.M. MacGregor BD | 1995 | 49 Deveron Park, Huntly AB54 8UZ
NMacGregor@churchofscotland.org.uk | 01466 792702

Tarves See Barthol Chapel

Udny and Pitmedden
Gillean P. MacLean (Ms) BA BD | 1994 2013 | The Manse, Manse Road, Udny Green, Ellon AB41 7RS
GMacLean@churchofscotland.org.uk | 01651 843794

Upper Donside (H)
Vacant | | **upperdonsideparishchurch@btinternet.com**
Session Clerk: Margaret Thomson | margaret.thomson9@btpenworld.com | 01464 861745

Christie, Andrew C. LTh	1975 2000	(Banchory-Devenick and Maryculter/Cookney) (Auxiliary Minister)	17 Broadstraik Close, Elrick, Aberdeen AB32 6JP	01224 746888
Craggs, Sheila (Mrs)	2001 2016		7 Morar Court, Ellon AB41 9GG	01358 723055

Craig, Anthony J.D. BD	1987 2009	(Glasgow: Maryhill)	4 Hightown, Collieston, Ellon AB41 8RS / craig.glasgow@gmx.net	01358 751247
Dryden, Ian MA DipEd	1988 2001	(New Machar)	16 Glenhome Gardens, Dyce, Aberdeen AB21 7FG / ian@idryden.freeserve.co.uk	01224 722820
Greig, Alan BSc BD	1977 2017	(Interim Minister)	1 Dunnydeer Place, Insch AB52 6HP / greig@kincair.free-online.co.uk	01464 820332
Groves, Ian B. BD CPS	1989 2016	(Inverurie West)	28 Parkhill Circle, Dyce, Aberdeen AB21 7FN / IGroves@churchofscotland.org.uk	01224 774380
Hawthorn, Daniel MA BD DMin	1965 2004	(Belhelvie)	7 Crimond Drive, Ellon AB41 8BT / danhawthorn@compuserve.com	01358 723981
Irvine, Carl J. BA	2017	Ordained Local Minister, Presbytery	Northside of Glack, Meikle Wartle, Inverurie AB51 5AR / CIrvine@churchofscotland.org.uk	01467 671135
Jones, Robert A. LTh CA	1966 1997	(Marnoch)	13 Gordon Terrace, Inverurie AB51 4GT	01467 622691
Macalister, Eleanor	1994 2006	(Ellon)	Quarryview, Ythan Bank, Ellon AB41 7TH / macal1ster@aol.com	01358 761402
Mack, John C. JP	1985 2008	(Auxiliary Minister)	The Willows, Auchleven, Insch AB52 6QB	01464 820387
McLeish, Robert S.	1970 2000	(Insch-Leslie-Premnay-Oyne)	19 Western Road, Insch AB52 6JR	01464 820749
Rodger, Matthew A. BD	1978 1999	(Ellon)	15 Meadowlands Drive, Westhill AB32 6EJ	01224 743184
Stoddart, A. Grainger	1975 2001	(Meldrum and Bourtie)	6 Mayfield Gardens, Insch AB52 6XL	01464 821124
Thomson, Iain U. MA BD	1970 2011	(Skene)	4 Keirhill Gardens, Westhill AB32 6AZ / iainuthomson@googlemail.com	01224 746743

(34) BUCHAN

Meets at St Kane's Centre, New Deer, Turriff on the first Tuesday of February, March, May, September, October, November and December; and on the third Tuesday of June.

| Clerk: | REV. SHEILA M. KIRK BA LLB BD | The Manse, Old Deer, Peterhead AB42 5JB / buchan@churchofscotland.org.uk | 01771 623582 |

Aberdour linked with Pitsligo
Vacant | 31 Blairmore Park, Rosehearty, Fraserburgh AB43 7NZ | 01346 571823

Auchaber United linked with Auchterless
Stephen J. Potts BA | 2012 | The Manse, Auchterless, Turriff AB53 8BA / SPotts@churchofscotland.org.uk | 01888 511058

Auchterless See Auchaber United

Banff linked with King Edward
David I.W. Locke MA MSc BD — 2000 2012 — 7 Colleonard Road, Banff AB45 1DZ
DLocke@churchofscotland.org.uk — 01261 812107 / 07776 448301

Crimond linked with Lonmay
Vacant
Session Clerk, Crimond: Irene Fowlie (Mrs) — The Manse, Crimond, Fraserburgh AB43 8QJ
fowlie@hotmail.com — 01346 532431
Session Clerk, Lonmay: Roy Kinghorn — strathelliefarm@btinternet.com — 01346 532436

Cruden (H)
Vacant
Session Clerk: Robert Esson — The Manse, Hatton, Peterhead AB42 0QQ
robertesson@btinternet.com — 01779 841229 / 01779 813049

Deer (H)
Sheila M. Kirk BA LLB BD — 2007 2010 — The Manse, Old Deer, Peterhead AB42 5JB
SKirk@churchofscotland.org.uk — 01771 623582

Fraserburgh: Old
Vacant — 4 Robbie's Road, Fraserburgh AB43 7AF — 01346 515332

Fraserburgh: South (H) linked with Inverallochy and Rathen: East
Vacant
Session Clerk, Fraserburgh: South: William J. Smith — 15 Victoria Street, Fraserburgh AB43 9PJ
bill.moira.smith@gmail.com — 01346 518244 / 01346 513991

Fraserburgh: West (H) linked with Rathen: West
Vacant
Session Clerk, Fraserburgh: West: Jill Smith (Mrs) — 4 Kirkton Gardens, Fraserburgh AB43 8TU
jill@fraserburgh-harbour.co.uk — 01346 513303 / 01346 517972
Session Clerk, Rathen: West: Ian J. Campbell — cicfarmers@hotmail.co.uk — 01346 532062

Fyvie linked with Rothienorman
Vacant
Session Clerk, Fyvie: Audrey Clark (Mrs) — The Manse, Fyvie, Turriff AB53 8RD
fyviechurch@hotmail.co.uk — 01651 891230 / 01651 891729
Session Clerk, Rothienorman: Isabel Forsyth (Mrs) — isabelmforsyth@btconnect.com — 07475 490052

Inverallochy and Rathen: East See Fraserburgh: South
King Edward See Banff

Longside
Robert A. Fowlie BD — 2007 — The Manse, Old Deer, Peterhead AB42 5JB
RFowlie@churchofscotland.org.uk — 01771 622228

Lonmay See Crimond

Macduff
Hugh O'Brien CSS MTheol — 2001 2016 — 10 Ross Street, Macduff AB44 1NS
HOBrien@churchofscotland.org.uk — 01261 832316

Marnoch
Alan Macgregor BA BD PhD — 1992 2013 — Marnoch Manse, 53 South Street, Aberchirder, Huntly AB54 7TS
AMacgregor@churchofscotland.org.uk — 01466 781143

Maud and Savoch linked with New Deer: St Kane's
Vacant — The Manse, New Deer, Turriff AB53 6TD
jwc707@hotmail.co.uk — 01771 644216 / 07870 572333 / 01771 644303
Session Clerk, Maud and Savoch: Janice Cruikshank (Mrs)
Session Clerk, New Deer St Kane's: Elsie Foubister (Mrs)

Monquhitter and New Byth linked with Turriff: St Andrew's
James M. Cook MA MDiv — 1999 2002 — St Andrew's Manse, Balmellie Road, Turriff AB53 4SP
JCook@churchofscotland.org.uk — 01888 560304

New Deer: St Kane's See Maud and Savoch

New Pitsligo linked with Strichen and Tyrie
Vacant — Kingsville, Strichen, Fraserburgh AB43 6SQ
William Stewart — 2015 2016 — Denend, Strichen, Fraserburgh AB43 6RN
(Ordained Local Minister) — billandjunes@live.co.uk — 01771 637365 / 01771 637256

Ordiquhill and Cornhill (H) linked with Whitehills
W. Myburgh Verster BA BTh LTh MTh — 1981 2011 — 6 Craigneen Place, Whitehills, Banff AB45 2NE
WVerster@churchofscotland.org.uk — 01261 861317

Peterhead: New
Vacant — 1 Hawthorn Road, Peterhead AB42 2DW
ursular@tiscali.co.uk — 01779 480680
Session Clerk: Ruth Mackenzie (Miss)

Peterhead: St Andrew's (H)
Guardianship of the Presbytery
Session Clerk: John Leslie   1 Landale Road, Peterhead AB42 1QN   01779 238200
eil.ian@btinternet.com   01779 470571

Pitsligo See Aberdour

Portsoy
Vacant   The Manse, 4 Seafield Terrace, Portsoy, Banff AB45 2QB   01261 842272

Rathen: West See Fraserburgh: West
Rothienorman See Fyvie

St Fergus
Jeffrey Tippner BA MDiv MCS PhD   1991   2012   26 Newton Road, St Fergus, Peterhead AB42 3DD   01779 838287
JTippner@churchofscotland.org.uk

Sandhaven
Guardianship of the Presbytery

Strichen and Tyrie See New Pitsligo
Turriff: St Andrew's See Monquhitter and New Byth

Turriff: St Ninian's and Forglen (H) (L)
Kevin R. Gruer BSc BA   2011   4 Deveronside Drive, Turriff AB53 4SP   01888 563850
KGruer@churchofscotland

Whitehills See Ordiquhill and Cornhill

Coutts, Fred MA BD	1973	1989	(Hospital Chaplain)	Ladebank, 1 Manse Place, Hatton, Peterhead AB42 0UQ fred.coutts@btinternet.com	01779 841320
Fawkes, G.M. Allan BA BSc JP	1979	2000	(Lonmay with Rathen: West)	3 Northfield Gardens, Hatton, Peterhead AB42 0SW afawkes@aol.com	01779 841814
McMillan, William J. CA LTh BD	1969	2004	(Sandsting and Aithsting with Walls and Sandness)	7 Ardinn Drive, Turriff AB53 4PR revbillymcmillan@aol.com	01888 560727
Macnee, Iain LTh BD MA PhD	1975	2011	(New Pitsligo with Strichen and Tyrie)	Wardend Cottage, Alvah, Banff AB45 3TR macneeiain4@googlemail.com	01261 815647
Noble, George S. DipTh	1972	2000	(Carfin with Newarthill)	Craigowan, 3 Main Street, Inverallochy, Fraserburgh AB43 8XX	01346 582749

Ross, David S. MSc PhD BD | 1978 2013 | (Chaplain: Scottish Prison Service) | 3–5 Abbey Street, Old Deer, Peterhead AB42 5LN | padsross@btinternet.com | 01771 623994

Thorburn, Robert J. BD | 1978 2017 | (Fyvie with Rothienorman) | 12 Slackadale Gardens, Turriff AB53 4UA | rjthorburn@aol.com

van Sittert, Paul BA BD | 1997 2011 | Chaplain: Army | 4Bn The Royal Regiment of Scotland, Bourlon Barracks, Plumer Road, Catterick Garrison DL9 3AD | padre.pvs@gmail.com

(35) MORAY

Meets at St Andrew's-Lhanbryd and Urquhart on the first Tuesday of February, March, May, September, October, November and December, and at the Moderator's church on the fourth Tuesday of June.

| Clerk: | REV. ALASTAIR H. GRAY MA BD | North Manse, Church Road, Keith AB55 5FX
moray@churchofscotland.org.uk | **01542 886840**
07944 287777 |

Aberlour (H)
Vacant
Session Clerk: Michelle Southgate | The Manse, Mary Avenue, Aberlour AB38 9QU
mas@btinternet.com | 01340 871687
07753 631507

Alves and Burghead linked with Kinloss and Findhorn
Vacant
Session Clerk: Alves and Burghead: Barrie Wallace | The Manse, 4 Manse Road, Kinloss, Forres IV36 3GH
abcsessionclerk@aim.com | 01309 690474
01343 850372
Session Clerk: Kinloss and Findhorn: Corinne Davies | cozzerdavies@gmail.com | 01309 690359

Bellie and Speymouth
Seoras I. Orr MSc MTh | 2018 | 11 The Square, Fochabers IV32 7DG
SOrr@churchofscotland.org.uk | 01343 820256

Birnie and Pluscarden linked with Elgin: High
Stuart M. Duff BA | 1997 2014 | The Manse, Daisy Bank, 5 Forteath Avenue, Elgin IV30 1TQ
SDuff@churchofscotland.org.uk | 01343 545703

Buckie: North (H) linked with Rathven
Isabel C. Buchan (Mrs) BSc BD RE(PgCE) | 1975 2013 | The Manse, 14 St Peter's Road, Buckie AB56 1DL
IBuchan@churchofscotland.org.uk | 01542 832118

Buckie: South and West (H) linked with Enzie
Vacant
Session Clerk, South and West: Alma Blackhall (Mrs) — Craigendarroch, 14 Cliff Terrace, Buckie AB56 1LX — almablackhall@btinternet.com — 01542 833775 / 01542 832758
Session Clerk, Enzie: Morag Aitken (Mrs) — moragaitken@btinternet.com — 01542 835128

Cullen and Deskford (www.cullen-deskford-church.org.uk)
Douglas F. Stevenson BD DipMin DipHE MCOSCA MBACP   1991   2010 — 14 Seafield Road, Cullen, Buckie AB56 4AF — DStevenson@churchofscotland.org.uk — 01542 841963

Dallas linked with Forres: St Leonard's (H) linked with Rafford
Donald K. Prentice BSc BD   1989   2010 — St Leonard's Manse, Nelson Road, Forres IV36 1DR — DPrentice@churchofscotland.org.uk — 01309 672380
John A. Morrison BSc BA PGCE   2013 — 35 Kirkton Place, Elgin IV30 6JR — JMorrison@churchofscotland.org.uk — 01343 550199
(Ordained Local Minister)

Duffus, Spynie and Hopeman (H) (www.duffusparish.co.uk)
Jennifer M. Adams BEng BD   2013 — The Manse, Duffus, Elgin IV30 5QP — JAdams@churchofscotland.org.uk — 01343 830276

Dyke and Edinkillie
Vacant
Session Clerk: Jane Foster — Dyke and Edinkillie Manse, Westview, Mundole, Forres IV36 2TA — jwaf2212@hotmail.co.uk — 01309 641257
New charge formed by union of Dyke and Edinkillie

Elgin: High   See Birnie and Pluscarden

Elgin: St Giles' (H) and St Columba's South
Deon Oelofse BA MDiv LTh MTh   2002   2017 — **Office: Williamson Hall, Duff Avenue, Elgin IV30 1QS** — **01343 551501**
18 Reidhaven Street, Elgin IV30 1QH — DOelofse@churchofscotland.org.uk — 01343 208786
Sonia Palmer RGN   2017 — 94 Ashgrove Park, Elgin IV30 1UT — Sonia.Palmer@churchofscotland.org.uk — 07748 700929
(Ordained Local Minister)

Enzie   See Buckie: South and West

Findochty linked with Portknockie
Vacant
Session Clerk, Findochty: David Pirie — 20 Netherton Terrace, Findochty, Buckie AB56 4QD — hdpirie@aol.com — 01542 833180
Session Clerk, Portknockie: Morag Ritchie (Mrs) — moragritchie8@btinternet.com — 01542 834123 / 01542 840951

Forres: St Laurence (H)
Barry J. Boyd LTh DPS   1993   12 Mackenzie Drive, Forres IV36 2JP   01309 672260
BBoyd@churchofscotland.org.uk   07778 731018 (Mbl)

Forres: St Leonard's   See Dallas

Keith: North, Newmill, Boharm and Rothiemay (H)
Alastair H. Gray MA BD   1978   2015   North Manse, Church Road, Keith AB55 5BR   **01542 886390**
AGray@churchofscotland.org.uk   01542 886840

Keith: St Rufus, Botriphnie and Grange (H)
Vacant   St Rufus' Manse, Church Road, Keith AB55 5BR   01542 882799
nicolasmith1099@gmail.com   01542 488673
Session Clerk: Nicola Smith (Ms)

Kinloss and Findhorn   See Alves and Burghead

Knockando, Elchies and Archiestown (H) linked with Rothes (www.moraykirk.co.uk)
Robert J.M. Anderson BD FInstLM   1993   2000   The Manse, Rothes, Aberlour AB38 7AF   01340 831381
RJMAnderson@churchofscotland.org.uk

Lossiemouth: St Gerardine's High (H) linked with Lossiemouth: St James
Geoffrey D. McKee BA   1997   2014   The Manse, St Gerardine's Road, Lossiemouth IV31 6RA   01343 208852
GMcKee@churchofscotland.org.uk

Lossiemouth: St James'   See Lossiemouth: St Gerardine's High

Mortlach and Cabrach (H)
Vacant   Mortlach Manse, Dufftown, Keith AB55 4AR   01340 820380
queenstreetmob@btinternet.com   01340 820049
Session Clerk: Elaine Clarke (Mrs)

Portknockie   See Findochty
Rafford   See Dallas
Rathven   See Buckie: North
Rothes   See Knockando, Elchies and Archiestown

St Andrew's-Lhanbryd (H) and Urquhart
Vacant
Session Clerk: Alastair Rossetter

39 St Andrews Road, Lhanbryde, Elgin IV30 8PU
alastair@rossetter.plus.com

01343 843765
07751 323975

Name	Years	Role	Address / Email	Phone
Anne Attenburrow BSc MB ChB	2006 2018	(Auxiliary Minister)	4 Jock Inksons Brae, Elgin IV30 1QE AAttenburrow@churchofscotland.org.uk	01343 552330
Bain, Brian LTh	1980 2007	(Gask with Methven and Logiealmond)	Bayview, 13 Stewart Street, Portgordon, Buckie AB56 5QT bricoreen@gmail.com	01542 831215
Buchan, Alexander MA BD PGCE	1975 1992	(North Ronaldsay with Sanday)	The Manse, 14 St Peter's Road, Buckie AB56 1DL revabuchan@bluebucket.org	01542 832118
Davidson, A.A.B. MA BD	1960 1997	(Grange with Rothiemay)	11 Sutors Rise, Nairn IV12 5BU	01343 820937
King, Margaret MA DCS	2002 2012	(Deacon)	56 Murrayfield, Fochabers IV32 7EZ margaretrking@tiscali.co.uk	
Legge, Rosemary (Mrs) BSc BD MTh	1992 2017	(Cushnie and Tough)	57 High Street, Archiestown, Aberlour AB38 7QZ revrl192@aol.com	01340 810304
Morton, Alasdair J. MA BD DipEd FEIS	1960 2000	(Bowden with Newtown)	16 St Leonard's Road, Forres IV36 1DW alasgilmor@hotmail.co.uk	01309 671719
Morton, Gillian M. (Mrs) MA BD PGCE	1983 1996	(Hospital Chaplain)	16 St Leonard's Road, Forres IV36 1DW gillianmorton@hotmail.co.uk	01309 671719
Munro, Sheila BD	1995 2016	RAF Station Chaplain	Chaplaincy Centre, RAF Wyton, Huntingdon PE28 2EA sheila.munro781@mod.gov.uk	
Poole, Ann McColl (Mrs) DipEd ACE LTh	1983 2003	(Dyke with Edinkillie)	Kirkside Cottage, Dyke, Forres IV36 2TF	01309 641046
Robertson, Peter BSc BD	1988 1998	(Dallas with Forres: St Leonard's with Rafford)	17 Ferryhill Road, Forres IV36 2GY peterrobertsonforres@talktalk.net	01309 676769
Rollo, George B. BD	1974 2010	(Elgin: St Giles' and St Columba's South)	'Struan', 13 Meadow View, Hopeman, Elgin IV30 5PL rollos@gmail.com	01343 835226
Ross, William B. LTh CPS	1988 2016	(Aberdour with Pitsligo)	5 Strathlene Court, Rathven AB55 3DD williamross278@btinternet.com	01542 834418
Smith, Hugh M.C. LTh	1973 2013	(Mortlach and Cabrach)	6 Concraig Walk, Kingswells, Aberdeen AB15 8DU	01224 745275
Smith, Morris BD	1988 2013	(Cromdale and Advie with Dulnain Bridge with Grantown-on-Spey)	1 Urquhart Grove, New Elgin IV30 8TB mosmith.themanse@btinternet.com	01343 545019
Watts, Anthony BD DipTechEd JP	1999 2013	(Glenmuick (Ballater))	7 Cumiskie Crescent, Forres IV36 2QB tony.watts6@btinternet.com	
Whyte, David LTh	1993 2011	(Boat of Garten, Duthil and Kincardine)	1 Lemanfield Crescent, Garmouth, Fochabers IV32 7LS whytedj@btinternet.com	01343 870667
Wright, David L. MA BD	1957 1998	(Stornoway: St Columba)	84 Wyvis Drive, Nairn IV12 4TP	01667 451613

(36) ABERNETHY

Meets at Boat of Garten on the first Tuesday of February, March, May, September, October, November and December, and on the last Tuesday of June.

| Clerk: | REV JAMES A.I. MacEWAN MA BD | Rapness, Station Road, Nethy Bridge PA25 3DN abernethy@churchofscotland.org.uk | 01479 821116 |

Abernethy (H) linked with Boat of Garten (H), Carrbridge (H) and Kincardine
Donald K. Walker BD   1979   2013   The Manse, Deshar Road, Boat of Garten PH24 3BN   01479 831252
DWalker@churchofscotland.org.uk

Alvie and Insh (H) linked with Rothiemurchus and Aviemore (H)
Vacant   The Manse, 8 Dalfaber Park, Aviemore PH22 1QF   01479 810280
Session Clerk, Alvie and Insh: Bill Steele   bill.steele-4@btopenworld.com   01450 661918
Session Clerk, Rothiemurchus and Aviemore: markduncan55@live.com   07766 002757
  Mark Duncan

Boat of Garten (H), Carrbridge (H) and Kincardine See Abernethy

Cromdale (H) and Advie linked with Dulnain Bridge (H) linked with Grantown-on-Spey (H)
Gordon I. Strang BSc BD   2014   The Manse, Golf Course Road, Grantown-on-Spey PH26 3HY   01479 872084
GStrang@churchofscotland.org.uk

Dulnain Bridge See Cromdale and Advie
Grantown-on-Spey See Cromdale and Advie

Kingussie (H)
Vacant   The Manse, 18 Hillside Avenue, Kingussie PH21 1PA   01540 662327
Session Clerk: Fraser Nicol   fraserandann2@yahoo.co.uk   07907 266007

Laggan (H) linked with Newtonmore: St Bride's (H)
Catherine A. Buchan (Mrs) MA MDiv   2002   2009   The Manse, Fort William Road, Newtonmore PH20 1DG   01540 673238
CBuchan@churchofscotland.org.uk

Newtonmore: St Bride's See Laggan
Rothiemurchus and Aviemore See Alvie and Insh

Tomintoul (H), Glenlivet and Inveraven
Vacant
Session Clerk: Margo Stewart (Mrs)

The Manse, Tomintoul, Ballindalloch AB37 9HA
margoandedward@hotmail.co.uk
01807 580254

Atkinson, Graham T. MA BD MTh	2006	2017	(Glasgow: Sandyhills)	15 Lockhart Place, Aviemore PH22 1SW gtatkinson75@yahoo.co.uk	07715 108837
Duncanson, Mary (Ms) BTh	2013	2017	(Ordained Local Minister: Presbytery Pastoral Support)	3 Balmenach Road, Cromdale, Grantown-on-Spey PH26 3LJ MDuncanson@churchofscotland.org.uk	01479 872165
MacEwan, James A.I. MA BD	1973	2012	(Abernethy with Cromdale and Advie)	Rapness, Station Road, Nethy Bridge PH25 3DN wurrus@hotmail.co.uk	01479 821116
Ritchie, Christine A.Y. (Mrs) BD DipMin	2002	2012	(Braes of Rannoch with Foss and Rannoch)	25 Beachen Court, Grantown-on-Spey PH26 3JD cayritchie@btinternet.com	01479 873419
Thomson, Mary Ellen (Mrs)	2013		Ordained Local Minister: Presbytery Chaplain to Care Homes	Riverside Flat, Gynack Street, Kingussie PH21 1EL Mary.Thomson@churchofscotland.org.uk	01540 661772

(37) INVERNESS

Meets at Inverness, in Inverness: Inshes (2018) on the third Saturday of September, the third Tuesday of November, (2019) the second Saturday in March and the last Tuesday in June; Saturday meetings preceded by a presbytery conference.

Clerk: REV. TREVOR G. HUNT BA BD 7 Woodville Court, Culduthel Avenue, Inverness IV2 6BX **01463 250355**
inverness@churchofscotland.org.uk **07753 423333**

Ardersier (H) linked with Petty
Robert Cleland 1997 2014 The Manse, Ardersier, Inverness IV2 7SX 01667 462224
RCleland@churchofscotland.org.uk

Auldearn and Dalmore linked with Nairn: St Ninian's (H)
Thomas M. Bryson BD 1997 2015 The Manse, Auldearn, Nairn IV12 5SX 01667 451675
TBryson@churchofscotland.org.uk

Cawdor (H) linked with Croy and Dalcross (H)
Robert E. Brookes BD 2009 2016 The Manse, Croy, Inverness IV2 5PH 01667 493717
RBrookes@churchofscotland.org.uk

Croy and Dalcross See Cawdor

Culloden: The Barn (H)
Michael Robertson BA — 2014 — 45 Oakdene Court, Culloden IV2 7XL — 01463 795430
Mike.Robertson@churchofscotland.org.uk — 07740 984395

Daviot and Dunlichity linked with Moy, Dalarossie and Tomatin
Vacant
Session Clerk, Daviot and Dunlichity: Kathleen Matheson (Mrs) — The Manse, Daviot, Inverness IV2 5XL — 01463 772242
k.matheson@btconnect.com — 01808 521767
Session Clerk, Moy, Dalarossie and Tomatin: Vivian Roden — 2018 — vroden@btinternet.com — 01808 511355

Dores and Boleskine
Vacant
Session Clerk: Iain King — kingdores@btinternet.com — 01463 751293

Inverness: Crown (H)
Vacant
Morven Archer (Mrs) — 2013 2018 — 39 Southside Road, Inverness IV2 4XA — **01463 231140**
(Ordained Local Minister) — 42 Firthview Drive, Inverness IV3 8QE — 01463 230537
MArcher@churchofscotland.org.uk — 01463 237840

Inverness: Dalneigh and Bona (GD) (H)
Vacant — 9 St Mungo Road, Inverness IV3 5AS — 01463 232339

Inverness: East (H)
Andrew T.B. McGowan (Prof.) — 1979 2009 — 2 Victoria Drive, Inverness IV2 3QD — 01463 238770
BD STM PhD — AMcGowan@churchofscotland.org.uk

Inverness: Hilton
Duncan A.C. MacPherson LLB BD — 1994 — 66 Culduthel Mains Crescent, Inverness IV2 6RG — 01463 231417
DMacPherson@churchofscotland.org.uk
Jonathan Fraser MA(Div) MTh ThM — 2012 — 9 Broom Drive, Inverness IV2 4EG — 07749 539981
(Associate Minister) — jonathan@hiltonchurch.org.uk

Inverness: Inshes (H)
David S. Scott MA BD — 1987 2013 — 48 Redwood Crescent, Milton of Leys, Inverness IV2 6HB — 01463 772402
David.Scott@churchofscotland.org.uk
Farquhar A.M. Forbes MA BD — 2016 — The Heights, Inverarnie, Inverness IV2 6XA — 01808 521450
(Associate Minister) — FForbes@churchofscotland.org.uk

Inverness: Kinmylies (H)
Vacant
2 Balnafettack Place, Inverness IV3 8TQ — 01463 224307

Inverness: Ness Bank (H)
Fiona E. Smith (Mrs) LLB BD   2010
15 Ballifeary Road, Inverness IV3 5PJ
FSmith@churchofscotland.org.uk — 01463 234653

Inverness: Old High St Stephen's
Peter W. Nimmo BD ThM   1996   2004
24 Damfield Road, Inverness IV2 3HU
PNimmo@churchofscotland.org.uk — 01463 250802

Inverness: St Columba (New Charge Development) (H)
Scott A. McRoberts BD MTh   2012
20 Bramble Close, Inverness IV2 6BS
SMcRoberts@churchofscotland.org.uk — 01463 230308 / 07535 290092

Inverness: Trinity (H)
Vacant
Session Clerk: Iain Macdonald
60 Kenneth Street, Inverness IV3 5PZ
iain2567@gmail.com — 01463 234756 / 01463 223238

Kilmorack and Erchless
Ian A. Manson BA BD   1989   2016
'Roselynn', Croyard Road, Beauly IV4 7DJ
IManson@churchofscotland.org.uk — 01463 783824

Kiltarlity linked with Kirkhill
Jonathan W. Humphrey BSc BD PhD   2015
4 Courtyard Cottages, Lentran IV4 8RL
JHumphrey@churchofscotland.org.uk — 07587 186424

Kirkhill See Kiltarlity
Moy, Dalarossie and Tomatin See Daviot and Dunlichity

Nairn: Old (H)
Alison C. Mehigan BD DPS   2003   2015
15 Chattan Gardens, Nairn IV12 4QP
AMehigan@churchofscotland.org.uk — 01667 452382 / 01667 453777

Nairn: St Ninian's See Auldearn and Dalmore
Petty See Ardersier

Urquhart and Glenmoriston (H)
Hugh F. Watt BD DPS DMin

	1986	1996	Blairbeg, Drummadrochit, Inverness IV3 6UG HWatt@churchofscotland.org.uk	01456 450231

Name	Years	Charge	Address / Email	Phone
Black, Archibald T. BSc	1964 1997	(Inverness: Ness Bank)	16 Elm Park, Inverness IV2 4WN	01463 230588
Brown, Derek G. BD DipMin DMin	1989 1994	Lead Chaplain: NHS Highland	Cathedral Manse, Cnoc-an-Lobht, Dornoch IV25 3HN derek.brown1@nhs.net	01862 810296
Buell, F. Bart BA MDiv	1980 1995	(Urquhart and Glenmoriston)	6 Towerhill Place, Cradlehall, Inverness IV2 5FN bartbuell@talktalk.net	01463 794634
Chisholm, Archibald F. MA	1957 1997	(Braes of Rannoch with Foss and Rannoch)	32 Seabank Road, Nairn IV12 4EU arch32@btinternet.com	01667 452001
Craw, John DCS	1998 2009	(Deacon)	5 Larchfield Court, Nairn IV12 4SS johncraw607@btinternet.com	07544 761653
Hunt, Trevor G. BA BD	1986 2011	(Evie with Firth with Rendall)	7 Woodville Court, Culduthel Avenue, Inverness IV2 6BX trevorhunt@gmail.com	01463 250355 07753 423333
Jeffrey, Stewart D. BSc BD	1962 1997	(Banff with King Edward)	10 Grigor Drive, Inverness IV2 4LP stewart.jeffrey@talktalk.net	01463 230085
Lyon, B. Andrew LTh	1971 2007	(Fraserburgh West with Rathen West)	20 Barnview, Culloden, Inverness IV2 7EX balyon2018@hotmail.com	01463 559609
MacKay, Stewart A.	2009	Chaplain: Army	3 Bn Black Watch, Royal Regiment of Scotland, Fort George, Ardersier, Inverness IV1 2TD	
Mackenzie, Seoras L. BD	1996 1998	Chaplain: Army	39 Engr Regt (Air Support), Kinloss Barracks, Kinloss, Forres IV36 3XL	
MacQuarrie, Donald A. BSc BD	1979 2012	(Fort William: Duncansburgh MacIntosh with Kilmonivaig)	Birch Cottage, 4 Craigrorie, North Kessock, Inverness IV1 3XH pdmacq@ukgateway.net	01463 731050
McRoberts, T. Douglas BD CPS FRSA	1975 2014	(Malta)	24 Redwood Avenue, Inverness IV2 6HA doug.mcroberts@btinternet.com	01463 772594
Mitchell, Joyce (Mrs) DCS	1994 2010	(Deacon)	Sunnybank, Farr, Inverness IV2 6XG joyce@mitchell71.freeserve.co.uk	01808 521285
Morrison, Hector BSc BD MTh	1981 2009	Principal: Highland Theological College	24 Oak Avenue, Inverness IV2 4NX	01463 238561
Rettie, James A. BTh	1981 1999	(Melness and Eriboll with Tongue)	2 Trantham Drive, Westhill, Inverness IV2 5QT	01463 798896
Ritchie, Bruce BSc BD PhD	1977 2014	(Dingwall: Castle Street)	16 Brinckman Terrace, Westhill, Inverness IV2 5BL brucezomba@hotmail.com	01463 791389
Robertson, Fergus A. MA BD	1971 2010	(Inverness: Dalneigh and Bona)	16 Druid Temple Way, Inverness IV2 6UQ faavrobertson@yahoo.co.uk	01463 718462
Stirling, G. Alan S. MA	1960 1999	(Leochel Cushnie and Lynturk with Tough)	97 Lochlann Road, Culloden, Inverness IV2 7HJ	01463 798313
Turner, Fraser K. LTh	1994 2007	(Killtarlity with Kirkhill)	20 Caulfield Avenue, Inverness IV2 5GA fraseratq@yahoo.co.uk	01463 794004
Warwick, Ivan C. MA BD TD	1980 2014	(Paisley St James')	Ardcruidh Croft, Heights of Dochcarty, Dingwall. IV15 9UF L70rev@btinternet.com	01349 861464 07787 535083

| Waugh, John L. LTh | 1973 | 2002 | (Ardclach with Auldearn and Dalmore) | 58 Wyvis Drive, Nairn IV12 4TP
jswaugh@gmail.com | Tel/Fax 01667 456397 |
| Younger, Alastair S. BScEcon ASCC | 1969 | 2008 | (Inverness: St Columba High) | 33 Duke's View, Slackbuie, Inverness IV2 6BB
younger873@btinternet.com | 01463 242873 |

INVERNESS ADDRESSES

Inverness

Crown	Kingsmills Road x Midmills Road
Dalneigh and Bona	St Mary's Avenue
East	Academy Street x Margaret Street
Hilton	Druid Road x Tomatin Road
Inshes	Inshes Retail Park
Kinmylies	Kinmylies Way
Ness Bank	Ness Bank x Castle Road
Old High	Church Street x Church Lane
St Columba	Drummond School
St Stephen's	Old Edinburgh Road x Southside Road
Trinity	Huntly Place x Upper Kessock Street

Nairn

| Old | Academy Street x Seabank Road |
| St Ninian's | High Street x Queen Street |

(38) LOCHABER

Meets at Caol, Fort William, in Kilmallie Church Hall at 6pm, on the first Tuesday of September and December, on the last Tuesday of October and on the fourth Tuesday of March. The June meeting is held at 6pm on the second Tuesday in the church of the incoming Moderator. The Presbytery Annual Conference is held in February.

| Clerk: | **REV DONALD G. B. McCORKINDALE
BD DipMin** | The Manse, 2 The Meadows, Strontian, Acharacle PH36 4HZ
lochaber@churchofscotland.org.uk | **01967 402234
07554 176580** |
| Treasurer: | **MRS CONNIE ANDERSON** | **Darach, Duror PA38 4BS**
faoconnie@gmail.com | **01631 740334** |

Acharacle (H) linked with Ardnamurchan

| Fiona M. Ogg (Mrs) BA BD | 2012 | The Church of Scotland Manse, Acharacle PH36 4JU
Fiona.Ogg@churchofscotland.org.uk | 01967 431654 |

Ardgour and Kingairloch linked with Morvern linked with Strontian

| Donald G.B. McCorkindale BD DipMin | 1992 | 2011 | The Manse, 2 The Meadows, Strontian, Acharacle PH36 4HZ
DMcCorkindale@churchofscotland.org.uk | 01967 402234
07554 176580 |

Ardnamurchan See Acharacle

Duror (H) linked with Glencoe: St Munda's (H)

| Alexander C. Stoddart BD | 2001 | 2016 | 9 Cameron Brae, Kentallen, Duror PA38 4BF
AStoddart@churchofscotland.org.uk | 01631 740285 |

Fort Augustus linked with Glengarry

Anthony M. Jones 1994 2018 The Manse, Fort Augustus PH32 4BH 01320 366210
BD DPS DipTheol CertMin FRSA AJones@churchofscotland.org.uk

Fort William: Duncansburgh MacIntosh (H) linked with Kilmonivaig

Richard Baxter MA BD 1997 2016 The Manse, The Parade, Fort William PH33 6BA 01397 702297
RBaxter@churchofscotland.org.uk 07958 541418

Morag Muirhead (Mrs) 2013 6 Dumbarton Road, Fort William PH33 6UU 01397 703643
(Ordained Local Minister) MMuirhead@churchofscotland.org.uk

Glencoe: St Munda's See Duror
Glengarry See Fort Augustus

Kilmallie

Richard T. Corbett BSc MSc PhD BD 1992 2005 Kilmallie Manse, Corpach, Fort William PH33 7JS 01397 772736
RCorbett@churchofscotland.org.uk

Kilmonivaig See Fort William: Duncansburgh MacIntosh

Kinlochleven (H) linked with Nether Lochaber (H)

Malcolm A. Kinnear MA BD PhD 2010 The Manse, Lochaber Road, Kinlochleven PH50 4QW 01855 831227
MKinnear@churchofscotland.org.uk

Morvern See Ardgour
Nether Lochaber See Kinlochleven

North West Lochaber

Stewart Goudie BSc BD 2010 2018 Church of Scotland Manse, Annie's Brae, Mallaig PH41 4RG 01687 462514
SGoudie@churchofscotland.org.uk

Strontian See Ardgour

Anderson, David M. MSc FCOptom 1984 2018 (Ordained Local Minister) 'Mirlos', 1 Dumfries Place, Fort William PH33 6UQ 01397 702091
david@mirlos.co.uk

Lamb, Alan H.W. BA MTh 1959 2005 (Associate Minister) Smiddy House, Arisaig PH39 4NH 01687 450227
h.a.lamb@handalamb.plus.com

Millar, John L. MA BD	1981 1990	(Fort William: Duncansburgh with Kilmonivaig)	Flat 0/1, 12 Chesterfield Gardens, Glasgow G12 0BF johnmillar123@btinternet.com	0141 339 4090
Varwell, Adrian P.J. BA BD PhD	1983 2011	(Fort Augustus with Glengarry)	19 Enrick Crescent, Kilmore, Drumnadrochit, Inverness IV63 6TP adrian.varwell@btinternet.com	01456 459352
Winning, A. Ann MA DipEd BD	1984 2006	(Morvern)	'Westering', 13C Carnoch, Glencoe, Ballachulish PH49 4HQ awinning009@btinternet.com	01855 811929

LOCHABER Communion Sundays Please consult the Presbytery website: www.lochaber.presbytery.org.uk

(39) ROSS

Meets on the first Tuesday of September in the church of the incoming Moderator; and in Dingwall: Castle Street Church on the first Tuesday of October, November, December, February, March and May, and on the last Tuesday of June.

| Clerk: | **MRS CATH CHAMBERS** | **184 Kirkside, Alness IV17 0RH ross@churchofscotland.org.uk** | **01349 882026** |

Alness
Vacant

| Michael J. Macdonald (Auxiliary Minister) | 2004 | 2014 | 27 Darroch Brae, Alness IV17 0SD 73 Firhill, Alness IV17 0RT Michael.Macdonald@churchofscotland.org.uk | 01349 882238 01349 884268 |

Avoch linked with Fortrose and Rosemarkie
Vacant
Session Clerk, Avoch: Robert S. Moore
Session Clerk, Rosemarkie: Jack Kernahan

| | | 5 Ness Way, Fortrose IV10 8SS bob@knockmuir.co.uk jackkernahan@aol.com | 01381 621433 |

Contin (H) linked with Fodderty and Strathpeffer (H)
Vacant

| James Bissett (Ordained Local Minister) | 2016 | The Manse, Contin, Strathpeffer IV14 9ES 14 First Field Avenue, North Kessock, Inverness IV1 3JB JBissett@churchofscotland.org.uk | 01997 421028 01463 731930 |

Cromarty linked with Resolis and Urquhart

| Terrance Burns BA MA | 2014 | 2017 | The Manse, Culbokie, Dingwall IV7 8JN TBurns@churchofscotland.org.uk | 01349 877452 |

Dingwall: Castle Street (H)
Vacant
Session Clerk: Richard Brown
16 Achany Road, Dingwall IV15 9JB
broons.northwood@btinternet.com
01349 866792
01349 877065

Dingwall: St Clement's (H)
Bruce Dempsey BD
1997   2014
8 Castlehill Road, Dingwall IV15 9PB
BDempsey@churchofscotland.org.uk
01349 292055

Fearn Abbey and Nigg linked with Tarbat
Robert G.D.W. Pickles
BD MPhil ThD
2003   2015
Church of Scotland Manse, Fearn, Tain IV20 1WN
RPickles@churchofscotland.org.uk
01862 832282

Ferintosh
Stephen Macdonald BD MTh
2008   2018
Ferintosh Manse, Leanaig Road, Conon Bridge,
  Dingwall IV7 8BE
SMacdonald@churchofscotland.org.uk
01349 861275
07570 804193

Fodderty and Strathpeffer See Contin
Fortrose and Rosemarkie See Avoch

Invergordon
Kenneth Donald MacLeod BD CPS
1989   2000
The Manse, Cromlet Drive, Invergordon IV18 0BA
KMacLeod@churchofscotland.org.uk
01349 852273

Killearnan (H) linked with Knockbain (H)
Susan Cord
2016
14 First Field Avenue, North Kessock, Inverness IV1 3JB
SCord@churchofscotland.org.uk
01463 731930

Kilmuir and Logie Easter
Vacant
Session Clerk: George Morrison
The Manse, Delny, Invergordon IV18 0NW
ga.morrison@virgin.net
01862 842280

Kiltearn (H)
Donald A. MacSween BD
1991   1998
The Manse, Swordale Road, Evanton, Dingwall IV16 9UZ
DMacSween@churchofscotland.org.uk
01349 830472

Knockbain See Killearnan

Lochbroom and Ullapool (GD)
Heidi J. Hercus — 2018 — The Manse, 11 Royal Park, Mill Street, Ullapool IV26 2XT
HHercus@churchofscotland.org.uk — 01854 613146

Resolis and Urquhart See Cromarty

Rosskeen
Vacant
Carol Rattenbury — 2017 — Rosskeen Manse, Perrins Road, Alness IV17 0XG
(Ordained Local Minister) — Balloan Farm House, Alcaig, Conon Bridge, Dingwall IV7 8HU
CRattenbury@churchofscotland.org.uk — 01349 882265 / 01349 877323

Tain
Andrew P. Fothergill BA — 2012 2017 — 14 Kingsway Avenue, Tain IV19 1NJ
AFothergill@churchofscotland.org.uk — 01862 892296

Tarbat See Fearn Abbey and Nigg

Urray and Kilchrist
Scott Polworth LLB BD — 2009 — The Manse, Corrie Road, Muir of Ord IV6 7TL
SPolworth@churchofscotland.org.uk — 01463 870259

Name			Charge	Address / Email	Tel
Archer, Nicholas D.C. BA BD	1971	1992	(Dores and Boleskine)	2 Aldie Cottages, Tain IV19 1LZ na.2ac777@btinternet.com	01862 821494
Bell, Graeme K. BA BD	1983	2017	(Glasgow: Carnwadric)	4 Munro Terrace, Rosemarkie, Fortrose IV10 8UR graemekbell@googlemail.com	07591 180101
Dupar, Kenneth W. BA BD PhD	1965	1993	(Christ's College, Aberdeen)	The Old Manse, The Causeway, Cromarty IV11 8XJ	01381 600428
Forsyth, James LTh	1970	2000	(Fearn Abbey with Nigg Chapelhill)	Rhives Lodge, Golspie, Sutherland KW10 6DD	
Greer, A. David C.	1956	1996	(Barra)	17 Duthac Wynd, Tain IV19 1LP greer2@talktalk.net	01862 892065
Horne, Douglas A. BD	1977	2009	(Tain)	151 Holm Farm Road, Culduthel, Inverness IV2 6BF douglas.horne@talktalk.net	01463 712677
Lincoln, John MPhil BD	1986	2014	(Balquhidder with Killin and Ardeonaig)	59 Obsdale Park, Alness IV17 0TR johnlincoln@minister.com	01349 882791
McDonald, Alan D. LLB BD MTh DLitt DD	1979	2016	(Cameron with St Andrews: St Leonard's)	7 Duke Street, Cromarty IV11 8YH alan.d.mcdonald@talk21.com	01381 600954
Mackinnon, R.M. LTh	1968	1995	(Kilmuir and Logie Easter)	27 Riverford Crescent, Conon Bridge, Dingwall IV7 8HL	01349 866293
MacLennan, Alasdair J. BD DCE	1978	2001	(Resolis and Urquhart)	Airdale, Seaforth Road, Muir of Ord IV6 7TA	01463 870704
Macleod, John MA	1959	1993	(Resolis and Urquhart)	'Benview', 19 Balvaird, Muir of Ord IV6 7RG sheilaandjohn@yahoo.co.uk	01463 871286

Munro, James A. BA BD DMS   1979 2013   (Port Glasgow: Hamilton Bardrainney)   1 Wyvis Crescent, Conon Bridge, Dingwall IV7 8BZ   01349 865752
james781munro@btinternet.com

Scott, David V. BTh   1994 2014   (Fearn Abbey and Nigg with Tarbat)   29 Sunnyside, Culloden Moor, Inverness IV2 5ES   01463 795802

Smith, Russel BD   1994 2013   (Dingwall: St Clement's)   1 School Road, Conon Bridge, Dingwall IV7 8AE   01349 861011
russanntwo@btinternet.com

(40) SUTHERLAND

Meets at Lairg on the first Tuesday of March, May, September, November and December, and on the first Tuesday of June at the Moderator's church.

Clerk: IAN W. McCREE BD   Tigh Ardachu, Mosshill, Brora KW9 6NG   01408 621185
sutherland@churchofscotland.org.uk

Altnaharra and Farr linked with Melness and Tongue (H)
Beverly W. Cushman MA MDiv BA PhD   1977   2017   The Manse, Bettyhill, Thurso KW14 7SS   01641 521208
BCushman@churchofscotland.org.uk

Assynt and Stoer
Vacant   Canisp Road, Lochinver, Lairg IV27 4LH   01571 844342

Clyne (H) linked with Kildonan and Loth Helmsdale (H)
Vacant   Golf Road, Brora KW9 6QS   01408 621239
Session Clerk, Clyne: Sydney L. Barnett   sydneylb43@gmail.com   01408 621569

Creich linked with Kincardine Croick and Edderton linked with Rosehall
Vacant   The Manse, Ardgay IV24 3BG   01863 766285
Session Clerk, Creich: Jeani Hunter (Mrs)   nielsonhunter@btinternet.com   01862 810544
Session Clerk, Kincardine Croick and Edderton: Rev. Mary J. Stobo   MStobo@churchofscotland.org.uk   01863 766868
Session Clerk, Rosehall: Lt. Col. Colin Gilmour   MBE DL   shenaval@btinternet.com   01549 441374

Dornoch Cathedral (H)
Susan M. Brown (Mrs) BD DipMin   1985   1998   Cathedral Manse, Cnoc-an-Lobht, Dornoch IV25 3HN   01862 810296
Susan.Brown@churchofscotland.org.uk

Durness and Kinlochbervie
Andrea M. Boyes (Mrs) RMN BA(Theol)   2013   2017   Manse Road, Kinlochbervie, Lairg IV27 4RG   01971 521287
ABoyes@churchofscotland.org.uk

Eddrachillis
John MacPherson BSc BD   1993   Church of Scotland Manse, Scourie, Lairg IV27 4TQ   01971 502431
JMacPherson@churchofscotland.org.uk

Golspie
John B. Sterrett BA BD PhD   2007   The Manse, Fountain Road, Golspie KW10 6TH   Tel/Fax 01408 633295
JSterret@churchofscotland.org.uk

Kildonan and Loth Helmsdale See Clyne

Kincardine Croick and Edderton See Creich

Lairg (H) linked with Rogart (H)
Vacant
Hilary M. Gardner (Miss)   2010   2018   The Manse, Lairg IV27 4EH   01863 766107
(Auxiliary Minister)   Cayman Lodge, Kincardine Hill, Ardgay IV24 3DJ
HGardner@churchofscotland.org.uk

Melness and Tongue See Altnaharra and Farr

Rogart See Lairg
Rosehall See Creich

Chambers, John OBE BSc   1972 2009   (Inverness: Ness Bank)   Bannlagan Lodge, 4 Earls Cross Gardens, Dornoch IV25 3NR   01862 811520
chambersdornoch@btinternet.com
Goskirk, J.L. LTh   1968 2010   (Lairg with Rogart)   Rathvilly, Lairgmuir, Lairg IV27 4ED   01549 402569
leslie_goskirk@sky.com
McCree, Ian W. BD   1971 2011   (Clyne with Kildonan and Loth Helmsdale)   Tigh Ardachu, Mosshill, Brora KW9 6NG   01408 621185
ianmccree@live.co.uk
McKay, Margaret (Mrs) MA BD MTh   1991 2003   (Auchaber United with Auchterless)   2 Mackenzie Gardens, Dornoch IV25 3RU   01862 811859
megsie38@gmail.com
Stobo, Mary J. (Mrs)   2013   Ordained Local Minister; Community Healthcare Chaplain   Druim-an-Sgairnich, Ardgay IV24 3BG   01863 766868
MStobo@churchofscotland.org.uk

(41) CAITHNESS

Meets alternately at Wick and Thurso on the first Tuesday of February, March, May, September, November and December, and the third Tuesday of June.

| Clerk: | REV. RONALD JOHNSTONE BD | 2 Comlifoot Drive, Halkirk KW12 6ZA
caithness@churchofscotland.org.uk | 01847 839033 |

Bower linked with Halkirk Westerdale linked with Watten

Vacant

Session Clerk, Bower: Nicola Milne (Mrs)	The Manse, Station Road, Watten, Wick KW1 5YN morgan.milne@btconnect.com	01955 621220 01955 641357
Session Clerk, Halkirk: Janet Mowat (Mrs)	jsmowat25@btinternet.com	01847 831638
Session Clerk, Watten: vacant		

Halkirk Westerdale See Bower

Latheron

| Vacant | | Central Manse, Main Street, Lybster KW3 6BN
parish-of-latheron@btconnect.com | 01593 721706 |
| Heather Stewart (Mrs)
(Ordained Local Minister) | 2013 2017 | Burnthill, Thrumster, Wick KW1 5TR
Heather.Stewart@churchofscotland.org.uk | 01955 651717
Work 01955 603333 |

North Coast

| David J.B. Macartney BA | 2017 | Church of Scotland Manse, Reay, Thurso KW14 7RE
DMacartney@churchofscotland.org.uk | 01847 811441 |

Pentland

Vacant

| Lyall Rennie
(Ordained Local Minister) | 2014 | The Manse, Canisbay, Wick KW1 4YH
Ruachmarra, Lower Warse, Canisbay, Wick KW1 4YB
LRennie@churchofscotland.org.uk | 01955 611756 |

New charge formed by union of **Canisbay, Dunnet, Keiss and Olrig**

Thurso: St Peter's and St Andrew's (H)

| David S.M. Malcolm BD | 2011 2014 | The Manse, 46 Rose Street, Thurso KW14 8RF
David.Malcolm@churchofscotland.org.uk | 01847 895186 |

Thurso: West (H)

| Ida Tenglerova Mgr | 2012 | 2017 | Thorkel Road, Thurso KW14 7LW | 01847 892663 |
| | | | ITenglerova@churchofscotland.org.uk | |

Watten See Bower

Wick: Pulteneytown (H) and Thrumster

| Andrew A. Barrie BD | 2013 | 2017 | The Manse, Coronation Street, Wick KW1 5LS | 01955 603166 |

Wick: St Fergus

| John Nugent BD | 1999 | 2011 | Mansfield, Miller Avenue, Wick KW1 4DF | 01955 602167 |
| | | | JNugent@churchofscotland.org.uk | 07511 503946 |

Duncan, Esme (Miss)	2013	2017	(Ordained Local Minister)	Avalon, Upper Warse, Canisbay, Wick KW1 4YD	01955 611455
				EDuncan@churchofscotland.org.uk	
Johnstone, Ronald BD	1977	2011	(Thurso: West)	2 Comlifoot Drive, Halkirk KW12 6ZA	01847 839033
				ronaldjohnstone@btinternet.com	
Warner, Kenneth BD	1981	2008	(Halkirk and Westerdale)	Kilearnan, Clayock, Halkirk KW12 6UZ	01847 831825
				wrnkenn@btinternet.com	

CAITHNESS Communion Sundays

Bower	1st Jul, Dec	Dunnet	last May, Nov
Halkirk Westerdale	Apr, Jul, Oct	Keiss	1st May, 3rd Nov
Latheron	Apr, Jul, Sep, Nov	Olrig	last May, Nov
North Coast	Mar, Easter, Jun, Sep, Dec	Thurso: St Peter's and	
Pentland:		St Andrew's	Mar, Jun, Sep, Dec
Canisbay	1st Jun, Nov	West	4th Mar, Jun, Nov
		Watten	1st Jul, Dec
		Wick: Pulteneytown and	1st Mar, Jun, Sep, Dec
		Thrumster	Apr, Oct
		St Fergus	

(42) LOCHCARRON – SKYE

Meets in Kyle on Tuesdays in August, September, November, December, February, March and June.

| Clerk: | REV. RODERICK A.R. MacLEOD | The Manse, 6 Upper Breakish, Isle of Skye IV42 8PY | 01471 822416 |
| | BA MBA BD DMin | lochcarronskye@churchofscotland.org.uk | |

Applecross, Lochcarron and Torridon (GD)
Anita Stutter Drs (MA) | 2008 | 2017 | The Manse, Colonel's Road, Lochcarron, Strathcarron IV54 8YG
AStutter@churchofscotland.org.uk | 01520 722783

Bracadale and Duirinish (GD)
Janet Easton-Berry BA (SocSc) BA (Theol) | 2016 | Duirinish Manse, Dunvegan, Isle of Skye IV55 8WQ
JEaston-Berry@churchofscotland.ork.uk | 01470 521668

Gairloch and Dundonnell
Stuart J. Smith BEng BD MTh | 1994 | 2016 | Church of Scotland Manse, The Glebe, Gairloch IV21 2BT
Stuart.Smith@churchofscotland.org.uk | 01445 712645

Glenelg Kintail and Lochalsh
Vacant | The Manse, Main Street, Kyle of Lochalsh IV40 8DA | 01599 534294

Kilmuir and Stenscholl (GD)
John W. Murray LLB BA | 2003 | 2015 | 1 Totescore, Kilmuir, Isle of Skye IV51 9YN
JMurray@churchofscotland.org.uk | 01470 542297

Portree (GD)
Sandor Fazakas BD MTh | 1976 | 2007 | Viewfield Road, Portree, Isle of Skye IV51 9ES
SFazakas@churchofscotland.org.uk | 01478 611868

Snizort (H) (GD)
Vacant | The Manse, Kensaleyre, Snizort, Portree, Isle of Skye IV51 9XE | 01470 532453

Strath and Sleat (GD)
Roderick A.R. MacLeod BA MBA BD DMin | 1994 | 2015 | The Manse, 6 Upper Breakish, Isle of Skye IV42 8PY
RMacLeod@churchofscotland.org.uk | 01471 822416

Anderson, Janet (Miss) DCS | 1979 | 2012 | (Deacon) | Creagard, 31 Lower Breakish, Isle of Skye IV42 8QA
jaskye@hotmail.co.uk | 01471 822403

Mackenzie, Hector M. | 2008 | Chaplain: Army | HQ Military Corrective Training Centre, Berechurch Hall Camp,
Berechurch Hall Road, Colchester CO2 9NU
mackenziehector@hotmail.com

Martin, George M. MA BD | 1987 | 2005 | (Applecross, Lochcarron and Torridon) | 8(1) Buckingham Terrace, Edinburgh EH4 3AA | 0131 343 3937

Morrison, Derek   1995 2013   (Gairloch and Dundonnell)   2 Cliffton Place, Poolewe, Achnasheen IV22 2JU   01445 781333
derekmorrison1@aol.com

LOCHCARRON – SKYE Communion Sundays

Applecross	1st Sep
Arnisort	3rd Mar, Sep
Bracadale	Last Feb
Broadford	3rd Jan, Easter, 3rd Sep
Duirinish	4th Jun
Dundonnell	
Elgol	1st Aug
Gairloch	3rd Jun, Nov
Glenelg	2nd Jun, Nov
Glenshiel	1st Jul
Kilmuir	1st Mar, Sep
Kinlochewe	
Kyle	2nd May, 1st Oct
Kyleakin	Last Nov
Lochalsh	4th Jan, Jun, Sep, Christmas, Easter
Lochcarron and Shieldaig	Easter; communion held on a revolving basis when there is a fifth Sunday in the month
Portree	Easter, Pentecost, Christmas, 2nd Mar, Aug, 1st Nov
Sleat	Last Sep
Snizort	1st Jan, 4th Mar
Stenscholl	1st Jun, Dec
Strath	4th Jan

In Strath and Sleat, joint Communions are held quarterly with local churches at 6pm in Kyleakin Village Hall.

(43) UIST

Meets on the first Tuesday of February, March, September and November in Lochmaddy, and on the third Tuesday of June in Leverburgh.

Clerk: REV. GAVIN J. ELLIOTT MA BD   5a Aird, Isle of Benbecula HS7 5LT   **01870 602726**
uist@churchofscotland.org.uk

Benbecula (GD) (H) linked with Carinish (GD) (H)
Andrew (Drew) P. Kuzma BA   2007   Church of Scotland Manse, Griminish, Isle of Benbecula HS7 5QA   01870 602180
AKuzma@churchofscotland.org.uk

Ishabel Macdonald,   2011   'Cleat Afe Ora', 18 Carinish, Isle of North Uist HS6 5HN   01876 580367
(Ordained Local Minister)   Ishie.Macdonald@churchofscotland.org.uk

Berneray and Lochmaddy (GD) (H) linked with Kilmuir and Paible (GD)
Alen J.R. McCulloch MA BD   1990 2017   Church of Scotland Manse, Paible, Isle of North Uist HS6 5HD   01876 510310
AMcCulloch@churchofscotland.org.uk

Carinish See Benbecula

Kilmuir and Paible See Berneray and Lochmaddy

Manish-Scarista (GD) (H)
Vacant
Session Clerk: Paul Alldred
Church of Scotland Manse, Scarista, Isle of Harris HS3 3HX   01859 550200
paul.alldred@outlook.com   01859 520494

Tarbert (GD) (H)
Ian Murdo M. MacDonald DPA BD   2001   2015
The Manse, Manse Road, Tarbert, Isle of Harris HS3 3DF   01859 502231
Ian.MacDonald@churchofscotland.org.uk

Elliott, Gavin J. MA BD   1976 2015   (Ministries Council)   5a Aird, Isle of Benbecula HS7 5LT   01870 602726
gavkondwani@gmail.com

MacIver, Norman BD   1976 2011   (Tarbert)   57 Boswell Road, Wester Inshes, Inverness IV2 3EW
norman@n-cmaciver.freeserve.co.uk

Morrison, Donald John   2001   Auxiliary Minister   22 Kyles, Tarbert, Isle of Harris HS3 3BS   01859 502341
DMorrison@churchofscotland.org.uk

Petrie, Jackie G.   1989 2011   (South Uist)   7B Malaclete, Isle of North Uist HS6 5BX   01876 560804
jackiegpetrie@yahoo.com

Smith, John M.   1956 1992   (Lochmaddy)   Hamersay, Clachan, Locheport, Lochmaddy,
Isle of North Uist HS6 5HD

Smith, Murdo MA BD   1988 2011   (Manish-Scarista)   Aisgeir, 15A Upper Shader, Isle of Lewis HS3 3MX   01876 580332

UIST Communion Sundays

Benbecula	2nd Mar, Sep
Berneray and Lochmaddy	4th Jun, last Oct
Carinish	4th Mar, Aug
Kilmuir and Paible	1st Jun, 3rd Nov
Manish-Scarista	3rd Apr, 1st Oct
Tarbert	2nd Mar, 3rd Sep

(44) LEWIS

Meets at Stornoway, in St Columba's Church Hall, on the second Tuesday of February, March, September and November. It also meets if required in April, June and December on dates to be decided.

Clerk: MR JOHN CUNNINGHAM   1 Raven's Lane, Stornoway, Isle of Lewis HS2 0EG   01851 709977
lewis@churchofscotland.org.uk   07789 878840

Barvas (GD) (H)
Dougie Wolf BA(Theol)   2017
Church of Scotland Manse, Lower Barvas, Isle of Lewis   HS2 0QY
mrdougiewolf@gmail.com
01851 840218

Carloway (GD) (H)
Vacant
Church of Scotland Manse, Knock, Carloway, Isle of Lewis   HS2 9AU
01851 643211
01851 643255

Cross Ness (GE) (H)
Vacant
Cross Manse, Swainbost, Ness, Isle of Lewis   HS2 0TB
01851 810375

Kinloch (GE) (H)
Iain M. Campbell BD   2004   2008
Laxay, Lochs, Isle of Lewis   HS2 9LA
i455@btinternet.com
01851 830218

Knock (GE) (H)
Guardianship of the Presbytery

Lochs-Crossbost (GD) (H)
Guardianship of the Presbytery

Lochs-in-Bernera (GD) (H) linked with Uig (GE) (H)   2008
Hugh Maurice Stewart DPA BD
Church of Scotland Manse, Uigen, Miavaig, Isle of Lewis   HS2 9HX
berneralwuig@btinternet.com
01851 672388

Stornoway: High (GD) (H)
Vacant
Session Clerk: John Cunningham
High Manse, 1 Goathill Road, Stornoway, Isle of Lewis   HS1 2NJ
lewis@churchofscotland.org.uk
01851 703106
07789 878840

Stornoway: Martin's Memorial (H)
Thomas MacNeil MA BD   2002
Matheson Road, Stornoway, Isle of Lewis   HS1 2LR
tommymacneil@hotmail.com
01851 700820
01851 704238

John M. Nicolson BD DipMin   1997   2017
(Assistant Minister)
33 Westview Terrace, Stornoway, Isle of Lewis   HS1 2HP
johnmurdonicolson@gmail.com
07899 235355

Stornoway: St Columba (GD) (H)
William J. Heenan BA MTh   2012
St Columba's Manse, Lewis Street, Stornoway, Isle of Lewis   HS1 2JF
wmheenan@hotmail.com
01851 701546
01851 705933
07837 770589

Uig See Lochs-in-Bernera

Amed, Paul LTh DPS		1992 2015	6 Scotland Street, Stornoway, Isle of Lewis H51 2JQ paul.amed@outlook.com	01851 706450
Johnstone, Ben MA BD DMin	(Strath and Sleat)	1973 2013	Loch Alainn, 5 Breaclete, Great Bernera, Isle of Lewis HS2 9LT benonbernera@gmail.com	01851 612445
Maclean, Donald A. DCS	(Deacon)	1988 1990	8 Upper Barvas, Isle of Lewis HS2 0QX	01851 840454
MacLennan, Donald Angus	(Kinloch)	1975 2006	4 Kestrel Place, Inverness IV2 3YH maclennankinloch@btinternet.com	01463 243750 07799 668270
Macleod, Gordon M. BA	Chaplain, Western Isles Hospital	2017	6 Laxdale Lane, Stornoway, Isle of Lewis HS2 0DR macleods@laxdaleholidaypark.com	07717 065739
Macleod, William	(Uig)	1957 2006	54 Lower Barvas, Isle of Lewis HS2 0QY	01851 840217
Shadakshari, T.K. BTh BD MTh	Head of Spiritual Care, Western Isles Health Board	1998 2006	23D Benside, Newmarket, Stornoway, Isle of Lewis HS2 0DZ tk.shadakshari@nhs.net	Home 01851 701727 Office 01851 704704 07403 697138

LEWIS Communion Sundays

Barvas	3rd Mar, Sep				
Carloway	1st Mar, last Sep	Knock	3rd Apr, 1st Nov	Stornoway: Martin's Memorial	3rd Feb, last Aug
Cross Ness	2nd Mar, Oct	Lochs-Crossbost	4th Mar, Sep	Stornoway: St Columba	1st Dec, Easter
Kinloch	3rd Mar, 2nd Jun, 2nd Sep	Lochs-in-Bernera	1st Apr, 2nd Sep	Uig	3rd Feb, last Aug 3rd Jun, 4th Oct
		Stornoway: High	3rd Feb, last Aug		

(45) ORKNEY

Normally meets at Kirkwall on the first Wednesday of September, November, February, April, and the third Wednesday of June.

Clerk: DR MICHAEL PARTRIDGE MA(Cantab) CPhys FInstP   Clook, Stromness, Orkney **KW16 3JP**   **01856 850810**
orkney@churchofscotland.org.uk

Depute Clerk: MS MARGARET A.B. SUTHERLAND LLB BA   13 Cursiter Crescent, Kirkwall, Orkney **KW15 1XN**   **01856 873747**
mabs2@tiscali.co.uk

Birsay, Harray and Sandwick
David G. McNeish MB ChB BSc BD   2015   The Manse, North Biggings Road, Dounby, Orkney KW17 2HZ   01856 771599
DMcNeish@churchofscotland.org.uk

East Mainland
Wilma A. Johnston MTheol MTh   2006   2014   The Manse, Holm, Orkney KW17 2SB   01856 781797
Wilma.Johnston@churchofscotland.org.uk

Eday
Vacant
Session Clerk: Johan Robertson   essonquoy@btinternet.com   01857   622251

Evie (H) linked with Firth (H) (01856 761117) linked with Rendall linked with Rousay
Vacant
The Manse, Finstown, Orkney KW17 2EG
rbdickey@hotmail.com   01856   761328
eileenocot@hotmail.co.uk   01856   761396
liznedyar@gmail.com   01856   761409
Session Clerk, Firth: Janis Dickey   01856   821477
Session Clerk, Rendall: Eileen Fraser
Session Clerk, Rousay: Elizabeth Firth

Firth See Evie

Flotta linked with Hoy and Walls linked with Orphir (H) and Stenness (H)
Vacant
Stenness Manse, Stenness, Stromness, Orkney KW16 3HH   01856   701219
Session Clerk, Flotta: Isobel Smith   01856   701363
Session Clerk, Hoy and Walls:
Anderson Sutherland

Hoy and Walls See Flotta

Kirkwall: East (H) linked with Shapinsay
Julia M. Meason MTh   2013
East Church Manse, Thoms Street, Kirkwall, Orkney KW15 1PF   01856   874789
JMeason@churchofscotland.org.uk

Kirkwall: St Magnus Cathedral (H)
G. Fraser H. Macnaughton MA BD   1982   2002
Berstane Road, Kirkwall, Orkney KW15 1NA   01856   873312
FMacnaughton@churchofscotland.org.uk

North Ronaldsay
Guardianship of the Presbytery
Presbytery Clerk: Mike Partridge
orkney@churchofscotland.org.uk   01856   850810

Orphir and Stenness See Flotta

Papa Westray linked with Westray
Iain D. MacDonald BD   1993
The Manse, Hilldavale, Westray, Orkney KW17 2DW   Tel/Fax   01857   677357
IMacDonald@churchofscotland.org.uk   07710   443780

Rendall See Evie
Rousay See Evie

Sanday
Vacant

Shapinsay See Kirkwall: East

South Ronaldsay and Burray
Vacant — St Margaret's Manse, Church Road, St Margaret's Hope, Orkney KW17 2SR — 01856 831670

Stromness (H)
John A. Butterfield BA BD MPhil   1990 2016 — 5 Manse Lane, Stromness, Orkney KW16 3AP — JButterfield@churchofscotland.org.uk — 01856 850203

Stronsay: Moncur Memorial
Vacant
Session Clerk: Elsie Dennison — elsie.dennison@live.co.uk — 01857 616238

Westray See Papa Westray

Name			Charge	Address	Telephone
Clark, Thomas L. BD	1985	2008	(Orphir with Stenness)	7 Headland Rise, Burghead, Elgin IV30 5HA toml.clark@btinternet.com	01343 830144
Cordukes, Roy BSc BD	2014	2018	(Evie with Firth with Rendall with Rousay)	Newhouse, Herston, St Margaret's Hope, Orkney KW17 2RH RCordukes@churchofscotland.org.uk	
Freeth, June BA MA	2015		Ordained Local Minister	Cumlaquoy, Birsay, Orkney KW17 2ND JFreeth@churchofscotland.org.uk	01856 721449
Graham, Jennifer D. (Mrs) BA MDiv PhD	2000	2011	(Eday with Stronsay: Moncur Memorial)	Lodge, Stronsay, Orkney KW17 2AN jdgraham67@gmail.com	01857 616487
Prentice, Martin W.M.	2013		Ordained Local Minister	Cott of Howe, Cairston, Stromness, Orkney KW16 3JU MPrentice@churchofscotland.org.uk	01856 851139 07795 817213
Tait, Alexander	1967	1995	(Glasgow: St Enoch's Hogganfield)	Ingermas, Evie, Orkney KW17 2PH	01856 751477
Wishart, James BD	1986	2009	(Deer)	Upper Westshore, Burray, Orkney KW17 2TE jwishart06@btinternet.com	01856 731672

(46) SHETLAND

Meets at Tingwall on the first Tuesday of February, April, June, September, November and December.

Clerk:	**REV DEBORAH J. DOBBY BD PGCE RGN RSCN**	**25 Hogalee, East Voe, Scalloway, Shetland ZE1 0UU** **shetland@churchofscotland.org.uk**	**01595 881184**

Burra Isle linked with Tingwall
Deborah J. Dobby (Mrs)
BA BD PGCE RGN RSCN   2014   25 Hogalee, East Voe, Scalloway, Shetland ZE1 0UU   01595 881184
DDobby@churchofscotland.org.uk

Delting linked with Northmavine
Vacant   The Manse, Grindwell, Brae, Shetland ZE2 9QJ   01806 522219
Session Clerk, Delting: Isobel Morrice (Ms)   isobelmorrice@btinternet.com

Dunrossness and St Ninian's inc. Fair Isle linked with Sandwick, Cunningsburgh and Quarff
Vacant   Compass House, Stove, Sandwick, Shetland ZE1 9HH   01595 431575
Session Clerk, Sandwick, Cunningsburgh and
Quarff: Dennis Buddle

Lerwick and Bressay
Vacant   The Manse, 82 St Olaf Street, Lerwick, Shetland ZE1 0ES   01595 692125
Session Clerk: James Halcrow   jim.halcrow@btinternet.com   01595 693024

Nesting and Lunnasting linked with Whalsay and Skerries
Irene A. Charlton (Mrs) BTh   1994   1997   The Manse, Marrister, Symbister, Whalsay, Shetland ZE2 9AE   01806 566767
ICharlton@churchofscotland.org.uk

Northmavine See Delting

Sandsting and Aithsting linked with Walls and Sandness
D. Brian Dobby MA BA   1999   2014   The Manse, 25 Hogalee, East Voe, Scalloway, Shetland ZE1 0UU   01595 881184
BDobby@churchofscotland.org.uk

Sandwick, Cunningsburgh and Quarff See Dunrossness and St Ninian's
Tingwall See Burra Isle

Unst and Fetlar linked with Yell
Vacant
Session Clerk, Yell: Will John Anderson — North Isles Manse, Gutcher, Yell, Shetland ZE2 9DF
willjohnanderson@gmail.com
01957 744258
01957 722231
07766 445487

Walls and Sandness See Sandsting and Aithsting
Whalsay and Skerries See Nesting and Lunnasting
Yell See Unst and Fetlar

Name			Charge / Note	Address	Tel
Greig, Charles H.M. MA BD	1976	2016	(Dunrossness and St Ninian's inc. Fair Isle with Sandwick, Cunningsburgh and Quarff)	6 Hayhoull Place, Bigton, Shetland ZE2 9GA chm.greig@btinternet.com	01950 422468
Kirkpatrick, Alice H. (Miss) MA BD FSAScot	1987	2000	(Northmavine)	1 Daisy Park, Baltasound, Unst, Shetland ZE2 9EA	
Knox, R. Alan MA LTh AInstAM	1965	2004	(Fetlar with Unst with Yell)	27 Killyvalley Road, Garvagh, Co. Londonderry, Northern Ireland BT51 5LX caroline.lockerbie@btinternet.com	02829 558925
Lockerbie, Caroline R. BA MDiv DMin	1978	2017	(Lerwick and Bressay: Transition Minister)		
Macintyre, Thomas MA BD	1972	2011	(Sandsting and Aithsting with Walls and Sandness)	Lappideks, South Voxter, Cunningsburgh, Shetland ZE2 9HF the2macs.macintyre@btinternet.com	01950 477549
Murray, B. Ian BD	2002	2018	Interim Minister, Shetland	Kilmorie House, 6 Institution Road, Elgin IV30 1RP BMurray@churchofscotland.org.uk	01343 546265
Smith, Catherine (Mrs) DCS	1964	2003	(Deacon)	21 Lingaro, Bixter, Shetland ZE2 9NN	01595 810207
Williamson, Magnus J.C.	1982	1999	(Fetlar with Yell)	Creekhaven, Houl Road, Scalloway, Shetland ZE1 0XA	01595 880023

(47) ENGLAND

Meets at London, in Crown Court Church, on the second Tuesday of February, and at St Columba's, Pont Street, on the second Tuesday of June and the second Saturday of October.

Clerk: REV. ALISTAIR CUMMING MSc CCS FInstLM — 64 Prince George's Avenue, London SW20 8BH — **england@churchofscotland.org.uk** — 07534 943986

Corby: St Andrew's (H)
A. Norman Nicoll BD   2003   2016   43 Hempland Close, Corby, Northants NN18 8LR — NNicoll@churchofscotland.org.uk — 07930 988863

Corby: St Ninian's (H)

Kleber Machado BTh MA MTh | 1998 | 2012 | The Manse, 46 Glyndebourne Gardens, Corby, Northants NN18 0PZ | **01536 265245**
KMachado@churchofscotland.org.uk | | | | 01536 669478

Guernsey: St Andrew's in the Grange (H)

Vacant | The Manse, Le Villocq, Castel, Guernsey GY5 7SB | 01481 257345

Jersey: St Columba's (H)

Graeme M. Glover BD | 2017 | 18 Claremont Avenue, St Saviour, Jersey JE2 7SF | 01534 730659
GGlover@churchofscotland.org.uk

London: Crown Court (H)

Philip L. Majcher BD | 1982 | 2007 | 53 Sidmouth Street, London WC1H 8IX | **020 7836 5643**
PMajcher@churchofscotland.org.uk | | | | 020 7278 5022

London: St Columba's (H) (020 7584 2321) linked with Newcastle: St Andrew's (H)

C. Angus MacLeod MA BD | 1996 | 2012 | 29 Hollywood Road, Chelsea, London SW10 9HT | Office | 020 7584 2321
Angus.MacLeod@churchofscotland.org.uk

Andrea E. Price (Mrs) | 1997 | 2014 | St Columba's, Pont Street, London SW1X 0BD | Home | 020 7610 6994
(Associate Minister) | APrice@churchofscotland.org.uk | | | | Office | 020 7584 2321

Anderson, Andrew F. MA BD	1981	2011	(Edinburgh: Greenside)	58 Reliance Way, Oxford OX4 2FG andrew.relianceway@gmail.com	01865 778397
Anderson, David P. BSc BD	2002	2007	Army Chaplain	padre.anderson180@mod.gov.uk	07590 507917
Binks, Mike	2007		Auxiliary Minister	Hollybank, 10 Kingsbrook, Corby NN18 9HY MBinks@churchofscotland.org.uk	
Cairns, W. Alexander BD	1978	2006	(Corby: St Andrew's)	Kirkton House, Kirkton of Craig, Montrose DD10 9TB sandy.cairns@btinternet.com	07808 588045
Cameron, R. Neil	1975	1981	(Chaplain: Community)	neilandminacameron@yahoo.co.uk	
Coulter, David G. CB OStJ QHC BA BD MDA PhD CF	1989	1994	Chaplain General, HM Land Forces	8 Ashdown Terrace, Tidworth, Wilts SP9 7SQ padredgcoulter@yahoo.co.uk	01980 842175
Cumming, Alistair MSc CCS FInstLM	2010	2013	Presbytery Clerk: Auxiliary Minister	64 Prince George's Avenue, London SW20 8BH ACumming@churchofscotland.org.uk	020 8540 7365 07534 943986
Francis, James MBE BD PhD	2002	2009	Army Chaplain	37 Millburn Road, Coleraine BT52 1QT	02870 353869
Lancaster, Craig MA BD	2004	2011	RAF Chaplain	52 Suffolk Avenue, RAF Honington, Bury St Edmunds IP31 1LW craig.lancaster102@mod.gov.uk	
Langlands, Cameron H. BD MTh ThM PhD MInstLM	1995	2012	Chaplain South London and Maudsley NHS Foundation Trust	Maudsley Hospital, Denmark Road, London SE5 8EZ	07989 642544
Lovett, Mairi F. BSc BA DipPS MTh	2005	2013	Hospital Chaplain	Royal Brompton Hospital, Sydney Street, London SW3 6NP m.lovett@rbht.nhs.uk	020 7352 8121 ext. 4736

Name	Years	Position	Address	Telephone
Lunn, Dorothy I.M.	2002 2017	(Auxiliary Minister)	14 Bellerby Drive, Ouston, Co.Durham DH2 1TW / dorothylunn@hotmail.com	0191 492 0647
Macfarlane, Peter T. BA LTh	1970 1994	(Chaplain: Army)	4 rue de Rives, 37160 Abilly, France	0141 579 1366
McIndoe, John H. MA BD STM DD	1966 2000	(London: St Columba's with Newcastle: St Andrew's)	5 Dunlin, Westerlands Park, Glasgow G12 0FE / johnandrev@mcindoe555.fsnet.co.uk	
MacLeod, Rory N. BA BD	1986 1992	Chaplain: Army	154 Regt RLC, Bothwell House, Elgin Street, Dunfermline KY12 7SB	01344 754098
McMahon, John K.S. MA BD	1998 2012	Head of Spiritual and Pastoral Care, West London Mental Health Trust	Broadmoor Hospital, Crowthorne, Berkshire RG45 7EG / john.mcmahonrev@wlmht.nhs.uk	
Mather, James BA DipArch MA MBA	2010	Auxiliary Minister: University Chaplain	24 Ellison Road, Barnes, London SW13 0AD / JMather@churchofscotland.org.uk	Home 020 8876 6540 / Work 020 7361 1670 / Mbl 07836 715655
Middleton, Paul (Prof) BMus BD ThM PhD	2000 2017	Biblical Studies, University of Chester	97B Whipcord Lane, Chester CH1 4DG	01704 543044
Munro, Alexander W. MA BD	1978	Chaplain and Teacher of Religious Studies	Columba House, 12 Alexandra Road, Southport PR9 0NB / revdj@gmail.com	020 8870 0953
Thom, David J. BD DipMin	1999 2015	Army Chaplain	Flat 5, 18 Northside Wandsworth Common, London SW18 2SL / revrfw@gmail.com	
Walker, R. Forbes BSc BD ThM	1987 2013	School Chaplain		
Wallace, Donald S.	1950 1980	(Chaplain: RAF)	7 Dellfield Close, Watford, Herts WD1 3BL	01923 223289
Ward, Michael J. BSc BD PhD MA PGCE	1983 2009	Training and Development Officer: Presbyterian Church of Wales	Apt 6, Bryn Hedd, Conwy Road, Penmaen-mawr, Gwynedd LL34 6BS / revmw@btopenworld.com	07765 598816
Wood, Peter J. MA BD	1993	(College Lecturer)	97 Broad Street, Cambourne, Cambridgeshire CB23 6DH / pejowood@tiscali.co.uk	01954 715558

ENGLAND – Church Addresses

Corby: St Andrew's	Occupation Road
Corby: St Ninian's	Beanfield Avenue
Guernsey:	The Grange, St Peter Port
Newcastle:	Sandyford Road
Jersey:	Midvale Road, St Helier
London: Crown Court	Crown Court WC2
London: St Columba's	Pont Street SW1

(48) PRESBYTERY OF INTERNATIONAL CHARGES

Meets over the weekend of the second Sunday of March and October, hosted by congregations in mainland Europe.

Clerk: REV. JAMES SHARP

102 Rue des Eaux-Vives, CH-1207 Geneva, Switzerland   0041 22 786 4847
clerk@internationalpresbytery.net
www.internationalpresbytery.net

Depute Clerk: REV. DEREK G. LAWSON

Schiedamse Vest 121, 3012BH, Rotterdam, The Netherlands   0031 10 412 5709
deputeclerk@internationalpresbytery.net

Amsterdam: English Reformed Church
Lance Stone BD MTh PhD
1980   2014
Jan Willem Brouwersstraat 9, NL-1071 LH Amsterdam, The Netherlands
minister@ercadam.nl
Church address: Begijnhof 48, 1012WV Amsterdam
0031 20 672 2288

Bermuda: Christ Church, Warwick (H)
Alistair G. Bennett BSc BD
1978   2016
The Manse, 6 Manse Road, Paget PG 01, Bermuda
Church address: Christ Church, Middle Road, Warwick, Bermuda
Mailing address: PO Box WK 130, Warwick WK BX, Bermuda
christchurch@logic.bm; www.christchurch.bm
001 441 236 1882
001 441 236 0400

Bochum (Associated congregation)
James M. Brown MA BD
1982
Neustrasse 15, D-44787 Bochum, Germany
j.brown56@gmx.de
Church address: Pauluskirche, Grabenstrasse 9, 44787 Bochum
0049 234 133 65

Brussels St Andrew's (H)
Andrew Gardner BSc BD PhD
1997   2004
23 Square des Nations, B-1000 Brussels, Belgium
minister@churchofscotland.be
Church address: Chaussée de Vieurgat 181, 1050 Brussels
secretary@churchofscotland.be
0032 2 649 02 19
0032 2 672 40 56

Budapest St Columba's
Aaron C. Stevens BA MDiv MACE
2006
Stefánia út 32, H-1143, Budapest, Hungary
revastevens@yahoo.co.uk
Church address: Vörösmarty utca 51, 1064 Budapest
0036 1 373 0725
0036 70 615 5394

Colombo, Sri Lanka: St Andrew's Scots Kirk
Vacant
73 Galle Road, Colpetty, Colombo 3, Sri Lanka
minister@standrewsscotskirk.org
chandan59@yahoo.com
0094 112 323 765
0094 112 386 774

Session Clerk: Chandan de Silva
0094 11 258 8687

Costa del Sol
Guardianship of the Presbytery
Avenida Jesus Santos Rein, 24 Edf. Lindamar 4 – 3Q, Fuengirola, 29640 Malaga, Spain
Church address: Lux Mundi Ecumenical Centre, Calle Nueva 3, 29460 Fuengirola
lillias@hotmail.com
0034 951 260 982

Session Clerk: Lillias Macfarlane
0034 951 273 333

Geneva Laurence H. Twaddle MA BD MTh	1977	2017	6 chemin Taverney, 1218 Geneva, Switzerland cofsg@pingnet.ch Church address: Auditoire de Calvin, 1 Place de la Tacomerie, Geneva	**0041 22 788 08 31** 0041 22 788 08 31
Gibraltar St Andrew's Ewen MacLean BA BD	1995	2009	St Andrew's Manse, 29 Scud Hill, Gibraltar scotskirk@gibraltar.gi Church address: Governor's Parade, Gibraltar	00350 200 77040
Lausanne: The Scots Kirk (H) Vacant			26 Avenue de Rumine, CH-1005 Lausanne, Switzerland minister@scotskirklausanne.ch	0041 21 323 98 28
Session Clerk: Janet Shaner			shaner.janet@gmail.com	
Lisbon St Andrew's Guardianship of the Presbytery			Rua Coelho da Rocha, N°75 - 1° Campa de Ourique, 1350-073 Lisbon, Portugal cofslx@netcabo.pt Church address: Rua da Arriaga, Lisbon	00351 213 951 165
Session Clerk: Nina O'Donnell			sessionclerklisbon@gmail.com	00351 21 483 8750
Malta St Andrew's Scots Church (H) Kim Hurst	2000	2014	La Romagnola, 15 Triq is-Seiqia, Misrah Kola, Attard ATD 1713, Malta minister@saintandrewsmalta.com Church address: 210 Old Bakery Street, Valletta, Malta	Tel/Fax 00356 214 15465
Paris: The Scots Kirk Jan J. Steyn	2011	2017	10 Rue Thimmonier, F-75009 Paris, France Church address: 17 Rue Bayard, 75009 Paris JSteyn@churchofscotland.org.uk	0033 1 48 78 47 94
Rome: St Andrew's Vacant			Via XX Settembre 7, 00187 Rome, Italy	Tel 0039 06 482 7627 Fax 0039 06 487 4370
Session Clerk: Inge Weustink			iweustink@hotmail.com	0039 320 478 3246

Rotterdam: Scots International Church

Derek G. Lawson LLB BD	1998	2016	Schiedamse Vest 121, 3012BH Rotterdam, The Netherlands	**0031 10 412 4779**
			DLawson@churchofscotland.org.uk	
			Church address: Schiedamsesingel 2, Rotterdam, The Netherlands	0031 10 412 5709
			info@scotsintchurch.com	

Trinidad: Greyfriars St Ann's, Port of Spain l/w Arouca and Sangre Grande

Vacant			50 Frederick Street, Port of Spain, Trinidad	001 868 623 6684
Interim Moderator: Rev Aaron Stevens, Budapest				

Name			Position	Address	Telephone
Bom, Irene	2008		Ordained Local Minister-Worship and Prayer Promoter	Bergpolderstraat 53A, NL-3038 KB Rotterdam, The Netherlands ibsalem@xs4all.nl	0031 10 265 1703
Evans-Boiten, Joanne H.G. BD	2004	2018	Retreat Centre Director	Colomba le Roc, 510 Chemin du Faurat, Belmontet, 46800 Montecuq, France Joanne.evansboiten@gmail.com	0033 5 65 22 13 11
Foggitt, Eric W. MA BSc BD	1991	2009	(Dunbar)	Christiaan de Wet Straat 19/2, 1091 NG Amsterdam, Netherlands ericleric3@btinternet.com	07981 294 326
Herbold Ross, Kristina M.	2008	2018	(Work Place Chaplain)	8 El-Abaseya, Al Izab, Al Waili, Cairo 11381, Egypt	07702 863342
Johnston, Colin D. MA BD	1986	2016	Evangelical Theological Seminary Cairo		00 200 100 955 7809
McGeoch, Graham G. MA BD MTh	2009	2017	Lecturer	Faculdade Unida de Vitoria, R.Eng. Fabio Ruschi, 161 Bento Ferreira, Vitoria ES 29050-670, Brazil	
Pitkeathly, Thomas C. MA CA BD	1984	2004	(Brussels)	77 St Thomas Road, Lytham St. Anne's FY8 1JP tpitkeathly@yahoo.co.uk	01253 789634
Reamonn, Paraic BA BD	1982	2018	(Jerusalem: St Andrew's)	395B Route de Mandement, 1281 Ruissin, Switzerland	0041 22 776 4834
Ross, Matthew Z. LLB BD MTh FSAScot	1998	2018	Programme Executive for Diakonia and Capacity Building, World Council of Churches	World Council of Churches, Route de Ferney 150, Case Postale 2100, CH-1211 Geneva 2, Switzerland Matthew.Ross@wcc-coc.org	
Sharp, James	2005	2013	Ordained Local Minister, Presbytery Clerk	102 Rue des Eaux-Vives, 1207 Geneva, Switzerland jim.sharp@churchofscotland.org.uk	0041 22 786 4847

(49) JERUSALEM

Clerk:	JOANNA OAKLEY-LEVSTEIN		St Andrew's, Galilee, PO Box 104, Tiberias 14100, Israel j-oak.lev@gmail.com	00972 50 5842517

Jerusalem: St Andrew's and Tiberias: St Andrew's (tiberias@churchofscotland.org.uk; https://standrewsgalilee.com)

John McCulloch BA BA (Theol) PhD	2018		St Andrew's Scots Memorial Church, 1 David Remez Street, PO Box 8619, Jerusalem 91086, Israel JMcCulloch@churchofscotland.org.uk	00972 2 673 2401
Katharine S. McDonald BA MSc BD MLitt (Associate Minister) (Scottish Episcopal Church)	2012	2015	St Andrew's, Galilee, 1 Gdud Barak Street, PO Box 104, Tiberias 14100, Israel kmcdonald@churchofscotland.org.uk	00972 4 671 0759

SECTION 6

Additional Lists of Personnel

LIST A – ORDAINED LOCAL MINISTERS

Those engaged in active service. Where only one date is given it is the year of ordination and appointment. Contact details may be found under the Presbytery in Section 5 to which an OLM belongs.

NAME	ORD	APP	APPOINTMENT	PRESBYTERY
Allardice, Michael MA MPhil PGCertTHE FHEA	2014	—	—	25 Kirkcaldy
Archer, Morven (Mrs)	2013	2018	Inverness: Crown	37 Inverness
Bellis, Pamela A. BA	2014	2014	Inch linked with Portpatrick linked with Stranraer: Trinity	9 Wigtown and Stranraer
Bissett, James	2016		Contin linked with Fodderty and Strathpeffer	39 Ross
Bom, Irene	2008		Worship Resourcing	48 International Charges
Breingan, Mhairi	2011	—	—	14 Greenock and Paisley
Brodie, Catherine J. MA BA MPhil PGCE	2017		Dundee: Fintry	29 Dundee
Brown, Kathryn I. (Mrs)	2014		Falkirk: Trinity	22 Falkirk
Crossan, Morag BA	2016		Dalmellington linked with Patna Waterside	10 Ayr
Crossan, William	2014	—	—	19 Argyll
Dee, Oonagh	2014	2016	Castle Douglas linked with The Bengairn Parishes	8 Dumfries and Kirkcudbright
Dempster, Eric T. MBA	2016	2018	Lockerbie: Dryfesdale, Hutton and Corrie	7 Annandale and Eskdale
Don, Andrew MBA	2006	2013	Newton	3 Lothian
Finnie, Bill H. BA PgDipSW CertCRS	2015		Kirkintilloch: Hillhead	16 Glasgow
Forsythe, Ruth (Mrs) MCS	2017		Glasgow: Broomhill Hyndland	16 Glasgow
Freeth, June BA MA	2015	—	—	45 Orkney
Fulcher, Christine P. BEd	2012	2014	Kilmore and Oban	19 Argyll
Geddes, Elizabeth (Mrs)	2013	2017	Langbank linked with Port Glasgow: St Andrew's	14 Greenock and Paisley
Gray, Ian	2013	2017	Monrose: Old and St Andrew's	30 Angus
Grieve, Leslie E.T.	2014		Glasgow: Colston Wellpark	16 Glasgow
Hardman Moore, Susan (Prof.) MA MAR PhD	2013		New College, University of Edinburgh	1 Edinburgh
Harrison, Frederick	2013	2016	Newbattle	3 Lothian
Harvey, Joyce (Mrs)	2013	2017	Kirkinner linked with Mochrum linked with Sorbie	9 Wigtown and Stranraer
Henderson, Derek R.	2017		Abercorn linked with Pardovan, Kingscavil and Winchburgh	2 West Lothian
Hickman, Mandy R. RGN	2013	2014	West Kilbride	12 Ardrossan
Hogg, James	2018		Troon: St Meddan's	10 Ayr
Hughes, Barry MA	2011	—	—	4 Melrose and Peebles
Hunt, Roland BSc PhD CertEd	2016		Glasgow: Carmyle linked with Glasgow: Mount Vernon	16 Glasgow
Irvine, Carl J. BA	2017		Presbytery-wide	33 Gordon
Johnston, June E. BSc MEd BD	2013	—	—	3 Lothian
Livingstone, Alan	2013		Scone and St Martins	28 Perth
McCutcheon, John	2014	—	—	18 Dumbarton

Name	Year	Congregation	Presbytery
Macdonald, Ishabel	2011	Benbecula linked with Carinish	43 Uist
MacDonald, Monica (Mrs)	2014	Slamannan	22 Falkirk
Mack, Lynne (Mrs)	2013 / 2014	Gargunnock linked with Kilmadock linked with Kincardine-in-Menteith	23 Stirling
McKenzie, Janet R. (Mrs)	2016	Edinburgh: The Tron Kirk (Gilmerton and Moredun)	1 Edinburgh
MacLeod, Iain A.	2012	Presbytery-wide	16 Glasgow
McLeod, Tom	2014	Craigie Symington linked with Prestwick: South	10 Ayr
Maxwell, David	2014	Cambuslang	16 Glasgow
Michie, Margaret (Mrs)	2013	Loch Leven Parish Grouping	28 Perth
Morrison, John A. BSc BA PGCE	2013	Dallas linked with Forres: St Leonard's linked with Rafford	35 Moray
Muirhead, Morag Y. (Mrs)	2014	Fort William: Duncansburgh MacIntosh linked with Kilmonivaig	38 Lochaber
Murphy, Jim	2013	East Kilbride: Mossneuk	17 Hamilton
Nicol, Robert D.	2013	—	27 Dunkeld and Meigle
Nutter, Margaret A.E.	2014	Clydebank: Waterfront linked with Dalmuir: Barclay	18 Dumbarton
Palmer, Sonia RGN	2017	Elgin: St Giles' and St Columba's South	35 Moray
Porteous, Brian	2018	Kirkcaldy: Torbain	25 Kirkcaldy
Prentice, Martin W.M.	2013	—	45 Orkney
Rattenbury, Carol	2017	Rosskeen	39 Ross
Rennie, Lyall	2014	Pentland	41 Caithness
Sarle, Andrew BSc BD	2013	Falkirk: Bainsford	22 Falkirk
Sharp, James	2005	Presbytery Clerk, International Charges	48 International Charges
Somevi, Joseph K. BSc MSc PhD MRICS MRTPI MIEMA CertCRS	2015	Aberdeen: Bridge of Don Oldmachar	31 Aberdeen
Steele, Grace M.F. MA BTh	2014	Paisley: St Ninian's Ferguslie	14 Greenock and Paisley
Stevenson, Stuart	2011	Latheron	41 Caithness
Stewart, Heather (Mrs)	2013	New Pitsligo linked with Strichen and Tyrie	34 Buchan
Stewart, William	2015	Community Healthcare Chaplain	40 Sutherland
Stobo, Mary J. (Mrs)	2013	Eddleston linked with Peebles: Old	4 Melrose and Peebles
Strachan, Pamela D. (Lady) MA (Cantab)	2015	Dundee: Lochee	29 Dundee
Strachan, Willie MBA DipY&C	2013	Glasgow: Baillieston Mure Memorial linked with Glasgow: Baillieston St Andrew's	16 Glasgow
Stuart, Alex P.	2014	Glasgow: Kelvinside Hillhead linked with Glasgow: Wellington	16 Glasgow
Sturrock, Roger D. (Prof.) BD MD FCRP	2014	Presbytery Chaplain to Care Homes	16 Glasgow
Thomson, Mary Ellen (Mrs)	2013	—	36 Abernethy
Thorburn, Susan (Mrs) MTh	2014	Falkland linked with Freuchie	26 St Andrews
Trewren, Norman	2018	Mearns Coastal	32 Kincardine and Deeside
Tweedie, Fiona J. BSc PhD	2011	Mission Statistics Co-ordinator, Church Offices	1 Edinburgh
Wallace, Mhairi (Mrs)	2013	Kirkmichael, Tinwald and Torthorwald	8 Dumfries and Galloway
Watson, Michael D.	2013	Musselburgh: St Andrew's High	3 Lothian
Watt, Kim	2015	Presbytery-wide	11 Irvine and Kilmarnock
Welsh, Rita M. BA PhD	2017	Edinburgh: Holy Trinity	1 Edinburgh
White, Ann BA DipTh	2018	Falkirk: Grahamston United	22 Falkirk

ORDAINED LOCAL MINISTERS (Retired)

Those who are retired and registered under the Registration of Ministries Act (Act 2, 2017, as amended) as 'O' or 'R' (Retaining). There are presently no OLMs registered as 'I'(Inactive). Contact details may be found under the Presbytery in Section 5 to which an OLM belongs.

NAME	ORD	RET	PRESBYTERY
Anderson, David M. MSc FCOptom	1984	2018	38 Lochaber
Duncan, Esme (Miss)	2013	2017	41 Caithness
Duncanson, Mary (Ms) BTh	2013	2017	36 Abernethy
Edwards, Dougal BTh	2013	2017	30 Angus
Kiehlmann, Peter BA (Dr)	2016	2018	47 England
Mathers, Alexena (Sandra)	2015	2018	22 Falkirk
McAllister, Anne C. (Mrs) BSc DipEd CCS	2013	2016	11 Irvine and Kilmarnock
McLaughlin, Cathie H. (Mrs)	2014	2018	16 Glasgow
Robertson, Ishbel A.R. MA BD	2013	2018	18 Dumbarton

LIST B – AUXILIARY MINISTERS

Those engaged in active service. Contact details may be found under the Presbytery in Section 5 to which an Auxiliary Minister belongs.

NAME	ORD	APP	APPOINTMENT	PRESBYTERY
Binks, Mike	2007	—	—	47 England
Buck, Maxine	2007	2015	Presbytery-wide	17 Hamilton
Cameron, Ann J. (Mrs) CertCS DCE TEFL	2005	2017	Craigrownie linked with Garelochhead linked with Rosneath St. Modan's	18 Dumbarton
Campbell, Gordon A. MA BD CDipAF DipHSM CMgr MCMI MIHM AssocCIPD AFRIN ARSGS FRGS FSAScot	2001	2004	An Honorary Chaplain, University of Dundee	29 Dundee
Cumming, Alistair MSc CCS FInstLM	2010	2013	Presbytery Clerk; England	47 England
Fletcher, Timothy E.G. BA FCMA	1998	2014	Perth: Kinnoull	28 Perth
Gardner, Hilary M. (Miss)	2010	2018	Lairg linked with Rogart	40 Sutherland
Griffiths, Ruth I. (Mrs)	2004		Dunoon: The High Kirk linked with Innellan linked with Toward	19 Argyll
Hood, Catriona A.	2006	2018	South Argyll	19 Argyll
Howie, Marion L.K. (Mrs) MA ARCS	1992	2016	Dalry: St Margaret's	12 Ardrossan
Jackson, Nancy	2009	—	—	10 Ayr

NAME	ORD	RET	PRESBYTERY	
Kemp, Tina MA	2005	2017	Helensburgh linked with Rhu and Shandon	18 Dumbarton
Macdonald, Michael	2004	2014	Alness	39 Ross
Mack, Elizabeth A. (Miss) DipPEd	1994	2018	Lochend and New Abbey	8 Dumfries and Kirkcudbright
Manson, Eileen (Mrs) DipCE	1994	2014	Greenock: Lyle Kirk	14 Greenock and Paisley
Mather, James BA DipArch MA MBA	2010	—	University Chaplain	47 England
Moore, Douglas T.	2003	2015	Coylton linked with Drongan: The Schaw Kirk	10 Ayr
Morrison, Donald John	2001	—	—	43 Uist
Paterson, Andrew E. JP	1994	2016	Presbytery-wide	24 Dunfermline
Perry, Marion (Mrs)	2009	2017	Blackbraes and Shieldhill linked with Muiravonside	22 Falkirk
Riddell, Thomas S. BSc CEng FIChemE	1993	1994	Linlithgow: St Michael's	2 West Lothian
Robson, Brenda PhD	2005	2014	Kirknewton and East Calder	2 West Lothian
Shearer, Anne F. BA DipEd	2004	—	Logie	23 Stirling
Vivers, Katherine A.	2008	2014	—	7 Annandale and Eskdale
Walker, Linda	1993	2017	Presbytery-wide	16 Glasgow
Wandrum, David C.	2011	—	Carriden	22 Falkirk
Whittaker, Mary	2011	2012	Aberdeen: St John's Church for Deaf People	31 Aberdeen
Wilkie, Robert F.	2011	2012	Perth: Craigie and Moncrieffe	28 Perth

AUXILIARY MINISTERS (Retired)

Those who are retired and registered under the Registration of Ministries Act (Act 2, 2017, as amended) as 'O', 'R' (Retaining) or 'I' (Inactive). Only those 'Inactive' Auxiliary Ministers who have given consent under the GDPR to publication of their details are included. Contact details may be found under the Presbytery in Section 5 to which an Auxiliary Minister belongs.

NAME	ORD	RET	PRESBYTERY	
Attenburrow, Anne BSc MB ChB	2006	2018	35	Moray
Birch, James PgDip FRSA FIOC	2001	2007	16	Glasgow
Brown, Elizabeth (Mrs) JP RGN	1996	2007	28	Perth
Cloggie, June (Mrs)	1997	2006	23	Stirling
Craggs, Sheila (Mrs)	2001	2016	33	Gordon
Harrison, Cameron	2006	2011	26	St Andrews
Kay, Elizabeth (Miss) DipYCS	1993	2007	29	Dundee
Landale, William S.	2005	2016	5	Duns
Lunn, Dorothy I. M.	2002	2017	47	England
McAlpine, John BSc	1988	2004	17	Hamilton
MacDonald, Kenneth BA MA	2001	2006	16	Glasgow
MacFadyen, Anne M. (Mrs) BSc BD FSAScot	1995	2003	16	Glasgow
Mack, John C. JP	1985	2008	33	Gordon

Mailer, Colin M.	1996	2005	22 Falkirk (not member of Presbytery) 25 Saltcoats Drive, Grangemouth FK3 9JP 01324 712401
Paterson, Maureen (Mrs) BSc	1992	2010	25 Kirkcaldy
Phillippo, Michael MTh BSc BVetMed MRCVS	2003	2011	31 Aberdeen
Pot, Joost BSc	1992	2004	48 International Charges (not member of Presbytery) joostpot@gmail.com
Ramage, Alastair E. MA BA ADB CertEd	1996	2016	18 Dumbarton
Shaw, Catherine A.M. MA	1998	2006	11 Irvine and Kilmarnock
Thomas, Shirley A. (Mrs) DipSocSci AMIA	2000	2006	30 Angus
Wilson, Mary D. (Mrs) RGN SCM DTM	1990	2004	27 Dunkeld and Meigle
Zambonini, James LIADip	1997	2015	17 Hamilton

LIST C – THE DIACONATE

Those engaged in active service. Contact details may be found under the Presbytery in Section 5 to which a Deacon belongs.

Prior to the General Assembly of 2002, Deacons were commissioned. In 2002 existing Deacons were ordained, as have been those subsequently.

NAME	ORD	APP	APPOINTMENT	PRESBYTERY
Beck, Isobel BD DCS	2014	2016	Kilwinning: Old	12 Ardrossan
Blair, Fiona (Miss) DCS	1994	2015	Ardrossan and Saltcoats: Kirkgate	12 Ardrossan
Buchanan, Marion (Mrs) MA DCS	1983	2006	Glasgow: Garthamlock and Craigend East; Glasgow: Ruchazie	16 Glasgow
Brydson, Angela (Mrs) DCS	2015	2014	Lochmaben, Moffat and Lockerbie Grouping	7 Annandale and Eskdale
Cathcart, John Paul (Mr) DCS	2000	2017	Glasgow: Castlemilk	16 Glasgow
Corrie, Margaret (Miss) DCS	1989	2013	Armadale	2 West Lothian
Crawford, Morag (Miss) MSc DCS	1977	1998	Rosyth	24 Dunfermline
Crocker, Liz (Mrs) DipComEd DCS	1985	2015	Edinburgh: The Tron Kirk (Gilmerton and Moredun)	1 Edinburgh
Cuthbertson, Valerie (Miss) DipTMus DCS	2003		Cumbernauld: Old	22 Falkirk
Evans, Mark (Mr) BSc MSc DCS	1988	2006	Head of Spiritual Care and Bereavement Lead, NHS Fife	1 Edinburgh
Gargrave, Mary S. (Mrs) DCS	1989	2002	Glasgow: Carnwadric	16 Glasgow
Getliffe, Dot (Mrs) BA BD DipEd DCS	2006	—	136 Ardness Place, Lochardil, Inverness IV2 4QY DGetliffe@churchofscotland.org.uk	37 Inverness
Hamilton, James (Mr) DCS	1997	2000	Glasgow: Maryhill	16 Glasgow
Hamilton, Karen M. (Mrs) DCS	1995	2014	Glasgow: Cambuslang	16 Glasgow
Love, Joanna (Ms) BSc DCS	1992	2009	Iona Community: Wild Goose Resource Group	16 Glasgow
Lyall, Ann (Miss) DCS	1980	2017	Interim Deacon, Avonbridge linked with Torphichen	2 West Lothian
MacDonald, Anne (Mrs) BA DCS	1980	2002	Healthcare Chaplain, Glasgow Royal Infirmary	16 Glasgow
McIntosh, Kay (Mrs) DCS	1990	2018	Edinburgh: Mayfield Salisbury	1 Edinburgh

Name				Presbytery
Mackay, Kenneth D. (Mr) DCS	1996	1998	Perth: Letham St Mark's	28 Perth
McLaren, Glenda M. (Mrs) DCS	1990	2006	Dunoon: St John's linked with Kirn and Sandbank	19 Argyll
McLellan, Margaret DCS	1986	2014	Glasgow: Merrylea	16 Glasgow
McPheat, Elspeth (Miss) DCS	1985	2001	CrossReach: Manager, St Margaret's House, Polmont	1 Edinburgh
Nicholson, David (Mr) DCS	1994	1993	Cumbernauld: Kildrum	22 Falkirk
Pennykid, Gordon J. BD DCS	2015		Livingston: Old	2 West Lothian
Philip, Elizabeth (Mrs) MA BA BA PGCSE DCS	2007		——	28 Perth
Porter, Jean T. (Mrs) BD DCS	2006	2008	Stirling: St Mark's	23 Stirling
Robertson, Pauline (Mrs) BA Cert'Theol DCS	2003	2016	Port Chaplain, Sailors' Society	1 Edinburgh
Scott, Pamela (Mrs) DCS	2017	2017	Lochgelly and Benarty: St Serf's	24 Dunfermline
Stewart, Marion G. (Miss) DCS	1991	1994	Skene	33 Gordon
Thomson, Jacqueline (Mrs) MTh DCS	2004	2008	Buckhaven and Wemyss	25 Kirkcaldy
Wallace, Catherine (Mrs) PGDipC DCS	1987	2017	Honorary Secretary, Diaconate Council	28 Perth
Wright, Lynda (Miss) BEd DCS	1979	2016	Community Chaplaincy Listening Co-ordinator, NHS Fife	25 Kirkcaldy

THE DIACONATE (Registered as Retaining or Inactive)

Those who are retired and registered under the Registration of Ministries Act (Act 2, 2017, as amended) as 'Retaining' or 'Inactive.' Only those 'Inactive' Deacons who have given consent under the GDPR to publication of their details are included. Contact details may be found under the Presbytery in Section 5 to which a Deacon belongs. Where a retired Deacon does not have a seat on Presbytery, contact details are given here. The list is shorter than in previous years, as some have not registered under the new arrangements.

NAME	COM/ORD	RET	PRESBYTERY
Allan, Jean (Mrs) DCS	1989	2011	29 Dundee
Anderson, Janet (Miss) DCS	1979	2012	42 Lochcarron-Skye
Beaton, Margaret S. (Miss) DCS	1989	2015	16 Glasgow
Buchanan, John (Mr) DCS	1988		3 Lothian
Craw, John (Mr) DCS	1998	2009	37 Inverness
Drummond, Rhoda (Miss) DCS	1960	1987	1 Edinburgh
Dunnett, Linda (Mrs) BA DCS	1976	2016	23 Stirling
Gordon, Margaret (Mrs) DCS	1998	2012	1 Edinburgh
Gray, Greta (Miss) DCS	1992	2014	14 Greenock and Paisley
Hughes, Helen (Miss) DCS	1977	2008	16 Glasgow
Johnston, Mary (Miss) DCS	1988	2003	14 Greenock and Paisley (not a member of Presbytery) 19 Lounsdale Drive, Paisley PA2 9ED 0141 849 1615
King, Margaret MA DCS	2002	2012	35 Moray
Lundie, Ann V. (Miss) DCS	1972	2007	31 Aberdeen

McCully, M. Isobel (Miss) DCS	1974	1999	14 Greenock and Paisley (not a member of Presbytery) 10 Broadstone Avenue, Port Glasgow PA14 5BB 01475 742240
MacKinnon, Ronald A. (Mr) DCS	1996	2012	12 Ardrossan
Maclean, Donald A. (Mr) DCS	1988	1990	44 Lewis
McNaughton, Janette (Miss) DCS	1982	2007	22 Falkirk (not a member of Presbytery) 4 Dunellan Avenue, Moodiesburn, Glasgow G69 0GB 01236 870180
McPherson, James B. (Mr) DCS	1988	2001	16 Glasgow
Martin, Janie (Miss) DCS	1979	2008	29 Dundee
Merrilees, Ann (Miss) DCS	1994	2006	2 West Lothian
Miller, Elsie M. (Miss) DCS	1974	2001	16 Glasgow
Mitchell, Joyce (Mrs) DCS	1994	2010	37 Inverness
Mulligan, Anne MA DCS	1974	2013	1 Edinburgh
Munro, Patricia BSc DCS	1986	2016	28 Perth
Nicol, Joyce (Mrs) BA DCS	1974	2006	14 Greenock and Paisley
Ogilvie, Colin (Mr) BA DCS	1998	2015	17 Hamilton (not a member of Presbytery) 21 Neilsland Drive, Motherwell ML1 3DZ 01698 321836; 07837 287804 colinogilvie2@gmail.com
Rennie, Agnes M. (Miss) DCS	1974	2012	1 Edinburgh
Rose, Lewis (Mr) DCS	1993	2010	29 Dundee
Ross, Duncan (Mr) DCS	1996	2015	14 Greenock and Paisley
Smith, Catherine (Mrs) DCS	1964	2003	46 Shetland
Steele, Marilynn J. (Mrs) BD DCS	1999	2012	3 Lothian
Steven, Gordon R. BD DCS	1997	2012	3 Lothian
Teague, Yvonne (Mrs) DCS	1965	2002	1 Edinburgh
Thomson, Phyllis (Miss) DCS	2003	2010	2 West Lothian
Trimble, Robert DCS	1988	1998	2 West Lothian
Urquhart, Barbara (Mrs) DCS	1986	2017	11 Irvine and Kilmarnock
Wallace, Sheila (Mrs) BA BD DCS	2009	2017	27 Dunkeld and Meigle
Wilson, Muriel (Miss) MA BD DCS	1997	2011	10 Ayr (not a member of Presbytery) 28 Bellevue Crescent, Ayr KA7 2DR 01292 264039 me.wilson28@btinternet.com

LIST D – MINISTERS NOT IN PRESBYTERIES REGISTERED AS RETAINING OR EMPLOYED

Those who are not members of a Presbytery but, under the Registration of Ministries Act (Act 2, 2017, as amended), are registered as 'Retaining' and authorised to perform the functions of ministry outwith an appointment covered by Category O or Category E. This list also includes a few ministers registered as 'Employed'(or 'O' for up to 3 years) who are not members of a Presbytery. The list is shorter than in previous years, as some have not registered under the new arrangements.

NAME	ORD	ADDRESS	TEL	PRES
Aitken, Ewan R. BA BD	1992	159 Restalrig Avenue, Edinburgh EH7 6PJ	0131 467 1660	1

Name	Year	Address / Email	Tel	No.
Alexander, James S. MA BD BA PhD	1966	5 Strathkinness High Road, St Andrews KY16 9RP	01334 472680	26
Anderson, David MA BD	1975	Rowan Cottage, Aberlour Gardens, Aberlour AB38 9LD maurvid@hotmail.com	01340 871906	35
Anderson, Susan M. (Mrs) BD	1997	32 Murrayfield, Bishopbriggs, Glasgow G64 3DS susanbbriggs32@gmail.com	0141 772 6338	16
Auld, A. Graeme (Prof.) MA BD PhD DLitt FSAScot FRSE	1973	Nether Swanshiel, Hobkirk, Bonchester Bridge, Hawick TD9 8JU a.g.auld@ed.ac.uk	01450 860636	6
Barclay, Neil W. BSc BEd BD	1986	4 Gibsongray Street, Falkirk FK2 7LN neil.barclay@virginmedia.com	01324 874681	22
Bardgett, Frank D. MA BD PhD	1987	Tigh an Iasgair, Street of Kincardine, Boat of Garten PH24 3BY iasgair1@icloud.com	01479 831751	36
Beattie, Warren R. BSc BD MSc PhD	1991	Director for Mission Research, OMF International, 2 Cluny Road, Singapore 259570 warren.beattie@omfmail.com	0065 6319 4550	1
Bradley, Andrew W. BD	1975	Flat 1/1, 38 Cairnhill View, Bearsden, Glasgow G61 1RP andrewwbradley@hotmail.com	0141 931 5344	16
Brown, R. Graeme BA BD	1961	Bring Deeps, Orphir, Orkney KW17 2LX graeme_sibyl@btinternet.com	01856 811707	45
Brown, Robert F. MA BD ThM	1971	55 Hilton Drive, Aberdeen AB24 4NJ Bjacob546@aol.com	01224 491451	31
Brown, Scott J. CBE QHC BD	1993	scott3568@gmail.com	07769 847876	47
Cowieson, Roy J. BD	1979	2160-15 Hawk Drive, Courtenay, BC V9N 9B2, Canada arjay1232@gmail.com	001 250 650 7568	13
Currie, David E.P. BSc BD	1983	42 Onslow Gardens, Muswell Hill, London N10 3JX davidepcurrie@gmail.com	01355 248510	17
Currie, Ian S. MBE BD	1975	ianscurrie@tiscali.co.uk		14
Davidson, Mark R. MA BD STM PhD RN	2005	The Manse, Main Street, Kippen FK8 3DN mark.davidson122@mod.uk	01786 871249	33
Dick, John H.A. (Ian) MA MSc BD	1982	18 Fairfield Road, Kelty KY4 0BY	01383 271147	24
Donaghy, Leslie G. BD DipMin PGCE FSAScot	1990	53 Oak Avenue, East Kilbride G75 9ED leslie@donaghy.org.uk	07809 484812	18
Douglas, Colin R. MA BD STM	1969	34 West Pilton Gardens, Edinburgh EH4 4EQ colin.r.douglas@gmail.com	0131 551 3808	1
Drake, Wendy F. (Mrs) BD	1978	21 William Black Place, South Queensferry EH30 9QR revwdrake@hotmail.co.uk	0131 331 1520	1
Earnshaw, Philip BA BSc BD	1986	22 Castle Street, St Monans, Anstruther KY10 2AP howardespie.me.com	01333 730640	26
Espie, Howard	2011	1 Sprucebank Avenue, Langbank, Port Glasgow PA14 6YX	01475 540391	1
Finlay, Quintin BA BD	1975	Ivy Cottage, Greenlees Farm, Kelso TD5 8BT	07901 981171	6
Forbes, John W.A. BD	1973	Little Ennochie Steading, Finzean, Banchory AB31 6LX jrbbbb@icloud.com	01330 850785	32
Gauld, Beverly G.D.D. MA BD	1972	7 Rowan View, Lanark ML11 9FQ	01555 665765	13
Gillies, Janet E. BD	1998	18 McIntyre Lane, Macmerry, Tranent EH33 1QL jan.gillies@yahoo.com	01875 824607	3

Name	Year	Address	Tel	No.
Grainger, Alison J. BD	1995	2 Hareburn Avenue, Avonbridge, Falkirk FK1 2NR, revajgrainger@btinternet.com	01324 861632	2
Harper, Anne J.M. (Miss) BD STM MTh CertSocPsych	1979	122 Greenock Road, Bishopton PA7 5AS	01505 862466	16
Haslett, Howard J. BA BD	1972	26 The Maltings, Haddington EH41 4EF, howard.haslett@btinternet.com	01620 481208	3
Hobson, Diane L. (Mrs) BA BD	2002	Buttercup Meadow, 5 Lower Westerland Barn, Marldon Village, Paignton TQ3 1RU, DHobson@churchofscotland.org.uk	07850 962007	31
Hudson, Eric V. LTh	1971	2 Murrayfield Drive, Bearsden, Glasgow G61 1JE	0141 942 6110	18
Hutcheson, Norman M. MA BD	1973	66 Maxwell Park, Dalbeattie DG5 4LS, norman.hutcheson@gmail.com	01556 610102	8
Hutchison, Alison M. (Mrs) BD DipMin	1988	Ashfield, Drumoak, Banchory AB31 5AG, ahutch@hotmail.co.uk	01330 811309	31
Jamieson, Esther M.M. (Mrs) BD	1984	1 Redburn, Bayview, Stornoway, Isle of Lewis HS1 2UU, iandejamieson@btinternet.com	01851 704789	44
Kerr, Hugh F. MA BD	1968	134C Great Western Road, Aberdeen AB10 6QE	01224 580091	16
Lawrie, Robert M. BD MSc DipMin LLCM(TD) MCMI	1994	West Benview, Main Road, Langbank PA14 6XP, rmlawrie66@gmail.com	01475 540240 / 07789 824479	1
Leishman, James S. LTh BD MA	1969	11 Hunter Avenue, Heathhall, Dumfries DG1 3UX	01387 249241	8
Logan, Thomas M. LTh	1971	3 Duncan Court, Kilmarnock KA3 7TF	01563 524398	11
McDonald, Ian J. M. BA BD	1984			48
McHaffie, Robin D. BD	1979	Shepherd's Cottage, Castle Heaton, Cornhill-on-Tweed TD12 4XQ, robinmchaffie@btinternet.com	01890 885946	5
MacKay, Alan H. BD	1974	Flat 1/1, 18 Newburgh Street, Glasgow G43 2XR, alanhmackay@aol.com	0141 632 0527	16
McKay, Johnston R. MA BA PhD	1969	15 Montgomerie Avenue, Fairlie, Largs KA29 0EE, johnston.mckay@btopenworld.com	01475 568802	16
McKean, Alan T. BD CertMin	1982	15 Park Road, Kirn, Dunoon PA23 8JL	01369 700016	39
McLay, Neil BA BD	2006	New Normandy Barracks, Evelyn Woods Road, Aldershot GU11 2LZ		48
McLean, Gordon LTh	1972	Beinn Dhorain, Kinnettas Square, Strathpeffer IV14 9BD, gmaclean@hotmail.co.uk	01997 421380	39
McWilliam, Thomas M. MA BD	1964	Flat 3, 13 Culduthel Road, Inverness IV2 4AG, tommcw@tommcwl.plus.com	01463 718981	39
Melville, David D. BD	1989	28 Porterfield, Comrie, Dunfermline KY12 9HJ, revddm@gmail.com	01383 850075	24
Messeder, Lee BD PgDipMin	2003	59 Miles End, Cavalry Park, Kilsyth G65 0BH, lee.messeder@gmail.com	07469 965934	23
Millar, Peter W. MA BD PhD	1971	6/5 Ettrickdale Place, Edinburgh EH3 5JN, ionacottage@hotmail.com	0131 557 0517	1
Mills, Peter W. CB BD DD CPS	1984			47
Monteith, W. Graham BD PhD	1974	20/3 Grandfield, Edinburgh EH6 4TL	0131 552 2564	1

Name	Year	Address / Email	Phone	No.
Muckart, Graeme W.M. MTh MSc FSAScot	1983	Kildale, Clashmore, Dornoch IV25 3RG / gw2m.kildale@gmail.com	01862 881715	40
Muir, Eleanor D. (Miss) MTheol DipPTheol	1986	eleanordmuir@tiscali.co.uk		28
Muir, Margaret A. (Miss) MA LLB BD	1989	59/4 South Beechwood, Edinburgh EH12 5YS	0131 313 3240	1
Munro, Flora BD DMin	1993	87 Gairn Terrace, Aberdeen AB10 6AY / floramunro@aol.com	07762 966393	31
Murray, George M. MTh	1995	6 Mayfield, Lesmahagow ML11 0FH / george.murray7@gmail.com	01555 895216	16
Newell, Alison M. (Mrs) BD	1986	1A Inverleith Terrace, Edinburgh EH3 5NS / alinewell@aol.com	0131 556 3505	1
Newell, J. Philip MA BD PhD	1982	1A Inverleith Terrace, Edinburgh EH3 5NS	0131 556 3505	28
Niven, William W. LTh	1982	4 Obsdale Park, Alness IV17 0TP	01349 884053	39
Parker, Carol Ann (Mrs) BEd BD	2009	The Cottages, Dornoch Firth Caravan Park, Meikle Ferry South, Tain IV19 1JX / CParker@churchofscotland.org.uk	01862 892292	39
Paterson, John L. MA BD STM	1964	9 The Pines, Murdoch's Loan, Alloway, Ayr KA7 4WD / revianpaterson@hotmail.co.uk	01292 443615	10
Patterson, Philip W. BMus BD	1999	Carver Barracks, Wimbish, Saffron Walden CB10 2YA	0131 664 0673	28
Penman, Iain D. BD	1977	33/5 Carnbee Avenue, Edinburgh EH16 6GA / iainpenmanklm@aol.com	07931 993427	1
Pieterse, Ben BA BTh LTh	2001	15 Bakeoven Close, Seaforth Sound, Simon's Town 7975, South Africa / benhp1@gmail.com		25
Provan, Iain W. (Prof.) MA BA PhD	1991	Regent College, 5800 University Boulevard, Vancouver BC V6T 2E4, Canada	001 604 224 3245	1
Reid, Alan A.S. MA BD STM	1962	Wayside Cottage, Bridgend, Ceres, Cupar KY15 5LS	01334 828509	26
Robertson, Blair MA BD ThM	1990	West End Guest House, 282 High Street, Elgin IV30 1AG / info@westendguesthouse.co.uk	01343 549629	35
Roderick, Maggie R. BA BD FRSA FTSI	2010	34 Craiglea, Stirling FK9 5EE / MRoderick@churchofscotland.org.uk		28
Saunders, Keith BD	1983	1/2, 10 Rutherford Drive, Lenzie G66 3US / revchap53@hotmail.com	0141 558 4338	16
Scotland, Ronald J. BD	1993	7A Rose Avenue, Elgin IV30 1NX / ronnieandjill@thescotlands.co.uk	01343 543086	35
Scouler, Michael D. MBE BSc BD	1988	Head of Spiritual Care, NHS Borders, Chaplaincy Centre, Borders General Hospital, Melrose TD6 9BS / michael.scouler@borders.scot.nhs.uk	01896 826565	6
Shackleton, Scott J.S. QCVS BA BD PhD RN	1993	Deputy Chaplain of the Fleet, Naval Command HQ, MP1.2 Leach Building, Whale Island, Portsmouth PO2 8BY / scott.shackleton674@mod.uk		47
Shanks, Norman J. MA BD DD	1983	1 Marchmont Terrace, Glasgow G12 9LT / rufuski@btinternet.com	0141 339 4421	16
Smith, Elizabeth (Mrs) BD	1996	smithrevb44@gmail.com		1
Smith, Hilary W. BD DipMin MTh PhD	1999	hilaryoxfordsmith1@gmail.com	0131 441 5858	35

NAME	ORD	ADDRESS	TEL	PRES
Stewart, Charles E. BSc BD MTh PhD	1976	105 Sinclair Street, Helensburgh G84 9HY / c.e.stewart@btinternet.com	01436 678113	18
Stewart, Fraser M.C. BSc BD	1980	12a Crowlista, Uig, Isle of Lewis HS2 9JF / fraserstewart1955@hotmail.com	01851 672413	39
Stewart, Margaret L. (Mrs) BSc MB ChB BD	1985	28 Inch Crescent, Bathgate EH48 1EU / famstewart@ormail.co.uk	01506 653428	2
Storrar, William F. (Prof.) MA BD PhD	1984	Director, Center of Theological Inquiry, 50 Stockton Street, Princeton, NJ 08540, USA		1
Strachan, Alexander E. MA BD	1974	2 Leafield Road, Dumfries DG1 2DS / aestrachan@aol.com	01387 279460	8
Strachan, David G. BD DPS	1978	1 Deeside Park, Aberdeen AB15 7PQ	01224 324101	31
Strachan, Ian M. MA BD	1959	'Cardenwell', Glen Drive, Dyce, Aberdeen AB21 7EN	01224 772028	31
Tallach, John MA MLitt	1970	29 Firthview Drive, Inverness IV3 8NS / johntallach@talktalk.net	01463 418721	48
Thomas, W. Colville ChLJ BTh BPhil DPS DSc	1964	11 Muirfield Crescent, Gullane EH31 2HN	01620 842415	3
Thomson, Alexander BSc BD MPhil PhD	1973	4 Munro Street, Dornoch IV25 3RA / alexander.thomson6@btinternet.com	01862 811650	40
Thrower, Charles D. BSc	1965	Grange House, Wester Grangemuir, Pittenweem, Anstruther KY10 2RB / charlesandsteph@btinternet.com	01333 312631	26
Turnbull, John LTh	1994	4 Rathmor Road, Biggar ML12 6QG / john.moiraturnbull62@btinternet.com	01899 221502	13
Whyte, Ron C. BD CPS	1990	13 Hillside Avenue, Kingussie PH21 1PA / ron4xst@btinternet.com	01540 661101 / 07979 026973	36
Wilson, Andrew G.N. MA BD DMin	1977	Auchintarph, Coull, Tarland, Aboyne AB34 4TT / agn.wilson@gmail.com	01339 880918	32
Wilson, Thomas F.	1984	55 Allison Close, Cove, Aberdeen AB12 3WG	01224 873501	31
Wood, James L.K.	1967	1 Glen Drive, Dyce, Aberdeen AB21 7EN	01224 722543	31

LIST E – MINISTERS NOT IN PRESBYTERIES (REGISTERED AS INACTIVE)

Those who are not members of a Presbytery but, under the Registration of Ministries Act (Act 2, 2017, as amended), are registered as 'Inactive'. Only those who have given consent under the GDPR to publication of their details are included. The list is shorter than in previous years, as some have not registered under the new arrangements.

NAME	ORD	ADDRESS	TEL	PRES
Alexander, Douglas N. MA BD	1961	West Morningside, Main Road, Langbank, Port Glasgow PA4 6XP	01475 540249	14

Name	Year	Address	Phone	
Campbell, J. Ewen R. MA BD	1967	20 St Margaret's Road, North Berwick EH39 4PJ	01620 890835 07840 353887	25
Chestnut, Alexander MBE BA	1948	5 Douglas Street, Largs KA30 8PS	01475 674168	14
Craig, Ronald A.S. BAcc BD	1983	29 Third Avenue, Auchinloch, Kirkintilloch, Glasgow G66 5EB rascraig@ntlworld.com	0141 573 9220	16
Dickson, Graham T. MA BD	1985	43 Hope Park Gardens, Bathgate EH48 2QT gtd194@googlemail.com	01506 237597	2
Donaldson, Colin V.	1982	3A Playfair Terrace, St Andrews KY16 9HX	01334 472889	3
Gale, Ronald A.A. LTh	1982	Dorset		5
Liddiard, F.G.B. MA	1957	34 Trinity Fields Crescent, Brechin DD9 6YF bernardliddiard@btinternet.com	01356 622966	30
Lithgow, Anne R. (Mrs) MA BD	1992	13 Cameron Park, Edinburgh EH16 5JY anne.lithgow@btinternet.com		3
McGillivray, A. Gordon MA BD STM	1951	36 Larchfield Neuk, Balerno EH14 7NL	0131 449 3901	1
McLachlan, Fergus C. BD	1982	46 Queen Square, Glasgow G41 2AZ	0141 423 3830	16
Minto, Joan E. (Mrs) MA BD	1993	1 Lochaber Cottages, Forres IV36 2RL joanminto.123@gmail.com	07800 669074	3
Murray, Douglas R. MA BD	1965	32 Forth Park, Bridge of Allan, Stirling FK9 5NT d-smurray@supanet.com	01786 831081	23
Olsen, Heather (Miss) BD	1978	4 Riverside Park, Lochyside, Caol, Fort William PH33 7RA	01397 700023	38
Prentice, George BA BTh	1964	46 Victoria Gardens, Corsebar Road, Paisley PA2 9AQ g.prentice04@talktalk.net	0141 842 1585	14
Ramsay, Alan MA	1967	12 Riverside Grove, Lochyside, Fort William PH33 7RD	01397 702054	38
Smith, Ronald W. BA BEd BD	1979	1F1, 2 Middlefield, Edinburgh EH7 4PF	0131 553 1174 07900 896954	1

LIST F – HEALTH AND SOCIAL CARE CHAPLAINS (NHS)

LOTHIAN

Lead Chaplain Spiritual Care	Rev. Canon Caroline Applegath carrie.applegath@nhslothian.scot.nhs.uk	Spiritual Care Office: 0131 242 1990
The Royal Infirmary of Edinburgh	51 Little France Crescent, Edinburgh EH16 4SA	0131 536 1000

Full details of chaplains and contacts in all hospitals: www.nhslothian.scot.nhs.uk > Services > Health Services A-Z > Spiritual Care

BORDERS

Head of Spiritual Care   Rev. Michael Scouler   01896 826565
michael.scouler@nhs.border.org

Chaplaincy Centre, Borders General Hospital, Melrose TD6 9BS

Further information: www.nhsborders.scot.nhs.uk > Patients and Visitors > Our services > Chaplaincy Centre

DUMFRIES AND GALLOWAY

Spiritual Care Lead   Dawn Allan   01387 246246 Ext 31544
dawnallan1@nhs.net   07795 120965

Dumfries and Galloway Royal Infirmary,
Sanctuary Office, Cargenbridge, Dumfries DG2 8RX

Further information: www.nhsdg.scot.nhs.uk > Focus on > Search > Chaplaincy

AYRSHIRE AND ARRAN

Service Lead for Chaplaincy and Staff Care   Rev. Judith A. Huggett   01563 577301
judith.huggett@aapct.scotnhs.uk

Crosshouse Hospital, Kilmarnock KA2 0BE

Chaplaincy Office, Ailsa Hospital, Dalmellington Road, Ayr KA6 6AB   01292 610556

Further information: www.nhsaaa.net > Services A-Z > Chaplaincy service

LANARKSHIRE

Chaplaincy Office   01698 377637
spiritualcare@lanarkshire.scot.nhs.uk

Law House, Airdrie Road, Carluke ML8 5EP

Further information: www.nhslanarkshire.org.uk > Our services A-Z > Palliative care > Palliative care support > Spiritual care

GREATER GLASGOW AND CLYDE

Chaplaincy and Spiritual Care		The Sanctuary, Queen Elizabeth University Hospital, Govan Road, Glasgow G51 4TF	0141 211 3026
chaplains@ggc.scot.nhs.uk			

Further information: www.nhsggc.org.uk > Services Directory (foot of page) > Spiritual Care

FORTH VALLEY

Spiritual Care Centre	Forth Valley Royal Hospital, Larbert FK5 4WR	01324 566071
		07824 460882

Further information: www.nhsforthvalley.com > Services A–Z > Spiritual Care Centre

FIFE

Head of Spiritual Care and Bereavement Lead	Mr Mark Evans DCS	Department of Spiritual Care, Queen Margaret Hospital, Whitefield Road, Dunfermline KY12 0SU	01383 623623 ext 24136
	mark.evans59@nhs.net		
Victoria Hospital, Kirkcaldy		Chaplain's Office	01592 648158
Queen Margaret Hospital, Dunfermline		Chaplain's Office	01383 674136
Mental Health and Community Chaplain	Adamson and Stratheden Hospitals		07976 918909
Glenrothes and Cameron Community Hospitals	Chaplain's Office		01592 643355 ext 21765
St Andrews Community Hospital	Rev Dr James Connolly		
	jamesconnolly@nhs.net		07711 177655
Community Chaplaincy Listening Co-ordinator (NHS Fife)	Miss Lynda Wright DCS		07835 303395
	lynda.wright1@nhs.net		

Further information: www.nhsfife.org > Your Health > Support Services > Spiritual Care

TAYSIDE

Senior Chaplains	Rev. Alan Gibbon and Rev David Gordon	The Wellbeing Centre, Royal Victoria Hospital, Dundee DD2 1SP	01382 423110
	lynne.downie@nhs.net		

Further information: www.nhstayside.scot.nhs.uk > Your Health/Wellbeing > Our Services A-Z > Spiritual Care

GRAMPIAN

| Lead Chaplain | Rev. Mark Rodgers | Chaplains' Office, Aberdeen Royal Infirmary, Foresterhill, Aberdeen AB25 2ZN
nhsg.chaplaincy@nhs.net | 01224 553166 |

Further information: www.nhsgrampian.co.uk > Home > Local Services and Clinics > Spiritual Care

HIGHLAND

| Lead Chaplain | Rev. Dr Derek Brown
derek.brown1@nhs.net | Raigmore Hospital, Old Perth Road, Inverness IV2 3UJ | 01463 704463 |

Further information: www.nhshighland.scot.nhs.uk/Services/Pages/Chaplaincy-Raigmore.aspx

WESTERN ISLES HEALTH BOARD

| **Lead Chaplain** | Rev. T. K. Shadakshari | 23D Benside, Newmarket, Stornoway, Isle of Lewis HS2 0DZ
tk.shadakshari@nhs.net | (Home) 01851 701727

(Office) 01851 704704
(Mbl) 07403 697138 |

NHS SCOTLAND

Head of Programme, Health & Social Care Chaplaincy & Spiritual Care, NHS Education for Scotland

| Vacant: contact in the interim: | Jane Davies jane.davies@nes.scot.nhs.uk
3rd Floor, 2 Central Quay,
89 Hydepark Street, Glasgow G3 8BW | 0141 223 1498 |

LIST G – CHAPLAINS TO HM FORCES

The three columns give dates of ordination and commissioning, and branch where the chaplain is serving: Royal Navy, Army, Royal Air Force, Royal Naval Reserve, Army Reserve, Army Cadet Force, or where the person is an Officiating Chaplain to the Military.

NAME	ORD	COM	BCH	ADDRESS
Anderson, David P. BSc BD	2002	2007	A	HQ 12 Armoured Infantry Brigade, Ward Barracks, Bulford, Wiltshire SP4 9NA padre.anderson180@mod.gov.uk
Begg, Richard MA BD	2008	2016	A	3 Signal Regiment, Kiwi Barracks, Bulford Barracks, Salisbury SP4 9NY
Berry, Geoff T. BD BSc	2009	2012	A	4 Regiment RA, Alanbrooke Barracks, Topcliffe, Thirsk YO7 3EY
Blackwood, Keith T. BD DipMin	1997	1977	ACF	Shetland Independent Battery, ACF, TA Centre, Fort Charlotte, Lerwick, Shetland ZE1 0JN
Blakey, Stephen A. BSc BD	1977	1977	AR	6 Bn The Royal Regiment of Scotland, Walcheran Barracks, 122 Hotspur Street, Glasgow G20 8LQ
Blakey, Stephen A. BSc BD	1977	1977	ACF	Lothian & Borders Bn ACF, Drumshoreland House, Broxburn EH52 5PF
Blakey, Stephen A. BSc BD	1977	1977	OCM	HQ (Scottish) Brigade; Tayforth University Officers 'Training Corps
Bryson, Thomas M. BD	1997		ACF	2 Bn The Highlanders, ACF, Cadet Training Centre, Rocksley Drive, Boddam, Peterhead AB42 3BA
Bryson, Thomas M. BD	1997		OCM	51 (Scottish) Brigade, Forthside, Stirling FK7 7RR
Campbell, Karen K. BD MTh DMin	1997		OCM	Personnel Recovery Unit, Edinburgh
Cobain, Alan R. BD	2000	2017	A	1 Yorks, Battlesbury Barracks, Woodcock Lane, Warminster BH12 9DT lyorks-ai-bhq-padre@mod.gov.uk
Connolly, Daniel BD DipTheol DipMin	1983	1994	AR	Scottish and North Irish Yeomanry, Redford Barracks, Colinton Road, Edinburgh EH13 0PP
Coulter, David G. CB OStJ QHC BA BD MDA PhD	1989		A	Chaplain General, MoD Chaplains (Army), HQ Land Forces, 2nd Floor Zone 6, Ramillies Building, Marlborough Lines, Andover, Hants SP11 8HJ
Dalton, Mark F. BD DipMin RN	2002		RN	The Chaplaincy, HMS Neptune, HM Naval Base Clyde, Faslane, Helensburgh G84 8HL mark.dalton242@mod.gov.uk
Davidson, Mark R. MA BD STM PhD RN	2005		RN	CNR Chaplain, Naval Chaplaincy Service, MP1.2 Leach Building, NCHQ, Whale Island, Portsmouth PO2 8BY mark.davidson122@mod.gov.uk
Dicks, Shuna M. BSc BD	2010		ACF	2 Bn The Highlanders, ACF, Cadet Training Centre, Rocksley Drive, Boddam, Peterhead AB42 3BA
Frail, Nicola BLE MBA MDiv	2000	2012	A	32 Engineer Regiment, Marne Barracks, Catterick Garrison DL10 7NP
Francis, James MBE BD PhD	2002	2009	A	Deputy Assistant Chaplain General, 38 (Irish) Brigade, Thiepval Barracks, Lisburn B28 3NP
Gardner, Neil N. MA BD RNR	1991	2015	OCM	Edinburgh Universities Officers' Training Corps
Gardner, Neil N. MA BD RNR	1991		RNR	Honorary Chaplain, Royal Navy
Goodison, Michael J. BSc BD	2013	2012	A	Royal Scots Dragoon Guards, Leuchars Station, Leuchars KY16 0JX
Kellock, Chris N. MA BD	1998	2000	A	Royal Memorial Chapel, Royal Military Academy, Haig Road, Camberley GU15 4PQ
Kennon, Stanley BA BD RN	1992		RN	Britannia Royal Naval College, Dartmouth TO6 0HJ
Kinsey, Louis BD DipMin TD	1991		AR	205 (Scottish) Field Hospital (V), Graham House, Whitefield Road, Glasgow G51 6JU
Lancaster, Craig MA BD	2004	2011	RAF	52 Suffolk Avenue, RAF Honington, Bury St Edmunds IP31 1LW craig.lancaster102@mod.gov.uk

Logan, David D.J. MStJ BD MA	2009	2009	ACF	Black Watch Bn, ACF, Queens Barracks, 131 Dunkeld Road, Perth PH1 5BT
Logan, David D.J. MStJ BD MA	2009	2011	OCM	7 SCOTS, Queens Barracks, 131 Dunkeld Road, Perth PH1 5BT
McCulloch, Alen J.R. MA BD	1990		ACF	Cornwall ACF, 7 Castle Canyke Road, Bodmin PL31 1DX
MacDonald, Roderick I.T. BD CertMin	1992		ACF	West Lowland Bn, ACF, Fusilier House, Seaforth Road, Ayr KA8 9HX
MacKay, Stewart A.	2009		A	3 Bn Black Watch, Royal Regiment of Scotland, Fort George, Ardersier, Inverness IV1 2TD
Mackenzie, Cameron BD	1997		ACF	Lothian and Borders Bn, ACF, Drumshoreland House, Broxburn EH52 5PF
Mackenzie, Hector M.	2008	2008	A	HQ Military Corrective Training Centre, Berechurch Hall Camp, Berechurch Hall Road, Colchester CO2 9NU
Mackenzie, Seoras L. BD	1996	1998	A	39 Engr Regt (Air Support), Kinloss Barracks, Kinloss, Forres IV36 3XL
McLaren, William MA BD	1990		ACF	Angus and Dundee Bn, ACF, Barry Buddon, Carnoustie DD7 7RY
McLaren, William MA BD	1990		OCM	225 GS Med Regt (V), Oliver Barracks, Dalkeith Road, Dundee DD4 7DL
McLay, Neil BA BD	2006	2012	A	New Normandy Barracks, Evelyn Woods Road, Aldershot GU11 2LZ
MacLeod, Rory N. BA BD	1986	1992	AR	154 Regt RLC, Bothwell House, Elgin Street, Dunfermline KY12 7SB
MacPherson, Duncan J. BSc BD	1993	2002	A	Army Personnel Centre, MP413, Kentigern House, 65 Brown Street, Glasgow G2 8EX
Mathieson, Angus R. MA BD	1988		OCM	Edinburgh Garrison & the Personnel Recovery Unit (PRU)
Milliken, Jamie BD	2005	2018	RN	45 Commando, RM Condor, Forfar Road, Arbroath DD11 3SP
Munro, Sheila BD	1995	2003	RAF	Chaplaincy Centre, RAF Wyton, Huntingdon PE28 2EA; sheila.munro781@mod.uk
Patterson, Philip W. BMus BD	1999	2017	A	29 EOD and SGSU, Carver Barracks, Wimbish, Saffron Walden CB10 2YA
Prentice, Donald K. BSc BD	1989		OCM	205 (Scottish) Field Hospital (V), Graham House, Whitefield Road, Glasgow G51 6JU
Rankin, Lisa-Jane BD CPS	2003		OCM	2 Bn Royal Regiment of Scotland, Glencorse Barracks, Penicuik EH26 0QH
Rowe, Christopher J. BA BD	2008	2008	AR	32 (Scottish) Signal Regiment, 21 Jardine Street, Glasgow G20 6JU
Selemani, Ecilo LTh MTh	1993	2011	ACF	Glasgow and Lanark Bn, ACF, Gilbertfield Road, Cambuslang, Glasgow G72 8YP
Selemani, Ecilo LTh MTh	1993	2011	OCM	51 Infantry Brigade, Forthside, Stirling FK7 7RR
Shackleton, Scott J.S. QCVS BA BD PhD RN	1993	2010	RN	Deputy Chaplain of the Fleet, Naval Command HQ, MP1.2 Leach Building, Whale Island, Portsmouth PO2 8BY; scott.shackleton674@mod.uk
Stewart, Fraser M.C. BSc BD	1980		ACF	1 Bn The Highlanders, ACF, Gordonville Road, Inverness IV2 4SU
Taylor, Gayle J.A. MA BD	1999	2015	OCM	3 Bn The Rifles, 1 SCOTS, Redford Barracks, Colinton Road, Edinburgh EH13 0PP
Thom, David J. BD DipMin	1999	2011	A	Royal Logistics Corps, Princess Royal Barracks, Deepcut, Camberley GU16 6RW
van Sittert, Paul BA BD	1997		A	4 Bn The Royal Regiment of Scotland, Bourlon Barracks, Plumer Road, Catterick Garrison DL9 3AD
Warwick, Ivan C. MA BD TD	1980		ACF	1 Bn The Highlanders, ACF, Gordonville Road, Inverness IV2 4SU
Warwick, Ivan C. MA BD TD	1980		ACF	Orkney Independent Battery, ACF, Territorial Army Centre, Weyland Park, Kirkwall KW15 LP
Warwick, Ivan C. MA BD TD	1980		OCM	Fort George and Cameron Barracks, Inverness
Wilson, Fiona A. BD	2008		ACF	West Lowland Battalion, ACF, Fusilier House, Seaforth Road, Ayr KA8 9HX
Young, David T. BA BD MTh	2007	2018	RNR	HMS Dalriada, Govan, Glasgow G51 3JH

LIST H – READERS

This list comprises active Readers only.

1. EDINBURGH

Devoy, Fiona (Mrs)
196 The Murrays Brae, Edinburgh EH17 8UH
fiona.devoy@yahoo.co.uk
0131 558 8210

Farrow, Edmund
14 Brunswick Terrace, Edinburgh EH7 5PG
edmundfarrow@blueyonder.co.uk
0131 664 2366

Jackson, Kate (Ms)
3 Kedslie Road, Edinburgh EH16 6NT
katejackson1252@gmail.com
0131 554 1326

Johnston, Alan
36 Foster Road, Penicuik EH26 0FL
alanacj2@gmail.com
07901 510819

Kerrigan, Herbert A. (Prof.) MA LLB QC
Airdene, 20 Edinburgh Road, Dalkeith EH22 1JY
kerrigan@kerriganqc.com
0131 660 3007
07725 953772

Pearce, Martin
4 Corbiehill Avenue, Edinburgh EH4 5DR
martin.j.pearce@blueyonder.co.uk
0131 336 4864

Sherriffs, Irene (Mrs)
22/2 West Mill Bank, Edinburgh EH13 0QT
reenie.sherriffs@blueyonder.co.uk
07801 717222
0131 466 9530

Tew, Helen (Mrs)
5/5/Moat Drive, Edinburgh EH14 1NU
helentew9@gmail.com
07986 170802

2. WEST LOTHIAN

Elliott, Sarah (Miss)
105 Seafield Rows, Seafield, Bathgate EH47 7AW
sarah.elliott6@btopenworld.com
01506 654950

Galloway, Brenda (Dr)
16 Baron's Hill Court, Linlithgow EH49 7SP
bhgallo@yahoo.co.uk
01506 842028

Holden, Louise (Mrs)
Am Batnach, Easter Breich, West Calder EH55 8PP
louise.holden@btinternet.com
01506 873030

Middleton, Alex
19 Cramond Place, Dalgety Bay KY11 9LS
alex.middleton@btinternet.com
01383 820800

Orr, Elizabeth (Mrs)
64a Marjoribanks Street, Bathgate EH48 1AL
liz-orr@hotmail.co.uk
01506 653116

Paxton, James
5 Main Street, Longridge, Bathgate EH47 8AE
jim_paxton@btinternet.com
01501 772192

Wilkie, David
55 Goschen Place, Broxburn EH52 5JH
david-fmu_09@tiscali.co.uk
01506 238644

3. LOTHIAN

Evans, W. John IEng MIIE(Elec)
Waterlily Cottage, 10 Fenton Steading, North Berwick EH39 5AF
jevans7is@hotmail.com
01620 842990

Hogg, David MA — 82 Eskhill, Penicuik EH26 8DQ, hogg-d2@sky.com — 01968 676350

Millan, Mary (Mrs) — 33 Polton Vale, Loanhead EH20 9DF, marymillan@gmail.com — 07821 693946 / 0131 440 1624

Trevor, A. Hugh MA MTh — 29A Fidra Road, North Berwick EH39 4NE, htrevor@talktalk.net] — 07814 466104 / 01620 894924

Yeoman, Edward T.N. FSAScot — 75 Newhailes Crescent, Musselburgh EH21 6EF, edwardyeoman6@aol.com — 0131 653 2291 / 07896 517666

4. MELROSE AND PEEBLES
Selkirk, Frances (Mrs) — 2 The Glebe, Ashkirk, Selkirk TD7 4PJ, f.selkirk@hillview2selkirk.plus.com — 01750 322040

5. DUNS
Landale, Alison (Mrs) — Green Hope Guest House, Ellemford, Duns TD11 3SG, alison@greenhope.co.uk — 01361 890242

6. JEDBURGH
Findlay, Elizabeth (Mrs) — 7e Rose Lane, Kelso TD5 7AP, findlay290@gmail.com — 01573 226641

Knox, Dagmar (Mrs) — 3 Stichill Road, Ednam, Kelso TD5 7QQ, dagmar.knox.riding@btinternet.com — 01573 224883

7. ANNANDALE AND ESKDALE
Boncey, David — Redbrae, Beattock, Moffat DG10 9RF, david.boncey613@btinternet.com — 01683 300613

Brown, Martin J. — Lochhouse Farm, Beattock, Moffat DG10 9SG, martin.j.brown1967@gmail.com — 01683 300451

Brown, S. Jeffrey BA — Skara Brae, Holm Park, 8 Ballplay Road, Moffat DG10 9JU, sjbrown@btinternet.com — 01683 220475

Dodds, Alan — Trinco, Battlehill, Annan DG12 6SN, alanandjen46@talktalk.net — 01461 201235

Jackson, Susan (Mrs) — 48 Springbells Road, Annan DG12 6LQ, peter-jackson24@sky.com — 07498 714675

Morton, Andrew A. BSc — 19 Sherwood Park, Lockerbie DG11 2DX, andrew_morton@mac.com — 01576 203164

8. DUMFRIES AND KIRKCUDBRIGHT
Corson, Gwen (Mrs) — 7 Sunnybrae, Borgue, Kirkcudbright DG6 4SJ, gwendolyn@hotmail.com — 01557 870328

Matheson, David — 44 Auchenkeld Avenue, Heathhall, Dumfries DG1 3QY / davidb.matheson44@btinternet.com — 01387 252042
Monk, Geoffrey — Hilbre Cottage, Laurieston, Castle Douglas DG7 2PW — 01644 450679
Smith, Nicola (Mrs) — Brightwater Lodge, Kelton, Castle Douglas DG7 1SZ / nickysasmith@btinternet.com — 01556 680453

9. WIGTOWN AND STRANRAER

Cash, Marlane (Mrs) — 5 Maxwell Drive, Newton Stewart DG8 6EL / marlaneg690@btinternet.com — 01671 401375, 07884 370419
McQuistan, Robert — Old Schoolhouse, Carsluith, Newton Stewart DG8 7DT / mcquistan@mcquistan.plus.com — 01671 820327

10. AYR

Anderson, James (Dr) BVMS PhD DVM FRCPath FIBiol MRCVS — 67 Henrietta Street, Girvan KA26 9AN / jc.anderson@tesco.net — 01465 710059
Jamieson, Iain A. — 2 Whinfield Avenue, Prestwick KA9 2BH / iain@jamieson4189.freeserve.co.uk — 07952 512720, 01242 476898
Morrison, James — 27 Monkton Road, Prestwick KA9 1AP / jim.morrison@talktalk.net — 01292 479313, 07773 287852
Murphy, Ian — 56 Lamont Crescent, Netherthird, Cumnock KA18 3DU / ianm_cumnock@yahoo.co.uk — 01290 423675
Ogston, Jean (Mrs) — 14 North Park Avenue, Girvan KA26 9DH / jeanogston@googlemail.com — 01465 713081
Riome, Elizabeth (Mrs) — Monkwood Mains, Minishant, Maybole KA19 8EY / aj.riome@btinternet.com — 01292 443440
Ronald, Glenn — 188 Prestwick Road, Ayr KA8 8NP / glenronald@btinternet.com — 01292 286861
Stewart, Christine (Mrs) — 52 Kilnford Drive, Dundonald KA2 9ET / christiestewart@btinternet.com — 01563 850486

11. IRVINE AND KILMARNOCK

Bircham, James F. — 8 Holmlea Place, Kilmarnock KA1 1UU / james.bircham@sky.com — 01563 532287
Cooper, Fraser — 5 Balgray Way, Irvine KA11 1RP / frasercooper1560@gmail.com — 01294 211235
Crosbie, Shona (Mrs) — 4 Campbell Street, Darvel KA17 0DA / fawltytowersdarvel@yahoo.co.uk — 01560 322229
Dempster, Ann (Mrs) — 20 Graham Place, Kilmarnock KA3 7JN / ademp99320@aol.com — 01563 529361, 07729 152945
Gillespie, Janice (Miss) — 12 Jeffrey Street, Kilmarnock KA1 4EB / janice.gillespie@tiscali.co.uk — 01563 540009
Graham, Barbara (Miss) MA MLit MPhil CertChSt — 42 Annanhill Avenue, Kilmarnock KA1 2LQ / barbara.graham74@btinternet.com — 01563 522108

Hamilton, Margaret A. (Mrs)	59 South Hamilton Street, Kilmarnock KA1 2DT tomhmltn@sky.com	01563 534431
Jamieson, John H. (Dr) BSc DEP DEdPsy AFBPsS CPsychol	22 Moorfield Avenue, Kilmarnock KA1 1TS johnhjamieson@tiscali.co.uk	01563 534065
McGeever, Gerard	23 Kinloch Avenue, Stewarton, Kilmarnock KA3 3HQ mcgeege1@gmail.com	01560 484331
MacLean, Donald	1 Four Acres Drive, Kilmaurs, Kilmarnock KA3 2ND donanmmac@yahoo.co.uk	01563 538475
Mills, Catherine (Mrs)	59 Crossdene Road, Crosshouse, Kilmarnock KA2 0JU cfmills5lib@hotmail.com	01563 535305
Raleigh, Gavin	21 Landsborough Drive, Kilmarnock KA3 1RY gavin.raleigh@lineone.net	01563 539377
Robertson, William	1 Archers Avenue, Irvine KA11 2GB willie.robert@yahoo.co.uk	01294 203577
Whitelaw, David	9 Kirkhill, Kilwinning KA13 6NB whitelawfam@talktalk.net	01294 551695

12. ARDROSSAN

Barclay, Elizabeth (Mrs)	2 Jacks Road, Saltcoats KA21 5NT mfiz98@dsl.pipex.com	01294 471855
Brookens, Aileen J. (Mrs)	Willow Cottage, Glenashdale, Whiting Bay, Isle of Arran KA27 8QW aileenbrokens@gmail.com	01770 700535
Bruce, Andrew	57 Dockers Gardens, Ardrossan KA22 8GB andrew_bruce2@sky.com	01294 605113
Clarke, Elizabeth (Mrs)	Swallowbrae, Torbeg, Isle of Arran KA27 8HE lizahclarke@gmail.com	01770 860219 07780 574367
Currie, Archie BD	55 Central Avenue, Kilbirnie KA25 6JP Archie.Currie@churchofscotland.org.uk	01505 681474 07881 452115
McCool, Robert	17 McGregor Avenue, Stevenston KA20 4BA	01294 466548
Macleod, Sharon (Mrs)	Creag Dhubh, Golf Course Road, Whiting Bay, Isle of Arran KA27 8QT macleodsharon@hotmail.com	01770 700353
Ross, Magnus M.B. BA MEd	39 Beachway, Largs KA30 8QH m.b.ross@btinternet.com	01475 689572

13. LANARK

Grant, Alan	25 Moss-side Avenue, Carluke ML8 5UG amgrant25@aol.com	01555 771419
Love, William	30 Barmore Avenue, Carluke ML8 4PE janbill30@tiscali.co.uk	01555 751243

14. GREENOCK AND PAISLEY

Banks, Russell
18 Aboyne Drive, Paisley PA2 7SJ
margaret.banks2@ntlworld.com
0141 884 6925

Bird, Mary Jane (Miss)
mjbird55@gmail.com

Boag, Jennifer (Miss)
11 Madeira Street, Greenock PA16 7UJ
jenniferboag@hotmail.com
01475 720125

Davey, Charles L.
16 Divert Road, Gourock PA19 1DT
charlesdavey16@hotmail.co.uk
01475 631544

Glenny, John C.
49 Cloch Road, Gourock PA19 1AT
jacklizg@aol.com
01475 636415

Hood, Eleanor (Mrs)
12 Clochoderick Avenue, Kilbarchan, Johnstone PA10 2AY
eleanor.hood.kilbarchan@ntlworld.com
01505 704208

MacDonald, Christine (Ms)
33 Collier Street, Johnstone PA5 8AG
christine.macdonald10@ntlworld.com
01505 355779

McFarlan, Elizabeth (Miss)
20 Fauldswood Crescent, Paisley PA2 9PA
elizabeth.mcfarlan@ntlworld.com
01505 358411

McHugh, Jack
'Earlshaugh', Earl Place, Bridge of Weir PA11 3HA
jackmchugh11@btinternet.com
01505 612789

Marshall, Leon M.
'Glenisla', Gryffe Road, Kilmacolm PA13 4BA
lm@stevenson-kyles.co.uk
01505 872417

Maxwell, Margaret A. (Sandra) (Mrs) BD
2 Grants Avenue, Paisley PA2 6AZ
sandra@maxwellmail.co.uk
0141 884 3710

Rankin, Kenneth
20 Bruntsfield Gardens, Glasgow G53 7QJ
krankin@hotmail.co.uk
0141 880 7474

Spooner, John R. BSc PGC(Mgt)
Onslow, Uplawmoor Road, Neilston, Glasgow G78 3LB
jrspooner@btopenworld.com
0141 881 5182
07481 008033

16. GLASGOW

Campbell, Jack T. BD BEd
40 Kenmure Avenue, Bishopbriggs, Glasgow G64 2DE
jack.campbell@ntlworld.com
0141 563 5837

Dickson, Hector M.K.
'Gwito', 61 Whitton Drive, Giffnock, Glasgow G46 6EF
hectordickson@hotmail.com
0141 637 0080

Fullarton, Andrew
2/2, 2263 Paisley Road West, Glasgow G52 3QA
0141 883 9518
01786 609594

Grant, George
8 Erskine Street, Stirling FK7 0QN
georgegrant@gmail.com
07921 168057

Horner, David J.
20 Ledi Road, Glasgow G43 2AJ
djhorner@btinternet.com
0141 637 7369

Joansson, Tordur (Todd)
1/2, 18 Eglinton Court, Glasgow G5 9NE
to41jo@yahoo.co.uk
0141 429 6733

Kilpatrick, Joan (Mrs)
39 Brent Road, Regent's Park, Glasgow G46 8JG
je-kilpatrick@sky.com
0141 621 1809

McChlery, Stuart
62 Grenville Drive, Cambuslang, Glasgow G72 8DP
s.mcchlery@gcu.ac.uk
0141 643 9730

McColl, John
solfolly11@gmail.com
07757 303195

McFarlane, Robert — 25 Avenel Road, Glasgow G13 2PB — robertmcfrln@yahoo.co.uk — 0141 954 5540

McInally, Gordon — 10 Melville Gardens, Bishopbriggs, Glasgow G64 3DF — gmcinally@sky.com — 0141 563 2685

Mackenzie, Norman — 55 Culzean Crescent, Newton Mearns, Glasgow G77 5SW — 07935 861530

Millar, Kathleen (Mrs) — 18 Greenwood Grove West, Stewarton Road, Glasgow G77 6ZF — 07793 203045

Morrison, Graham — 1/1, 40 Gardner Street, Glasgow G11 5DF — 0141 579 4772

Morrison, Katie (Miss) — 3b Lennox Court, 16 Stockiemuir Avenue, Bearsden G61 3JL — katiemorrison2003@hotmail.co.uk — 07852 373840

Nicolson, John — 2 Lindsaybeg Court, Chryston, Glasgow G69 9DD — john.c.nicolson@btinternet.com — 0141 942 3024 / 0141 779 2447

Phillips, John B. — 2/3, 30 Handel Place, Glasgow G5 0TP — johnphillips@fish.co.uk — 0141 429 7716

Robertson, Lynne M. (Mrs) MA MEd — 2 Greenhill, Bishopbriggs, Glasgow G64 1LE — emrobertsonmed@btinternet.com — 0141 772 1323 / 07720 053981

Roy, Shona (Mrs) — 81 Busby Road, Clarkston, Glasgow G76 8BD — theroyfamily@yahoo.co.uk — 0141 644 3713

Smith, Ann — 52 Robslee Road, Thornliebank, Glasgow G46 7BX — 0141 621 0638

Stead, May (Mrs) — 9A Carrick Drive, Mount Vernon, Glasgow G32 0RW — maystead@hotmail.co.uk — 07917 785109

Stewart, James — 45 Airthrey Avenue, Glasgow G14 9LY — jmstewart325@btinternet.com — 0141 959 5814

Tindall, Margaret (Mrs) — 23 Ashcroft Avenue, Lennoxtown, Glasgow G65 7EN — margaretindall@aol.com — 01360 310911

17. HAMILTON

Allan, Angus J. — Blackburn Mill, Chapelton, Strathaven ML10 6RR — angus.allan@hotmail.com — 01357 300916

Beattie, Richard — 4 Bent Road, Hamilton ML3 6QB — richardbeattie1958@hotmail.com — 01698 420806

Chirnside, Peter — 141 Kyle Park Drive, Uddingston, Glasgow G71 7DB — petefiona@btinternet.com — 01698 813769

Codona, Joy (Mrs) — Dykehead Farm, 300 Dykehead Road, Airdrie ML6 7SR — jcodona772@btinternet.com — 01236 767063 / 07810 770609 / 07742 022423

Douglas, Ian — 24 Abbotsford Crescent, Strathaven ML10 6EQ — lDouglas@churchofscotland.org.uk — 07929 031068

Fyfe, Lorna — 8b Glenavon Court, Larkhall, ML9 2WA — lorna.fyfe@yahoo.com

Haggarty, Francis — 46 Glen Road, Caldercruix, ML6 7PZ — frank_h@fsmail.net — 01236 842182

Hastings, William Paul — 186 Glen More, East Kilbride, Glasgow G74 2AN — wphastings@hotmail.co.uk — 01355 521228 / 07954 167158

Hislop, Eric	1 Castlegait, Strathaven ML10 6FF eric.hislop@tiscali.co.uk	01357 520003
Jardine, Lynette	1 Hume Drive, Uddingston, Glasgow G71 4DW lpjardine@blueyonder.co.uk	01698 812404
Leckie, Elizabeth	8 Montgomery Place, Larkhall ML9 2EZ elizleckie@blueyonder.co.uk	01698 325625
McCleary, Isaac	719 Coatbridge Road, Bargeddie, Glasgow G69 7PH isaacmccleary@gmail.com	07908 547040
Preston, Steven J.	24 Glen Prosen, East Kilbride, Glasgow G74 3TA steven.preston1@btinternet.com	01355 237359 07752 120536
Stevenson, Thomas	34 Castle Wynd, Quarter, Hamilton ML3 7XD weetangtr@gmail.com	01698 282263
White, Ian T.	4 Gilchrist Walk, Lesmahagow ML11 0FQ iantwhite@aol.com	01555 890704

18. DUMBARTON

Galbraith, Iain B. MA MPhil MTh ThD FTCL	Beechwood, Overton Road, Alexandria G83 0LJ iainbg@icloud.com	01389 753563
McEwan, Alex	Flat 1/1 The Riggs, Milngavie G62 8LX aleximcewan@gmail.com	0141 384 0274
Morgan, Richard	Annandale, School Road, Rhu, Helensburgh G84 8RS themorgans@hotmail.co.uk	01436 821269

19. ARGYLL

Alexander, John	11 Cullipool Village, Isle of Luing, Oban PA34 4UB jandjalex@gmail.com	01852 314242
Allan, Douglas	1 Camplen Court, Rothesay PA20 0NL douglasallan984@btinternet.com	
Binner, Aileen (Mrs)	Ailand, North Connel, Oban PA37 1QX binners@ailand.plus.com	01631 710264
Garrett, William	7 Creag Ghlas, Lochgilphead PA31 8UE we.garrett@btinternet.com	
Logue, David	3 Braeface, Tayvallich, Lochgilphead PA31 8PN david@loguenet.co.uk	01546 870647
McFie, David	1/1 33 Victoria Street, Rothesay PA20 0AJ waverley710@gmx.co.uk	01700 500048
MacKellar, Janet BSc	Laurel Bank, 23 George Street, Dunoon PA23 8JT jkmackellar@aol.com	01369 705549
McLellan, James A.	West Drimvore, Lochgilphead PA31 8SU james.mclellan8@btinternet.com	
Mills, Peter A.	Northton, Ganavan, Oban PA34 5TU peter@peteramills.com	01546 606403

Morrison, John L. — Tigh na Barnashaig, Tayvallich, Lochgilphead PA31 8PN / jolomo@thejolomostudio.com — 01546 870637

Ramsay, Matthew M. — Portnastorm, Carradale, Campbeltown PA28 6SB / kintyre@fishermensmission.org.uk — 01583 431381

Scouller, Alastair — 15 Allanwater Appartments, Bridge of Allan, Stirling FK9 4DZ / scouller@globalnet.co.uk — 01786 832496

Sinclair, Margaret (Ms) — 2 Quarry Place, Furnace, Inveraray PA32 8XW / margaret_sinclair@btinternet.com — 01499 500633

Stather, Angela (Ms) — 1 Dunlossit Cottages, Port Askaig, Isle of Islay PA46 7RB / angstat@btinternet.com — 01496 840726

Thornhill, Christopher R. — 4 Ardfern Cottages, Ardfern, Lochgilphead PA31 8QN / c.thornhill@btinternet.com — 01852 300011

Waddell, Martin — Fasgadh, Clachan Seil, Oban PA34 4TJ / waddell715@btinternet.com — 01852 300395

Zielinski, Jeneffer C. (Mrs) — 7 Wallace Court, Ferguslie Street, Sandbank, Dunoon PA23 8QA / jenefferzielinski@gmail.com — 01369 706136

22. FALKIRK

Duncan, Lorna M. (Mrs) BA — Richmond, 28 Solway Drive, Head of Muir, Denny FK6 5NS / ell.dee@blueyonder.co.uk — 01324 813020

McMillan, Isabelle (Mrs) — Treetops, 17 Castle Avenue, Airth FK2 8GA — 07896 433314 / 01324 812667

Stewart, Arthur MA — 51 Bonnymuir Crescent, Bonnybridge FK4 1GD / arthur.stewart1@btinternet.com

Struthers, Ivar B. — 7 McVean Place, Bonnybridge FK4 1QZ / ivar.struthers@btinternet.com — 01324 841145 / 07921 778208

23. STIRLING

Grier, Hunter — 17 Station Road, Bannockburn, Stirling FK7 8LG / anneandhunter@gmail.com — 01786 815192

McPherson, Alistair M. — Springpark, Doune Road, Dunblane FK15 9AR — 01786 826850 / 01324 812395

Scoular, Iain W. — 15 Bonnyside Road, Bonnybridge FH4 2AD / iain@iwsconsultants.com — 07717 131596

24. DUNFERMLINE

Brown, Gordon — Nowell, Fossoway, Kinross KY13 0UW / brown.nowell@hotmail.co.uk — 01577 840248

Conway, Bernard — 4 Centre Street, Kelty KY4 0EQ — 01383 830442

McCaffery, Joyce (Mrs) — 53 Foulford Street, Cowdenbeath KY4 9AS / mccafferyjo@tiscali.co.uk — 01383 515775

Meiklejohn, Barry — 40 Lilac Grove, Dunfermline KY11 8AP / meiklejohn.ib@gmail.com — 01383 731550

Mitchell, Ian G. QC — 17 Carlingnose Point, North Queensferry, Inverkeithing KY11 1ER — 01383 416240
igmitchell@easynet.co.uk

Monk, Alan — 36 North Road, Saline KY12 9UQ — 01383 851283
alanmonk@talktalk.net

25. KIRKCALDY

Biernat, Ian — 2 Formonthills Road, Glenrothes KY6 3EF — 01592 741487
ian.biernat@btinternet.com

26. ST ANDREWS

Elder, Morag Anne (Ms) — 5 Provost Road, Tayport DD6 9JE — 01382 552218
benardin@tiscali.co.uk

Grant, Allan — 6 Normandy Place, Rosyth KY11 2HJ — 01383 428760 / 07449 278378
allan75@talktalk.net

King, C. Mary (Mrs) — 8 Bankwell Road, Anstruther KY10 3DA — 01333 310017

Peacock, Graham — 6 Balgove Avenue, Gauldry, Newport-on-Tay DD6 8SQ — 01382 330124
grahampeacock6@btinternet.com

Smith, Elspeth (Mrs) — Glentarkie Cottage, Glentarkie, Strathmiglo, Cupar KY14 7RU — 01337 860824
elspeth.smith@btinternet.com

27. DUNKELD AND MEIGLE

Howat, David P. — Lilybank Cottage, Newton Street, Blairgowrie PH10 6HZ — 01250 874715
david@thehowats.net

Patterson, Rosemary (Mrs) — Rowantree, Golf Course Road, Blairgowrie PH10 6LJ — 01250 876607
pattersonrose.c@gmail.com

Theaker, Phillip D. (Dr) — 5 Altamount Road, Blairgowrie PH10 6QL — 01250 871162
ptheaker@talktalk.net

28. PERTH

Archibald, Michael — Wychwood, Culdeesland Road, Methven, Perth PH1 3QE — 01738 840995
michael.archibald@gmail.com

Begg, James — 8 Park Village, Turretbank Road, Crieff PH7 4JN — 01764 655907
Bjimmy37@aol.com

Benneworth, Michael — 7 Hamilton Place, Perth PH1 1BB — 01738 628093
mbenneworth@hotmail.com

Davidson, Andrew — 95 Needless Road, Perth PH2 0LD — 01738 620839
a.r.davidson.91@cantab.net

Laing, John — 10 Graybank Road, Perth PH2 0GZ — 01738 623888
johnandmarylaing@hotmail.co.uk

Ogilvie, Brian — 67 Whitecraigs, Kinnesswood, Kinross KY13 9JN — 01592 840823 / 07815 759864
brianj.ogilvie1@btopenworld.com

Stewart, Anne — Ballcraine, Murthly Road, Stanley, Perth PH1 4PN — 01738 828637
anne.stewart13@btinternet.com

Yellowlees, Deirdre (Mrs) — Ringmill House, Gannochy Farm, Perth PH2 7JH — d.yellowlees@btinternet.com — 01738 633773 / 07920 805399

29. DUNDEE

Sharp, Gordon — 6 Kelso Street, Dundee DD2 1SJ — gordonsharp264@gmail.com — 01382 643002

Xenophontos-Hellen, Tim — Aspro Spiti, 23 Ancrum Drive, Dundee DD2 2JG — tim.xsf@btinternet.com — (Work) 01382 630355 / 01382 567756

30. ANGUS

Beedie, Alexander W. (William) — 6B Carnegie Street,, Arbroath DD11 1TX — a.wbeedie38@gmail.com — 01241 875001

Gray, Linda (Mrs) — 8 Inchgarth Street, Forfar DD8 3LY — lindamgray@sky.com — 01307 464039

Walker, Eric — 12 Orchard Brae, Kirriemuir DD8 4JY — 01575 572082
Walker, Pat (Mrs) — 12 Orchard Brae, Kirriemuir DD8 4JY — pat.line15@btinternet.com — 01575 572082

31. ABERDEEN

Cooper, Gordon — 4 Springfield Place, Aberdeen AB15 7SF — ga_cooper@hotmail.co.uk — 01224 316667

Gray, Peter (Prof.) — 165 Countesswells Road, Aberdeen AB15 7RA — pmdgray@bcs.org.uk — 01224 318172

32. KINCARDINE AND DEESIDE

Bell, Robert — 27 Mearns Drive, Stonehaven AB39 2DZ — r.bell282@btinternet.com — 01569 767173 / 07733 014826 / 01339 880058

Broere, Teresa (Mrs) — 3 Balnastraid Cottages, Dinnet, Aboyne AB34 5NE — broere@btinternet.com

Coles, Stephen — 43 Mearns Walk, Laurencekirk AB30 1FA — steve@sbcco.com — 01561 378400

McCafferty, W. John — Lynwood, Cammachmore, Stonehaven AB39 3NR — wjmccafferty@yahoo.co.uk — 01569 730281 / 07768 925122 / 01339 755489

McLuckie, John — 7 Monaltrie Close, Ballater AB35 5PT — johnemcluckie@btinternet.com

Middleton, Robin B. (Capt.) — 7 St Ternan's Road, Newtonhill, Stonehaven AB39 3PF — robbiemiddleton7@hotmail.co.uk — 01569 730852

Platt, David — 2 St Michael's Road, Newtonhill, Stonehaven AB39 3RW — daveplatt01@btinternet.com — 01569 730465

Simpson, Elizabeth (Mrs) — Connemara, 33 Golf Road, Ballater AB35 5RS — connemara33@yahoo.com — 01339 755597

33. GORDON

Bichard, Susanna (Mrs) — Beechlee, Haddo Lane, Tarves, Ellon AB41 7JZ
smbichard@aol.com — 01651 851345

Crouch, Simon — Greenbank, Corgarff, Strathdon AB36 8YL
scassents@aol.com — 01975 651779 / 07713 101358

Doak, Alan B. — 17 Chievres Place, Ellon AB41 9WH
alanbdoak@aol.com — 01358 721819

Findlay, Patricia (Mrs) — Douglas View, Tullynessle, Alford AB33 8QR
p.a.findlay@btopenworld.com — 01975 562379

Lord, Noel (Dr) — drnolly@gmail.com — 01467 643937

Mitchell, Jean (Mrs) — 6 Cowgate, Oldmeldrum, Inverurie AB51 0EN
j.g.mitchell@btinternet.com — 01651 872745

Robb, Margaret (Mrs) — Chrislouan, Keithhall, Inverurie AB51 0LN
mdmrobb@btinternet.com — 01651 882310

34. BUCHAN

Barker, Tim — South Silverford Croft, Longmanhill, Banff AB45 3SB
tbarker05@aol.com — 01261 851839

Brown, Lillian (Mrs) — 45 Main Street, Aberchirder, Huntly AB54 7ST
mabroon64@gmail.com — 01466 780330

Forsyth, Alicia (Mrs) — Rothie Inn Farm, Forgue Road, Rothienorman, Inverurie AB51 8YH
aliciaforsyth56@gmail.com — 01651 821359

Givan, James — Zimra, Longmanhill, Banff AB45 3RP
jim_givan@btinternet.com — 01261 833318 / 07753 458664

Grant, Margaret (Mrs) — 22 Elphin Street, New Aberdour, Fraserburgh AB43 6LH
mgrant3120@gmail.com — 01346 561341

Lumsden, Vera (Mrs) — 8 Queen's Crescent, Portsoy, Banff AB45 2PX
veralumsden53@gmail.com — 01261 842712

McColl, John — East Cairnchina, Lonmay, Fraserburgh AB43 8RH
solfolly11@gmail.com — 07757 303195

McDonald, Rhoda (Miss) — 16 St Andrew's Drive, Fraserburgh AB43 2PX
techmc@callnetuk.com — 01346 514052

MacLeod, Ali (Ms) — 11 Pitfour Crescent, Fetterangus, Peterhead AB42 4EL
aliowl@hotmail.com — 01771 622992 / 07821 670705

Macnee, Anthea (Mrs) — Wardend Cottage, Alvah, Banff AB45 3TR
macneeiain4@googlemail.com — 01261 815647

Mair, Dorothy L.T. (Miss) — Flat F, 15 The Quay, Newburgh, Ellon AB41 6DA
dorothymair2@aol.com — 01358 788832 / 07505 051305

Noble, John M. — 44 Henderson Park, Peterhead AB42 2WR
john_m_noble@hotmail.co.uk — 01779 472522

Ogston, Norman — Rowandale, 6 Rectory Road, Turriff AB53 4SU
norman.ogston@gmail.com — 01888 560342

Simpson, Andrew C. — 10 Wood Street, Banff AB45 1JX
andy.louise1@btinternet.com — 01261 812538

Sneddon, Richard — 100 West Road, Peterhead AB42 2AQ
richard.sneddon@btinternet.com — 01542 831646 / 07974 760337

35. MORAY
Forbes, Jean (Mrs) — Greenmoss, Drybridge, Buckie AB56 5JB
dancingfeet@tinyworld.co.uk

36. ABERNETHY
Bardgett, Alison (Mrs) — Tigh an Iasgair, Street of Kincardine, Boat of Garten PH24 3BY
iasgair10@icloud.com — 01479 831751
Black, Barbara J. (Mrs) — Carn Eilrig, Nethy Bridge PH25 3EE
bblack7550@aol.com — 01479 821641

37. INVERNESS
Appleby, Jonathan — 91 Cradlehall Park, Inverness IV2 5DB
jon.wyvis@gmail.com — 01463 791470
Cazaly, Leonard — 9 Moray Park Gardens, Culloden, Inverness IV2 7FY
len_cazaly@lineone.net — 01463 794469
Cook, Arnett D. — 66 Millerton Avenue, Inverness IV3 8RY
arnett.cook@btinternet.com — 01463 224795
Dennis, Barry — 5 Loch Ness View, Dores, Inverness IV2 6TW
barrydennis@live.co.uk — 01463 751393
MacInnes, Ailsa (Mrs) — Kilmartin, 17 Southside Road, Inverness IV2 3BG
ailsa.macinnes@btopenworld.com — 01463 230321 / 07704 485055
Robertson, Hendry — Park House, 51 Glenurquhart Road, Inverness IV3 5PB
hendryrobertson046@btinternet.com — 01463 231858 / 07929 766102
Robertson, Stewart J.H. — 6 Raasay Road, Inverness IV2 3LR
sjhro@tiscali.co.uk — 01463 417937
Roden, Vivian (Mrs) — 15 Old Mill Road, Tomatin, Inverness IV13 7YW
vroden@btinternet.com — 01808 511355 / 07887 704915

38. LOCHABER
Gill, Ella (Mrs) — 5 Camus Inas, Acharacle PH36 4JQ
ellagill768@gmail.com — 01967 431834
Skene, William — Tiree, Gairlochy, Spean Bridge PH34 4RQ
billskene@aol.com — 01397 712594

39. ROSS
Finlayson, Michael R. — Amberlea, Glenskiach, Evanton, Dingwall IV16 9UU
finlayson935@btinternet.com — 01349 830598

Greer, Kathleen (Mrs) MEd — 17 Duthac Wynd, Tain IV19 1LP — 01862 892065
greer2@talktalk.net

Jamieson, Patricia A. (Mrs) — 9 Craig Avenue, Tain IV19 1JP — 01862 893154
hapijam179@yahoo.co.uk

McAlpine, James — 5 Cromlet Park, Invergordon IV18 0RN — 01349 852801
jmca2@tiscali.co.uk

Munro, Irene (Mrs) — 1 Wyvis Crescent, Conon Bridge, Dingwall IV7 8BZ — 01349 865752
irenemunro@rocketmail.com

40. SUTHERLAND

Baxter, A. Rosie (Dr) — Daylesford, Invershin, Lairg IV27 4ET — 01549 421326
drrosiereid@yahoo.co.uk — 07748 761694

Roberts, Irene (Miss) — Flat 4, Harbour Buildings, Main Street, Portmahomack, Tain IV20 1YG — 01862 871166
ireneroberts43@hotmail.com — 07854 436854

Weidner, Karl — 6 St Vincent Road, Tain IV19 1JR — 01862 894202
kweidner@btinternet.com

41. CAITHNESS

MacDonald, Morag (Dr) — Orkney View, Portskerra, Melvich KW14 7YL — 01641 531281
liliasmacdonald@btinternet.com

O'Neill, Leslie — Holytree Cottage, Parkside, Lybster KW3 6AS — 01593 721738
leslie_oneill@hotmail.co.uk

O'Neill, Maureen (Mrs) — Holytree Cottage, Parkside, Lybster KW3 6AS — 01593 721738
oneill.maureen@yahoo.com

42. LOCHCARRON – SKYE

Lamont, John H. BD — 6 Tigh na Filine, Aultbea, Achnasheen IV22 2JE — 07714 720753
jhlamont@btinternet.com

MacRae, Donald E. — Nethania, 52 Strath, Gairloch IV21 2DB — 01445 712235
Dmgair@aol.com

43. UIST

MacNab, Ann (Mrs) — Druim Skilivat, Scolpaig, Lochmaddy, Isle of North Uist HS6 5DH — 01876 510701
annabhan@hotmail.com

44. LEWIS

Macleod, Donald — 14 Balmerino Drive, Stornoway, Isle of Lewis HS1 2TD — 01851 704516
donaldmacleod25@btinternet.com

Macmillan, Iain — 34 Scotland Street, Stornoway, Isle of Lewis HS1 2JR — 01851 704826
macmillan@brocair.fsnet.co.uk — 07775 027987

Murray, Angus — 4 Ceann Chilleagraidh, Stornoway, Isle of Lewis HS1 2UJ — 01851 703550
angydmurray@btinternet.com

45. ORKNEY

Dicken, Marion (Mrs) — 12 MacDonald Park, St Margaret's Hope, Orkney KW17 2AL / mj44@hotmail.co.uk — 01856 831687

Gillespie, Jean (Mrs) — 16 St Colm's Quadrant, Eday, Orkney KW16 3PH / jrw2810@btinternet.com — 01856 701406

Jones, Josephine (Mrs) BA Cert Ed LRAM — Moorside, Firth, Orkney KW17 2JZ / yetminstermusic@googlemail.com — 01856 761899

Pomfret, Valerie (Mrs) — 3 Clumly Avenue, Kirkwall, Orkney KW15 1YU / vpomfret@btinternet.com

Robertson, Johan (Mrs) — Essonquoy, Eday, Orkney KW17 2AB / essonquoy@btinternet.com — 01857 622251

46. SHETLAND

Harrison, Christine (Mrs) BA — Gerdavatn, Baltasound, Unst, Shetland ZE2 9DY / chris4242@btinternet.com — 01957 711578

47. ENGLAND

Menzies, Rena (Mrs) — 49 Elizabeth Avenue, St Brelade's, Jersey JE3 8GR / menzfamily@jerseymail.co.uk — 01534 741095

Milligan, Elaine (Mrs) — 16 Surrey Close, Corby, Northants NN17 2TG / elainemilligan@ntlworld.com — 01536 205259

48. INTERNATIONAL CHARGES

49. JERUSALEM

Oakley-Levstein, Joanna (Mrs) BA — Mevo Hamma, 12934, Israel / j.oak.lev@gmail.com — 00972 50584 2517

LIST I – MINISTRIES DEVELOPMENT STAFF

Ministries Development Staff support local congregations, parish groupings and presbyteries in a wide variety of ways, bringing expertise or experience to pastoral work, development, and outreach in congregation and community. Some may be ministers and deacons undertaking specialist roles: they are listed also in Section 5 (Presbyteries), with deacons further in List C of the present section.

1. EDINBURGH

Ball, Timothy — Edinburgh: Meadowbank – Research and Communications Worker — TBall@churchofscotland.org.uk

Crocker, Liz DipComEd DCS — Edinburgh: Tron Kirk (Gilmerton and Moredun) – Parish Assistant — ECrocker@churchofscotland.org.uk

Fejszes, Violetta (Dr)	Edinburgh: Old Kirk and Muirhouse – Parish Development Worker	VFejszes@churchofscotland.org.uk
de Jager, Lourens (Rev) PgDip MDiv BTh	Edinburgh: Portobello and Joppa – Associate Minister	LDeJager@churchofscotland.org.uk
Lennox, Gigha K.	Edinburgh: St David's Broomhouse – Children and Family Worker	GLennox@churchofscotland.org.uk
Logie, Duncan A.	Edinburgh: St Margaret's – Children, Youth and Family Worker	DLogie@churchofscotland.org.uk
McMullin, Michael BA	Edinburgh: Gorgie Dalry Stenhouse – Community Outreach Worker	MMcMullin@churchofscotland.org.uk
Marshall, Zoe	Edinburgh: Willowbrae – Community Development Worker	ZMarshall@churchofscotland.org.uk
Midwinter, Alan	Edinburgh: St David's Broomhouse – Pastoral Assistant	AMidwinter@churchofscotland.org.uk
Moodie, David	Edinburgh: Granton – Parish Assistant	DMoodie@churchofscotland.org.uk
Richardson, Ian (Dr)	Edinburgh: Holy Trinity – Discipleship Team Leader	IRichardson@churchofscotland.org.uk
Robertson, Douglas S. BEng BA MTh	Edinburgh: Gracemount – Church Leader	Douglas.Robertson@churchofscotland.org.uk
Stark, Jennifer MA MATheol	Edinburgh: Richmond Craigmillar – Community Development Worker	JStark@churchofscotland.org.uk

2. WEST LOTHIAN

Brown, Kenneth (Rev)	Livingston United – Church and Community Development Worker	Kenneth.Brown@churchofscotland.org.uk
Corrie, Margaret (Miss) DCS	Armadale – Mission Development Worker	MCorrie@churchofscotland.org.uk
Johnston, Ashley L.	Abercorn linked with Pardovan, Kinscavil and Winchburgh – Child, Young Person and Family Worker	AJohnston@churchofscotland.org.uk
Pennykid, Gordon J. BD DCS	Livingston: Old – Parish Assistant	GPennykid@churchofscotland.org.uk
Philip, Darren BSc	Livingston United – Youth and Children's Worker	DPhilip@churchofscotland.org.uk
Safrany, Zoltan (Rev)	Bathgate: St John's – Parish Development Worker	ZSafrany@churchofscotland.org.uk

3. LOTHIAN

Glen, Ewen A.	Tranent Cluster and Presbytery – Family and Youth Development Worker	EGlen@churchofscotland.org.uk
Middlemass, Deborah	Tranent Cluster – Family and Youth Development Worker	DMiddlemass@churchofscotland.org.uk
Muir, Malcolm T. (Rev)	Newbattle – Associate Minister	MMuir@churchofscotland.org.uk
Pryde, Erica	Newbattle – Mission and Outreach Co-ordinator	EPryde@churchofscotland.org.uk

4. MELROSE AND PEEBLES

5. DUNS

6. JEDBURGH

7. ANNANDALE AND ESKDALE

Brydson, Angela (Mrs) DCS	Lochmaben, Moffat and Lockerbie grouping – Deacon	ABrydson@churchofscotland.org.uk
Campbell, Alasdair D. BA	Annan and Gretna grouping – Parish Assistant	Alasdair.Campbell@churchofscotland.org.uk
Hislop, Donna	Canonbie, Langholm & Border grouping - Youth Worker	DHislop@churchofscotland.org.uk

8. DUMFRIES AND KIRKCUDBRIGHTSHIRE

Temple, Tracy	Dumfries: Northwest – Parish Assistant	TTemple@churchofscotland.org.uk

9. WIGTOWN AND STRANRAER

10. AYR
Crossan, Morag (Rev) BA — Dalmellington linked with Patna Waterside – Youth and Childen's Worker — MCrossan@churchofscotland.org.uk

11. IRVINE AND KILMARNOCK
Wardrop, Elaine — Kilmarnock: St Andrew's and St Marnock's: Mission Development Worker — EWardrop@churchofscotland.org.uk

12. ARDROSSAN
Beck, Isobel BD DCS — Kilwinning Old – Deacon — IBeck@churchofscotland.org.uk
Blair, Fiona DCS — Beith – Parish Assistant — FBlair@churchofscotland.org.uk
Boyd, Carol — Kilwinning Mansefield Trinity – Young Adults Community Development W. — CBoyd@churchofscotland.org.uk
Currie, Archie — Ardrossan: Park – Outreach and Family Worker — archie.currie.currie@churchofscotland.org.uk
Hunter, Jean C.Q. BD — Brodick linked with Corrie linked with Lochranza and Pirmmill linked with Shiskine – Parish Assistant — JHunter@churchofscotland.org.uk
McKay, Angus — Cumbrae linked with Largs St John's – Parish Assistant — AMcKay@churchofscotland.org.uk

13. LANARK

14. GREENOCK AND PAISLEY
McCallum, Graham — Paisley St Ninian's Ferguslie – Outreach Worker — GMcCallum@churchofscotland.org.uk
Murphy, Natasha C. — Greenock Parish Grouping – Youth and Children's Worker — NMurphy@churchofscotland.org.uk

16. GLASGOW
Baird, Janette Y. — Glasgow: Castlemilk – Community Development Worker — JBaird@churchofscotland.org.uk
Buchanan, Marion (Mrs) MA DCS — Glasgow: Garthamlock and Craigend East – Deacon — MBuchanan@churchofscotland.org.uk
Cameron, Lisa — Glasgow: St James' (Pollok) – Youth and Children's Ministry Leader — LCameron@churchofscotland.org.uk
Campbell, Julie — Glasgow: Drumchapel St Andrew's – Parish Assistant — Julie.Campbell@churchofscotland.org.uk
Cathcart, John Paul DCS — Glasgow: Castlemilk – Deacon — Paul.Cathcart@churchofscotland.org.uk
Crumlin, Melodie BA PGMgt DipBusMgt — PEEK (Possibilities for Each and Every Kid) – Project Development Manager — MCrumlin@churchofscotland.org.uk
Dinsmore, Yvonne — Glasgow: Colston Wellpark – Parish Project Development Worker — YDinsmore@churchofscotland.org.uk
Durning, Ashley — Glasgow: Possilpark – Youth Development Worker — ADurning@churchofscotland.org.uk
Evans, Andrew — Glasgow: Gorbals – Community Development Worker — AEvans@churchofscotland.org.uk
Gargrave, Mary S. (Mrs) DCS — Glasgow: Carnwadric – Deacon — Mary.Gargrave@churchofscotland.org.uk
Goodwin, Jamie — Glasgow: Govan and Linthouse – Research and Development Facilitator — Jgoodwin@churchofscotland.org.uk
Hamilton, James DCS — Glasgow: Maryhill – Parish Assistant — James.Hamilton@churchofscotland.org.uk
Hamilton, Karen (Mrs) DCS — Cambuslang – Deacon — KHamilton@churchofscotland.org.uk
Hyndman, Graham — Church House, Bridgeton – Youth Worker — GHyndman@churchofscotland.org.uk
Kelly, Ewan R. (Rev) MB ChB BD PhD — Glasgow: Queen's Park Govanhill – Associate Minister — EKelly@churchofscotland.org.uk

McMahon, Deborah	Glasgow: Easterhouse – Children's Development Worker	DKeenan@churchofscotland.org.uk
McDougall, Hilary N. (Rev) MA PGCE BD	Presbytery Congregational Facilitator (Glasgow)	HMcDougall@churchofscotland.org.uk
McGreechin, Anne	Glasgow: Cranhill, Ruchazie and Garthamlock and Craigend East Parish Grouping – Congregational Support Worker	AMcGreechin@churchofscotland.org.uk
McIlreavy, Gillian M.	Glasgow: Govan and Linthouse – Communication Co-ordinator	GMcIlreavy@churchofscotland.org.uk
McKeown, Mark W.J. (Rev) MEng MDiv	Glasgow: Chryston – Associate Minister	MMcKeown@churchofscotland.org.uk
Marshall, Kirsteen	Glasgow: St Christopher's Priesthill and Nitshill – Parish Assistant	KMarshall@churchofscotland.org.uk
Miller, Susan	Glasgow: Shettleston New – Youth and Children's Worker	SMiller@churchofscotland.org.uk
Morrin, Jonathan	Glasgow: Barlanark Greyfriars – Youth and Children's Worker	JMorrin@churchofscotland.org.uk
Morrison, Iain J.	Glasgow: Colston Milton – Community Arts Worker	IMorrison@churchofscotland.org.uk
Pettigrove, Kaila	Glasgow: Wallacewell – Children and Youth Development Worker	KPettigrove@churchofscotland.org.uk
Robertson, Douglas J.	Glasgow: Baillieston churches – Children and Families Worker	DJRobertson@churchofscotland.org.uk
Sutton, Naomi	Glasgow: St Christopher's Priesthill and Nitshill – Children and Family Worker	NSutton@churchofscotland.org.uk
Thomas, Jay MA BA	Glasgow: Springburn – Parish Project Development Worker	JThomas@churchofscotland.org.uk
Thomson, Andrew (Rev) BA	Glasgow: Govan and Linthouse – Pastoral Assistant	AThomson@churchofscotland.org.uk
Usher, Eileen	Glasgow: Cranhill, Ruchazie, Garthamlock and Craigend East Parish Grouping – Family Worker	EUsher@churchofscotland.org.uk
Willis, Mags	Glasgow: Easterhouse – Youth Development Worker	MWillis@churchofscotland.org.uk
Young, Neil J.	Glasgow: St Paul's – Youth Worker	NYoung@churchofscotland.org.uk

17. HAMILTON

Binnie, Michelle	Hamilton: Gilmour and Whitehill linked with Hamilton: West -	MBinnie@churchofscotland.org.uk
Douglas, Ian	Motherwell: Crosshill linked with St Margaret's – Parish Assistant	IDouglas@churchofscotland.org.uk

18. DUMBARTON

Burke, Maureen	Dumbarton churches - Pastoral Assistant	MBurke@churchofscotland.org.uk
Dungavell, Marie Claire	Dumbarton: Riverside linked with West, Development Worker	MCDungavell@churchofscotland.org.uk
Graham, Gillian	Clydebank Waterfront linked with Dalmuir Barclay – Children, Young People and Family Worker	GGraham@churchofscotland.org.uk
Kemp, Tina (Rev) MA	Helensburgh linked with Rhu and Shandon – Ministries Assistant	TKemp@churchofscotland.org.uk
White, David M. (Rev) BA BD DMin	Baldernock linked with Milgavie St Paul's – Associate Minister	drdavidmwhite@btinternet.com

19. ARGYLL

Beautyman, Paul H. (Rev) MA BD	Presbytery – Youth Adviser	PBeautyman@churchofscotland.org.uk
Burton, Rebecca A.	Presbytery - Youth and Children's Worker	RBurton@churchofscotland.org.uk
Fulcher, Christine P. (Rev) BEd	Kilmore and Oban – Parish Assistant	CFulcher@churchofscotland.org.uk
Hay, Alison	North and East Argyll Hub-style Ministries Co-ordinator	AHay@churchofscotland.org.uk
Hood, Catriona A. (Rev)	South Argyll Hub-style Ministries Co-ordinator	CHood@churchofscotland.org.uk
McLaren, Glenda M. (Ms) DCS	Dunoon: St John's linked with Kirn and Sandbank – Deacon	Glenda.McLaren@churchofscotland.org.uk
Wilson, John K. (Kenny)	Presbytery - Youth and Children's Worker	KWilson@churchofscotland.org.uk

22. FALKIRK

Archer, Janice — Cumbernauld: Kildrum – Admin Support Worker

Bogle, Albert O. (Very Rev) BD MTh — Sanctuary First (Presbytery Mission Initiative) – Pioneer Minister — albertbogle@mac.com

Boland, Susan (Mrs) DipHE(Theol) — Cumbernauld: Abronhill – Family Development Worker — SBoland@churchofscotland.org.uk

Cuthbertson, Valerie S. (Miss) DCS — Cumbernauld: Old – Deacon — VCuthbertson@churchofscotland.org.uk

Nicholson, David DCS — Cumbernauld: Kildrum – Deacon — DNicholson@churchofscotland.org.uk

23. STIRLING

Allen, Valerie L (Rev) BMus MDiv DMin — Presbytery – Chaplain — VL2allen@btinternet.com

Anderson, Dorothy U. (Rev) LLB DipPL BD — Dunblane: Cathedral – Associate Minister — DAnderson@churchofscotland.org.uk

McDowell, Bonnie J. — Presbytery - Dementia Project Co-ordinator — BMcDowell@churchofscotland.org.uk

Porter, Jean T. (Mrs) BD DCS — Stirling: St Mark's – Deacon — JPorter@churchofscotland.org.uk

24. DUNFERMLINE

Christie, Aileen — Lochgelly and Benarty: St Serf's – Outreach Worker — Aileen.Christie@churchofscotland.org.uk

Crawford, Morag (Miss) MSc DCS — Rosyth – Deacon — MCrawford@churchofscotland.org.uk

Scott, Pamela (Mrs) DCS — Lochgelly and Benarty: St Serf's – Parish Assistant — PScott@churchofscotland.org.uk

25. KIRKCALDY

Hutchison, John BA — Rothes Trinity Parish Grouping – Families Worker and Parish Assistant — JHutchison@churchofscotland.org.uk

Livingstone, Ruth M. — Glenrothes: St Margaret's – Congregational Support Worker — RLivingstone@churchofscotland.org.uk

Pringle, Iona M. BD — Kennoway, Windygates and Balgonie: St Kenneth's – Parish Assistant — IPringle@churchofscotland.org.uk

Stark, Alastair BA — Glenrothes and Leslie churches: Youth and Children's Worker — AStark@churchofscotland.org.uk

Thomson, Jacqueline (Mrs) MTh DCS — Buckhaven and Wemyss – Deacon — Jaqueline.Thomson@churchofscotland.org.uk

26. ST ANDREWS

27. DUNKELD AND MEIGLE

28. PERTH

Mackay, Kenneth D. DCS — Perth: Letham St Mark's – Pastoral Worker — Kenneth.Mackay@churchofscotland.org.uk

Stewart, Alexander T. (Rev) MA BD FSAScot — Perth: St John's Kirk of Perth linked with Perth: St Leonard's-in-the-Fields – Associate Minister — alex.t.stewart@blueyonder.co.uk

Wellstood, Keith A. PGDipCG MICG — Perth: Riverside – Community Worker — KWellstood@churchofscotland.org.uk

29. DUNDEE

Berry, Gavin R. — Dundee: Camperdown/Lochee - Parish Assistant — GBerry@churchofscotland.org.uk

Campbell, Neil MA — Dundee: Craigiebank linked with Douglas and Mid Craigie – Youth and Young Adult Development Worker — Neil.Campbell@churchofscotland.org.uk

Clark, Ross — Dundee: Fintry – Discipleship, Mission and Development Worker — Ross.Clark@churchofscotland.org.uk

McKenzie, Matthew — Dundee: Lochee / Dundee: Camperdown – Youth and Families Worker — MMcKenzie@churchofscotland.org.uk

Stirling, Diane BSc DipCPC BTh — Dundee: Craigiebank linked with Douglas and Mid Craigie – Parish Assistant — DStirling@churchofscotland.org.uk

30. ANGUS

Grimmond, Shona — Arbroath: Knox's linked with Arbroath St Vigeans – Family Worker — SGrimmond@churchofscotland.org.uk

Stevens, Linda (Rev) BSc BD PgDip — The Glens and Kirriemuir: Old – West Angus Area Team Minister — LStevens@churchofscotland.org.uk

31. ABERDEEN

Amalanand, John — Aberdeen: Garthdee – Parish Assistant — JAmalanand@churchofscotland.org.uk

Angus, Natalie — Dyce – Youth and Family Worker — NAngus@churchofscotland.org.uk

Broere, Teresa — Aberdeen: Mastrick – Parish Assistant — PBroere@churchofscotland.org.uk

Lightbody, Philip (Rev) — Presbytery - Mission Development Leader and Presbytery Planning Officer — PLightbody@churchofscotland.org.uk

Mitchell, William — Aberdeen: St George's Tillydrone / Middlefield – Community Development Worker — WMitchell@churchofscotland.org.uk

Taylor, Valerie AssocCIPD PGDip — Aberdeen: Torry St Fittick's – Ministry Assistant — VTaylor@churchofscotland.org.uk

32. KINCARDINE AND DEESIDE

33. GORDON

Adam, Pamela BD — Ellon – Parish Assistant — PAdam@churchofscotland.org.uk

Bruce, Nicola P.S. BA MTh — Ellon – Parish Assistant, Mission Development — NBruce@churchofscotland.org.uk

Cross, Peter — Ellon – Parish Assistant — PCross@churchofscotland.org.uk

Mikelson, Heather (Rev) — Presbytery - Mission Development Worker — HMikelson@churchofscotland.org.uk

Stewart, Marion G. (Miss) DCS — Skene – Deacon — MStewart@churchofscotland.org.uk

Stigant, Victoria J. — Presbytery - Youth Work Facilitator — VStigant@churchofscotland.org.uk

34. BUCHAN

35. MORAY

Baker, Paula (Mrs) — Birnie and Pluscarden linked with Elgin: High – Parish Assistant — PBaker@churchofscotland.org.uk

Bosch, Eckhardt — Keith churches – Parish Assistant — EBosch@churchofscotland.org.uk

36. ABERNETHY

Orr, Gillian BA — Presbytery - Youth Worker — GOrr@churchofscotland.org.uk

37. INVERNESS

Haringman, Paul MSc — Culloden: The Barn – Community Worker — Paul.Haringman@churchofscotland.org.uk

Lynch, David J. — Inverness: Trinity – Children and Family Worker — DLynch@churchofscotland.org.uk

38. LOCHABER

39. ROSS

40. SUTHERLAND

41. CAITHNESS
MacArthur, Neil (Archie)   Pentland – Parish Assistant   AMacArthur@churchofscotland.org.uk

42. LOCHCARRON-SKYE

43. UIST

44. LEWIS

45. ORKNEY

46. SHETLAND
Weir, K. Ellen   Presbytery – Youth and Children's Worker   EWeir@churchofscotland.org.uk

47. ENGLAND
Price, Andrea E. (Rev)   London: St Columba's – Associate Minister   APrice@churchofscotland.org.uk

48. INTERNATIONAL CHARGES

LIST J – OVERSEAS LOCATIONS

AFRICA
MALAWI

Church of Central Africa Presbyterian
Synod of Livingstonia
Mr Linus Malu (2018)   Legal Officer, Church and Society Department, Church and Society Department, PO Box 112, Mzuzu, Malawi   +265 265 1 311 133   www.ccapsolinia.org
nnabuikemalu@yahoo.com

Vacant (2018)   Resource, Mobilisation & Communications Manager, Church and Society Department, PO Bix 112, Mzuzu, Malawi   +265 265 1 311 133   www.ccapsolinia.org
churchsociety@sdnp.org.mw

Location	Name	Address	Contact
ZAMBIA	**Synod of Nkhoma** Dr David Morton (2009)	Nkhoma Hospital, PO Box 48, Nkhoma, Malawi kuluva2@gmail.com	00265 9940 74022 www.nkhomahospital.org
	United Church of Zambia Mr Keith and Mrs Ida Waddell (2016)	UCZ Synod, Nationalist Road at Burma Road, P.O. Box 50122, 15101 Ridgeway, Lusaka, Zambia keithida2014@gmail.com	00260 964 761 039 http://uczsynod.org
	Ms Jenny Featherstone (Ecumenical appointment) (2007)	Principal, Chodort Training Centre, PO Box 630451, Choma, Zambia jenny.featherstone@googlemail.com	00260 979 703 130
ASIA NEPAL	Mr Joel Hasvenstein (2015)	c/o United Mission to Nepal, PO Box 126, Kathmandu, Nepal ed@umn.org.np	00 977 1 4228 118 www.umn.org.np
LAOS	Mr Tony and Mrs Catherine Paton (2009)	Church Mission Society, Church of the Holy Spirit, Vientiane Lao People's Democratic Republic	www.the-chs.org.
EUROPE PRAGUE	Rev Dr David I. Sinclair (2017)	Evangelical Church of the Czech Brethren, Jungmannova 9, CZ111 21, Prague 1 DSinclair@churchofscotland.org.uk	00 420 224 999 230
ROME	Ms Fiona Kendall (2017)	Mediterranean Hope, Federation of Protestant Churches in Italy, Via Firenze 38, 00138 Roma, Italy FKendall@churchofscotland.org.uk	00 39 (0)6 4825 120 www.mediterraneanhope.com
MIDDLE EAST EGYPT	Rev Colin D. Johnston (2016)	Evangelical Theological Seminary Cairo, 8 El-Abaseya, Al Izab, Al Waili, Cairo 11381, Egypt CDJohnston@churchofscotland.org.uk	00 200 100 955 7809 http://etsc.org/new/
BEIRUT	Rev Dr Hedda Klip (2017)	Near East School of Theology, PO Box 13-5780, Sourati Street, Chouran, Beirut, Lebanon Boekli2010@gmail.com	00 961 134 990 1131 www.theonest.edu.lb/en/Home

For other European, Middle Eastern and other locations, see the Presbyteries of International Charges and Jerusalem (Section 5: 48 and 49)

LIST K – PRISON CHAPLAINS

ADVISER TO SCOTTISH PRISON SERVICE (NATIONAL)	Rev. Sheena Orr	SPS HQ, Carlton House, 5 Redheughs Rigg, South Gyle, Edinburgh EH12 9DQ sheena.orr@sps.pnn.gov.uk	0131 244 8745

For a list of Prisons and Chaplains see: www.churchofscotland.org.uk > Resources > Yearbook > Section 6-K

LIST L – UNIVERSITY CHAPLAINS

For a list of Universities and Chaplains see: www.churchofscotland.org.uk > Resources > Yearbook > Section 6-L

LIST M – WORK PLACE CHAPLAINS

CHIEF EXECUTIVE	Rev. Iain McFadzean	iain.mcfadzean@wpcscotland.co.uk	07969 227694

For a full list of Regional Organisers, Team Leaders and Chaplaincy Locations see: www.wpcscotland.co.uk > Contact Us

LIST N – REPRESENTATIVES ON COUNCIL EDUCATION COMMITTEES

For a full list see: www.churchofscotland.org.uk > Resources > Yearbook > Section 6-N

LIST O – MINISTERS ORDAINED FOR SIXTY YEARS AND UPWARDS

For a full list see: www.churchofscotland.org.uk > Resources > Yearbook > Section 6-O

LIST P – DECEASED MINISTERS AND DEACONS

The Editor has been made aware of the following ministers and deacons who have died since the compilation of the previous volume of the Year Book.

Aitken, Eric Douglas	(Clackmannan)
Black, Andrew Graham	(Gladsmuir with Longniddry)
Bowie, Adam McCall	(Cavers and Kirkton with Hobkirk and Southdean)
Bowie, Alexander Glen	(Principal Chaplain to the Royal Air Force)
Brain, Isobel Jarvie	(Ballantrae)
Bristow, William Henry Greenway	(Chaplain, Army)
Brown, William	(Edinburgh: Polwarth)
Bryden, William Anderson	(Glasgow: Yoker Old with Glasgow: Yoker St Matthew's)
Campbell, William Frank	(Ale and Teviot)
Craig, Eric	(Edinburgh: Chalmers Lauriston)
Crombie, William Duncan	(Glasgow: Calton New with Glasgow: St Andrew's)
Dowswell, James Adrian Miller	(Lerwick and Bressay)
Forrest, Kenneth Peat	Auxiliary Minister, Langbank with Port Glasgow: St Andrew's
Fraser, Ian Masson	(Selly Oak Colleges, Birmingham)
Galloway, Robert Wood Clark	(Cromarty)
Garden, Margaret Jay	(Cushnie and Tough)
Gibson, Francis Symington	(Kilarrow with Kilmeny)
Gibson, Herbert Marshall	(Glasgow: St Thomas' Gallowgate)
Gillespie, Irene Cameron	(Tiree)
Graham, Alexander David Moore	(Aberdeen: Rosemount)
Gregson, Elizabeth Mills	(Glasgow: Drumchapel St Andrew's)
Grubb, George Darlington Wilson	(Edinburgh: Corstorphine Craigsbank)
Harbison, David John Hislop	(Beith: High with Beith: Trinity)
Hawdon, John Edward	(Dundee: Clepington)
Hutchison, Alan E. W. DCS	(Deacon)
Irvine, Euphemia Helen Clouston	(Milton of Campsie)
Jenkinson, John Harley	(Auxiliary Minister, Cumbernauld Kildrum)
Kellas, David John	(Kilfinan with Kyles)
Kerr, Andrew	(Kilbarchan: West)
Lugton, George Lockhart	(Guernsey: St Andrew's in the Grange)
Lynn, Robert	(Ayr: St Leonard's with Dalrymple)
McCreadie, David White	(Kirkmabreck)
MacDonald, James Mackay	(Kilmarnock: St John's Onthank)
Macfarlane, Alwyn James Cecil	(Glasgow: Newlands South)
MacFarlane, David Cockburn	(Eddleston with Peebles: Old)
MacInnes, David	(Kilmuir and Paible)
MacMahon, Janet Phillips Hotchkies	(Kilmaronock Gartocharn)
MacQuien, Duncan DCS	(Deacon)
Macrae, Jennifer	Haddington: St Mary's
Millar, Archibald Edmunds	(Perth: St Stephen's)

Philip, Michael Robert	(Falkirk: Bainsford)
Ross, Alan Chalmers	(Eskdalemuir with Hutton and Corrie with Tundergarth)
Sangster, Ernest George	(Alva)
Shaw of Chapelverna, Duncan	(Edinburgh: Craigentinny St Christopher's)
Sherratt, Arthur	(Saltcoats: St Cuthbert's)
Sherry, George Taylor	(Menstrie)
Souter, David Iain	(Perth: Kinnoull)
Stewart, Gordon Grant	(Perth: St Leonard's-in-the-Fields and Trinity)
Stirling, Alexander Douglas	(Rhu and Shandon)
Trevorrow, James Aird	(Glasgow: Cranhill)
Whyte, John Henry	(Gourock: Ashton)
Wilkinson, Arrick Dempster	(Fisherton with Kirkoswald)
Yule, Ronald Fraser	Fraserburgh: South with Inverallochy and Rathen: East

SECTION 7

Legal Names and Scottish Charity Numbers for Congregations

All congregations in Scotland, and congregations furth of Scotland which are registered with OSCR, the Office of the Scottish Charity Regulator

For a complete list of legal names see:
www.churchofscotland.org.uk > Resources > Yearbook > Section 7

Further information

All documents, as defined in the Charities References in Documents (Scotland) Regulations 2007, must specify the Charity Number, Legal Name of the congregation, any other name by which the congregation is commonly known and the fact that it is a Charity. For more information, please refer to the Law Department circular on the Regulations on the Church of Scotland website.

www.churchofscotland.org.uk > Resources > Subjects > Law Department Circulars > Charity Law

SECTION 8

Church Buildings: Ordnance Survey National Grid References

Please go to: www.churchofscotland.org.uk > Resources > Yearbook > Section 8

SECTION 9

Parish and Congregational Changes

The parish structure of the Church of Scotland is constantly being reshaped as the result of unions, linkages and the occasional dissolution.

Section 9A, 'Parishes and Congregations: names no longer in use', records one of the inevitable consequences of these changes, the disappearance of the names of many former parishes and congregations. There are, however, occasions when for legal and other reasons it is important to be able to identify the present-day successors of those parishes and congregations whose names are no longer in use and which can therefore no longer be easily traced. A list of all such parishes and congregations, with full explanatory notes, may be found at:

www.churchofscotland.org.uk/Resources/Yearbook > Section 9A

Section 9B, 'Recent Readjustment and other Congregational Changes', printed below, incorporates all instances of union, linkage and dissolution, together with certain other congregational changes, which have taken place since the publication of the 2017–18 Year Book.

1 Edinburgh	**Edinburgh: Craigmillar Park** linked with **Edinburgh: Reid Memorial**
	Edinburgh: Leith Wardie renamed **Edinburgh: Wardie**
6 Jedburgh	**Kelso Country Churches** linked with **Oxnam**: linkage severed
11 Irvine and Kilmarnock	**Irvine: Girdle Toll** linked with **Irvine: St Andrew's**
13 Lanark	**Coalburn** and **Lesmahagow: Old** united as **Coalburn and Lesmahagow: Old**
16 Glasgow	**Glasgow: Mosspark** and **Glasgow: Sherbrooke St Gilbert's** united as **Glasgow: Sherbrooke Mosspark**
	Netherlee linked with **Stamperland**

17 Hamilton	**Chapelton, Glassford, Strathaven: East** and **Strathaven: Rankin** united as **Strathaven: Trinity**
	Motherwell: North linked with **Wishaw: Craigneuk and Belhaven**
	Wishaw: Craigneuk and Belhaven linked with **Wishaw: Old**: linkage severed
18 Dumbarton	**Dumbarton: Riverside** linked with **Dumbarton: West Kirk** additionally linked with **Dumbarton: St Andrew's**
19 Argyll	**Kilchoman, Kilmeny** and **Portnahaven** united as **North and West Islay**
26 St Andrews	**Abdie and Dunbog** and **Newburgh** united as **Lindores**
	Auchtermuchty and **Edenshead and Strathmiglo** united as **Edenshead**
29 Dundee	**Dundee: Meadowside St Paul's** linked with **Dundee: St Andrew's**
31 Aberdeen	**Aberdeen: Queen Street** and **Aberdeen: St Mark's** united as **Aberdeen: St Mark's**
35 Moray	**Dyke** and **Edinkillie** united as **Dyke and Edinkillie**
40 Sutherland	**Altnaharra and Farr** linked with **Melness and Tongue**
41 Caithness	**Canisbay, Dunnet, Keiss** and **Olrig** united as **Pentland**
47 England	**Liverpool: St Andrew's** dissolved
49 Jerusalem	**Jerusalem: St Andrew's** and **Tiberias: St Andrew's** united as **Jerusalem: St Andrew's and Tiberias: St Andrew's**

SECTION 10

Congregational
Statistics
2017

Comparative Statistics: 1977–2017

	2017	*2007*	*1997*	*1987*	*1977*
Communicants	336,831	489,118	660,954	838,659	1,002,945
Elders	27,494	38,534	44,922	46,808	48,454

NOTES ON CONGREGATIONAL STATISTICS

Com Number of communicants at 31 December 2017.

Eld Number of elders at 31 December 2017.

G Membership of the Guild including Young Woman's Groups and others as recorded on the 2017 annual return submitted to the Guild Office.

In 17 Ordinary General Income for 2017. Ordinary General Income consists of members' offerings, contributions from congregational organisations, regular fund-raising events, income from investments, deposits and so on. This figure does not include extraordinary or special income, or income from special collections and fund-raising for other charities.

M&M Final amount allocated to congregations to contribute for Ministries and Mission after allowing for Presbytery-approved amendments up to 31 December 2017, but before deducting stipend endowments and normal allowances given for locum purposes in a vacancy or guardianship.

–18 This figure shows 'the number of children and young people aged 17 years and under who are involved in the life of the congregation'.

NB: Figures may not be available for new charges created or for congregations which have entered into readjustment late in 2017 or during 2018. Figures might also not be available for congregations which failed to submit the appropriate schedule.

Congregation	Com	Eld	G	In 17	M&M	–18
1. Edinburgh						
Balerno	544	72	23	135,826	68,142	25
Barclay Viewforth	316	29	-	162,197	123,105	60
Blackhall St Columba's	677	67	-	202,363	113,290	24
Bristo Memorial Craigmillar	56	6	-	49,807	30,385	70
Broughton St Mary's	175	23	-	65,521	47,359	52
Canongate	336	33	-	154,583	71,673	12
Carrick Knowe	353	46	59	63,690	40,107	260
Colinton	827	51	-	198,207	119,248	75
Corstorphine: Craigsbank	408	30	-	101,627	62,214	91
Corstorphine: Old	393	34	40	136,930	71,819	60
Corstorphine: St Anne's	358	56	61	113,180	67,475	21
Corstorphine: St Ninian's	643	75	63	164,702	98,205	-
Craiglockhart	368	47	28	139,829	96,155	12
Craigmillar Park	188	14	21	69,362	49,801	3
Reid Memorial	291	15	-	119,458	55,532	21
Cramond	982	93	-	247,368	172,534	75
Currie	474	28	52	149,020	89,524	76
Dalmeny	91	12	-	20,694	22,815	7
Queensferry	531	44	52	118,951	65,386	165
Davidson's Mains	434	70	-	-	118,107	60
Drylaw	71	15	-	16,233	6,559	3
Duddingston	419	42	-	109,808	68,585	126
Fairmilehead	509	58	31	106,724	79,388	49
Gorgie Dalry Stenhouse	226	24	-	-	80,061	29
Gracemount	23	4	-	20,959	2,567	8
Liberton	706	50	40	219,884	126,847	80
Granton	173	20	-	-	24,195	10
Greenbank	691	82	37	255,338	142,093	213
Greenside	126	26	-	-	29,263	6
Greyfriars Kirk	301	32	-	-	92,179	20
High (St Giles')	469	34	-	329,096	178,773	17
Holy Trinity	210	28	-	-	109,265	165
Inverleith St Serf's	329	37	22	110,258	77,891	150
Juniper Green	297	24	-	97,674	65,991	30
Kirkliston	234	31	45	89,931	58,736	10
Leith: North	172	22	-	77,886	51,569	20
Leith: St Andrew's	186	22	-	81,531	55,014	42
Leith: South	308	54	-	174,239	77,768	132
Liberton Northfield	172	10	-	54,001	28,904	241
Marchmont St Giles'	215	30	19	113,896	71,574	68
Mayfield Salisbury	511	61	-	251,819	143,428	50
Meadowbank	82	4	-	37,803	94,975	3
Morningside	426	62	-	197,720	122,702	78
Morningside United	99	12	-	64,872	5,502	15
Murrayfield	492	42	-	150,495	94,123	80
Newhaven	147	16	-	81,693	49,107	120
Old Kirk and Muirhouse	96	18	-	30,081	18,574	65
Palmerston Place	379	36	-	169,000	106,804	97

Congregation	Com	Eld	G	In 17	M&M	–18
Pilrig St Paul's	216	17	22	46,360	27,726	31
Polwarth	180	21	12	91,693	55,205	15
Portobello and Joppa	829	78	78	234,617	134,061	199
Priestfield	111	16	18	89,769	48,804	-
Ratho	184	16	-	43,094	31,692	10
Richmond Craigmillar	91	9	-	-	5,130	20
St Andrew's and St George's West	329	47	-	274,040	160,382	52
St Andrew's Clermiston	184	11	-	-	29,733	11
St Catherine's Argyle	104	7	-	67,234	35,812	31
St Cuthbert's	291	40	-	129,936	94,625	9
St David's Broomhouse	119	16	-	30,005	16,458	37
St John's Colinton Mains	218	18	-	58,511	38,924	48
St Margaret's	212	28	19	51,816	37,565	87
St Martin's	83	12	-	23,818	4,604	15
St Michael's	317	26	28	68,845	51,764	14
St Nicholas' Sighthill	333	20	-	-	25,914	30
St Stephen's Comely Bank	174	10	-	95,080	57,421	21
Slateford Longstone	192	11	32	35,546	28,377	21
Stockbridge	186	19	-	80,133	58,088	38
Tron Kirk (Gilmerton and Moredun)	87	8	-	-	8,789	118
Wardie	513	47	44	158,048	89,110	70
Willowbrae	111	16	-	42,081	46,869	3

2. West Lothian

Abercorn	64	8	-	16,659	10,228	-
Pardovan, Kingscavil and Winchburgh	260	29	-	72,527	40,565	214
Armadale	491	41	24	84,710	48,125	202
Avonbridge	66	7	-	14,157	7,163	6
Torphichen	224	16	-	31,016	26,532	5
Bathgate: Boghall	224	27	22	96,122	52,504	146
Bathgate: High	458	34	32	94,691	52,000	70
Bathgate: St John's	341	21	30	60,774	34,000	108
Blackburn and Seafield	371	30	-	79,219	44,693	85
Blackridge	70	8	-	20,266	9,700	2
Harthill: St Andrew's	185	10	22	57,739	33,154	52
Breich Valley	108	11	18	34,914	22,876	40
Broxburn	353	27	32	84,132	45,900	20
Fauldhouse: St Andrew's	184	11	-	43,470	36,249	12
Kirknewton and East Calder	296	36	22	99,927	65,030	62
Kirk of Calder	512	40	19	89,541	49,378	24
Linlithgow: St Michael's	1,289	105	51	-	171,121	175
Linlithgow: St Ninian's Craigmailen	390	40	43	70,321	43,348	115
Livingston: Old	320	30	19	91,699	58,704	60
Livingston: United	290	28	-	77,923	40,067	180
Polbeth Harwood	161	17	-	47,700	15,226	9
West Kirk of Calder	248	18	13	56,904	43,610	70
Strathbrock	281	25	17	98,134	70,419	60
Uphall South	190	25	-	55,815	39,428	25
Whitburn: Brucefield	208	20	25	99,379	50,563	90
Whitburn: South	342	26	29	79,755	52,049	87

Congregation	Com	Eld	G	In 17	M&M	–18
3. Lothian						
Aberlady	197	18	-	51,434	20,891	6
Gullane	353	25	22	69,887	34,826	40
Athelstaneford	200	13	-	26,124	17,606	20
Whitekirk and Tyninghame	133	13	-	-	22,060	15
Belhaven	555	43	62	80,937	52,420	39
Spott	99	7	-	14,652	9,190	4
Bilston	87	3	15	13,269	5,871	-
Glencorse	290	13	19	25,586	15,524	5
Roslin	222	9	-	29,772	16,093	16
Bonnyrigg	605	58	40	112,317	67,758	12
Cockenzie and Port Seton: Chalmers M'rl	168	28	25	84,080	52,786	90
Cockenzie and Port Seton: Old	217	18	23	-	32,795	14
Cockpen and Carrington	190	25	46	42,043	23,844	12
Lasswade and Rosewell	267	21	-	29,399	24,113	10
Dalkeith: St John's and King's Park	466	38	26	146,995	67,092	65
Dalkeith: St Nicholas' Buccleuch	324	19	-	62,433	32,158	4
Dirleton	219	17	-	-	36,127	17
North Berwick: Abbey	257	29	38	92,479	53,109	27
Dunbar	335	20	31	104,740	69,708	67
Dunglass	269	10	-	25,745	21,336	20
Garvald and Morham	36	9	-	-	7,171	9
Haddington: West	212	17	28	55,933	36,608	10
Gladsmuir	164	17	-	-	15,228	-
Longniddry	327	43	30	75,600	49,054	10
Gorebridge	124	11	-	113,935	65,218	100
Haddington: St Mary's	502	39	-	-	64,261	47
Howgate	28	6	-	22,050	12,419	8
Penicuik: South	85	9	-	-	41,444	13
Humbie	69	8	-	-	16,669	15
Yester, Bolton and Saltoun	275	34	-	50,468	38,309	25
Loanhead	290	23	28	-	42,566	40
Musselburgh: Northesk	296	25	25	64,923	39,045	102
Musselburgh: St Andrew's High	276	24	14	64,558	42,662	-
Musselburgh: St Clement's & St Ninian's	76	10	-	15,428	16,338	-
Musselburgh: St Michael's Inveresk	364	36	-	80,168	50,823	8
Newbattle	334	25	15	72,362	38,773	136
Newton	98	1	-	13,966	14,124	9
North Berwick: St Andrew Blackadder	569	38	34	173,063	93,956	70
Ormiston	143	9	23	-	26,624	15
Pencaitland	153	4	-	-	18,494	9
Penicuik: North	405	30	-	74,180	46,721	52
Penicuik: St Mungo's	303	20	18	71,492	41,661	21
Prestonpans: Prestongrange	251	18	18	67,169	35,195	12
Tranent	233	16	33	56,054	33,116	68
Traprain	403	29	29	70,104	52,181	43
Tyne Valley	294	23	-	74,112	53,926	94
4. Melrose and Peebles						
Ashkirk	34	4	-	11,487	5,434	1

Congregation	Com	Eld	G	In 17	M&M	–18
Selkirk	361	17	-	69,805	43,653	36
Bowden and Melrose	685	59	22	123,472	76,722	20
Broughton, Glenholm and Kilbucho	139	-	20	18,153	12,015	-
Skirling	59	5	-	7,461	5,277	-
Stobo and Drumelzier	85	7	-	19,356	13,823	3
Tweedsmuir	37	4	-	-	4,476	1
Caddonfoot	162	-	-	18,750	9,810	-
Galashiels: Trinity	392	-	27	60,802	40,257	-
Carlops	52	-	-	28,666	11,292	-
Kirkurd and Newlands	85	12	9	14,454	15,963	15
West Linton: St Andrew's	180	-	-	-	23,302	-
Channelkirk and Lauder	390	20	18	-	39,677	25
Earlston	363	22	9	50,196	34,908	37
Eddleston	99	5	-	-	9,745	12
Peebles: Old	435	-	-	109,865	59,255	-
Ettrick and Yarrow	172	-	-	40,635	32,563	6
Galashiels: Old and St Paul's	252	-	29	63,116	41,701	-
Galashiels: St John's	183	10	-	42,303	24,558	-
Innerleithen, Traquair and Walkerburn	326	26	43	52,464	36,005	12
Lyne and Manor	89	7	-	25,059	21,837	3
Peebles: St Andrew's Leckie	531	34	-	-	64,787	72
Maxton and Mertoun	80	11	-	14,750	11,220	-
Newtown	116	8	-	16,938	9,152	-
St Boswells	177	20	18	31,967	19,076	4
Stow: St Mary of Wedale and Heriot	176	12	-	30,508	24,116	9

5. Duns

Ayton and District Churches	293	17	11	17,496	33,844	4
Berwick-upon-Tweed: St Andrew's Wallace Green & Lowick	289	19	-	58,188	35,197	20
Chirnside	88	5	11	16,697	8,882	-
Hutton and Fishwick and Paxton	59	4	16	15,270	11,028	4
Coldingham and St Abbs	66	11	-	33,328	26,225	20
Eyemouth	104	15	21	41,961	23,795	31
Coldstream and District Parishes	422	33	-	52,114	46,503	-
Eccles and Leitholm	147	13	13	24,684	16,952	2
Duns and District Parishes	629	37	41	82,267	77,601	65
Fogo	44	3	-	9,946	7,011	6
Gordon: St Michael's	59	5	-	-	6,922	7
Greenlaw	85	8	19	19,741	12,135	-
Legerwood	61	6	-	8,006	5,426	4
Westruther	38	6	-	5,664	4,338	25

6. Jedburgh

Ale and Teviot United	384	25	16	39,629	43,478	12
Cavers and Kirkton	100	8	-	11,175	9,903	-
Hawick: Trinity	502	34	43	52,321	30,589	-
Cheviot Churches	293	23	32	-	51,611	-
Hawick: Burnfoot	71	13	-	29,485	15,877	65
Hawick: St Mary's and Old	368	20	22	42,697	28,693	91

Congregation	Com	Eld	G	In 17	M&M	–18
Hawick: Teviot and Roberton	256	8	9	49,001	33,700	10
Hawick: Wilton	274	22	-	-	26,123	51
Teviothead	55	5	-	4,912	3,562	-
Hobkirk and Southdean	128	19	14	15,259	13,123	2
Ruberslaw	241	19	11	37,902	24,925	4
Jedburgh: Old and Trinity	624	-	31	-	49,414	-
Kelso Country Churches	183	15	18	23,356	33,300	11
Oxnam	122	10	-	14,294	8,047	6
Kelso: North and Ednam	951	71	27	122,407	85,253	8
Kelso: Old and Sprouston	462	28	-	53,366	28,818	12

7. Annandale and Eskdale

Congregation	Com	Eld	G	In 17	M&M	–18
Annan: Old	353	46	40	66,164	44,728	20
Dornock	106	10	-	-	6,157	3
Annan: St Andrew's	579	40	49	64,526	40,473	81
Brydekirk	46	4	-	-	6,180	-
Applegarth, Sibbaldbie and Johnstone	118	6	17	8,443	8,818	-
Lochmaben	247	18	35	67,271	39,089	20
Canonbie United	86	16	-	35,922	18,657	14
Liddesdale	97	8	18	29,497	21,415	-
Dalton and Hightae	173	8	-	20,239	15,415	7
St Mungo	73	9	-	13,385	10,380	-
Gretna: Old, Gretna: St Andrew's Half Morton & Kirkpatrick Fleming	302	23	19	-	37,371	22
Hoddom, Kirtle-Eaglesfield and Middlebie	199	19	14	28,221	15,849	59
Kirkpatrick Juxta	99	7	-	13,009	6,249	-
Moffat: St Andrew's	334	30	22	73,855	42,728	63
Wamphray	54	5	-	9,159	4,989	8
Langholm Eskdalemuir Ewes and Westerkirk	423	26	12	69,778	51,833	45
Lockerbie: Dryfesdale, Hutton and Corrie	687	40	33	62,538	47,050	15
The Border Kirk	292	45	22	60,563	39,389	28
Tundergarth	28	6	-	-	6,460	-

8. Dumfries and Kirkcudbright

Congregation	Com	Eld	G	In 17	M&M	–18
Balmaclellan and Kells	55	5	16	15,634	14,256	3
Carsphairn	85	8	-	10,047	6,784	4
Dalry	70	12	-	24,984	12,725	2
Caerlaverock	108	7	-	12,408	7,349	-
Dumfries: St Mary's-Greyfriars	349	29	29	-	44,000	15
Castle Douglas	352	20	19	62,170	40,586	11
The Bengairn Parishes	180	15	-	26,733	25,382	2
Closeburn	179	12	-	27,838	17,000	20
Kirkmahoe	234	12	-	25,398	19,611	1
Colvend, Southwick and Kirkbean	201	12	18	92,797	56,629	-
Corsock and Kirkpatrick Durham	83	12	7	24,675	14,500	6
Crossmichael, Parton and Balmaghie	205	10	17	25,462	25,331	-
Cummertrees, Mouswald and Ruthwell	177	18	-	28,762	19,900	-
Dalbeattie and Kirkgunzeon	491	26	39	-	36,264	0
Urr	172	10	-	-	14,620	-
Dumfries: Maxwelltown West	526	29	34	82,860	56,850	147

Congregation	Com	Eld	G	In 17	M&M	–18
Dumfries: Northwest	329	9	-	33,761	29,040	18
Dumfries: St George's	478	50	25	126,157	71,057	72
Dumfries: St Michael's and South	691	43	22	-	63,200	73
Dumfries: Troqueer	243	20	24	105,186	59,065	55
Dunscore	181	16	-	25,283	21,405	1
Glencairn and Moniaive	151	12	-	41,431	25,490	7
Durisdeer	144	6	-	22,969	13,626	10
Penpont, Keir and Tynron	148	10	-	-	18,292	10
Thornhill	124	10	-	-	24,832	-
Gatehouse and Borgue	275	18	-	69,028	35,000	12
Tarff and Twynholm	140	12	26	24,692	18,306	14
Irongray, Lochrutton and Terregles	163	22	-	22,315	20,253	-
Kirkconnel	227	13	-	36,760	23,200	-
Sanquhar: St Bride's	379	23	16	42,488	28,463	5
Kirkcudbright	487	19	-	91,404	54,504	78
Kirkmichael, Tinwald & Torthorwald	375	38	22	-	40,619	11
Lochend and New Abbey	203	14	11	36,268	17,930	-
9. Wigtown and Stranraer						
Ervie Kirkcolm	175	13	-	22,214	13,011	24
Leswalt	260	16	-	28,547	17,684	8
Glasserton and Isle of Whithorn	94	7	-	-	10,482	-
Whithorn: St Ninian's Priory	295	6	16	36,229	27,260	24
Inch	179	16	10	13,593	14,802	-
Portpatrick	211	10	21	23,584	16,599	-
Stranraer: Trinity	478	42	34	89,535	59,487	35
Kirkcowan	110	-	-	34,933	21,093	-
Wigtown	154	16	12	33,375	23,148	45
Kirkinner	126	7	7	21,454	9,156	-
Mochrum	228	15	21	23,914	15,678	30
Sorbie	108	8	-	21,887	14,893	-
Kirkmabreck	125	9	25	19,050	11,775	-
Monigaff	211	-	-	20,349	19,921	-
Kirkmaiden	204	21	-	33,589	23,272	18
Stoneykirk	284	27	14	-	26,245	8
Luce Valley	219	19	27	53,931	34,508	10
Penninghame	397	21	21	94,757	55,840	31
Stranraer: High Kirk	511	34	-	74,419	55,859	200
10. Ayr						
Alloway	979	91	-	247,592	124,280	430
Annbank	251	17	14	26,001	21,298	1
Tarbolton	171	29	20	49,951	38,755	8
Auchinleck	315	16	22	-	27,284	3
Catrine	104	11	-	22,241	16,760	-
Ayr: Auld Kirk of Ayr	483	52	26	75,777	54,215	10
Ayr: Castlehill	576	-	47	83,732	62,547	-
Ayr: Newton Wallacetown	380	-	45	113,153	71,292	-
Ayr: St Andrew's	228	20	12	-	48,111	86
Ayr: St Columba	1,296	-	82	326,284	154,296	-

Congregation	Com	Eld	G	In 17	M&M	–18
Ayr: St James'	339	37	29	71,062	48,685	131
Ayr: St Leonard's	513	-	21	102,767	48,403	-
Dalrymple	124	10	-	-	12,258	1
Ayr: St Quivox	228	21	-	42,212	37,498	-
Ballantrae	241	16	13	37,657	25,405	8
St Colmon (Arnsheen Barrhill and Colmonell)	204	8	-	-	17,101	3
Barr	66	-	-	2,118	3,167	-
Dailly	129	-	-	18,497	11,436	-
Girvan: South	299	23	29	33,954	20,952	10
Coylton	323	-	-	38,500	25,535	-
Drongan: The Schaw Kirk	186	-	14	37,957	22,886	-
Craigie and Symington	274	22	20	49,168	38,250	13
Prestwick: South	270	-	31	87,910	53,776	-
Crosshill	173	-	33	10,749	10,161	-
Maybole	319	-	17	65,914	46,815	-
Dalmellington	211	12	-	21,964	22,118	9
Patna: Waterside	135	-	-	-	15,086	-
Dundonald	456	-	42	-	52,496	-
Fisherton	106	-	-	14,246	8,158	-
Kirkoswald	212	-	16	34,434	18,898	-
Girvan: North (Old and St Andrew's)	599	36	-	70,762	45,661	68
Kirkmichael	202	14	19	26,010	13,829	7
Straiton: St Cuthbert's	161	11	17	13,745	12,862	10
Lugar	157	10	15	26,870	7,946	4
Old Cumnock: Old	331	17	33	61,022	42,927	12
Mauchline	435	-	33	-	49,444	-
Sorn	138	12	14	15,228	11,476	3
Monkton and Prestwick: North	313	-	21	94,327	59,067	-
Muirkirk	154	13	-	22,042	11,513	7
Old Cumnock: Trinity	314	-	25	50,390	36,178	-
New Cumnock	461	31	26	72,344	45,326	50
Ochiltree	207	21	11	31,028	23,217	18
Stair	210	14	18	39,735	24,641	20
Prestwick: Kingcase	651	-	57	111,378	77,402	-
Prestwick: St Nicholas'	588	71	38	106,526	72,878	94
Troon: Old	903	63	-	139,397	84,047	125
Troon: Portland	491	51	22	130,552	80,450	23
Troon: St Meddan's	590	80	29	142,982	98,383	116

11. Irvine and Kilmarnock

Caldwell	217	15	-	66,165	40,740	4
Dunlop	369	35	25	81,340	49,457	20
Crosshouse	255	28	19	63,645	36,735	70
Darvel	298	25	26	54,666	32,591	45
Dreghorn and Springside	368	41	24	83,341	56,092	30
Fenwick	283	26	26	-	34,552	14
Kilmarnock: Riccarton	225	24	17	66,196	42,115	56
Galston	563	50	68	94,761	65,827	10
Hurlford	296	24	28	62,687	41,383	5
Irvine: Fullarton	351	28	52	108,548	61,258	278

Congregation	Com	Eld	G	In 17	M&M	–18
Irvine: Girdle Toll	154	16	20	-	22,808	117
Irvine: Mure	285	26	16	65,350	43,789	46
Irvine: Old	340	21	-	72,257	49,579	15
Irvine: Relief Bourtreehill	207	21	18	44,438	27,457	15
Irvine: St Andrew's	223	17	25	57,029	30,232	50
Kilmarnock: Kay Park	466	77	27	145,667	81,176	17
Kilmarnock: New Laigh Kirk	794	78	48	227,307	124,626	160
Kilmarnock: St Andrew's & St Marnock's	753	94	36	173,644	104,485	415
Kilmarnock: St John's Onthank	185	23	17	-	32,253	110
Kilmarnock: St Kentigern's	262	23	-	52,371	32,731	95
Kilmarnock: South	233	7	20	32,973	24,207	-
Kilmaurs: St Maur's Glencairn	280	14	28	55,643	32,237	50
Newmilns: Loudoun	173	6	-	42,415	27,626	6
Stewarton: John Knox	244	19	25	122,638	56,915	60
Stewarton: St Columba's	400	40	39	76,379	55,308	129

12. Ardrossan

Ardrossan: Park	382	30	35	-	48,108	139
Ardrossan and Saltcoats Kirkgate	224	35	27	95,996	51,390	2
Beith	676	58	22	97,987	69,233	49
Brodick	119	18	-	57,187	33,838	12
Corrie	34	5	-	20,046	11,553	1
Lochranza and Pirnmill	58	12	8	-	15,178	2
Shiskine	60	10	14	32,096	21,691	11
Cumbrae	232	-	33	44,972	39,668	-
Largs: St John's	650	40	47	139,591	78,489	25
Dalry: St Margaret's	503	57	29	-	95,370	24
Dalry: Trinity	184	19	-	85,730	49,840	86
Fairlie	204	24	27	67,274	50,005	26
Largs: St Columba's	339	29	50	81,536	63,032	9
Kilbirnie: Auld Kirk	286	30	-	37,309	40,872	12
Kilbirnie: St Columba's	494	31	-	65,727	38,673	34
Kilmory	32	5	-	-	8,024	-
Lamlash	90	12	23	41,983	22,414	5
Kilwinning: Mansefield Trinity	181	13	28	53,278	36,477	-
Kilwinning: Old	548	51	37	110,087	68,942	14
Largs: Clark Memorial	678	86	45	163,751	85,184	136
Saltcoats: North	267	24	23	50,171	30,773	12
Saltcoats: St Cuthbert's	233	34	13	84,576	50,894	111
Stevenston: Ardeer	197	29	29	43,881	29,972	132
Stevenston: Livingstone	250	29	20	61,562	36,523	7
Stevenston: High	220	20	17	83,306	56,400	40
West Kilbride	421	47	18	111,507	77,327	132
Whiting Bay and Kildonan	77	9	-	44,676	29,274	6

13. Lanark

Biggar	302	24	27	100,712	60,266	24
Black Mount	69	5	13	16,276	11,764	5
Cairngryffe	143	15	11	24,317	20,886	4
Libberton and Quothquan	79	12	-	17,912	10,044	15

Congregation	Com	Eld	G	In 17	M&M	–18
Symington	146	15	18	33,899	22,291	4
Carluke: Kirkton	717	55	30	136,346	77,568	365
Carluke: St Andrew's	189	13	15	49,292	32,694	17
Carluke: St John's	566	43	30	95,696	57,375	81
Carnwath	123	11	19	-	13,321	3
Carstairs	178	14	21	44,498	30,835	122
Coalburn and Lesmahagow Old	458	30	31	74,465	64,958	15
Crossford	138	5	-	38,546	21,515	52
Kirkfieldbank	73	6	-	-	9,284	-
Forth: St Paul's	319	24	35	61,694	37,138	108
Kirkmuirhill	146	8	45	78,905	45,704	30
Lanark: Greyfriars	517	47	30	98,494	52,554	195
Lanark: St Nicholas'	478	41	17	95,209	65,852	62
Law	170	11	13	45,582	25,008	110
Lesmahagow: Abbeygreen	116	13	-	61,016	44,068	150
The Douglas Valley Church	280	24	32	48,612	36,739	5
Upper Clyde	176	7	20	-	22,022	13

14. Greenock and Paisley

Barrhead: Bourock	426	36	31	-	59,409	200
Barrhead: St Andrew's	427	42	32	-	91,679	273
Bishopton	602	55	-	106,374	62,033	73
Bridge of Weir: Freeland	384	49	-	124,130	80,176	126
Bridge of Weir: St Machar's Ranfurly	316	29	27	94,129	58,868	15
Erskine Kirk	435	41	41	105,122	65,334	156
Erskine	332	29	52	97,984	64,525	150
Gourock: Old Gourock and Ashton	614	59	20	124,799	73,251	210
Gourock: St John's	427	53	11	136,898	72,737	255
Greenock: East End	55	6	-	16,506	6,322	15
Greenock: Mount Kirk	306	32	-	61,134	41,541	130
Greenock: Lyle Kirk	743	53	27	-	89,814	81
Greenock: St Margaret's	164	34	-	46,783	19,719	25
Greenock: St Ninian's	219	16	-	27,408	17,823	39
Greenock: Wellpark Mid Kirk	461	46	13	-	60,291	77
Greenock: Westburn	570	65	23	-	82,558	38
Houston and Killellan	657	64	57	140,564	86,474	160
Howwood	136	10	15	42,696	26,129	6
Inchinnan	253	32	25	62,889	40,478	45
Inverkip	293	30	20	79,137	45,319	27
Skelmorlie and Wemyss Bay	241	31	-	71,568	52,824	-
Johnstone: High	198	31	22	98,522	60,423	83
Johnstone: St Andrew's Trinity	196	27	-	40,116	26,289	61
Johnstone: St Paul's	359	64	-	81,273	48,565	150
Kilbarchan	422	55	43	105,828	78,009	120
Kilmacolm: Old	381	42	-	-	77,059	20
Kilmacolm: St Columba	161	17	-	95,341	62,245	4
Langbank	122	14	-	33,454	26,053	8
Port Glasgow: St Andrew's	419	61	26	79,272	51,145	337
Linwood	180	21	29	49,677	34,365	14
Lochwinnoch	88	11	-	36,821	29,770	158

Congregation	Com	Eld	G	In 17	M&M	–18
Neilston	441	31	23	113,750	68,829	196
Paisley: Abbey	688	40	-	160,800	106,808	88
Paisley: Glenburn	146	13	-	45,766	29,869	8
Paisley: Lylesland	275	39	28	92,103	59,925	53
Paisley: Martyrs' Sandyford	389	57	25	108,536	74,545	110
Paisley: Oakshaw Trinity	450	66	-	152,408	63,456	37
Paisley: St Columba Foxbar	155	16	-	28,451	21,367	41
Paisley: St Luke's	186	23	-	-	33,360	11
Paisley: St Mark's Oldhall	429	54	45	116,180	71,050	28
Paisley: St Ninian's Ferguslie	43	3	-	-	5,000	5
Paisley: Sherwood Greenlaw	533	64	32	129,132	71,653	154
Paisley: Stow Brae Kirk	329	-	45	96,900	65,497	-
Paisley: Wallneuk North	332	31	-	59,520	40,560	15
Port Glasgow: Hamilton Bardrainney	218	18	15	46,189	28,821	54
Port Glasgow: St Martin's	139	10	-	-	16,748	16
Renfrew: North	620	69	33	119,341	78,883	174
Renfrew: Trinity	327	23	37	95,065	65,526	49

16. Glasgow

Congregation	Com	Eld	G	In 17	M&M	–18
Banton	60	8	-	9,865	5,796	6
Twechar	69	12	-	21,619	9,693	6
Bishopbriggs: Kenmure	244	17	41	90,355	67,101	91
Bishopbriggs: Springfield Cambridge	581	39	86	143,580	78,644	154
Broom	472	51	24	118,715	80,052	448
Burnside Blairbeth	514	40	77	260,863	143,927	239
Busby	220	34	20	76,420	48,028	20
Cadder	618	73	50	-	93,835	137
Cambuslang	622	-	37	113,223	86,788	-
Cambuslang: Flemington Hallside	307	28	34	69,946	35,338	54
Campsie	143	14	20	61,372	37,335	43
Chryston	570	23	10	204,606	113,490	75
Eaglesham	490	42	40	142,588	88,454	185
Fernhill and Cathkin	232	23	15	49,198	34,518	103
Gartcosh	137	13	-	24,489	17,282	84
Glenboig	105	9	-	20,406	9,167	6
Giffnock: Orchardhill	419	41	12	182,454	92,102	224
Giffnock: South	592	63	44	180,016	101,182	35
Giffnock: The Park	243	-	-	72,589	45,390	-
Greenbank	781	71	68	234,850	134,287	350
Kilsyth: Anderson	249	22	50	-	46,760	81
Kilsyth: Burns and Old	355	28	30	79,276	52,442	47
Kirkintilloch: Hillhead	66	9	9	22,885	8,743	-
Kirkintilloch: St Columba's	205	32	33	87,018	56,122	30
Kirkintilloch: St David's Memorial Park	510	49	30	-	54,062	97
Kirkintilloch: St Mary's	660	41	25	114,968	72,001	27
Lenzie: Old	409	3	-	130,862	64,924	80
Lenzie: Union	553	59	64	190,040	108,081	230
Maxwell Mearns Castle	258	28	-	166,211	96,940	200
Mearns	701	47	-	206,000	124,222	44
Milton of Campsie	301	30	41	66,221	47,975	104

Congregation	Com	Eld	G	In 17	M&M	–18
Netherlee	600	64	32	190,970	116,019	266
Newton Mearns	364	31	30	105,533	69,449	86
Rutherglen: Old	224	26	-	65,733	39,183	20
Rutherglen: Stonelaw	296	-	-	136,626	85,518	-
Rutherglen: West and Wardlawhill	436	43	40	-	50,143	164
Stamperland	281	27	19	78,157	48,282	15
Stepps	206	20	-	59,391	35,185	65
Thornliebank	122	12	27	45,046	27,395	9
Torrance	203	19	-	92,500	59,905	107
Williamwood	401	66	31	-	65,686	601
Glasgow: Anderston Kelvingrove	46	6	-	-	21,665	6
Glasgow: Baillieston Mure Memorial	340	37	65	85,786	55,960	273
Glasgow: Baillieston St Andrew's	259	22	27	58,981	43,987	140
Glasgow: Balshagray Victoria Park	132	27	15	96,341	64,932	29
Glasgow: Barlanark Greyfriars	91	-	9	28,534	19,781	-
Glasgow: Blawarthill	166	21	20	-	14,842	64
Glasgow: Bridgeton St Francis in the East	74	14	14	36,064	22,045	13
Glasgow: Broomhill Hyndland	591	-	38	209,506	138,174	-
Glasgow: Calton Parkhead	84	-	-	-	4,984	-
Glasgow: Cardonald	330	-	-	107,462	71,032	-
Glasgow: Carmunnock	278	22	19	49,137	32,378	55
Glasgow: Carmyle	80	5	-	21,783	12,212	27
Glasgow: Kenmuir Mount Vernon	120	10	22	64,094	36,968	40
Glasgow: Carntyne	-	-	35	57,572	55,144	-
Glasgow: Carnwadric	81	13	-	32,760	21,860	60
Glasgow: Castlemilk	137	-	16	-	17,339	-
Glasgow: Cathcart Old	252	-	27	-	58,058	-
Glasgow: Cathcart Trinity	342	48	32	221,000	106,851	85
Glasgow: Cathedral (High or St Mungo's)	394	-	-	91,781	72,989	-
Glasgow: Causeway (Tollcross)	163	29	26	43,821	49,414	140
Glasgow: Clincarthill	215	33	36	-	61,824	11
Glasgow: Colston Milton	58	-	-	13,983	7,028	-
Glasgow: Colston Wellpark	90	12	-	-	17,935	48
Glasgow: Cranhill	43	8	-	12,717	3,879	93
Glasgow: Croftfoot	262	39	31	-	47,702	105
Glasgow: Dennistoun New	163	33	-	82,213	61,911	87
Glasgow: Drumchapel St Andrew's	143	32	-	-	29,624	47
Glasgow: Drumchapel St Mark's	73	-	-	17,709	1,484	-
Glasgow: Easterhouse	47	5	-	-	11,632	130
Glasgow: Eastwood	180	40	18	80,499	61,350	91
Glasgow: Gairbraid	119	-	-	31,382	20,072	-
Glasgow: Gallowgate	50	-	-	26,922	15,044	-
Glasgow: Garthamlock and Craigend East	55	13	-	-	2,429	85
Glasgow: Gorbals	93	14	-	58,730	16,871	13
Glasgow: Govan and Linthouse	169	45	39	93,392	61,698	118
Glasgow: Hillington Park	261	32	36	63,403	40,783	110
Glasgow: Ibrox	116	29	17	-	30,434	64
Glasgow: John Ross Memorial (For Deaf People)	52	4	-	-	-	-
Glasgow: Jordanhill	357	61	24	164,710	99,181	40
Glasgow: Kelvinbridge	62	24	-	36,755	32,983	45

Congregation	Com	Eld	G	In 17	M&M	–18
Glasgow: Kelvinside Hillhead	151	-	-	70,845	46,365	-
Glasgow: King's Park	555	62	33	140,832	86,650	131
Glasgow: Kinning Park	125	13	-	31,002	21,846	-
Glasgow: Knightswood St Margaret's	159	19	-	48,201	29,026	10
Glasgow: Langside	199	-	-	116,504	57,446	-
Glasgow: Maryhill	141	15	9	-	23,043	90
Glasgow: Merrylea	261	32	24	74,994	47,062	23
Glasgow: Mosspark	96	22	22	-	30,665	48
Glasgow: Newlands South	410	53	-	144,247	88,421	25
Glasgow: Partick South	120	-	-	58,205	43,182	-
Glasgow: Partick Trinity	167	-	-	-	57,892	-
Glasgow: Pollokshaws	109	22	-	42,287	26,034	13
Glasgow: Pollokshields	155	28	20	-	57,080	60
Glasgow: Possilpark	101	14	12	-	15,808	25
Glasgow: Queen's Park Govanhill	227	29	32	95,008	74,734	15
Glasgow: Renfield St Stephen's	134	16	17	-	43,158	-
Glasgow: Robroyston	45	2	-	39,372	3,500	20
Glasgow: Ruchazie	26	-	-	-	3,845	-
Glasgow: Ruchill Kelvinside	73	-	-	-	34,908	-
Glasgow: St Andrew and St Nicholas	324	-	12	79,155	57,213	-
Glasgow: St Andrew's East	61	15	22	33,848	19,604	60
Glasgow: St Christopher's Priesthill and Nitshill	195	17	-	31,178	27,236	34
Glasgow: St Columba	135	-	-	-	13,727	-
Glasgow: St David's Knightswood	200	17	24	81,183	53,191	30
Glasgow: St Enoch's Hogganfield	110	15	27	29,456	23,809	2
Glasgow: St George's Tron	-	-	-	-	1,307	-
Glasgow: St James' (Pollok)	152	22	37	41,729	32,014	83
Glasgow: St John's Renfield	294	43	-	143,693	83,100	147
Glasgow: St Paul's	34	5	-	10,750	2,923	216
Glasgow: St Rollox	74	6	-	43,701	24,394	40
Glasgow: Sandyford Henderson Memorial	113	16	-	131,968	111,118	12
Glasgow: Sandyhills	229	27	39	76,651	47,407	20
Glasgow: Scotstoun	98	-	-	62,657	36,823	-
Glasgow: Shawlands Trinity	300	33	-	92,222	90,894	107
Glasgow: Sherbrooke St Gilbert's	252	-	-	-	88,251	-
Glasgow: Shettleston New	205	30	21	-	49,532	78
Glasgow: Springburn	187	27	27	-	42,077	57
Glasgow: Temple Anniesland	262	21	-	-	57,827	113
Glasgow: Toryglen	58	10	-	12,908	8,653	6
Glasgow: Trinity Possil and Henry Drummond	58	5	-	60,200	36,751	3
Glasgow: Tron St Mary's	88	17	-	-	26,984	25
Glasgow: Wallacewell	126	-	-	12,376	1,463	-
Glasgow: Wellington	169	30	-	83,426	73,974	18
Glasgow: Whiteinch	80	5	-	-	34,293	36
Glasgow: Yoker	94	-	-	18,644	15,207	-

17. Hamilton

Airdrie: Cairnlea	523	49	27	-	89,253	110
Calderbank	113	9	15	26,920	12,074	-
Airdrie: Clarkston	332	35	17	72,001	45,489	119

Congregation	Com	Eld	G	In 17	M&M	–18
Airdrie: High	281	33	-	85,316	40,553	140
Caldercruix and Longriggend	163	9	-	58,322	36,516	65
Airdrie: Jackson	333	48	23	92,287	52,987	208
Airdrie: New Monkland	284	29	23	71,708	38,933	64
Greengairs	118	9	-	23,437	13,830	6
Airdrie: St Columba's	209	11	-	17,150	12,294	2
Airdrie: The New Wellwynd	705	93	-	181,241	89,093	97
Bargeddie	85	7	-	-	42,904	8
Bellshill: Central	157	25	22	55,510	33,022	14
Bellshill: West	459	34	15	78,638	41,748	23
Blantyre: Livingstone Memorial	199	21	21	53,059	30,673	225
Blantyre: St Andrew's	172	20	-	51,932	32,428	12
Blantyre: Old	254	17	26	67,699	45,193	38
Bothwell	478	53	47	204,535	63,974	117
Chapelhall	192	21	27	43,689	27,941	46
Kirk o' Shotts	164	10	-	-	18,026	12
Chapelton	151	16	-	36,713	17,215	32
Strathaven: Rankin	490	56	36	98,021	56,740	190
Cleland	145	11	-	28,817	15,161	12
Wishaw: St Mark's	277	30	40	71,617	44,984	136
Coatbridge: Blairhill Dundyvan	245	22	22	55,709	33,120	87
Coatbridge: Middle	299	33	39	46,700	33,814	120
Coatbridge: Calder	285	18	18	49,338	36,179	-
Coatbridge: Old Monkland	100	19	-	40,106	34,535	40
Coatbridge: New St Andrew's	571	74	29	115,924	77,572	220
Coatbridge: Townhead	123	17	-	33,068	25,351	69
Dalserf	188	17	21	57,490	54,104	7
East Kilbride: Claremont	403	44	-	139,872	76,727	60
East Kilbride: Greenhills	172	13	20	36,320	22,073	6
East Kilbride: Moncrieff	578	58	54	128,413	74,494	190
East Kilbride: Mossneuk	250	12	-	25,520	17,822	3
East Kilbride: Old	660	61	41	-	71,636	26
East Kilbride: South	216	30	-	-	49,054	112
East Kilbride: Stewartfield	26	4	-	14,403	7,000	13
East Kilbride: West	282	25	24	-	41,943	35
East Kilbride: Westwood	328	31	-	-	51,051	40
Glassford	82	5	16	21,080	12,958	-
Strathaven: East	213	34	-	55,724	38,512	30
Hamilton: Cadzow	399	60	41	116,323	83,034	89
Hamilton: Gilmour and Whitehill	121	24	-	34,778	29,452	8
Hamilton: West	193	36	-	67,503	38,345	50
Hamilton: Hillhouse	358	38	-	78,116	58,626	195
Hamilton: Old	472	73	17	-	87,187	45
Hamilton: St John's	506	53	64	-	73,420	262
Hamilton: South	180	21	24	57,930	40,294	15
Quarter	94	10	-	27,728	14,531	-
Hamilton: Trinity	276	17	-	54,899	34,598	76
Holytown	149	16	17	50,040	31,120	75
New Stevenston: Wrangholm Kirk	87	11	16	33,983	23,428	6
Larkhall: Chalmers	99	9	21	30,691	20,194	60

Congregation	Com	Eld	G	In 17	M&M	–18
Larkhall: St Machan's	390	59	38	-	62,030	120
Larkhall: Trinity	155	16	31	49,833	30,213	123
Motherwell: Crosshill	293	38	46	84,232	59,298	60
Motherwell: St Margaret's	351	15	-	48,620	26,098	12
Motherwell: Dalziel St Andrew's	474	62	33	134,464	77,798	230
Motherwell: North	123	25	30	58,067	35,077	92
Motherwell: St Mary's	670	94	62	-	87,753	312
Motherwell: South	384	51	63	94,385	67,993	120
Newarthill and Carfin	256	28	16	-	42,782	67
Newmains: Bonkle	114	17	-	38,118	21,255	34
Newmains: Coltness Memorial	183	20	15	-	39,740	46
Overtown	242	32	50	57,362	28,022	108
Shotts: Calderhead Erskine	405	34	30	89,271	55,495	10
Stonehouse: St Ninian's	393	50	37	-	22,478	200
Strathaven: Avendale Old and Drumclog	534	51	36	131,769	79,923	16
Uddingston: Burnhead	262	19	9	49,582	33,864	47
Uddingston: Old	431	48	32	139,224	80,435	25
Uddingston: Viewpark	403	66	16	-	62,290	170
Wishaw: Cambusnethan North	412	32	-	71,740	46,603	85
Wishaw: Cambusnethan Old & Morningside	378	35	16	68,280	61,177	140
Wishaw: Craigneuk and Belhaven	122	27	-	51,633	29,199	10
Wishaw: Old	185	26	-	35,224	22,758	48
Wishaw: South Wishaw	289	30	26	82,924	58,580	50

18. Dumbarton

Alexandria	244	23	22	73,489	38,442	20
Arrochar	58	13	6	-	11,834	-
Luss	88	15	9	81,594	27,589	-
Baldernock	178	15	-	36,402	24,212	1
Milngavie: St Paul's	839	81	100	206,538	118,225	165
Bearsden: Baljaffray	348	24	34	-	51,001	40
Bearsden: Cross	763	-	29	-	97,276	-
Bearsden: Killermont	578	52	48	157,103	89,060	70
Bearsden: New Kilpatrick	1,304	124	105	321,134	180,968	35
Bearsden: Westerton Fairlie Memorial	344	41	48	103,955	58,874	45
Bonhill	495	-	-	-	40,394	-
Renton: Trinity	244	-	-	31,787	20,533	-
Cardross	380	-	31	-	51,684	-
Clydebank: Faifley	177	-	33	49,516	25,274	-
Clydebank: Kilbowie St Andrew's	246	21	22	51,629	18,524	122
Clydebank: Radnor Park	132	-	16	44,514	27,326	-
Clydebank: Waterfront	164	23	-	63,169	34,564	38
Dalmuir: Barclay	175	15	-	43,157	20,317	32
Craigrownie	142	17	-	30,714	29,735	-
Garelochhead	146	-	-	-	40,279	-
Rosneath: St Modan's	113	12	32	28,761	16,415	3
Dumbarton: Riverside	470	61	50	112,132	69,739	235
Dumbarton: West Kirk	204	23	-	-	31,316	157
Dumbarton: St Andrew's	105	18	-	32,764	18,202	-
Duntocher: Trinity	194	26	47	36,328	23,024	-

Congregation	Com	Eld	G	In 17	M&M	–18
Helensburgh	978	73	40	204,754	132,441	20
Rhu and Shandon	265	-	28	58,657	37,143	-
Jamestown	177	21	15	-	28,242	-
Kilmaronock Gartocharn	208	10	-	34,441	19,841	6
Milngavie: Cairns	351	34	-	-	79,797	13
Milngavie: St Luke's	361	17	-	72,714	54,731	27
Old Kilpatrick Bowling	224	20	-	-	39,825	71

19. Argyll

Appin	86	12	21	21,460	16,258	5
Lismore	39	-	-	13,319	5,976	-
Ardchattan	95	9	-	-	18,451	12
Ardrishaig	124	18	28	38,709	21,593	-
South Knapdale	31	4	-	-	6,076	-
Barra	31	3	-	12,323	9,316	-
South Uist	49	7	-	15,952	11,019	6
Campbeltown: Highland	372	35	-	41,497	29,597	14
Campbeltown: Lorne and Lowland	738	49	26	96,626	53,122	72
Coll	19	3	-	5,944	2,193	-
Connel	113	19	10	-	27,484	13
Colonsay and Oronsay	12	2	-	-	5,552	-
Craignish	46	8	-	-	5,113	5
Kilbrandon and Kilchattan	92	17	-	18,001	20,446	23
Kilninver and Kilmelford	54	5	-	-	6,600	10
Cumlodden, Lochfyneside and Lochgair	83	15	17	24,480	12,791	-
Glenaray and Inveraray	101	-	-	28,992	19,894	-
Dunoon: St John's	122	20	32	46,689	29,274	-
Kirn and Sandbank	288	24	-	42,888	40,906	14
Dunoon: The High Kirk	297	-	29	-	41,476	-
Innellan	53	5	-	18,446	10,892	2
Toward	49	8	-	-	13,464	31
Gigha and Cara	33	7	-	7,938	6,746	4
Kilcalmonell	41	12	11	9,892	6,185	1
Killean and Kilchenzie	120	13	17	22,087	12,972	30
Glassary, Kilmartin and Ford	93	10	-	20,084	16,296	10
North Knapdale	48	8	-	26,566	20,589	22
Glenorchy and Innishael	44	6	-	-	7,182	-
Strathfillan	43	6	-	11,299	5,652	-
Iona	13	6	-	-	8,053	2
Kilfinichen & Kilvickeon & the Ross of Mull	28	4	-	9,108	4,475	-
Jura	24	5	-	5,842	3,780	-
Kilarrow	43	14	-	25,909	18,295	5
Kildalton and Oa	81	14	-	-	26,447	10
Kilchoman	67	12	-	18,290	17,387	12
Kilmeny	25	5	-	12,617	7,368	-
Portnahaven	25	5	11	-	3,966	4
Kilchrenan and Dalavich	28	7	-	14,540	10,721	12
Muckairn	117	19	7	25,256	17,738	-
Kilfinan	29	4	-	8,347	4,219	-
Kilmodan and Colintraive	77	10	-	16,121	13,413	15

Congregation	Com	Eld	G	In 17	M&M	–18
Kyles	92	20	-	33,023	19,857	5
Kilmore and Oban	440	43	26	84,028	58,297	35
Kilmun, Strone and Ardentnny: The Shore Kirk	175	22	14	37,948	36,571	-
Kilninian and Kilmore	24	-	-	11,353	5,756	-
Salen and Ulva	29	5	-	-	10,267	8
Tobermory	61	12	-	26,720	19,510	12
Torosay and Kinlochspelvie	25	4	-	-	4,563	1
Lochgilphead	216	-	26	34,520	23,316	-
Lochgoilhead and Kilmorich	57	9	-	27,934	21,699	6
Strachur and Strachlachlan	113	11	11	23,123	20,884	-
Rothesay: Trinity	312	35	13	59,865	39,726	52
Saddell and Carradale	178	15	21	38,019	23,763	12
Southend	219	11	10	30,555	18,004	5
Skipness	19	4	-	12,099	3,430	2
Tarbert, Loch Fyne and Kilberry	106	12	20	35,232	23,579	5
The United Church of Bute	478	36	36	72,239	51,746	18
Tiree	73	-	-	-	14,144	-
22. Falkirk						
Airth	140	9	19	-	25,420	40
Blackbraes and Shieldhill	150	21	21	32,507	19,440	-
Muiravonside	181	22	-	-	28,260	3
Bo'ness: Old	308	24	6	53,820	38,125	20
Bo'ness: St Andrew's	364	17	-	58,831	52,482	6
Bonnybridge: St Helen's	293	16	-	-	35,980	10
Bothkennar and Carronshore	201	18	-	40,496	21,287	13
Brightons	594	34	59	133,046	80,909	190
Carriden	374	49	21	60,444	41,557	-
Cumbernauld: Abronhill	191	13	25	56,705	44,380	45
Cumbernauld: Condorrat	293	23	38	73,572	46,165	100
Cumbernauld: Kildrum	252	28	-	72,906	38,748	200
Cumbernauld: Old	304	42	-	-	48,364	72
Cumbernauld: St Mungo's	171	33	-	48,800	31,182	14
Denny: Old	305	40	25	63,541	43,705	35
Haggs	224	23	-	-	25,027	48
Denny: Westpark	417	32	28	92,844	63,623	118
Dunipace	325	19	-	59,973	36,566	75
Falkirk: Bainsford	121	13	-	-	22,592	90
Falkirk: Camelon	183	15	-	82,403	47,165	16
Falkirk: Grahamston United	292	41	25	-	41,083	45
Falkirk: Laurieston	204	17	22	-	23,378	4
Redding and Westquarter	140	13	-	27,634	15,720	-
Falkirk: St Andrew's West	406	29	-	74,759	54,465	28
Falkirk: St James'	220	21	-	-	24,737	-
Falkirk: Trinity	506	65	15	209,409	102,982	78
Grangemouth: Abbotsgrange	330	51	-	66,208	47,562	109
Grangemouth: Kirk of the Holy Rood	319	-	-	55,932	34,575	15
Grangemouth: Zetland	532	73	64	117,774	69,237	200
Larbert: East	606	57	33	132,048	78,326	234
Larbert: Old	297	20	-	77,717	46,981	61

Congregation	Com	Eld	G	In 17	M&M	−18
Larbert: West	345	32	32	77,678	47,087	110
Polmont: Old	350	25	47	106,698	55,253	75
Slamannan	208	5	-	-	18,502	22
Stenhouse and Carron	324	26	-	-	48,227	10

23. Stirling

Congregation	Com	Eld	G	In 17	M&M	−18
Aberfoyle	75	7	15	16,564	11,715	3
Port of Menteith	52	7	-	12,410	5,693	-
Alloa: Ludgate	286	20	17	-	44,842	12
Alloa: St Mungo's	327	-	36	-	44,262	-
Alva	444	50	37	-	47,366	65
Balfron	129	15	12	49,033	24,690	20
Fintry	102	12	16	24,799	19,797	3
Balquhidder	54	2	-	13,591	14,595	-
Killin and Ardeonaig	83	8	8	23,181	14,555	6
Bannockburn: Allan	271	34	-	53,849	29,307	-
Cowie and Plean	156	9	-	17,312	12,737	-
Bannockburn: Ladywell	371	18	-	-	17,039	6
Bridge of Allan	662	51	76	109,562	80,403	77
Buchanan	95	8	-	-	11,704	4
Drymen	250	22	-	82,418	39,820	33
Buchlyvie	158	15	14	27,125	20,185	18
Gartmore	58	13	-	16,603	16,609	2
Callander	513	20	30	94,746	68,641	56
Cambusbarron: The Bruce Memorial	288	20	-	83,513	35,501	32
Clackmannan	356	24	23	-	49,514	55
Dollar	227	26	58	90,778	59,959	2
Glendevon	34	3	-	3,782	3,425	-
Muckhart	83	8	-	21,777	14,731	11
Dunblane: Cathedral	786	70	40	220,097	125,512	235
Dunblane: St Blane's	304	33	36	105,231	61,542	30
Lecropt	150	16	-	44,877	26,177	12
Fallin	245	7	-	-	21,254	70
Gargunnock	124	9	-	20,767	22,662	14
Kilmadock	87	12	-	18,424	15,911	23
Kincardine-in-Menteith	75	5	-	18,861	11,480	8
Killearn	335	21	41	80,668	64,995	40
Kippen	194	15	16	28,834	21,690	-
Norrieston	96	9	10	20,844	16,241	2
Logie	515	57	28	98,225	63,433	22
Menstrie	338	20	29	59,503	46,216	15
Sauchie and Coalsnaughton	417	24	14	58,601	39,052	11
Stirling: Allan Park South	162	23	-	50,325	27,083	105
Stirling: Church of The Holy Rude	137	16	-	-	30,826	-
Stirling: Viewfield Erskine	226	22	23	34,595	22,156	7
Stirling: North	332	20	21	64,653	50,672	42
Stirling: St Columba's	444	55	-	102,887	62,023	100
Stirling: St Mark's	158	10	-	29,880	16,397	39
Stirling: St Ninian's Old	612	62	-	96,114	58,793	70
Strathblane	167	17	41	69,387	40,901	41

Congregation	Com	Eld	G	In 17	M&M	–18
Tillicoultry	557	61	32	91,359	59,993	80
Tullibody: St Serf's	321	20	25	-	34,525	8

24. Dunfermline

Congregation	Com	Eld	G	In 17	M&M	–18
Aberdour: St Fillan's	350	18	-	75,979	49,152	10
Beath and Cowdenbeath: North	202	21	18	61,904	40,360	14
Cairneyhill	97	17	-	27,275	16,422	10
Limekilns	228	31	-	75,206	45,772	15
Carnock and Oakley	160	20	27	60,551	35,340	8
Cowdenbeath: Trinity	280	25	9	71,922	46,140	16
Culross and Torryburn	54	12	-	48,710	34,183	20
Dalgety	495	46	22	132,619	77,961	126
Dunfermline: Abbey	618	63	-	136,732	84,645	-
Dunfermline: East	76	6	-	64,986	11,209	60
Dunfermline: Gillespie Memorial	153	26	15	-	34,868	20
Dunfermline: North	145	15	-	28,050	22,810	1
Dunfermline: St Andrew's Erskine	171	21	13	54,036	31,941	4
Dunfermline: St Leonard's	302	26	24	74,673	47,732	43
Dunfermline: St Margaret's	225	29	9	-	50,729	127
Dunfermline: St Ninian's	155	18	24	45,924	31,194	32
Dunfermline: Townhill and Kingseat	219	23	28	-	44,518	59
Inverkeithing	220	20	-	60,415	44,930	24
North Queensferry	51	6	-	18,816	9,599	6
Kelty	252	21	32	61,225	51,772	14
Lochgelly and Benarty: St Serf's	368	34	-	63,734	46,458	14
Rosyth	200	20	-	34,353	22,298	4
Saline and Blairingone	145	19	15	38,934	29,967	19
Tulliallan and Kincardine	271	29	36	61,206	39,181	68

25. Kirkcaldy

Congregation	Com	Eld	G	In 17	M&M	–18
Auchterderran Kinglassie	295	-	15	52,347	37,007	-
Auchtertool	62	6	-	12,062	5,967	6
Kirkcaldy: Linktown	226	29	29	60,157	39,624	38
Buckhaven and Wemyss	232	22	21	57,964	34,141	6
Burntisland	279	-	16	-	44,335	10
Dysart: St Clair	413	24	13	-	32,817	20
Glenrothes: Christ's Kirk	191	20	26	33,518	30,421	-
Glenrothes: St Columba's	435	38	-	70,091	39,148	84
Glenrothes: St Margaret's	260	25	31	66,667	38,163	50
Glenrothes: St Ninian's	215	32	20	73,409	38,744	39
Kennoway, Windygates and Balgonie St Kenneth's	608	47	52	99,142	60,916	18
Kinghorn	285	-	-	78,388	42,191	4
Kirkcaldy: Abbotshall	450	40	-	76,498	47,502	7
Kirkcaldy: Bennochy	412	39	21	88,523	55,277	12
Kirkcaldy: Pathhead	334	35	41	78,841	48,241	140
Kirkcaldy: St Bryce Kirk	331	30	26	78,604	65,805	31
Kirkcaldy: Templehall	141	12	14	38,147	25,320	-
Kirkcaldy: Torbain	212	33	-	45,758	28,013	60
Leslie: Trinity	158	14	-	-	18,224	5
Leven	471	-	36	102,166	67,638	-

Congregation	Com	Eld	G	In 17	M&M	–18
Markinch and Thornton	562	33	-	93,830	60,989	9
Methil: Wellesley	298	27	17	57,788	27,059	142
Methilhill and Denbeath	181	19	33	37,075	22,704	12

26. St Andrews

Abdie and Dunbog	151	18	-	22,508	15,206	6
Newburgh	188	12	-	17,112	16,179	-
Anstruther and Cellardyke: St Ayle	381	34	40	97,222	53,896	8
Kilrenny	102	13	-	31,806	20,675	-
Auchtermuchty	237	18	12	36,414	25,101	-
Edenshead and Strathmiglo	132	10	-	-	14,290	-
Balmerino	114	14	-	27,164	14,960	-
Wormit	171	15	36	35,182	24,028	26
Boarhills and Dunino	137	7	-	24,969	16,299	-
St Andrews: Holy Trinity	315	23	38	-	73,383	15
Cameron	89	13	11	22,841	13,416	6
St Andrews: St Leonard's	525	45	21	134,838	80,907	22
Carnbee	85	12	14	14,271	10,707	1
Pittenweem	233	12	14	20,885	16,199	2
Ceres, Kemback and Springfield	338	27	21	68,201	68,415	41
Crail	318	22	41	46,909	31,014	8
Kingsbarns	62	9	-	17,531	8,775	-
Creich, Flisk and Kilmany	76	9	-	21,106	20,257	6
Cupar: Old and St Michael of Tarvit	486	27	23	-	83,526	51
Monimail	87	12	-	21,393	14,259	4
Cupar: St John's and Dairsie United	645	50	29	-	71,073	11
East Neuk Trinity	314	27	60	94,011	55,647	10
St Monans	243	14	24	84,285	43,740	18
Falkland	123	14	-	35,469	22,742	3
Freuchie	131	19	18	25,271	14,043	1
Howe of Fife	290	21	-	57,971	38,661	25
Largo	307	34	29	-	53,621	3
Largoward	21	6	-	8,314	5,854	2
Leuchars: St Athernase	286	22	20	-	37,946	-
Newport-on-Tay	337	34	-	73,008	49,807	33
St Andrews: Hope Park and Martyrs'	526	44	25	177,914	90,548	10
Strathkinness	89	14	-	22,144	10,348	-
Tayport	237	13	18	-	37,668	6

27. Dunkeld and Meigle

Aberfeldy	165	12	-	-	25,962	129
Dull and Weem	129	12	15	-	18,590	3
Grantully, Logierait and Strathtay	128	9	6	25,638	27,800	2
Alyth	646	34	26	82,092	53,595	20
Ardler, Kettins and Meigle	381	24	36	-	33,324	12
Bendochy	76	12	-	22,857	16,027	-
Coupar Angus: Abbey	270	15	-	-	25,880	57
Blair Atholl and Struan	111	14	-	17,262	21,018	-
Braes of Rannoch	17	4	-	10,142	8,157	-

Congregation	Com	Eld	G	In 17	M&M	–18
Foss and Rannoch	80	8	-	11,474	10,643	3
Blairgowrie	821	46	41	122,334	74,045	117
Caputh and Clunie	140	16	8	22,304	21,168	-
Kinclaven	131	13	14	20,845	13,457	5
Dunkeld	324	31	-	88,616	70,680	55
Fortingall and Glenlyon	50	8	-	18,726	12,685	4
Kenmore and Lawers	55	6	20	-	20,182	10
Kirkmichael, Straloch and Glenshee	90	5	-	15,420	13,369	5
Rattray	293	15	-	43,992	22,156	7
Pitlochry	334	32	17	88,465	56,220	27
Tenandry	40	9	-	21,501	18,120	-

28. Perth

Congregation	Com	Eld	G	In 17	M&M	–18
Aberdalgie and Forteviot	171	13	-	32,815	10,231	12
Aberuthven and Dunning	192	18	-	48,656	29,928	52
Abernethy & Dron & Arngask	275	28	28	33,782	35,784	18
Almondbank Tibbermore	257	14	23	-	28,074	3
Methven and Logiealmond	163	14	-	-	18,913	8
Ardoch	167	17	30	47,204	19,925	26
Blackford	99	12	-	26,071	15,464	40
Auchterarder	528	27	46	-	82,540	46
Auchtergaven and Moneydie	478	24	20	71,748	36,638	48
Redgorton and Stanley	317	15	39	41,858	29,308	40
Cargill Burrelton	120	22	22	29,740	23,178	9
Collace	109	6	17	16,255	9,539	8
Cleish	202	11	11	41,767	28,116	17
Fossoway St Serf's and Devonside	199	16	-	44,163	36,184	15
Comrie	404	-	23	88,266	63,113	-
Dundurn	52	8	-	19,179	10,147	-
Crieff	605	36	26	87,241	64,230	27
Dunbarney and Forgandenny	524	29	17	93,341	54,384	38
Errol	248	20	30	-	28,742	37
Kilspindie and Rait	64	6	-	10,100	7,889	-
Fowlis Wester, Madderty & Monzie	271	19	12	46,783	31,364	19
Gask	78	8	12	16,639	21,034	-
Kinross	664	40	45	137,342	69,215	141
Muthill	247	22	14	41,103	31,119	31
Trinity Gask and Kinkell	46	-	-	-	6,177	-
Orwell and Portmoak	419	-	27	76,326	52,594	32
Perth: Craigie and Moncrieffe	577	35	37	-	61,176	89
Perth: Kinnoull	369	34	23	113,115	51,575	42
Perth: Letham St Mark's	468	9	27	118,578	69,716	70
Perth: North	909	47	35	229,783	126,527	67
Perth: Riverside	63	-	-	51,396	21,900	-
Perth: St John's Kirk of Perth	443	30	-	101,242	66,644	-
Perth: St Leonard's-in-the-Fields	419	37	-	-	54,239	4
Perth: St Matthew's	726	31	19	107,349	63,252	175
St Madoes and Kinfauns	273	26	-	55,031	44,753	50
Scone and St Martins	852	41	47	115,330	71,576	51

Congregation	Com	Eld	G	In 17	M&M	–18
29. Dundee						
Abernyte	85	11	-	16,935	13,519	4
Inchture and Kinnaird	151	28	-	39,759	29,044	10
Longforgan	172	19	17	-	31,982	6
Auchterhouse	140	14	15	27,360	18,598	10
Monikie & Newbigging and Murroes & Tealing	449	22	11	54,738	36,860	7
Dundee: Balgay	326	32	23	66,870	40,404	14
Dundee: Barnhill St Margaret's	712	51	58	158,937	99,578	26
Dundee: Broughty Ferry New Kirk	653	46	37	107,416	64,153	97
Dundee: Broughty Ferry St James'	130	10	15	33,257	19,245	34
Dundee: Broughty Ferry St Luke's and Queen Street	372	40	15	-	46,321	12
Dundee: Broughty Ferry St Stephen's and West	300	24	-	55,344	30,008	-
Dundee: Dundee (St Mary's)	516	41	-	85,297	59,363	-
Dundee: Camperdown	125	9	-	21,102	19,608	10
Dundee: Chalmers Ardler	161	16	-	87,638	51,270	83
Dundee: Coldside	203	15	-	59,133	36,148	112
Dundee: Craigiebank	147	12	-	32,706	19,854	40
Dundee: Douglas and Mid Craigie	113	10	-	21,332	16,088	96
Dundee: Downfield Mains	359	23	23	87,525	54,972	128
Dundee: Fintry	90	7	-	53,133	31,624	60
Dundee: Lochee	471	22	30	77,967	43,940	201
Dundee: Logie and St John's Cross	191	13	21	17,224	50,821	-
Dundee: Meadowside St Paul's	276	25	20	70,674	33,687	26
Dundee: St Andrew's	426	42	26	112,199	69,736	17
Dundee: Menzieshill	244	12	-	40,584	26,280	170
Dundee: St David's High Kirk	207	42	22	48,098	34,875	40
Dundee: Steeple	197	29	-	125,906	74,686	27
Dundee: Stobswell	393	37	-	65,017	43,839	-
Dundee: Strathmartine	233	22	23	55,938	30,237	3
Dundee: Trinity	405	31	23	-	34,219	63
Dundee: West	270	27	22	72,304	53,505	-
Dundee: Whitfield	39	6	-	-	8,216	46
Fowlis and Liff	139	12	8	-	26,721	43
Lundie and Muirhead	274	27	-	44,980	27,292	52
Invergowrie	271	48	35	92,938	42,457	15
Monifieth	989	60	45	239,419	87,287	84
30. Angus						
Aberlemno	196	10	-	26,457	14,762	14
Guthrie and Rescobie	211	9	11	27,559	15,200	10
Arbirlot	136	9	-	-	16,675	12
Carmyllie	98	12	-	-	20,068	-
Arbroath: Knox's	262	19	23	33,499	24,915	30
Arbroath: St Vigeans	471	37	15	62,180	45,083	80
Arbroath: Old and Abbey	431	34	-	82,029	67,627	40
Arbroath: St Andrew's	523	43	40	136,158	83,549	90
Arbroath: West Kirk	693	74	40	94,729	68,834	18
Barry	184	7	18	24,945	16,736	3
Carnoustie	300	18	13	78,097	46,277	9
Brechin: Cathedral	443	30	24	-	53,182	10

Congregation	Com	Eld	G	In 17	M&M	–18
Brechin: Gardner Memorial	437	17	-	48,286	37,409	15
Farnell	109	12	-	8,404	10,084	10
Carnoustie: Panbride	629	32	-	72,489	48,328	28
Colliston	166	5	10	26,259	12,223	4
Friockheim Kinnell	132	10	22	21,321	12,543	1
Inverkeilor and Lunan	108	6	15	16,889	17,324	4
Dun and Hillside	382	42	33	-	40,481	6
Dunnichen, Letham and Kirkden	237	18	18	40,964	26,345	1
Eassie, Nevay and Newtyle	198	15	17	23,724	21,597	30
Edzell Lethnot Glenesk	334	27	20	35,572	32,727	8
Fern Careston Menmuir	99	9	-	13,768	13,454	14
Forfar: East and Old	608	45	42	94,911	72,108	35
Forfar: Lowson Memorial	590	46	27	120,112	64,538	225
Forfar: St Margaret's	464	24	20	86,051	44,910	85
Glamis, Inverarity and Kinettles	348	25	-	50,264	47,064	16
Kirriemuir: St Andrew's	254	17	24	42,898	32,294	30
Oathlaw Tannadice	119	7	-	17,578	17,782	3
Montrose: Old and St Andrew's	591	42	20	80,540	58,281	25
Montrose: South and Ferryden	381	22	-	51,893	39,408	4
The Glens and Kirriemuir Old	923	69	35	-	74,248	150
The Isla Parishes	133	18	11	27,191	30,003	7

31. Aberdeen

Aberdeen: Bridge of Don Oldmachar	187	8	-	52,719	34,168	10
Aberdeen: Craigiebuckler	726	69	27	-	71,533	110
Aberdeen: Ferryhill	322	44	17	80,561	53,486	110
Aberdeen: Garthdee	171	13	-	26,952	21,577	35
Aberdeen: High Hilton	305	29	18	51,688	33,997	41
Aberdeen: Holburn West	387	45	30	100,960	68,663	22
Aberdeen: Mannofield	949	100	45	-	95,269	15
Aberdeen: Mastrick	214	18	-	37,243	31,596	-
Aberdeen: Middlefield	94	5	-	5,251	3,102	-
Aberdeen: Midstocket	444	41	38	-	64,639	31
Aberdeen: Northfield	144	11	18	27,540	17,489	1
Aberdeen: Queen's Cross	406	43	21	-	96,987	8
Aberdeen: Rubislaw	422	58	30	144,970	87,201	23
Aberdeen: Ruthrieston West	312	32	17	74,309	44,908	6
Aberdeen: St Columba's Bridge of Don	219	17	-	-	52,781	100
Aberdeen: St George's Tillydrone	93	11	-	13,510	3,641	8
Aberdeen: St John's Church for Deaf People	88	1	-	-	-	-
Aberdeen: St Machar's Cathedral	518	39	-	148,572	86,166	12
Aberdeen: St Mark's	523	42	53	167,083	133,707	17
Aberdeen: St Mary's	302	35	-	70,045	45,871	70
Aberdeen: St Nicholas Kincorth, South of	324	26	21	74,232	43,658	120
Aberdeen: St Nicholas Uniting, Kirk of	320	27	15	129,913	14,113	6
Aberdeen: St Stephen's	149	20	13	-	44,950	39
Aberdeen: South Holburn	439	40	66	-	64,716	10
Aberdeen: Stockethill	87	6	-	32,309	7,868	21
Aberdeen: Summerhill	122	17	-	28,907	18,882	7
Aberdeen: Torry St Fittick's	306	16	19	61,913	43,923	-

Congregation	Com	Eld	G	In 17	M&M	–18
Aberdeen: Woodside	244	-	20	46,631	33,969	-
Bucksburn Stoneywood	391	12	-	33,385	25,256	-
Cults	714	71	42	-	99,476	94
Dyce	905	52	30	-	61,432	140
Kingswells	320	23	16	50,808	34,332	8
Newhills	379	28	31	-	74,183	12
Peterculter	547	46	-	110,318	65,830	152

32. Kincardine and Deeside

Congregation	Com	Eld	G	In 17	M&M	–18
Aberluthnott	105	8	10	12,059	11,999	3
Laurencekirk	359	8	21	25,498	22,125	-
Aboyne and Dinnet	286	9	17	45,476	32,779	45
Cromar	199	14	-	25,809	26,542	-
Arbuthnott, Bervie and Kinneff	465	-	24	92,158	51,007	-
Banchory-Ternan East	546	-	32	89,121	64,482	-
Banchory-Ternan West	576	-	27	133,885	67,118	-
Birse and Feughside	207	16	-	-	31,813	30
Braemar and Crathie	195	-	7	-	40,795	-
Drumoak - Durris	369	15	-	67,565	41,884	22
Glenmuick (Ballater)	249	20	-	40,435	26,382	9
Maryculter Trinity	140	14	9	44,983	30,882	60
Mearns Coastal	222	-	-	20,166	19,480	-
Mid Deeside	571	39	21	64,787	44,985	8
Newtonhill	228	12	16	30,268	20,232	100
Portlethen	281	17	-	54,101	49,649	46
Stonehaven: Dunnottar	543	23	21	64,495	45,637	12
Stonehaven: South	232	11	-	-	24,396	12
Stonehaven: Fetteresso	552	-	23	-	94,938	-
West Mearns	428	-	25	54,953	38,924	-

33. Gordon

Congregation	Com	Eld	G	In 17	M&M	–18
Barthol Chapel	75	9	10	10,914	6,224	23
Tarves	256	17	32	48,499	26,224	80
Belhelvie	342	32	21	87,875	55,237	71
Blairdaff and Chapel of Garioch	314	27	8	41,879	22,029	6
Cluny	181	11	-	31,022	19,380	20
Monymusk	97	5	-	23,154	13,920	41
Culsalmond and Rayne	158	6	-	10,366	10,897	10
Daviot	139	8	-	12,591	8,517	10
Cushnie and Tough	241	10	-	26,192	18,497	1
Echt and Midmar	268	13	-	-	26,532	4
Ellon	1,366	70	-	174,836	98,694	309
Fintray Kinellar Keithhall	153	12	12	29,504	25,372	-
Foveran	281	12	-	54,322	37,645	23
Howe Trinity	479	25	32	79,227	50,561	116
Huntly Cairnie Glass	592	10	11	-	38,132	-
Insch-Leslie-Premnay-Oyne	329	25	17	-	26,539	85
Inverurie: St Andrew's	784	33	-	-	67,716	10
Inverurie: West	593	42	23	80,094	57,176	13
Kemnay	459	32	-	70,034	51,109	137

Congregation	Com	Eld	G	In 17	M&M	–18
Kintore	659	35	-	80,966	59,264	50
Meldrum and Bourtie	391	25	30	68,456	50,431	26
Methlick	327	24	21	60,799	33,088	51
New Machar	401	18	-	51,096	50,086	30
Noth	221	8	-	27,033	18,489	1
Skene	1,135	67	44	157,080	87,061	165
Strathbogie Drumblade	412	35	29	59,439	43,515	15
Udny and Pitmedden	245	30	11	80,724	45,155	8
Upper Donside	334	18	-	42,500	28,956	25

34. Buchan

Congregation	Com	Eld	G	In 17	M&M	–18
Aberdour	104	9	13	13,696	8,060	14
Pitsligo	79	7	-	16,550	12,016	4
Auchaber United	107	11	10	14,912	13,347	2
Auchterless	176	17	10	19,157	16,943	3
Banff	540	28	-	70,519	49,670	125
King Edward	137	14	9	21,777	11,950	-
Crimond	152	12	-	25,448	15,290	12
Lonmay	100	12	12	13,839	10,672	-
Cruden	368	20	18	45,923	31,746	38
Deer	652	19	20	53,112	47,453	30
Fraserburgh: Old	468	50	48	109,893	74,160	135
Fraserburgh: South	254	18	-	-	30,671	6
Inverallochy and Rathen: East	73	8	-	-	10,170	15
Fraserburgh: West	443	45	-	64,901	47,773	-
Rathen: West	70	8	-	12,865	7,336	2
Fyvie	190	-	15	40,288	27,650	-
Rothienorman	114	8	-	15,946	8,431	20
Longside	405	25	-	77,966	38,896	56
Macduff	599	-	31	100,121	54,953	-
Marnoch	364	-	12	36,433	26,547	-
Maud and Savoch	176	-	-	27,524	19,113	-
New Deer: St Kane's	310	11	14	40,738	35,873	-
Monquhitter and New Byth	267	17	11	21,654	19,247	2
Turriff: St Andrew's	449	26	14	-	27,461	90
New Pitsligo	248	5	-	-	16,254	-
Strichen and Tyrie	377	14	20	58,115	33,941	21
Ordiquihill and Cornhill	137	10	13	11,054	7,490	32
Whitehills	265	18	20	44,304	26,303	4
Peterhead: New	532	33	32	53,261	87,295	22
Peterhead: St Andrew's	411	24	20	49,529	33,098	25
Portsoy	286	14	25	48,344	24,424	20
St Fergus	164	-	6	18,165	8,770	-
Sandhaven	67	-	-	-	3,006	-
Turriff: St Ninian's and Forglen	553	24	17	70,194	49,381	8

35. Moray

Congregation	Com	Eld	G	In 17	M&M	–18
Aberlour	262	18	28	44,931	31,658	20
Alves and Burghead	145	-	29	43,695	23,869	-
Kinloss and Findhorn	74	19	11	30,178	22,019	-

Congregation	Com	Eld	G	In 17	M&M	–18
Bellie and Speymouth	336	23	29	62,755	50,803	85
Birnie and Pluscarden	243	22	24	-	29,663	-
Elgin: High	425	38	-	69,406	37,157	37
Buckie: North	363	32	32	57,188	38,060	12
Rathven	73	15	14	-	11,691	6
Buckie: South and West	209	20	29	38,450	23,073	-
Enzie	69	-	-	9,886	8,440	-
Cullen and Deskford	264	17	18	53,888	37,710	-
Dallas	44	6	8	13,761	9,249	1
Forres: St Leonard's	175	-	29	-	30,708	-
Rafford	58	-	-	15,083	10,566	-
Duffus, Spynie and Hopeman	223	-	12	64,954	33,406	-
Dyke	114	10	12	24,167	18,749	12
Edinkillie	78	10	-	12,369	14,800	9
Elgin: St Giles' & St Columba's South	423	42	42	122,416	73,548	32
Findochty	38	8	12	-	11,379	16
Portknockie	57	9	16	22,658	7,088	41
Forres: St Laurence	372	-	21	73,997	49,579	-
Keith: North, Newmill, Boharm and Rothiemay	464	46	19	42,176	66,252	-
Keith: St Rufus, Botriphnie and Grange	875	-	32	-	60,300	-
Knockando, Elchies and Archiestown	222	15	6	36,194	27,299	16
Rothes	278	17	13	39,655	26,937	18
Lossiemouth: St Gerardine's High	186	11	29	52,486	32,640	-
Lossiemouth: St James'	193	15	30	53,449	34,996	7
Mortlach and Cabrach	277	10	14	-	24,844	2
St Andrew's-Lhanbryd and Urquhart	336	38	21	63,358	48,432	17

36. Abernethy

Abernethy	138	-	-	60,194	29,612	-
Boat of Garten, Carrbridge and Kincardine	137	-	28	45,378	22,356	-
Alvie and Insh	67	6	-	38,230	22,457	25
Rothiemurchus and Aviemore	66	6	-	14,799	10,524	8
Cromdale and Advie	62	-	-	18,065	14,981	-
Dulnain Bridge	31	-	-	12,197	8,862	-
Grantown-on-Spey	185	-	-	52,919	24,247	-
Kingussie	91	-	-	-	17,002	-
Laggan	37	-	-	20,427	10,629	-
Newtonmore	66	12	-	35,053	18,464	20
Tomintoul, Glenlivet and Inveraven	125	-	-	-	16,423	-

37. Inverness

Ardersier	51	11	-	19,586	8,736	14
Petty	45	-	11	-	8,290	-
Auldearn and Dalmore	52	7	-	10,879	7,119	5
Nairn: St Ninian's	170	11	27	49,058	31,061	6
Cawdor	152	12	-	26,401	17,810	15
Croy and Dalcross	57	-	15	20,212	9,417	-
Culloden: The Barn	225	16	-	92,324	60,368	125
Daviot and Dunlichity	52	5	8	14,219	10,909	8
Moy, Dalarossie and Tomatin	28	-	8	8,306	7,111	-

Congregation	Com	Eld	G	In 17	M&M	–18
Dores and Boleskine	70	-	-	16,582	9,509	-
Inverness: Crown	510	-	28	-	75,927	99
Inverness: Dalneigh and Bona	153	12	15	58,084	45,763	69
Inverness: East	230	25	-	122,979	79,554	44
Inverness: Hilton	225	10	-	84,075	50,308	37
Inverness: Inshes	227	15	-	145,351	84,469	151
Inverness: Kinmylies	71	8	-	43,957	39,933	55
Inverness: Ness Bank	539	58	31	148,156	89,361	156
Inverness: Old High St Stephen's	398	35	-	99,230	77,526	-
Inverness: St Columba	62	4	-	57,900	12,000	33
Inverness: Trinity	191	25	15	63,660	43,140	-
Kilmorack and Erchless	95	11	19	58,681	33,287	30
Kiltarlity	57	6	-	27,488	12,380	15
Kirkhill	70	10	14	25,943	14,447	9
Nairn: Old	415	-	21	117,441	63,746	-
Urquhart and Glenmoriston	102	9	-	51,389	34,182	10

38. Lochaber

Acharacle	36	5	-	21,115	10,194	15
Ardnamurchan	14	5	-	10,573	6,769	-
Ardgour and Kingairloch	47	6	13	12,796	7,065	2
Morvern	36	5	8	9,174	7,244	15
Strontian	25	3	-	7,665	4,859	11
Duror	30	6	13	14,424	8,927	-
Glencoe: St Munda's	41	8	-	-	9,357	-
Fort Augustus	64	9	-	20,244	13,664	-
Glengarry	28	5	12	-	8,030	15
Fort William: Duncansburgh MacIntosh	331	24	18	81,302	51,495	36
Kilmonivaig	59	6	14	-	16,663	10
Kilmallie	98	14	22	31,399	24,649	2
Kinlochleven	48	7	14	24,805	10,871	-
Nether Lochaber	43	9	-	17,529	13,141	-
North West Lochaber	82	14	10	29,727	19,933	12

39. Ross

Alness	67	10	-	31,690	17,120	14
Avoch	17	5	-	14,519	9,488	4
Fortrose and Rosemarkie	58	5	-	22,670	25,736	4
Contin	47	-	-	12,491	14,580	-
Fodderty and Strathpeffer	92	-	-	30,336	18,027	-
Cromarty	40	6	-	16,192	5,162	-
Resolis and Urquhart	74	-	-	34,550	26,407	-
Dingwall: Castle Street	145	-	16	48,566	28,724	-
Dingwall: St Clement's	171	31	15	73,547	36,077	24
Fearn Abbey and Nigg	40	5	-	-	18,543	-
Tarbat	34	-	-	-	9,064	-
Ferintosh	129	19	17	48,353	34,262	8
Invergordon	135	9	-	56,548	38,864	10
Killearnan	110	-	-	28,291	33,671	-
Knockbain	43	-	-	15,919	14,165	-

Congregation	Com	Eld	G	In 17	M&M	–18
Kilmuir and Logie Easter	57	8	17	32,916	23,614	1
Kiltearn	53	7	-	37,211	18,903	8
Lochbroom and Ullapool	38	-	-	29,622	19,487	-
Rosskeen	114	-	11	52,916	38,060	-
Tain	98	-	17	54,446	30,605	-
Urray and Kilchrist	79	-	-	57,853	32,250	-

40. Sutherland

Altnaharra and Farr	22	1	-	-	5,623	-
Assynt and Stoer	9	2	-	14,800	6,289	4
Clyne	55	13	-	28,596	18,334	3
Kildonan and Loth Helmsdale	30	6	-	7,046	8,325	3
Creich	17	4	-	10,852	13,965	-
Kincardine Croick and Edderton	34	10	-	18,647	15,764	4
Rosehall	21	3	-	9,785	7,123	3
Dornoch: Cathedral	296	34	51	-	70,062	70
Durness and Kinlochbervie	20	3	-	14,638	12,237	1
Eddrachillis	6	2	-	16,935	7,931	1
Golspie	56	8	4	36,599	28,824	-
Lairg	23	3	10	22,622	15,004	-
Rogart	12	4	-	8,432	8,463	-
Melness and Tongue	35	6	-	-	13,988	9

41. Caithness

Bower	28	-	-	6,097	7,499	-
Halkirk Westerdale	43	6	9	9,412	9,800	-
Watten	19	2	-	8,694	8,215	-
Canisbay	30	4	14	17,084	10,862	16
Dunnet	18	-	5	6,568	5,246	-
Keiss	27	-	-	8,208	4,659	-
Olrig	45	3	5	-	4,928	-
Latheron	57	12	6	24,847	16,999	21
North Coast	39	10	20	24,873	13,359	5
Thurso: St Peter's and St Andrew's	118	13	15	-	33,006	22
Thurso: West	172	23	20	57,148	33,012	14
Wick: Pulteneytown and Thrumster	183	12	25	58,140	38,283	15
Wick: St Fergus	196	31	20	46,266	37,604	2

42. Lochcarron-Skye

Applecross, Lochcarron and Torridon	54	6	8	-	21,297	2
Bracadale and Duirinish	43	8	6	27,165	20,463	3
Gairloch and Dundonnell	80	6	-	61,775	41,999	9
Glenelg Kintail and Lochalsh	86	8	8	41,347	35,766	-
Kilmuir and Stenscholl	46	6	-	46,154	21,372	15
Portree	92	11	-	68,522	40,771	15
Snizort	29	2	-	-	21,272	-
Strath and Sleat	123	5	-	92,249	56,847	24

43. Uist

Benbecula	56	10	18	45,336	24,950	22

Congregation	Com	Eld	G	In 17	M&M	–18
Carinish	75	11	13	47,154	27,066	11
Berneray and Lochmaddy	44	3	10	15,923	11,775	1
Kilmuir and Paible	27	4	-	32,429	17,297	9
Manish-Scarista	29	3	-	30,350	23,172	11
Tarbert	72	7	-	82,721	40,694	20

44. Lewis

Barvas	68	8	-	56,575	51,162	23
Carloway	43	2	-	24,131	14,401	27
Cross Ness	59	4	-	49,758	32,788	60
Kinloch	32	5	-	37,900	25,833	25
Knock	25	1	-	38,859	17,082	8
Lochs-Crossbost	10	3	-	17,431	13,951	9
Lochs-in-Bernera	24	3	-	18,445	13,292	14
Uig	21	2	-	-	14,996	2
Stornoway: High	86	3	-	65,738	35,817	20
Stornoway: Martin's Memorial	315	11	-	151,065	79,013	70
Stornoway: St Columba	139	9	40	93,040	58,559	160

45. Orkney

Birsay, Harray and Sandwick	300	-	36	36,044	25,047	-
East Mainland	195	19	12	24,752	18,253	7
Eday	11	3	-	-	2,228	2
Evie	23	-	-	4,753	8,280	-
Firth	83	4	-	21,161	14,536	15
Rendall	44	-	-	14,785	7,481	-
Rousay	14	-	-	1,575	3,696	-
Flotta	23	5	-	4,854	3,108	3
Hoy and Walls	50	9	10	6,867	4,169	4
Orphir and Stenness	145	-	-	20,047	18,674	-
Kirkwall: East	347	-	25	64,609	43,580	-
Shapinsay	39	7	-	8,420	4,189	9
Kirkwall: St Magnus Cathedral	504	-	28	76,279	42,984	-
North Ronaldsay	7	-	-	-	993	-
Papa Westray	7	4	-	9,219	4,451	3
Westray	82	16	26	23,151	18,264	40
Sanday	48	4	7	8,485	6,596	-
South Ronaldsay and Burray	121	11	14	19,250	12,069	-
Stromness	284	30	16	-	27,283	4
Stronsay: Moncur Memorial	50	7	-	10,964	9,315	8

46. Shetland

Burra Isle	31	6	14	10,971	6,619	12
Tingwall	48	12	12	28,799	21,843	18
Delting	65	6	13	13,080	14,204	8
Northmavine	57	5	-	6,486	8,856	-
Dunrossness and St Ninian's	39	-	-	14,300	10,845	-
Sandwick, Cunningsburgh & Quarff	53	6	12	24,327	15,657	7
Lerwick and Bressay	320	24	5	63,964	49,068	32
Nesting and Lunnasting	29	6	-	5,516	5,122	-

Congregation	Com	Eld	G	In 17	M&M	–18
Whalsay and Skerries	166	14	17	16,761	12,804	20
Sandsting and Aithsting	22	7	-	8,458	5,654	14
Walls and Sandness	29	11	-	9,407	5,843	1
Unst and Fetlar	75	8	17	20,986	12,793	5
Yell	42	8	12	-	7,641	-

47. England

Corby: St Andrew's	223	13	-	39,416	28,553	2
Corby: St Ninian's	291	12	-	44,537	25,869	10
Guernsey: St Andrew's in the Grange	180	20	-	76,696	44,479	21
Jersey: St Columba's	114	14	-	55,866	40,070	9
London: Crown Court	211	30	3	-	59,763	18
London: St Columba's	842	55	-	338,557	205,270	25
Newcastle: St Andrew's	105	13	-	-	8,372	22

48. International Charges

Amsterdam	364	15	-	-	-	25
Bermuda	-	-	-	-	-	-
Brussels	385	20	-	-	-	45
Budapest	-	-	-	-	-	-
Colombo	122	12	-	-	-	5
Costa del Sol	21	6	-	-	-	-
Geneva	219	10	-	-	-	40
Gibraltar	26	6	-	-	-	4
Lausanne	125	14	-	-	-	10
Lisbon	58	5	-	-	-	5
Malta	-	-	-	-	-	-
Paris	75	8	-	-	-	7
Rome	100	8	-	-	-	18
Rotterdam	189	10	-	-	-	25

INDEX OF MINISTERS

Ministers who are members of a Presbytery are designated 'A' if holding a parochial appointment in that Presbytery, or 'B' if otherwise qualifying for membership. 'A-1, A-2' etc. indicate the numerical order of congregations in the Presbyteries of Edinburgh, Glasgow, and Hamilton.

Also included are ministers listed in Section 6:

(1) Ministers who have resigned their seat in Presbytery but registered as Retaining or Employed (List 6-D);

(2) Ministers who have resigned their seat in Presbytery but registered as Inactive (List 6-E);

(3) Ministers serving overseas (List 6-J) – see also Presbyteries 48 and 49;

(4) Ordained Local Ministers and Auxiliary Ministers, who are listed both in Presbyteries and in List 6-A and List 6-B respectively; and

(5) Ministers who have died since the publication of the last *Year Book* (List 6-P)

For a list of the Diaconate, see List 6-C.

Simpson, R.R.	Lothian 3B	Stewart, C.E.	List 6-D	Taylor, W.R.	Edinburgh 1B
Sinclair, B.H.	Glasgow 16A-79	Stewart, D.	Greenock/Paisley 14B	Tchaikovsky, S.	Argyll 19A
Sinclair, C.A.M.	Edinburgh 1 A-47	Stewart, D.E.	Glasgow 16B	Teasdale, J.R.	Glasgow 16A-70
Sinclair, D.I.	List 6-J	Stewart, D.J.	Aberdeen 31A	Telfer, A.B.	Hamilton 17A-63
Sinclair, J.H.	Stirling 23B	Stewart, F.M.C.	List 6-D	Telfer, I.J.M.	Edinburgh 1B
Sinclair, T.D.	Glasgow 16A-91	Stewart, G.G.	List 6-P	Telfer, T.	Argyll 19A
Singh, A.R.	Glasgow 16A-13	Stewart, H.	Caithness 41A	Templeton, J.L.	Kirkcaldy 25B
Siroky, S.	Melrose/Peebles 4B	Stewart, H.M.	Lewis 44A	Tenglerova, I.	Caithness 41A
Slater, D.G.	Glasgow 16A-14	Stewart, J.	Argyll 19B	Thain, G.M.	Glasgow 16A-104
Sloan, R.	Dunkeld/Meigle 27B	Stewart, J.C.	Aberdeen 31B	Thom, D.J.	England 47B
Sloan, R.P.	Perth 28B	Stewart, J.C.	Perth 28A	Thom, I.G.	Dunfermline 24A
Smart, V.E.	Edinburgh 1 A-17	Stewart, L.	Dunkeld/Meigle 27A	Thomas, M.R.H.	Angus 30B
Smillie, A.M.	Greenock/Paisley 14B	Stewart, L.J.	Edinburgh 1B	Thomas, S.A.	Angus 30B
Smith, A.	Edinburgh 1B	Stewart, M.L.	List 6-D	Thomas, W.C.	List 6-D
Smith, A.E.	Kincardine/Deeside 32B	Stewart, N.D.	Glasgow 16B	Thomson, A.	Glasgow 16A-75
Smith, B.D.	Kincardine/Deeside 32A	Stewart, R.J.	Perth 28B	Thomson, A.	List 6-D
Smith, D.J.	Kirkcaldy 25A	Stewart, U.B.	Jedburgh 6B	Thomson, D.M.	Edinburgh 1B
Smith, E.	List 6-D	Stewart, W.	Buchan 34A	Thomson, I.U.	Gordon 33B
Smith, E.W.	Glasgow 16A-95	Stewart, W.T.	Hamilton 17B	Thomson, J.B.	Perth 28B
Smith, F.E.	Inverness 37A	Steyn, J.J.	Int. Charges 48A	Thomson, J.D.	Kirkcaldy 25B
Smith, G.S.	Glasgow 16B	Stirling, A.D.	List 6-P	Thomson, J.M.A.	Hamilton 17B
Smith, G.W.	West Lothian 2B	Stirling, G.A.S.	Inverness 37B	Thomson, M.	Ardrossan 12A
Smith, H.C.	Argyll 19A	Stirling, I.R.	Ayr 10A	Thomson, M.E.	Abernethy 36B
Smith, H.G.	Angus 30B	Stitt, R.J.M.	Edinburgh 1B	Thomson, P.D.	Perth 28B
Smith, H.M.C.	Moray 35B	Stobo, M.J.	Sutherland 40B	Thomson, R.	Stirling 23B
Smith, H.W.	List 6-D	Stoddart, A.C.	Lochaber 38A	Thomson, S.	St Andrews 26A
Smith, J.M.	Uist 43B	Stoddart, A.G.	Gordon 33B	Thomson, W.	Falkirk 22A
Smith, M.	Moray 35B	Stone, L.	Int. Charges 48A	Thorburn, R.J.	Buchan 34A
Smith, M.	Uist 43B	Storrar, W.F.	List 6-D	Thornburn, S.	St Andrews 26A
Smith, N.A.	Edinburgh 1 A-25	Stott, K.D.	Dundee 29A	Thornthwaite, A.P.	Dundee 29A
Smith, R.	Falkirk 22B	Strachan, A.E.	List 6-D	Thrower, C.D.	List 6-D
Smith, R.	Ross 39B	Strachan, D.G.	List 6-D	Tippner, J.	Buchan 34A
Smith, R.L.	Aberdeen 31A	Strachan, I.M.	List 6-D	Todd, J.F.	Falkirk 22A
Smith, R.W.	List 6-E	Strachan, P.D.	Melrose/Peebles 4A	Tomlinson, B.L.	Kirkcaldy 25B
Smith, S.J.	Greenock/Paisley 14A	Strachan, W.	Dundee 29A	Too, D.I.K.	Falkirk 22A
Smith, S.J.	Lochcarron/Skye 42A	Strang, G.I.	Abernethy 36A	Torrance, A.J.	St Andrews 26B
Smith, Y.	Greenock/Paisley 14A	Strickland, A.	Dundee 29B	Torrance, D.J.	Lothian 3A
Somevi, J.K.	Aberdeen 31A	Strong, C.	St Andrews 26B	Torrance, D.W.	Lothian 3B
Sorensen, A.K.	Greenock/Paisley 14A	Strong, C.A.	Irvine/Kilmarnock 11A	Torrance, I.R.	Edinburgh 1B
Souter, D.I.	List 6-P	Stuart, A.P.	Glasgow 16A-43	Torrens, S.A.R.	Edinburgh 1 A-3
Souter, L.M.	Lothian 3A	Sturrock, R.D.	Glasgow 16A-81, 123	Travers, R.	Ardrossan 12B
Speirs, A.	Greenock/Paisley 14A	Stutter, A.	Lochcarron/Skye 42A	Trevorrow, J.A.	List 6-P
Spence, E.G.B.	Lothian 3A	Suchanek-Seitz, B.V.	Ayr 10A	Trewren, N.	Kincardine/Deeside 32A
Spence, S.M.	Hamilton 17B	Sutherland, C.A.		Turnbull, J.	List 6-D
Spencer, J.	Glasgow 16B		Dumfries/Kirkcudbright 8B	Turnbull, S.L.A.	Hamilton 17A-42
Stalder, W.A.	Gordon 33A	Sutherland, D.A.	Ardrossan 12A	Turner, A.	Glasgow 16B
Stark, C.	Hamilton 17A-10	Sutherland, S.J.	Aberdeen 31A	Turner, F.K.	Inverness 37B
Stark, S	Edinburgh 1B	Sutton, P	Edinburgh 1A-59	Tuton, R.M.	Glasgow 16B
Steel, G.H.B.	Aberdeen 31A	Swan, D.	Aberdeen 31B	Twaddle, L.H.	Int. Charges 48A
Steele, G.M.F.	Dunkeld/Meigle 27B	Sweetin, B.A.	Angus 30A	Tweedie, F.J.	Edinburgh 1B
Steele, H.D.	Dunfermline 24A	Swindells, A.I.	Gordon 33A		
Steele, L.M.	Melrose/Peebles 4B	Swindells, S.	Gordon 33A	Unsworth, R.	St Andrews 26B
Steele, M.D.J.	Melrose/Peebles 4A	Swinton, J.	Aberdeen 31B	Urquhart, J.A.	Irvine/Kilmarnock 11A
Steell, S.C.	Greenock/Paisley 14A	Symington, A.H.	Ayr 10B	Urquhart, J.C.C.	Lothian 3A
Steenbergen, P.	Annandale/Eskdale 7B			Urquhart, N.	Irvine/Kilmarnock 11A
Stein, J.	Lothian 3B	Tait, A.	Orkney 45B		
Stein, M.E.	Lothian 3B	Tait, J.M.	Edinburgh 1B	van Sittert, P.	Buchan 34B
Stenhouse, E.M.	Perth 28A	Tait, T.W.	Dunkeld/Meigle 27B	van Welie, D.L.	Falkirk 22A
Stenhouse, W.D.	Perth 28B	Tallach, J.	List 6-D	Varwell, A.P.J.	Lochaber 38B
Stephen, A.A.	Kincardine/Deeside 32A	Taverner, D.J.	Duns 5A	Verster, W.M.	Buchan 34A
Stephen, D.M.	Edinburgh 1B	Taverner, G.R.	Melrose/Peebles 4B	Vidits, G.	Edinburgh 1 A-66
Sterrett, J.B.	Sutherland 40A	Taylor, A.S.	Ardrossan 12B	Vint, A.S.	Glasgow 16A-20
Steven, H.A.M.	Dumbarton 18B	Taylor, A.T.	Argyll 19B	Vischer, J.	Lothian 3A
Stevens, A.C.	Int. Charges 48A	Taylor, B.S.C.	Aberdeen 31A	Vivers, K.A.	Annandale/Eskdale 7B
Stevens, L.	Angus 30A	Taylor, C.	Dundee 29B		
Stevenson, D.F.	Moray 35A	Taylor, C.G.D.	Dundee 29A	Waddell, E.A.	Hamilton 17B
Stevenson, G.	Lothian 3A	Taylor, G.J.A.	Edinburgh 1 A-9	Walker, D.K.	Abernethy 36A
Stevenson, J.	Edinburgh 1B	Taylor, I.	Glasgow 16A-3	Walker, I.	West Lothian 2B
Stevenson, J.	Hamilton 17B	Taylor, J.	Kirkcaldy 25A	Walker, J.B.	St Andrews 26B
Stevenson, S.	Greenock/Paisley 14A	Taylor, J.C.	Dumbarton 18B	Walker, K.D.F.	Duns 5B
Stewart, A.E.	Perth 28B	Taylor, M.A.	Duns 5A	Walker, L.	Glasgow 16B
Stewart, A.T.	Perth 28A	Taylor, T.A.	Hamilton 17A-31	Walker, R.F.	England 47B

INDEX OF PARISHES AND PLACES

Numbers on the right of the column refer to the Presbytery in which the district lies. Names in brackets are given for ease of identification. They may refer to the name of the parish, which may be different from that of the district, or they distinguish places with the same name, or they indicate the first named place within a union.

INDEX OF SUBJECTS